# Inkscape

## Guide to a Vector Drawing Program

### Fourth Edition

**Tavmjong Bah**

PRENTICE
HALL

Upper Saddle River, NJ • Boston • Indianapolis • San Francisco
New York • Toronto • Montreal • London • Munich • Paris • Madrid
Capetown • Sydney • Tokyo • Singapore • Mexico City

The publisher offers excellent discounts on this book when ordered in quantity for bulk purchases or special sales, which may include electronic versions and/or custom covers and content particular to your business, training goals, marketing focus, and branding interests. For more information, please contact:

U.S. Corporate and Government Sales
(800) 382-3419
corpsales@pearsontechgroup.com

For sales outside the United States, please contact:

International Sales
international@pearson.com

Visit us on the Web: informit.com/ph

*Library of Congress Catalog-in-Publication Data*

Bah, Tavmjong.
  Inkscape : guide to a vector drawing program /Tavmjong Bah—4th ed.
      p. cm.
  Includes index.
  ISBN-13: 978-0-13-276414-8 (pbk.)
  ISBN-10: 0-13-276414-8 (pbk.)
 1. Computer graphics.  2. Inkscape (Electronic resource)  I. Title.
  T385.B297 2011
  006.6'8—dc22

                                      2011010197

ISBN-13: 978-0-13-276414-8
ISBN-10:   0-13-276414-8
Text printed in the United States at Edwards Brothers in Ann Arbor, Michigan.
First printing, May 2011

# Table of Contents

# Acknowledgments

First and foremost, thanks to the many authors of Inkscape! Here are the top 15 in terms of "commits" to the source code since the v0.48 release: Jon A. Cruz, JazzyNico, Krzysztof Kosiński, Diederik van Lierop, Johan Engelen, Tavmjong Bah, Alexandre Prokoudine, Ted Gould, Josh Andler, Chris Morgan, Kris De Gussem, buliabyak, Alvin Penner, helix84, Aurelio A. Heckert. A special thanks to the students at Ecole Centrale de Lyon who implemented the new *Spray Tool*. I would also like to thank Ted Gould, who put me in touch with Joe Brockmeier, who put me in touch with Prentice Hall. And a thanks to all the readers (especially Jon A. Cruz and Loïc Guégant) who have sent me comments and corrections.

This book was produced using emacs [http://www.gnu.org/software/emacs/], DocBook [http://www.docbook.org/], xsltproc [http://xmlsoft.org/XSLT/xsltproc2.html], fop [http://xmlgraphics.apache.org/fop/], and, of course, Inkscape [http://www.inkscape.org/].

# About the Author

**Tavmjong Bah** is a physicist living in Paris whose writing combines his love for technology and culture. An active member of the community, Tav is an Inkscape developer and is responsible for the improvements to the Text Tool between versions 0.47 and 0.48. He represents Inkscape as an invited expert in the W3C SVG working group. His *nom-de-plume* is the title granted to him by the paramount chief of the Nso, a Cameroonian people.

# Overview of What Is in This Book

*Inkscape, Guide to a Vector Drawing Program* is ***the guide*** to the Inkscape program. The shorter, web-based, version is linked directly under the program's Help menu. This book is both an introduction and reference for the Inkscape drawing program. With Inkscape, one can produce a wide variety of art, from photo-realistic drawings to organizational charts. Inkscape uses *SVG*, a powerful vector-based drawing language and W3C web standard, as its native format. *SVG* drawings can be directly viewed by all the major web browsers, including Firefox, Opera, Safari, Chrome, and Internet Explorer (starting with version 9). With the advent of *HTML5*, *SVG* will be easily embedded in web pages. Inkscape is available free for Windows, Macintosh, and Linux operating systems.

The first third of the book is devoted to twelve tutorials that progress in difficulty from very basic to highly complex. The remainder of the book covers each facet of Inkscape in detail. Updated for Inkscape v0.48, the book includes complete coverage of new features, including: updated Node tool with multipath editing, new Spray tool, improved Text tool, and many new extensions. Advance topics covered include the use of Inkscape's powerful tiling tool, built-in bitmap tracing, and *SVG* use on the Web including in *HTML5*. The book includes plenty of tips (and warnings) about the use of Inkscape and *SVG*.

# Introduction

This book serves as both a textbook and a reference for using Inkscape to produce high-quality drawings. It includes a series of tutorials followed by chapters that cover completely each facet of the Inkscape program. The book is full of tips and notes to enable the user to make the best use of the program.

Inkscape is an open source, *SVG*-based[1] vector drawing program. It is useful for drawing:

- Illustrations for the Web

- Graphics for mobile phones

- Simple line drawings

- Cartoons

- Complex works of art

- Figures for articles and books

- Organization charts

The file format that Inkscape uses is compact and quickly transmittable over the Internet. Yet it is powerful and can describe complex drawings that are scalable to any size. Support for the format has been added to web browsers and is already included in many mobile phones.

Inkscape supports the drawing of regular shapes (rectangles, circles, etc.), arbitrary paths, and text. These *objects* can be given a wide variety of attributes such as color, gradient or patterned fills, alpha blending, and markers. Objects can be transformed, cloned, and grouped. Hyperlinks can be added for use in web browsers. The Inkscape program aims to be fully *XML*, *SVG*, and *CSS* compliant.

Inkscape is available prepackaged for the Windows, Macintosh, and Linux operating systems. The program and its source code are freely available. They can be obtained from the Inkscape website [http://www.inkscape.org/].

Inkscape is undergoing very rapid development with new features being added and compliance to the *SVG* standard being constantly improved. This manual documents versions 0.47 and 0.48.

# How to Use This Book

Following this introduction, there is a set of tutorials. The tutorials are designed to cover the basics of all the important features found in Inkscape and to lead the reader from the beginning to end of the drawing process.

The bulk of the book is devoted to a detailed discussion of all of Inkscape's features, including examples of solving common drawing problems. Both the strengths and weaknesses of Inkscape are pointed out.

Depending on one's background, one may use the book as a reference or read the book from front to back. In general, the more fundamental topics are covered first. Novices are encouraged to work through each of the tutorials sitting in front of their computer. At the end of the book are a few drawing challenges.

Conventions:

- *Click*: Click on icon, object, and so forth with the **Left Mouse** button (unless another mouse button is indicated) with immediate release.

---

[1] All acronyms are defined in the Glossary.

- *Click-drag*: Click on icon, object, and so forth with the **Left Mouse** button (unless another mouse button is indicated) and hold the button down while moving the mouse.

- Select the option in the pull-down menu. Example: File → 🖾 Document Properties... (**Shift+Ctrl+D**): Select "Document Properties..." under the "File" pull-down menu. **Shift**+**Ctrl**+**D** is the keyboard shortcut corresponding to this option.

### One-button Mice

Users of one-button mice might want to upgrade to a multi-button mouse. Inkscape makes good use of a three-button mouse with a scroll wheel. (Inkscape also makes good use of graphics tablets.) In the meantime, the button on a one-button mouse corresponds to the **Left Mouse** button.

### Icons

The icons used in this book are in general those provided by Inkscape's default icon theme. Some icons, however, are provided by the operating system. It is possible that the icons you see in your version of Inkscape are different depending upon the source of your version. Regardless of what icons are used, the functionality remains the same.

### Book Website and Color Addendum

The book has a website [http://tavmjong.free.fr/INKSCAPE/] with some *SVG* examples and tests as well as graphics for use with the tutorials.

Being a drawing program, color is very important in Inkscape. You can download from the website a color addendum, which has many of the book's figures in color. Figures in the book that have a color version in the addendum are marked with the symbol ✪.

# Vector Graphics

There are two basic types of graphic images: *bitmap* (or *raster*) images and *vector* images. In the first case, the image is defined in terms of rows and columns of individual pixels, each with its own color. In the second case, the image is defined in terms of lines, both straight and curved. A single straight line is described in terms of its two end points. The difference in these types of graphic images becomes readily apparent when a drawing is enlarged.

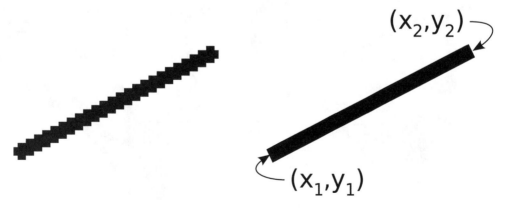

The same line is shown on the left and right. On the left it is displayed as a bitmap image, while on the right it is displayed as a vector. In both cases, the line has been scaled up by a factor of four from its nominal size.

When the bitmap resolution of a drawing matches the display resolution, the objects in the drawing look smooth.

The same drawing, but defined as a bitmap image on the left and a vector image on the right. If the output device has the same resolution as the bitmap image, there is little difference between the appearance of the two images.

If the bitmap resolution is significantly less than the display resolution, the display will show jagged lines.

The head of the gentleman in the above drawings has been scaled up by a factor of five. Now one can see a difference in the quality of the bitmap drawing (left) and the vector drawing (right). Note that the bitmap image uses *anti-aliasing*, a method of using grayscale to attempt to smooth the drawing.

All output devices, with few exceptions, use a raster or bitmap image to display graphics.[2] The real difference between drawing with bitmap graphics and vector graphics is the point at which the image is converted into a bitmap. In the case of vector graphics, this conversion is done at the very last step before display, ensuring that the final image matches exactly the resolution of the output device.

# SVG

*SVG* stands for *Scalable Vector Graphics*. *Scalable* refers to the notion that a drawing can be scaled to an arbitrary size without losing detail.

*Scalable* also refers to the idea that a drawing can be composed of an unlimited number of smaller parts, parts that can be reused many times.

The *SVG* standard is directed toward a complete description of two-dimensional graphics, including animation in an *XML* (eXtensible Markup Language) format. *XML* is an open standard for describing a document in a way that can be easily extended and is resistant to future changes in the document specification. A drawing saved in one version of *SVG* by one version of a drawing program should be viewable, to the full extent possible, by any previous or future version of any drawing program that adheres to the *SVG* standard. If a program doesn't support something in the *SVG* standard, it should just skip over any part of a drawing that uses it, rendering the rest correctly.

*SVG* files are small, and drawings described by the standard adapt well to different presentation methods. This has led to great interest in the standard. Support is included in many web browsers (Firefox, Chrome, Opera, Safari, and Internet Explorer from version 9), or is available through plug-ins (e.g., Adobe [http://www.adobe.com/svg/viewer/install/], Ssrc SVG [http://www.savarese.com/software/svgplugin/], svgweb [http://code.google.com/p/svgweb/] and Google [http://www.google.com/chromeframe]). Over a dozen companies including Apple (iPhone), Blackberry, LG, Motorola, Nokia, Samsung, and Sony Ericsson produce mobile phones that utilize a subset of the full *SVG* standard (SVG Tiny) that has been tailored for devices with limited resources.

# The Inkscape Program

Inkscape has its roots in the program Gill (GNOME Illustrator application) created by Raph Levian [http://www.levien.com/] of Ghostscript fame. This project was expanded on by the Sodipodi [http://sourceforge.net/projects/sodipodi] program. A different set of goals led to the split-off of the current Inkscape development effort.

The goal of the writers of Inkscape is to produce a program that can take full advantage of the *SVG* standard. This is not a small task. A link to the road map for future development can be found on the Inkscape website [http://www.inkscape.org/]. Of course, you are welcome to contribute!

Instructions on installing Inkscape can be found on the Inkscape website. Full functionality of Inkscape requires additional *helper* programs to be installed, especially for *importing* and *exporting* files in different graphic formats. Check the log file extensions-errors.log located on Linux at ~/.config/inkscape/ and on Windows at %userprofile%\Application Data\Inkscape\ for missing programs.

### Inkscape on the Mac

On the Mac OS X operating system, the Inkscape interface uses the *X11*-window layer, available on the 10.4, 10.5, and 10.6 installation disks. The non-native interface lacks the look and feel of "normal" Mac programs. Fear not, it will still work, although starting Inkscape may take a bit longer than other programs, especially the first time. A number of the keyboard shortcuts may also not work out of the box. You can consult InkscapeForum.com [http://www.inkscapeforum.com/viewtopic.php?t=800>f=5] for how to get the **Alt** keys to work properly and for other Mac related issues.

---

[2] The few vector output devices include large plotters for engineering and architectural drawings and archaic Tektronix terminals.

# Help

The first place to look for help is under the *Help* menu. Here you will find links to: this book (!), a web page containing all the *Keyboard* and *Mouse* commands (Help → *Keys and Mouse Reference*), tutorials, and a FAQ. Some of the items require a web browser and that you be connected to the Internet.

If you encounter a problem that is not covered by this book or the other resources under the *Help* menu, here are some other places to look:

- Inkscape website [http://www.inkscape.org/]. A variety of information is available, but it is not always well organized.

- Inkscape FAQ [http://wiki.inkscape.org/wiki/index.php/FAQ]. A good place to look for answers to common questions.

- Official Mailing Lists [http://www.inkscape.org/mailing_lists.php]. Inkscape has a friendly *Users* list. Lists also exist in a variety of languages, including Italian, Spanish, French, and Portuguese.

- The "unofficial" Inkscape Forums [http://www.inkscapeforum.com/].

# Chapter 1. Quick Start

Let's get started. Inkscape is a very powerful program. However, you need to understand only a small part of it to begin drawing. This section gives you an overview of parts of the Inkscape user interface and then leads you through the creation of a few drawings. We will use a number of examples:

- Swedish Flag: A basic introduction to Inkscape using simple rectangles.

- European Flag: Includes drawing stars and precisely placing objects.

- Hiking Club Logo: Introduces text and is a serious foray into paths.

- Northern Pacific Railway Logo: Shows how to create a drawing from a photograph with the help of the auto-tracing routine. Layers are also introduced.

- Box of Playing Cards: Shows how to use Inkscape to draw a simple isometric projection of a three-dimensional object. It utilizes precise transformations of objects.

- Can of Soup: Another demonstration of how to simulate a 3D object in a 2D drawing. It introduces gradients.

- Vine Design: Demonstrates how to create a pattern that can be used as a base tile for a repeating pattern. It introduces the powerful *Create Tiled Clones* feature of Inkscape.

- Button: Creates an *SVG* button for use on a web page and demonstrates how the button can be used. *SMIL*, JavaScript, and *CSS* styling are covered.

- Neon Sign: Introduces using Inkscape for animation.

- Bank Note: Uses a variety of Inkscape features to produce a "secure" bank note. Patterns and scroll work are featured.

- Bottle: Creates a photorealistic drawing of a spritzer bottle. Tracing, gradients, and blurring are used.

# The Anatomy of the Inkscape Window

*Updated for v0.48.*

Start by opening Inkscape. You will see a single window. This window contains several major areas, many containing clickable icons or pull-down menus. The following figure shows this window and labels key parts.

The *Command Bar*, *Snap Bar*, *Tool Controls*, and *Tool Box* are detachable by dragging on the handles (highlighted in blue) at the far left or top. They can be returned to their normal place by dragging them back. *New in v0.48:* Some of the bars change position depending on which option is selected at the bottom of the View menu. When *Default* is selected, the *Command Bar* is on the top while the *Snap Bar* is on the right. When *Custom* is selected, the *Command Bar* and the *Snap Bar* are both on the top. When *Wide* is selected, the *Command Bar* and the *Snap Bar* are both on the right. By default, *Default* is used if you are not using a "Wide Screen" display while *Wide* is used if you are. A width to height aspect ratio of greater than 1.65 is defined to be wide. These bars, as well as the *Palette* and *Status Bar*, can be hidden using the View → Show/Hide submenu.

As Inkscape has grown more complex, the area required to include icons and entry boxes for all the various items has also grown leading to problems when Inkscape is used on small screens. The *Command Bar*, *Snap Bar*, *Tool Controls*, and *Tool Box* have variable widths or heights. If there are too many items to be shown in the width (height) of the Inkscape window, a small down arrow will appear on the right side or bottom of the bars. Clicking on this arrow will open a drop-down menu with access to the missing items.

One can also choose to use smaller icons. These options can be found in the *Interface* section of the *Inkscape Preferences* dialog. Note that the *Secondary toolbar icon size* refers to the *Snap Bar*. Using the smallest icons, the smallest possible Inkscape window becomes 505 pixels wide by 451 pixels high in v0.48 and 573 pixels wide by 506 pixels high in v0.47. The smallest size may depend on which operating system you are using and the availability of a small icon set. By hiding all the various window components (*Command Bar*, *Palette*, etc.), you can get an Inkscape window just 505 by 281 in v0.48 and 525 by 287 in v0.47.

## Missing Icons in Menus

The authors of the Gnome windowing system used by Inkscape have in their infinite wisdom decided that icons do not belong in drop-down menus and buttons. They have disabled icons and even removed the option to restore them from the Gnome Preferences menus in the latest versions of the Gnome libraries. If you wish to restore icons to menus, you will need to use the program `gconf-editor` or "Configuration Editor" (which you may need to install). Navigate to `desktop → gnome → interface` and check the "menus_have_icons" box. You can also check the "buttons_have_icons" box if you wish.

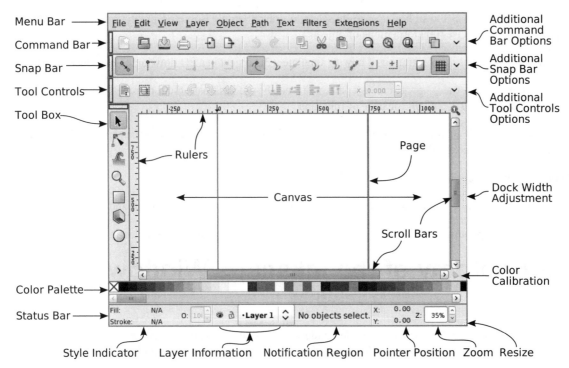

The default Inkscape window with the key parts labeled.✪(The star symbol indicates that a figure can be found in the color addendum, downloadable from the book's website.)

| | |
|---|---|
| Canvas | The drawing area. It may extend outside the viewable area. It can be panned (scrolled left/right and up/down) and zoomed. |
| Page | The part of the *Canvas* area corresponding to a printed page or other predefined area. Useful for setting an output region in printing or exporting a bitmap image. It may extend outside the viewable area. |
| Menu Bar | Contains the main pull-down menus. |
| Command Bar | Contains shortcuts to many of the items located in the menus. Click on the *Down arrow* on the right end to access entries missing due to space. |
| Snap Bar | Contains clickable icons that control snapping. See the section called *Snapping* in Chapter 5, *Positioning and Transforming*. |

Tool Controls

Contains entry boxes and clickable icons that are specific to the selected tool. For example, when the *Rectangle Tool* is in use, an entry box to specify a selected rectangle's width appears. Click on the *Down arrow* on the right end to access entries that may be missing due to space. If there is no arrow, then all options are being shown.

Tool Box

Contains "Tools" for selecting, drawing, or modifying objects. Clicking on an icon selects a tool. Double-clicking brings up that tool's preference dialog. The cursor (pointer) changes shape when placed over the canvas depending on which tool is selected.

Available tools: ⬉ , ⬈ , ⬕ , ⬕ , ◻ , ◻ , ◯ , ✿ , ◎ , ⬕ , ⬕ , ⬕ , **A** , ⬕ , ⬕ , ⬕ , ⬕ , ⬕ , ⬕ .

Color Palette

Contains a color palette. Colors can be dragged from the palette onto objects to change their *Fill*. Using the **Shift** key while dragging will change the *Stroke* color instead. The color used by some tools can be set by clicking on a color swatch. The palette can be changed by clicking on the arrow icon at the right end of the palette. Many predefined palettes are included. If the number of color swatches in a palette exceeds the space allocated, the scroll bar beneath the palette can be used to access the hidden swatches.

Status Bar

Contains several areas, including the *Style Indicator*, current drawing layer, pointer position, current drawing layer (and if it is visible or locked), current zoom level, window resize handle, and a *Notification Region* that describes context dependent options.

Style Indicator

Shows the style (*Fill* and *Stroke*) of a selected object, text fragment, or gradient stop. A **Left Mouse Click** on the *Fill* or *Stroke paint* part of the indicator opens the *Fill and Stroke* dialog. A **Right Mouse Click** opens up a pop-up menu. See the section called *Style Indicator* in Chapter 10, *Attributes* for details and more uses.

Notification Region

Contains context dependent information. If the region is too small to view all the text, placing the cursor over the region will display a *tool tip* with the full text.

 **Notification Region**

The *Notification Region* contains very useful information. Pay close attention to it when using an unfamiliar tool.

Rulers

Show the *x*- and *y*-axis coordinates of the drawing. Use **Ctrl+R** to toggle on/off. A **Left Mouse Drag** from a *Ruler* onto the *Canvas* creates a *Guide Line*.

Scroll Bars

Allows scrolling to adjust which part of the *Canvas* is viewable.

Color Calibration

Button toggles on/off use of a *Color Profile* [228] (if set up).

# Dockable Dialogs

Inkscape implements *Dockable Dialogs*. With this feature, opened dialogs are placed inside the main Inkscape window on the right side as seen in the next figure.

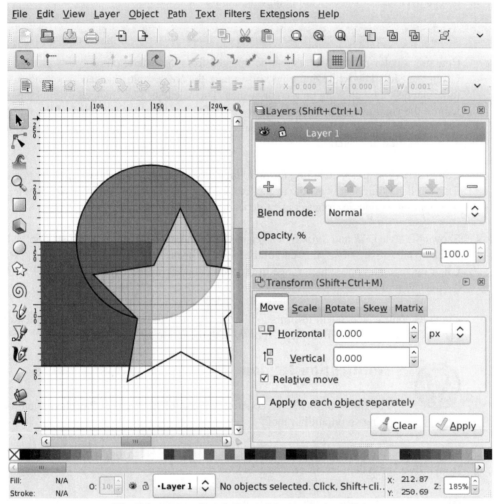

The Inkscape main window with two docked dialogs.

The docked dialogs can be rearranged, resized (if space permits), stacked, and iconified. To move a dialog, **Left Mouse Drag** in the dialog's title bar. Dialogs can also be dragged off of the main window into their own window. Each dialog can have its own window or they can be grouped in floating docks.

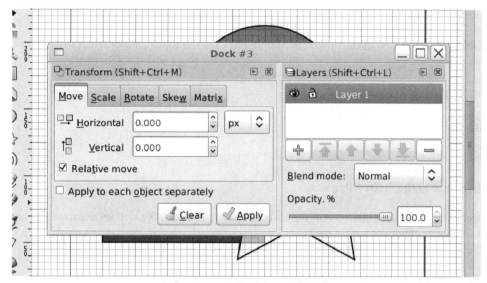

A floating *Dock* with two dialogs.

Selecting *Floating* under *Dialog behavior* in the *Windows* section of the *Inkscape Preferences* dialog (File → [image] Inkscape Preferences... (**Shift+Ctrl+P**)) disables the use of docks. Instead, all dialogs will be opened in their own window.

There is still some work to be done on the implementation of dockable dialogs. For example, a few dialogs have yet to be converted to be dockable (e.g., *Text*, *Object properties*). Bugs may also be encountered.

# The Swedish Flag—A Short Example

We will use Inkscape to draw a simple flag, that of Sweden. This example will cover: setting a custom drawing size, setting up a *Grid* to help precisely place objects, the use of the *Rectangle Tool*, changing the color of objects, and finally saving a drawing and exporting the drawing into a form suitable for use on a web page.

Flag of Sweden. ✪

The steps we'll take are:

- Start Inkscape.

- Set the drawing size.

- Set up a *Grid* to guide drawing objects.

- Draw the flag background.

- Draw the cross.

- Set the colors of the background and cross.

- Save and export the drawing.

It is assumed that you know how to start Inkscape and to use a mouse, touch pad, or tablet to select menu items and move scroll bars.

## Procedure 1.1. Drawing the Swedish Flag

1. **Start Inkscape.**

   The program will open a single window with a default page size.

2. **Set the page size to the desired flag size.**

   The correct width to height proportion of the Swedish flag is 16 to 10. We will set the page size to a 320 by 200 pixel area. What is important here is the ratio. The size of drawing when printed or exported to a bitmap can be changed later (by default, a pixel corresponds to a screen pixel when exported).

   a. **Open the *Document Properties* dialog.**

      Open the *Document Properties* dialog by selecting File → 🗎 Document Properties... (**Shift+Ctrl+D**).

   b. **Set page size.**

      In the newly opened window, set *Custom size*: *Units* to "px" using the drop-down menus. Then set the flag size by changing *Custom size*: *Width* to 320, and *Height* to 200. This can be done by typing the numbers into the entry boxes next to the labels (one could use the small up and down arrows to change the entered value, but this does not work well when an entered number could be non-integer). Note that when you type in new values, changes don't take effect until you hit **Return**, click on a different entry box, or move the cursor from the *Document Properties* dialog to another Inkscape window. *Page orientation* will automatically change to *Landscape*.

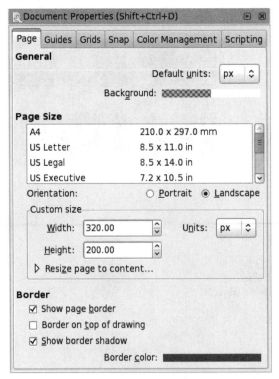

*Document Properties* dialog.

c. **Fit the page into the drawing area.**

The page is now a small rectangle at the bottom of the drawing area. To fit the page to the drawing area, click on the *Zoom-Page* icon ⊕ in the *Command Bar*, or use the keyboard shortcut: **5**. The Inkscape window should then look like this:

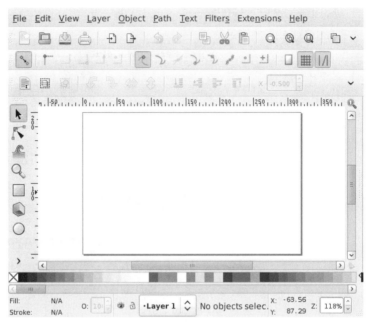

The Inkscape window after you have adjusted the page size and zoom level.

3. **Set a *Grid*.**

While the *Document Properties* dialog is open, we will make one more change that will make drawing the background and cross easier. A *Grid* is a set of (usually) horizontal and vertical lines that provide a guide for drawing objects. Optionally, objects will "snap" to a *Grid* when being drawn or moved, enabling accurate drawing. A *Grid* will not show when the drawing is printed or exported as a bitmap.

a. **Create a *Grid*.**

Select the *Grids* tab in the *Document Properties* dialog. Under the *Creation* section, select *Rectangular grid* from the drop-down menu (if not already selected) and then click on the *New* button. You should see a grid of blue lines on the canvas. If you don't, make sure both the *Enabled* and the *Visible* boxes are checked in the *Defined grids* section. If they are checked, toggle on the global visibility of *Grids* using the command View → ▦ Grid (#).

b. **Adjust the *Grid* spacing.**

You can now adjust the *Grid* to match the cross. The dimension and position of the cross is given by Swedish law. The vertical bar is to be placed between 5/16ths and 7/16ths of the flag width, while the horizontal bar is to be placed between 4/10ths and 6/10ths of the flag height.

The default *Grid* has minor divisions every pixel and major divisions every 5 pixels. Depending on the zoom level, not all divisions may be displayed. A more useful *Grid* for drawing the flag would be one with divisions every 20 pixels so that the *Grid* lines divide the flag width into 16 parts and the flag height into 10 parts.

To change the scale of the *Grid* go back to the *Grids* tab of the *Document Properties* window.

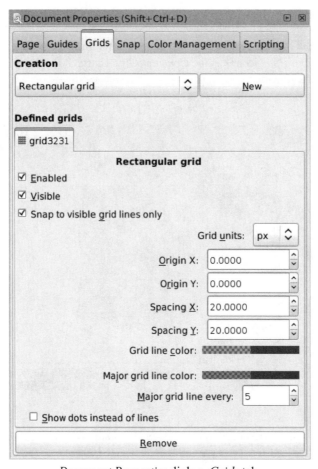

*Document Properties* dialog, *Grids* tab.

Set both *Spacing X* and *Spacing Y* to 20.

To help draw the flag accurately, we will turn on the snapping of nodes to the grid lines. First select the *Snap* tab. Check the *Always snap* option under the *Snap to grids* section. This will force snapping regardless of the distance the cursor is from a *Grid* line. Enable overall snapping by highlighting the Snap ( ✎ ) icon in the *Snap Bar*. Enable snapping of nodes by highlighting the Snap Nodes ( ↺ ) icon in the *Snap Bar*. Next make sure the Snap to Grid ( ⊞ ) icon is highlighted in the *Snap Bar* (you may have to widen/heighten the Inkscape window if the icon is not shown depending on the orientation of the *Snap Bar*, or you can use the drop-down menu opened with the the *Down arrow* at the right end or bottom of the bar and check the *Grids* box). Finally, make sure the Snap Bounding Box ( ⌐ ) icon is not highlighted.

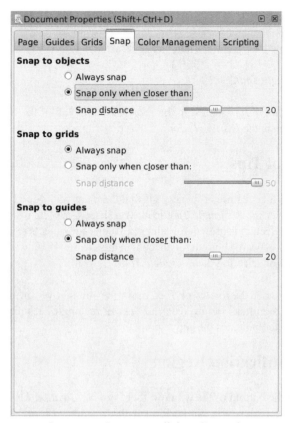

*Document Properties* dialog, *Snap* tab.

After making the changes, you may close the *Document Properties* window. The Inkscape window should look like this:

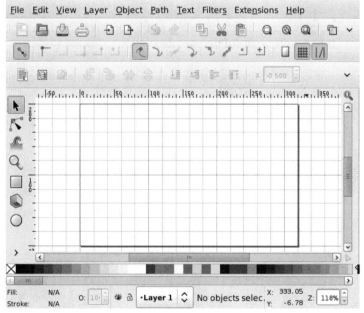

Drawing area with *Grid* turned on and adjusted. Note the *Snap Bar* settings.

4. **Draw the flag background.**

The flag has a light-blue background. There are several ways to accomplish this; we'll use a filled rectangle.

a. **Select the *Rectangle Tool*.**

Click on the *Rectangle Tool* icon ▢ in the *Tool Box* on the left of the Inkscape window (or use the keyboard shortcut **F4**) to select the *Rectangle Tool*.

# Tool Tips

One nice feature of Inkscape is that there are very good built-in hints. While the mouse pointer is over the *Rectangle Tool* icon, you'll see a *tool tip* describing the use of the *Rectangle Tool*. This feature is present for almost all icons and objects in Inkscape. The *tool tip* usually includes the keyboard shortcut for an icon, in this case (F4), indicating that pressing **F4** would be another way of selecting the *Rectangle Tool*.

Once you have selected the *Rectangle Tool*, move the pointer over the drawing area. The pointer will become a rectangle. This signifies you are ready to draw a rectangle or square. The small cross at the upper-left corner of the pointer indicates the active point.

# Notification Region

At the bottom of the window, there is a *Notification Region* (in the *Status Bar*). This tells you what actions you can perform with the selected tool. Note that the region isn't always large enough to show all the options. Moving the mouse over the region will pop up a *tool tip* showing the full content. One could also widen the Inkscape window to see more of the region. When the *Select Tool* is in use, the *Notification Region* will also tell you the number and type of objects that are currently selected.

b. **Draw the background rectangle.**

To draw the background rectangle, follow the hint in the *Notification Region*. Click-drag the pointer from one corner to the opposite corner of the page area.

Note how the corners of the rectangle snap to the *Grid*. If your rectangle doesn't match the page size, you can use one of the drag handles (little squares) in the upper left or lower right of the rectangle to adjust the size of the rectangle. (The circle at the upper-right corner has a different function. It is used to round the four corners of a rectangle.) As you drag the squares around, they will snap to the *Grid*.

If you make a mistake, you can click on the *Undo* icon ↺ in the *Command Bar*, use Edit → ↺ Undo (**Ctrl+Z**) from the *Menu Bar*, or use the keyboard shortcut **Ctrl+Z** to undo the change.

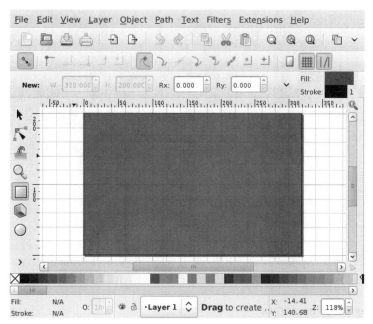

Background rectangle.

The background color will need to be changed. One could do that now, but it is easier to wait and change it at the same time the cross color is set.

5.  **Draw the cross.**

    The cross consists of a horizontal bar and a vertical bar.

    a.  **Draw the horizontal bar.**

        With the *Rectangle Tool* still selected, create a bar by starting six grid lines from the bottom of the background rectangle on the left side of the flag and click-dragging the pointer until four grid lines from the bottom on the right side of the flag. The rectangle corners should snap to the grid. Notice that the rectangle *Fill* color is the same as the background color but you should still be able to see the new bar. Make any corrections to the size and position of the rectangle that are necessary.

        **If you can't see the horizontal bar ...** don't panic! Inkscape often uses the *Current style* (attributes: color, line style, etc.) to draw new objects. The *Current style* is set to that of the last object where the style was modified (including that of a previous Inkscape session). If the border color matches the *Fill* color of the rectangle or if drawing the border has been turned off, AND if the *transparency* or *Alpha* is set to 100% you will have the same situation as a polar bear in a snow storm. There are many fixes but the easiest one is to change the horizontal bar color to be different from the background color. This can be done by clicking on any of the color samples in the *Palette* while the newly drawn bar is still selected (indicated by the dashed line around the perimeter). If a color sample in the *Palette* is clicked on when no object is selected, the *Current style* will be changed to use that color for the *Fill* of the next *Rectangle* drawn.

    b.  **Draw the vertical bar.**

        The vertical bar should extend between 5 and 7 grid lines from the left of the background rectangle.

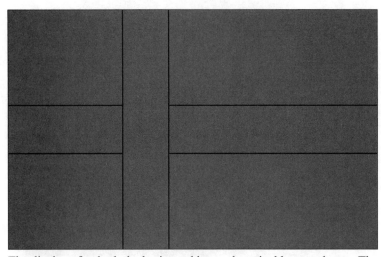

The display after both the horizontal bar and vertical bar are drawn. The border lines show how one rectangle of the cross overlaps the other.

c.  **Merge the bars into a cross.**

One could stop here. After removing the border for the bars, one would have the desired cross. But it might be better (and at least more pedagogical) to merge the bars into a cross, so that the cross is one *object* rather than two.

i.  **Select both the rectangles.**

Both bars need to be selected at once. This can be done with the *Select Tool* and the **Shift** key. Enable the *Select Tool* by clicking on the ⬉ icon in the *Tool Box* or by using one of the keyboard shortcuts **F1** or **s**.

After changing to the *Select Tool* (indicated by the pointer changing to an arrow when over the canvas or crossed arrows when over an object), click on one of the rectangles in the cross. Then, while holding the **Shift** key down, click on the other rectangle in the cross. Both rectangles should be selected as indicated by their dotted borders. Note that the background rectangle is not surrounded by a dotted border and that the *Notification Region* reports that two objects are selected.

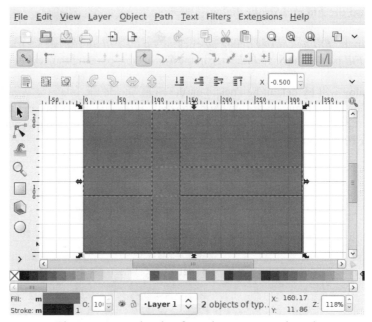

The two rectangles that form the cross are selected.

ii. **Merge paths.**

The two rectangles can be combined by merging their *Paths*. (Here, the *Path* is the border of the rectangle.) To merge the two rectangles, select Path → Union (**Ctrl++**) from the *Menu Bar*. The rectangles are now merged into one object.

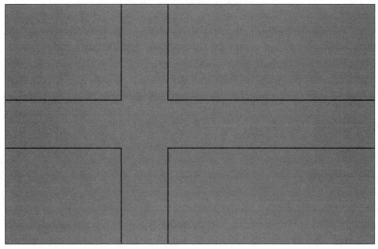

The cross after the rectangles have been merged.

The cross is no longer made of *Rectangle* objects but is instead defined as a *Path*.

6. **Set the colors of the background and cross.**

The next step is to adjust the colors of the background and cross to the colors of the Swedish flag. We'll use the *Fill and Stroke* dialog so that we can precisely set the correct colors.

a.  **Bring up the *Fill and Stroke* dialog.**

Open up the *Fill and Stroke* dialog by clicking on the *Fill and Stroke* icon ◢ in the *Command Bar*, clicking on the *Fill* part of the *Style Indicator* in the *Status Bar*, or using the keyboard shortcut **Shift+Ctrl+F**.

The dialog will by default be docked on the right, inside the Inkscape window. If you have room, undock the dialog by dragging on the top bar of the dialog (the gray bar with *Fill and Stroke* written in it). Drop the dialog outside of the Inkscape window. Hit **5** to recenter the drawing inside the main window (or use the **Middle Mouse** button to drag the drawing back to the center).

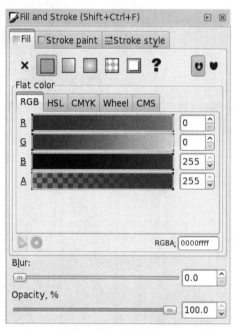

*Fill and Stroke* dialog.

Make sure that the *Fill* tab is highlighted at the top of the dialog; if not, click on the tab. The parameters in the *Fill and Stroke* dialog apply to the currently selected drawing object(s).

b.  **Set the *Fill* background color.**

Select the background rectangle by clicking on it with the *Select Tool*. The *Notification Region* should report that one rectangle is selected and the *Style Indicator* will show the *Fill* color and the *Stroke* color of the rectangle. The *Flat Color* ■ icon should be highlighted. If not, click on it.

There are several ways to specify the desired *Fill* color. We'll use the *Red-Green-Blue (RGB)* mode (select the *RGB* tab if not already highlighted). In this mode, a color is specified by setting the amount of each of the three primary colors. The scale extends from 0 to 255. One can change the amount of each primary color via sliding the little triangles left or right on the bars labeled R, G, B, or by changing the numbers in the boxes to the right of the bars (via typing or using the up/down arrows). For the Swedish flag, the background color is specified by the NIS standard color 4055-R95B, which is equivalent to the values: Red: 0, Green: 90, Blue: 173. The fourth entry is *Alpha* (A) or transparency, which indicates how opaque the object should be. We want our flag to have a solid, non–see-through background, so *Alpha* should be set to 255 (range is 0 to 255). Likewise, the *Master opacity* slide should be set to 100%.

One additional step is to turn off any *Stroke* (border) color. In the *Fill and Stroke* dialog, select the *Stroke paint* tab and click on the *No paint* × icon to turn off the stroke.

c.   **Set the cross *Fill* color.**

Select the cross and change the *Fill* color following the previous instructions. When the cross is selected, the *Notification Region* will report that a *Path* with 12 nodes is selected. You'll need to reselect the *Fill* tab. This time, set the colors to R: 255, G: 194, and B: 0. Also turn off the border as done previously.

7.   **Save and export your work.**

Now is the time to save your work. Select File → 💾 Save As... (**Shift+Ctrl+S**). The dialog that appears will depend on your operating system. Select the folder or directory where the drawing should be saved and give the drawing an appropriate name. Finally, click on the *Save* button.

One last step is to export your file as a *PNG (Portable Network Graphic)* bitmap that can be used by other graphics programs or on a web page. Bring up the *Export Bitmap* dialog: (File → 📄 Export Bitmap... (**Shift+Ctrl+E**)).

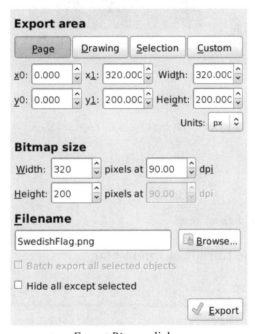

*Export Bitmap* dialog.

There are four options for choosing the area to export: *Page*, *Drawing*, *Selection*, and *Custom*. In our case, the *Page* and *Drawing* areas are the same. Select either one, then enter or select a filename at the bottom and click on the *Export* button to save the drawing as a *PNG*. You should now have a *PNG* file with a flag as shown at the beginning of this section. Note, the dialog will remain on the screen even after a successful export.

# The European Flag—A More Elaborate Example

We will use Inkscape to draw a more complicated flag, that of the European Union [http://www.coe.int/T/E/Com/ About_Coe/flag_guide.asp] (EU). This tutorial will cover using the *Star Tool* to draw a regular star, using *Guide Lines* for positioning, making copies or clones of an object, and precisely moving those copies to their proper places.

Flag of the European Union.✪

The steps are:

- Set basic drawing parameters (flag size, grid, background color).

- Add *Guide Lines*.

- Draw a single star.

- Duplicate the star and position the duplicates.

## Procedure 1.2. Drawing the European Union Flag

1.  **Set up the drawing.**

    To begin, start Inkscape. The page size needs to be set to the correct proportions for the EU flag, which has a 3 to 2 width to height ratio. We will use a 270 by 180 pixel area. This will facilitate drawing and placing of the stars to the EU specifications.

    Follow the instructions for setting the page size and creating a grid given in the Swedish flag example but set the flag width to 270 and the flag height to 180 pixels. Also set the grid spacing to 10 pixels rather than 20 (so we can snap to the flag width which is not divisible by 20). Enable snapping of nodes in the *Snap* tab.

    Draw a rectangle for the flag background that covers the entire page. Next use the *Fill and Stroke* dialog (Object → ✏ Fill and Stroke... (**Shift+Ctrl+F**)) to set the color of the background to the officially prescribed *RGB* color: 0, 51, 153. Check that the *Alpha* (A) value is 255 and the *Master opacity* is 100%.

2.  **Add *Guide Lines*.**

    For placing the stars, it is easiest to draw the first star at the center of the flag (at 135, 90). You can then use simple translations to move the stars to their final positions. You can make it easier to keep track of the center point by adding *Guide Lines*. The *Guide Lines* are lines that, like the *Grid*, are not part of the actual drawing.

    To add a *Guide Line*, click-drag starting on a *Ruler* near the middle and finishing at the desired point on the canvas. (If you start near the edge, an angled *Guide Line* will be created.) The *Guide Line* can be moved by selecting (with the *Select Tool*) and dragging. Be careful not to move the background! If you do, just undo the move ( ↶ or **Ctrl+Z**). To precisely place the *Guide Line*, double-click on the *Guide Line* using the *Select Tool*. A dialog will open where you can type in the exact position required.

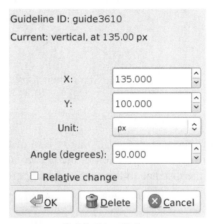

*Guide Line* dialog.

The *Guide Lines* can be turned on and off by using the *Guide Line* ( |/| ) icon in the *Snap Bar* (recall that you may need to enlarge the Inkscape window to see the icon) or via the command View → ⌐ Guides (|). Checking the box *Snap guides while dragging* under the *Guides* tab will allow *Guide Lines* to snap to the *Grid*.

Add both a horizontal *Guide Line* at $y = 90$ px and a vertical *Guide Line* at $x = 135$ px.

3.  **Draw a star.**

We need to draw a five-pointed star that will be duplicated to create the 12 stars of the flag. To avoid drawing a blue star on a blue background, click to the side of the drawing to deselect the background rectangle, then click on one of the colors in the *Palette*. When no object is selected, clicking on a color in the *Palette* will set the default *Fill* to that color.

a.  **Select *Star Tool* and set up the star parameters.**

To draw a star, select the *Star Tool* ✩ (keyboard shortcut **\***) in the *Tool Box*. You may need to click on the small right-arrow at the bottom of the *Tool Box* if the icon is not shown to access the pop-up menu. According to the EU flag specification, the stars on the flag are five-pointed with one point straight up. The easiest way to get the star the exact shape is to use the *Tool Controls*.

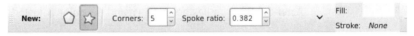

The *Star Tool-Tool Controls*.

In the *Tool Controls*, set the number of *Corners* to 5. Select the *Star* icon ( ✩ ) to enable drawing of a star. The *Spoke Ratio* is the ratio of the radius of the innermost point to the radius of the outermost point of a star (R2/R1). For a "regular" five-pointed star this should be 0.382. If you don't see the *Spoke Ratio* entry box, you can either widen the Inkscape window or access the parameter by clicking on the down-arrow at the right of the *Tool Controls*; select *Spoke Ratio* from the menu and then *0.382: pentagram* from the new drop-down menu.) The other entries in the *Tool Controls*, *Rounded* and *Randomized*, should both be zero.

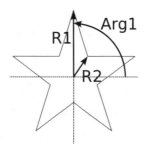

The Star dimensions.

b. **Draw the star.**

The specified radius (R1) of the star on the EU flag is 1/18 of the flag height, or 10 pixels with our flag size. Starting with the mouse at the intersection of the *Guide Lines*, click drag upward for 10 pixels. You must move the cursor half the distance to the next grid line before you'll see a star. The upper point will snap to the *Grid*.

Adjust the color of the star to a RGB value of (255, 204, 0). Make sure *Alpha* (A) is 255 and the *Master opacity* is 100%.

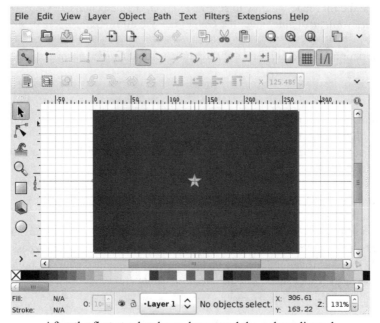

After the first star has been drawn and the color adjusted.

4. **Duplicate and place the 12 stars.**

a. **Clone a star.**

Either click on the icon 🖻 in the *Command Bar* or use Edit → Clone → 🖻 Create Clone (**Alt+D**) to make a *Clone* of the star. A *Clone* is a copy that is linked to the original so that if you modify the original, the *Clone* will also change. This is handy if you need to make a common adjustment to all the stars (change color, enlarge, etc.).

b. **Place a cloned star.**

The EU flag specifies that the stars be evenly distributed on a circle that is one third of the flag height and at positions corresponding to the hours of a clock. The easiest way to place the stars properly is to use the move feature on the *Move* tab of the *Transform* dialog (Object → Transform... (**Shift+Ctrl+M**)). Open the dialog, and if you have room, drag it out of the Inkscape window. To move the cloned star to the 12 o'clock position, set the *Vertical* (*y*) direction to 60 pixels. Make sure the *Relative move* box is checked and the units are set to pixels (px), then click the *Apply* button.

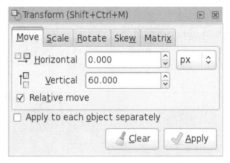

The *Transform* dialog, set to move the first cloned star into place.

Next, select the original star and make a new *Clone*. This time move the *Clone* 60 pixels down (−60). Repeat for the *Horizontal* (*x*) direction. For the rest of the stars, use the eight permutations of *x*(*y*) = ±30 and *y*(*x*) = ±52 pixels (60 times the sine and cosine of 30°, respectively).

After all 12 stars are placed, you can delete the original star. The links between the clones and the original star are automatically broken.

If desired, save your work and export a bitmap as for the Swedish flag.

# A Hiking Club Logo—An Exercise in Paths

We will use Inkscape to draw a logo for the Fuji Hiking and Mountaineering Club, as shown below. This tutorial will cover the use of text, importing a bitmap for use as a guide in drawing, and manipulation of paths.

Logo for the Fuji Hiking and Mountaineering Club.✪

The steps are:

- Start Inkscape and set the drawing size.

- Create the text for the logo.

- Import a bitmap with the shape of Fuji mountain.

- Convert the text to a path and manipulate that path.

- Trace the Fuji mountain picture to obtain a path.

- Trim the text to the mountain shape using Fuji mountain path.

- Add snow to the mountain top.

- Add finishing touches.

## Procedure 1.3. Creating the Fuji Hiking and Mountaineering Club Logo

1. **Set up the drawing.**

   To begin, start Inkscape.

   Follow the instructions for setting the page size and grid spacing given in the Swedish flag example, but set drawing size to a width of 500 and a height of 300 pixels. Do *not* create a *Grid*.

2. **Create the text.**

   a. **Enter the text.**

      Select the *Text Tool* **A** from the *Tool Box* (keyboard shortcut **F8**). Click on the left side of the page to establish a starting point for the text. You should see a blinking bar. Type the initials for the club "FHMC"; the text should appear in a small size on the page.

   b. **Adjust the text.**

      The text is too small and may not use the most suitable font. To change the attributes of the text, use the items in the *Text Tool-Tool Controls*.

The *Text Tool-Tool Controls* (v0.48).

The *Text Tool-Tool Controls* (v0.47).

With the text selected, choose a suitable font from the pull-down menu on the left. Nimbus Roman No9 L is a good freely available font with the wide serifs needed for the logo. If you do not have this font installed on your system, you can choose a similar font such as Times or Times New Roman. Select the **Bold** style by clicking on the Bold ( **a** ) icon in the bar, and set the *Font size* to 144. The changes to the text are shown immediately.

Finally, center the text near the bottom of the drawing by using the *Select Tool* and dragging the text down.

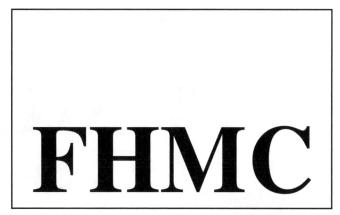

The text for the logo, sized and positioned.

3. **Import the guide for the mountain shape.**

We'll use as a basis for the shape of Fuji San a bitmap tracing of the mountain. You could use any suitable drawing or picture of the mountain (in *PNG*, *GIF*, or *JPEG* format). You can download the same image used here from the book's website (http://tavmjong.free.fr/INKSCAPE/).

a. **Import the bitmap.**

Import the bitmap using the *Import* dialog (File → ⊡ Import... (**Ctrl+I**)). *New in v0.48:* A dialog will pop up asking if you wish to *embed* or *link* to the image. Since we will not need to keep the image around, it is better to simply link to the file.

b. **Adjust the bitmap.**

The bitmap's image size doesn't match well with the text. The easiest way to adjust the size is to select the image with the *Select Tool* ⬉ (keyboard shortcut **F1**). When the image is selected, a set of double-headed arrows appears around the *bounding box* (dotted line) of the image. Dragging on the handles will scale the image. Dragging while holding down the **Ctrl** key will keep the width to height ratio constant. Dragging on a non-transparent part of the image will move the whole image. Note that if you click on the image twice with the *Select Tool*, the corner arrows change to rotation arrows. Just click on the image one more time to restore the scale arrows. One can also use the **Arrow** keys to move the image. Note: You may want to decrease the zoom a bit (**3** when image selected) or widen the Inkscape window before enlarging the image.

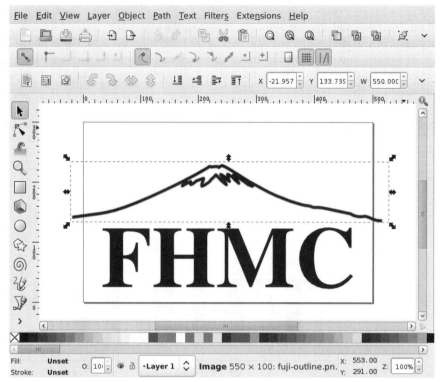

Image selected and with arrows, ready for scaling.

Drag on the corner arrows while holding down the **Ctrl** key and drag the image until you are happy with the scale and placement. I have chosen to center the top of Fuji over the right side serif of the H.

The outline of Fuji San, sized and positioned.

4. **Manipulate the text.**

In this section, we will convert the text to a *Path* so we can alter the shape of the letters. The text needs to be extended upward, above the outline of the mountain so that we can *Clip* it to match the shape of the mountain. We will also make a few additional cosmetic changes to the letters.

a. **Convert the text to a path.**

The text, stored as a text object, needs to be converted to a path object for editing. This process is not reversible and the text will lose its memory of being text. To convert the text to a path, select the text with the

*Select Tool* and use the Path → 🗗 Object to Path (**Shift+Ctrl+C**) command. Each letter is converted into a separate path and all the paths are placed in a *Group* (when objects are in a *Group* they can be manipulated as if they were one object). This is normally a good thing, but for our purposes it would be better if all the letters were not grouped and were composed of one path. So, with the text selected, use the Object → 🖾 Ungroup (**Shift+Ctrl+G**) command to remove the group and then Path → 🗗 Combine (**Ctrl+K**) to combine the paths.

b.   **Extend the text upward.**

    i.   **Extend the F and H up.**

We'll start with extending the F and H. Select the *Node Tool* 🖈 (**F2**). And click on the letters to select the text path.

The text is now surrounded by a series of small diamonds. These are the *nodes* of the path. They define places where the path changes direction or curvature. The path is edited by manipulating these nodes.

At this point, it is easier if you zoom in on the drawing. There are multiple ways to *zoom*. Using the **Ctrl** key with the scroll wheel of a scrolling mouse is one way. The drawing will zoom around the cursor position. Another way is to use the + or = keys. In this case, the zoom is around the center of the viewable canvas. The scroll bars can be used to pan the drawing (i.e., change the viewable region).

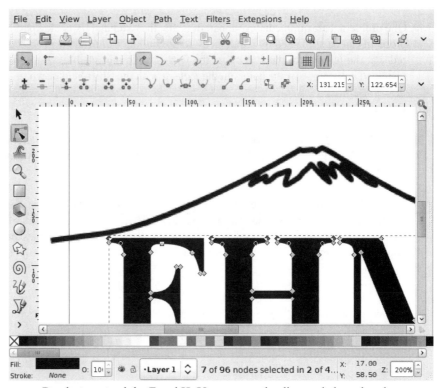

Ready to extend the F and H. You can see the diamond-shaped nodes.

To select a node, click on it with the *Node Tool*. Holding the **Shift** key down allows nodes to be added (or removed) from the selection. One can also use a *rubber-band* selection technique to select multiple nodes at one time. To do this, click-drag from one point to another. All nodes within the box defined by the starting and stopping points will be selected. The click-drag must not begin on a node. The selected nodes will change from gray to blue and yellow when selected.

Select the top nodes of the F and of both sides of the H. A total of seven nodes are selected in this example (there are two on top of each other at the upper-right corner of the F). If you have chosen a different font you may have to select a different number.

Now click-drag on any of the selected nodes upward, holding the **Ctrl** key down to constrain the direction of the drag to vertical. Drag until all the selected nodes are above the outline of the mountain.

After the F and H have been extended.

One problem that is immediately apparent is that the extended parts hide part of the bitmap image. This problem can be alleviated by temporarily removing the *Fill* of the text objects. To do this, click on the red *x* at the left end of the *Palette*. If the text is no longer visible, you will need to make the *Stroke* visible. Click on one of the colors in the *Palette* with the **Shift** held down.

ii.  **Extend the M.**

Extending the M may be more difficult than extending the first two letters, it depends on the font selected. For Nimbus Roman No9 L, we need to add two extra nodes in order to preserve the shape of the stems of the M.

Use the *Node Tool* to select the four nodes at the top of the M. Click on the ⚓ icon (*Insert New Node*) in the *Tool Controls*. This will add two nodes, each halfway between the pairs of adjacent selected nodes. Click on the background to deselect all the nodes, then click-drag the new node on the left side to be above the rightmost node of the left serif, as shown next.

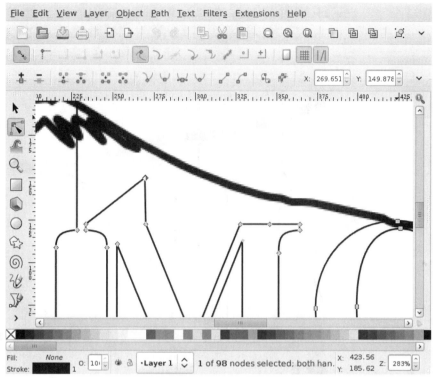

In the middle of the process to extend the M.

Do the equivalent for the new node on the right side.

Now select the four top nodes of the serifs (the two new nodes replacing two of the previous top nodes) and drag them up, holding the **Ctrl** key down to constrain their movement in the vertical direction. Move the nodes above the mountain.

iii. **Extend the C.**

Extending the C also requires a bit of node manipulation. Select the leftmost node and the top-center node of the C. Convert these to *Corner* nodes by clicking on the ⋎ icon in the *Tool Controls*. This will allow the path to have an abrupt change in direction at the nodes. Click on the ⌀ icon in the *Tool Controls* to convert the selected segment to a line. Click on the background to deselect both nodes, then click-drag the topmost node of the line to move it above the lower node of the line, as shown next.

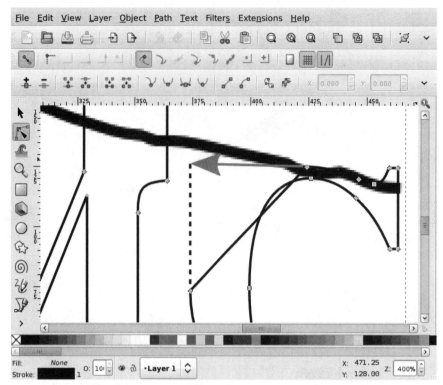

In the middle of the process to extend the C. The arrow shows the movement of the node and the dotted line, the new position of the line segment.

Select all the nodes along the top of the C and drag them above the mountain, again using the **Ctrl** key to constrain the movement in the vertical direction.

The text path should now look like this:

After all the characters in the text have been extended above the mountain image.

c.   **Adjust kerning.**

The *kerning* of the text isn't quite right. The C is too far from the M. This could have been corrected while the text was still a *Text* object, but it would have been hard to get correct spacing without seeing the newly extended parts.

To move the C, use the *Node Tool* to select all the nodes in the C, then use the left and right **Arrow** keys to move the C until the gap between the C and M matches the gaps between the F and H, and the H and M. If the movement step is too large, use **Alt+Arrow** to make smaller movements.

Adjust the spacing between the other letters if needed.

d.  **Fill in the gap in the M.**

The gap between the two extensions of the M is a bit wide. To reduce the visual effect of the gap we will add a block in between.

i.  **Add the rectangle.**

Select the *Rectangle Tool* ▢ (**F4**) and click drag a rectangle between the extensions of the M as shown below. Use the rectangle handles to adjust the position.

The text after adding a rectangle between the extensions of the M.

ii.  **Merge the rectangle with text.**

For later steps, the rectangle object must be merged with the text path. Select with the *Select Tool* both the rectangle and the text path. Then use the command: Path → ⬗ Combine (**Ctrl+K**) to create one path out of the two. The rectangle object is automatically converted to a path object before the merge.

5.  **Trace the bitmap mountain to form a new path.**

The top of the extended text will be trimmed with the shape of Fuji San. To do this, the bitmap image of the mountain must be converted to a path. But first, make any last-minute adjustments to the position of the mountain using the *Select Tool*.

Inkscape includes a tool to trace the bitmap automatically (Chapter 20, *Tracing Bitmaps*) but the path produced is too complicated for our use.

Instead, we will use the *Pencil Tool* ✐ (**F6**). In the *Tool Controls* make sure that *Mode* is set to *Bezier* ( ⌐ ) and that *Shape* is set to *None*. A *Smoothing* value of about 30 will give you a reasonable number of nodes. Starting at one end of the mountain, click-drag the pointer along the top edge of the mountain to create a new path. When you reach the far end, loop the path back to the starting point, as shown next.

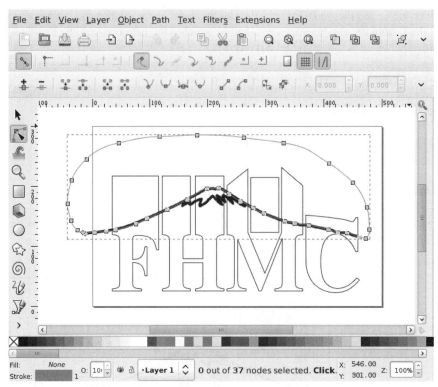

After tracing the mountain to form a path, the stroke color has been changed to red to make it easier to see.

It is not important that the ends of the path meet exactly. It is important that the loop encloses all of the tops of the letters. The path can be tweaked by using the *Node Tool* to reposition any wayward nodes. It helps to make the path a different color using the *Fill and Stroke* dialog.

6.  **Trim the tops of the letters.**

We'll use the *Path Difference* command to subtract the overlap between the mountain path and the text path from the text path. It is important that the mountain path be on top of the text path because this command subtracts the top path from the bottom path. As the mountain path was created after the text path, it should already be on top.

To do the path subtraction, select both the mountain path and the text path using the *Select Tool* (hold the **Shift** key down while selecting the second object) and then use the *Path Difference* command: Path → 🖉 Difference (**Ctrl+-**). The mountain path will disappear and the text path should look like below.

The text after trimming to the outline of the mountain.

7.    **Adding the snow to the mountain top.**

You could now delete the bitmap of Fuji San, change the fill of the text object to solid black, and call it a day, as shown next.

The logo without snow on Fuji San's top.

But it might look better if the logo included a snow cap.

To create a snow cap, zoom in on the bitmap image of the snow and the use the *Pencil Tool* to trace the snow, creating a loop as with the mountain top below.

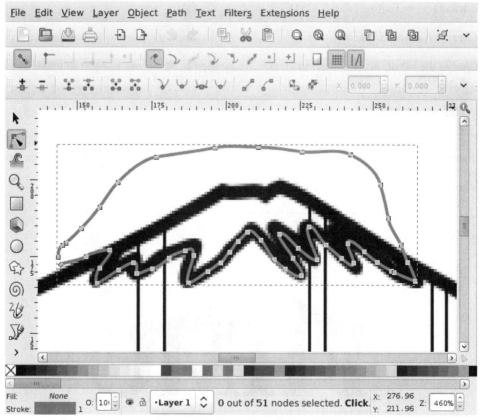

After tracing the snow to form a path.

The next step is to create a copy of the text object, with which to cut the snow path. To create a copy, select the text and then click on the *Duplicate* 🗐 icon in the *Command Bar* or use the menu entry Edit → 🗐 Duplicate (**Ctrl+D**).

With the **Shift** key down, select the snow path. Both the duplicate text path and snow path should be selected. Use the *Path Intersection* command: Path → 🗐 Intersection (**Ctrl+\***) to combine the two paths. The logo should look like:

The logo after adding a path for snow.

8. **Finishing touches.**

   a. **Delete the Fuji San bitmap.**

   The bitmap is no longer needed. Delete it by selecting it and then using Edit → 🗑 Delete (**Delete or Backspace**) or Edit → ✂ Cut (**Ctrl+X**).

   b. **Correct *Fill* and *Stroke*.**

   Change the fill of the text object to black. Change the *Fill* of the snow object to white and the *Stroke paint* to black.

   c. **Widen the snow outline.**

   The snow outline looks a bit thin. To give it more definition, use the *Stroke style* tab of the *Fill and Stroke* dialog. Change the width to 3 pixels. The width of the text path must also be changed to 3 pixels to match.

The logo is now finished. Save your work as in the previous tutorials.

The finished logo.

# The Northern Pacific Railway Logo—A Tracing Example

Inkscape's *auto-tracing* capability is very useful for turning existing artwork into *SVG* drawings. In this example, we will create the artwork for a logo from a photograph. The logo is for the Northern Pacific (or NP) railroad, which features the *Yin and Yang* symbol. This tutorial will cover use of the *Trace Bitmap* dialog as well as manipulation of paths. The use of *Layers* is also introduced.

Logo for the Northern Pacific Railroad featuring the Yin and Yang (Monad) symbol.✪

The steps are:

• Start Inkscape and set the drawing size.

• Import the source photo.

• Auto trace the logo.

• Clean up the logo paths.

## Procedure 1.4. Creating the Northern Pacific Logo

1. **Set up the drawing.**

   To begin, start Inkscape.

   Follow the instructions for setting the page size and grid spacing given in the Swedish flag example but set drawing size to a width of 500 and a height of 500 pixels. Do *not* turn on the *Grid*.

2. **Import the photograph.**

   You can use any photograph (in *PNG*, *GIF*, or *JPEG* form) with a logo for this exercise. However, sharp, high resolution photographs work best. I will use part of a photograph from the railroad photographer James M. Fredrickson. The photograph has been cropped to show only the logo. If you wish to use the same photograph as used in the exercise, you can download it from the book's website: http://tavmjong.free.fr/INKSCAPE/.

The end of a passenger car showing the Northern Pacific logo.

The NP logo, cropped and zoomed from the previous photograph.

a.  **Import the photograph.**

Import the photograph using the File → 🗁 Import... (**Ctrl+I**) dialog. *New in v0.48:* A dialog will pop up asking if you wish to *embed* or *link* to the image. Since we will not need to keep the image around, it is better to simply link to the file.

b.  **Adjust the size and position of the photograph.**

Adjust the photograph's size and position to match the Inkscape page with the *Select Tool* ↖ (keyboard shortcut **F1**). Drag the corners while holding down the **Ctrl** key to preserve the aspect ratio. Drag the body to translate the photo.

3.  **Trace the logo.**

Inkscape utilizes the *Potrace* tracing library to create *SVG* paths from bitmap images. To trace the picture, call up the *Trace Bitmap* dialog (Path → ◎ Trace Bitmap... (**Shift+Alt+B**)).

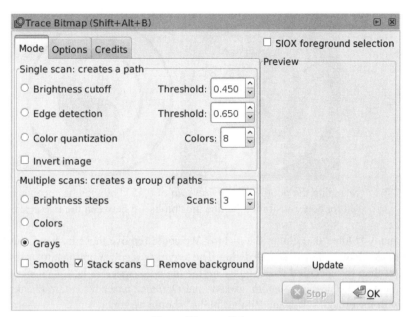

*Trace Bitmap* dialog.

The *Trace Bitmap* dialog presents a number of choices for how the tracing is done. Looking at the image, we see that there are three different grayscale levels. This suggests that we use one of the *Multiple scans* methods. As this is a monochrome photograph, we'll try the *Grays* option with *Scans* set to three. This will give us three regions, each corresponding to one of the grayscale levels. There is the possibility to smooth the bitmap prior to tracing by checking the *Smooth* box. This is not necessary as our starting photograph doesn't have any speckle. Finally, there is an option to generate paths for mutually exclusive areas or that include all darker regions. The latter is more useful for us, so we check the *Stack scans* option box. The resulting traces are shown below.

Results of scanning using the *Multiple scans, Grays* option. On the far left is the output of the scan. The three paths that make up the scan are shown separately to the right. As each path includes all darker regions, the path for the lightest region is just a square covering the entire page.

The paths generated with the *Grays* option are usable as a starting point for the NP logo. However, we might be able to do better if we use the *Single scan, Brightness cutoff* method, optimizing the threshold for each scan.

Select the *Brightness cutoff* option in the *Trace Bitmap* dialog. Adjust the *Threshold* to create a well-defined Yin and Yang path. Pressing the *Update* button will create a preview. A threshold of 0.15 seems to work well. After finding a good value, click on the *OK* button to generate the path.

Scanning the photo with a *Threshold* of 0.15. The scan has been shifted for better visibility. Notice the "blobs" in between the two circles.

The scan has many "blobs" that clutter the picture. We could remove these by hand, but there is an easier way.
Select the *Options* tab in the *Trace Bitmap* dialog. The *Suppress speckles* option allows the automatic suppression
of paths smaller than the specified size. Make sure the *Suppress speckles* box is checked and set the *Size* to 50.
While you're at it, make sure the *Smooth corners* and *Optimize paths* boxes are checked. This will result in a
smooth scan with fewer nodes. Rescan and the "blobs" should be gone.

It will be easier to edit the traces separately. To do so, we'll temporarily move the path. This requires a precise
move which can be done with the *Transform* dialog (Object → ✣ Transform... (**Shift+Ctrl+M**)). Bring up the
dialog and select the *Move* tab. Move the path a page width to the right by setting the *Horizontal* entry to 500
pixels, setting the *Vertical* entry to 0 pixels, selecting the *Relative move* option, and then clicking on the *Apply*
button. (One could also move the path using the **Shift**+**Arrow** keys to move the path 20 pixels at a time. This
may be faster than calling up the *Transform* dialog but there is a small risk of making a mistake in the shifts.)

Next, repeat the trace with a new threshold. This time optimize the threshold for the lettering. A threshold of 0.65
looks good. Execute the trace. The following figure shows what you should see.

Results of scanning using the *Image Brightness* twice. A threshold of 0.15
was used for the path in the right while a threshold of 0.65 was used for
the path on the left. The original photo is still under the tracing on the left.

4.  **Clean up the traces.**

    a.  **Move the photograph to a different layer.**

        Objects in Inkscape can be selected by clicking on them. This leads to a small problem when using a *rub-
        ber-band* selection technique where one click-drags to select multiple objects as we will want to do a few
        times. If the click-drag begins over the photograph, the photograph will be moved. One can avoid this by
        holding the **Shift** key down while starting the click-drag, but this is a bit of a pain to do every time. One

could *lock* the picture in place by checking the *Lock* box in the *Object Properties* dialog but this isn't recommended. It is nontrivial to select and unlock a locked object.

The preferred solution is to put the picture on a separate *Layer*. *Layers* can be thought of as separate drawings on transparent sheets that are stacked on top of each other. The final drawing is what one sees through the stack. In Inkscape, the *Layers* can be easily locked and unlocked against modification. They can also be made invisible. We'll put the photograph on a locked *Layer* by itself. Then there is no chance of it moving while we work on cleaning up the tracings.

First, create a new *Layer* for the photograph. This is done through the *Add Layer* dialog (Layer → ⮥ Add Layer... (**Shift+Ctrl+N**)). Enter the name "Photograph", select *Below current* in the *Position* drop-down menu, and then click on the *Add* button. The new layer is created below the old layer. It is selected automatically. The layer name is shown in the *Status Bar*.

Select the photograph by clicking on an opening in the tracing (check the *Notification Region* to see what is selected). Note that the layer is automatically changed back to the original layer (Layer 1) when the photograph is selected. Move the photograph to the new layer by using the command Layer → ⬃ Move Selection to Layer Below (**Shift+Page Down**). The current layer changes automatically to "Photograph". Lock this layer by clicking on the 🔓 icon next to the layer name. The icon should change to the locked state 🔒 . The photograph now cannot be moved.

b.  **Clean up the Yin and Yang.**

Select the path for the circles and the Yin and Yang. The current layer will switch to "Layer 1". Zoom in the paths by hitting the **3** key. Each trace creates one path. Each path is made up of many sub-paths. It is generally easier to clean up a tracing by converting the sub-paths into independent paths. Do this by using the Path → 🖋 Break Apart (**Shift+Ctrl+K**) command.

The first thing you will notice is that the Yin and Yang symbol becomes all black. Don't panic! This is because the Yin and Yang has been broken into two pieces, one for the outer circle and one for the Yin shape. Each path takes on the attributes of the prior combined path and thus both have black *Fill*. Select the Yang (left side) path by first clicking on the background to deselect the paths and then clicking inside the area of the Yang path (look at the original photo). You can tell you've selected the correct path by the shape of the bounding box that is shown when the path is selected. If you got the wrong path, try again moving the cursor a bit. It may be necessary to hold down the **Alt** key while clicking. This will cycle through selecting each object under the cursor in turn. (If the cycling doesn't work, your window manager may be stealing the **Alt** key. See the section called *Alternative Alt Key* in Chapter 24, *Customization*, for ways to work around this problem.)

The Yang path is selected.

While the photograph is in black and white, the Yang part of the monad in the NP logo should be red. Set the *Fill* color of the path by clicking on the red square in the *Palette* (or using the *Fill and Stroke* dialog).

After the Yin and Yang has been cleaned up.

c.   **Clean up circles.**

Next we will replace the complicated path for the outer circle with ... you guessed it, a circle. Select the *Ellipse Tool* ○ from the *Tool Controls*. To create a circle, hold down the **Ctrl** key while click-dragging the mouse from one corner of an imaginary box (the *bounding box*) that encloses the outer circle, to the opposite corner of the imaginary box. Don't worry about getting the size and position correct at this point.

Turn off the *Fill* by clicking on the red *x* at the right end of the *Palette*. It is easier to adjust the circle if the circle *Stroke* is a different color than the original and is semi-transparent. Set the *Stroke* color by holding the **Shift** while clicking on the red square in the *Palette*. Set the opacity to 50% using the entry box marked *O:* in the *Style Indicator* at the lower left of the Inkscape window.

Now we are ready to adjust the circle. Set the stroke width to match the width of the original circle by either selecting the width from the pop-up menu accessed by a **Right Mouse Click** on the number next to the *Stroke* color in the *Style Indicator* (a *tool tip* will display *Stroke width: x px* when the cursor is over the number) or, if finer control is required, by setting using the *Width* entry box under the *Stroke style* tab of the *Fill and Stroke* dialog (Object → ✏ Fill and Stroke... (**Shift+Ctrl+F**)).

Next, adjust the size of the circle by dragging either of the two square handles (on left and top of circle). The handles are visible (by default) when any of the *shape tools* or the *Node Tool* is selected. Hold down the **Ctrl** down while dragging to preserve the circle shape. Tapping the **Space** bar will change to the *Select Tool* for repositioning the circle. Fine adjustments to the position can be made by holding the **Alt** key down while using the arrow keys. Tapping the **Space** bar a second time will reselect the *Ellipse Tool*.

The new outer circle (semi-transparent red), sized and positioned.✪

By this time, you will have realized that the original outer circle is not a true circle. This is because the logo in the photograph is at an angle with respect to the plane of the photograph so the original circle is distorted. We will keep the true circle for the logo but keep in mind that we may need to make other corrections.

The final steps for the outer circle are to delete the original circle and change the stroke of the new circle to a solid black.

The inner solid black circle can also be replaced following the same steps as for replacing the outer circle with two minor changes: 1. Use a filled circle without a stroke. 2. Place the new circle behind the Yang object with the Object → ⬜ Lower (**Page Down**) command (also available from the *Select Tool-Tool Controls*).

The new inner circle (semi-transparent red), sized and positioned but before moving behind the Yang object.⊘

d. **Clean up the lettering.**

It is now time to clean up the letters. Again we must break up the path into pieces. After doing so, you'll see one big black square. I don't have to remind you not to panic, do I? Select the square and delete it; you should now see a big black circle. Delete that too (select it by clicking its edge). You should now see letters. While we are at it, delete the center black circle leaving only the letters.

Notice that the A, O, P, and two R's are missing their holes. (You are not panicking, right?) This is because they are each composed of two paths that need to be put back together. We can do this for each of the letters, but in this case it is more convenient to select all the letter paths and merge them into one path using the Path → ⬜ Combine (**Ctrl+K**) command. (A *rubber-band* selection would work well here.)

After extracting only the lettering on the left.

e. **Final steps.**

It is time to rejoin the Yin and Yang as well as the circles with the text. Select the Yin and Yang, and the circles and use the *Transform* dialog to move them −500 pixels in the horizontal direction.

One can now see that the lettering isn't quite spaced correctly. This is again due to the orientation of the logo in the original picture. The lettering needs to be widened a little bit. Select the lettering path and scale it by 3% in the horizontal direction using the *Scale* tab of the *Transform* dialog.

The logo is now finished. You can either delete or hide the original photograph. (Select the "Photograph" *Layer* in the *Status Bar* and then either click on the 🔒 icon to unlock the layer and then select and delete the photograph, or click on the ✋ icon to hide the *Layer*.) You can also make fine adjustments to the Yin path with the *Node Tool* if desired. Save your work as in the previous tutorials.

# A Box for Cards—An Isometric Projection

Inkscape is a two-dimensional drawing program. It can, however, be used to create simple three-dimensional drawings. We will create in this tutorial a simple *Isometric Projection* [http://en.wikipedia.org/wiki/Isometric_projection].

A box of playing cards.✪

An isometric projection is a view of an object such that there is an equal opening angle between the three projected orthogonal axes, as shown below.

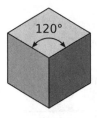

The isometric projection of a cube. The angle between each pair of projected axes is 120°.

Inkscape includes axonometric *Grids* that can be used to rapidly draw isometrically projected boxes. However, the method described here works best when drawings are included on the sides of the boxes as distorting the sides requires two precise transformations (scaling and skewing).

The steps are:

- Start Inkscape and set the drawing size.

- Create the three sides of the box, unfolded.

- Add designs to box sides.

- Transform each box side into place.

## Procedure 1.5. Creating an Isometric Projection

1. **Set up the drawing.**

   To begin, start Inkscape.

   Follow the instructions for setting the page size and defining a *Grid* given in the Swedish flag example but set drawing size to a width of 500 pixels and a height of 500 pixels. Set the *Grid* spacing to 10 pixels. In the *Snap Bar*, enable snapping ( ✎ ), enable snapping to the *Grid* ( ▦ ), and turn off snapping of *bounding boxes* ( 𝌆 ).

2. **Create the three sides of the box.**

   We need the front, side, and top of the box in the ratio 6:4:1, similar to the dimensions for a deck of cards. Create one rectangle with a width of 200 pixels and height of 300 pixels with the lower edge 100 pixels from the bottom of the page. Create a rectangle to the right of the first with width of 50 pixels and height of 300. Create another rectangle above the first rectangle with width of 200 pixels and a height of 50 pixels. The paths of the rectangles should overlap.

   Turn on the *Fill* of the rectangles with the *Palette* or *Fill and Stroke* dialog (Object → ▱ Fill and Stroke... (**Shift+Ctrl+F**)) and set the *Fill* to white. Turn on the *Stroke* and set the *Stroke* color to black and the width to one pixel. Set the *Stroke Join* to *Round* by clicking on the ▱ icon under the *Stroke style* tab in the *Fill and Stroke* dialog. This will make the corners where the rectangles touch neater.

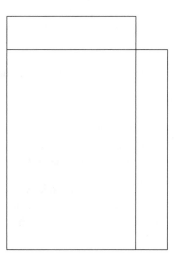

The sides of the box laid out flat.

3. **Add designs to the box sides.**

   You can add any designs you want to the box sides. I will use the NP logo created in the previous tutorial as well as some text.

Import the logo using the File → ⬚ Import... (**Ctrl+I**) command. The logo will need to be scaled smaller. You can do this by click-dragging on one of its corners. Hold the **Ctrl** key down to keep the height to width ratio constant. Once you have it sized appropriately, you can center the logo within the large rectangle by using the Object → ⬚ Align and Distribute... (**Shift+Ctrl+A**) dialog. To add the large rectangle to the logo selection, click on it while holding down the **Shift** key. In the *Align and Distribute* dialog, select from the *Relative to* drop-down menu *Last selected*. Since the rectangle was the last object selected, it will remain fixed and the logo will move. Click on the *Center on vertical axis* icon ( ⬚ ) and the *Center on horizontal axis* icon ( ⬚ ).

Add some text to the sides as you wish. When finished, group each box side with the objects on that side by first selecting the box side with all the objects inside and the using the Object → ⬚ Group (**Ctrl+G**) command. When objects are placed in a *Group*, they can be manipulated as if they are just one object. This will ensure that when the box sides are transformed, the logo and text will be transformed as well.

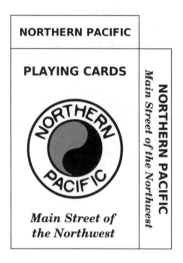

The sides after adding logo and text.

4.  **Transform each box side into place.**

    Now the fun begins. We would like to distort each box side into a rhombus with the edges keeping the same length. This cannot be done directly. The distortions require several steps. The steps are to make the box sides narrower and then to skew them. The box top will also have to be rotated.

    When the sides are narrowed, we will want to keep the stroke width from narrowing at the same time. The option to scale stroke width when an object is scaled can be toggled on and off in the *Tool Controls* when the *Select Tool* is in use. Make sure the *Scale Stroke Width* ⬚ icon is not highlighted (or if the icon is not shown because the window is too narrow, that the *Scale stroke width* box is not checked). If it is, toggle off the option.

    Select the box front (largest side). We want to be precise when we narrow the sides so we'll use the Object → ⬚ Transform... (**Shift+Ctrl+M**) dialog. Bring up the dialog and select the *Scale* tab. Set the *Width* box to 86.603%. This is equal to cos(30°). Click on the *Apply* button. Use the *Select Tool* to drag the box front back against the other lower box side. It should snap into place.

    Next we need to skew the box front by 30°. This is easiest done with the *Select Tool*. Click on the box front a second time to change the *scaling* handles into *rotating* and *skewing* handles. When you do so, a small cross, the

*Rotation center*, should appear in the center of the selection. This is the reference point for rotation or skewing. Click-drag this cross to the upper-right corner of the box front. Be careful that it doesn't snap to the corner of the *bounding box*. The cross should be centered in the middle of the *Stroke*. If it isn't, it will lead to small alignment problems at end. You can zoom in to check.

Now click-drag the *scaling* handle (double headed vertical arrow) on the left side of the box front upward while holding down the **Ctrl** key. Using the **Ctrl** key will snap the skewing to multiples of 15°. Drag until the skew is −30° (watch the *Notification Region*).

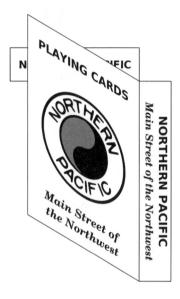

After transforming the front of the box into place. The front of the box may be in front (as shown) or behind the top of the box depending on the order in which you grouped the sides.

Repeat the last steps with the box side on the lower right, just interchanging "left" and "right."

The box top also needs to be narrowed by the same amount as the others, but this time in the vertical direction. Set the *Width* back to its default value and the *Height* to 86.603% before scaling the rectangle. Before skewing, move the *Rotation center* to the lower right corner of the box top. Again make sure the cross is in the middle of the stroke width, aligned with the grid. Skew the rectangle 30° by dragging the top skewing handle right while using the **Ctrl** key. Finally, rotate the box top 30° clockwise by dragging the upper-left rotation handle while holding the **Ctrl** key down.

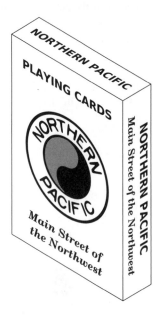

The finished box of playing cards.

The box of playing cards is now finished. Save your work as in the previous tutorials.

If you did not place the *Rotation center* exactly as specified (e.g., on the *bounding box* rather than the middle of the stroke), you may have a small misalignment in the box sides. One can either redo the steps or simply nudge the offending side into place using the **Arrow** keys while holding the **Alt** key down.

The corner of the top of the box inside the red circle doesn't meet the other corner correctly. This was the result of aligning the *Rotation center* to the *bounding box*.

# A Can of Soup—A Three-Dimensional Drawing with Gradients

We will use Inkscape to draw a soup can. This example will cover: combining and dividing paths, using *Gradients*, making shadows, and distorting text.

A souped-up soup can.✪

The steps we'll take are:

- Start Inkscape, set the drawing size, and specify a grid.

- Draw the can shape.

- Add a gradient.

- Add a shadow.

- Add a label background.

- Add the label text.

- Spiff up the can top.

## Procedure 1.6. Drawing a Soup Can

1.  **Set the canvas parameters.**

    Start Inkscape. Set the drawing size to 200 by 200 pixels. Set up a *Grid* with spacing of 5 pixels. Enable snapping of nodes to the *Grid*, disable snapping of *bounding boxes*.

2.  **Draw the can shape.**

    The can will be composed of two lines connecting parts of two ellipses. (One could use a rectangle to obtain the straight lines but that has the tendency of producing extra nodes.)

a. **Draw the top of the can.**

Click on the *Ellipse Tool* icon ⊙ in the *Tool Box* on the left of the Inkscape window (or use one of the keyboard shortcuts: **F5** or **e**) to select the *Ellipse Tool*. Draw an ellipse to represent the top of the can by click-dragging between the 50 and 150 pixel marks on the horizontal axis and between the 150 and 180 pixel marks on the vertical axis. Give the ellipse a solid color *Fill* by clicking on a colored square in the *Palette* (I've used light red).

b. **Draw the bottom of the can.**

Duplicate the ellipse by selecting the ellipse (if not selected) and clicking on the 🗐 icon in the *Command Bar* or using the menu entry Edit → 🗐 Duplicate (**Ctrl+D**). A copy of the ellipse will be placed on top of the original ellipse. The new ellipse will be left selected.

Move the ellipse down by click-dragging it while holding down the **Ctrl** key to constrain the movement to the vertical direction. Move it down until the top is at the 50 pixel mark on the vertical axis. You now have the top and bottom of the can.

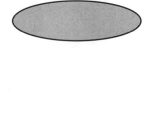

The top and the bottom of the soup can.

c. **Draw the side of the can.**

The side of the can will be formed by joining the bottom half of the top ellipse to the bottom half of the bottom ellipse. In the process, we will sacrifice both ellipses. Because we still need a separate top for the can as it will be colored differently from the body, we'll duplicate the top ellipse and sacrifice the new copy.

Select the top ellipse and duplicate it as above. Then with the duplicate ellipse still selected, convert the ellipse into a path object by using the Path → ⬡ Object to Path (**Shift+Ctrl+C**) command. The object will not appear to have changed but the underlying description is now an editable path.

To edit the path, select the *Node Tool* by clicking on the ⬚ icon (**F2** or **n**) in the *Tool Box*. Select the top node of the path and delete it by clicking on the ≞ icon (Delete selected nodes) in the *Tool Controls* or by using one of the keyboard shortcuts: **Backspace** or **Delete**.

Open the path up by selecting the two side nodes and clicking on the ⁑ (Delete segment between two non-endpoint nodes) icon in the *Tool Controls*.

Repeat the previous steps for the bottom ellipse (except for duplicating it). You should have a drawing that looks like the following one if you change the color of the still intact top ellipse:

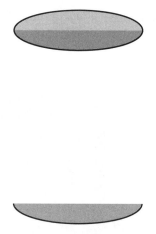

The two half ellipses that will form the can side along with a full ellipse (color changed) for the can top.

Next the top and bottom half ellipses need to be joined together. Select both and combine into one path with the Path → ⵁ Combine (**Ctrl+K**) command.

With the *Node Tool*, select the two leftmost nodes, one from the top and one from the bottom. Join them by clicking on the ⵁ (Join selected endnodes with a new segment) icon in the *Tool Controls*. Repeat for the two rightmost nodes.

You should now have a well-constructed can side, as shown below.

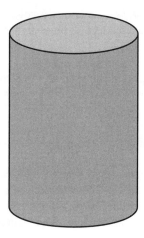

The side of the can after completing the side's path.

3.   **Add a gradient for a 3D effect.**

A *Gradient* can represent the reflections off the curved part of the can. There are two ways to add a gradient, the first is to use the *Gradient Tool* and the second to use the *Fill and Stroke* dialog. To add a *Gradient* using the

*Gradient Tool*, select the tool by clicking on the ⬚ icon (**Ctrl+F1** or **g**) in the *Tool Box*. Then with the can side selected, click-drag from the left side of the can to the right side. To add a *Gradient* using the *Fill and Stroke* dialog, open the dialog (Object → ▱ Fill and Stroke... (**Shift+Ctrl+F**)). Select the *Fill* tab, if not already selected, and with the can side selected, click on the *Linear gradient* ( ▢ ) icon. Both methods create a default *Gradient* across the can side using the preexisting *Fill* color.

The *Gradient* needs a bit of work to make it look proper which is easiest done with the *Gradient Tool*. Two *Gradient* handles will appear when the can side is selected.

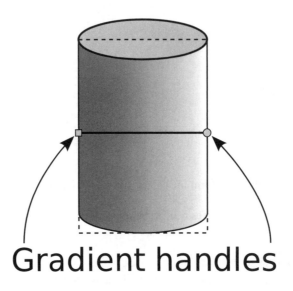

## Gradient handles

After changing the *Fill* of the can side to a *Gradient*. Note the *Gradient* handles. They are displayed when a selected object has a *Gradient* and the *Gradient Tool*, *Node Tool*, *Dropper Tool* or one of the *shape tools* is in use.

*Gradients* are defined in terms of *Stops*. A *Stop* has a color and position (offset) in the *Gradient*. The default *Gradient* has two *Stops*, both with the same color but with different transparencies. For the side of the can, we'll use three *Stops*.

Add a third *Stop* by double-clicking on the line connecting the two existing *Stops* with the *Gradient Tool* enabled and the can side selected. The cursor will have an extra + sign when it is possible to add *Stops*. When you add a *Stop* it takes on the color of the *Gradient* at the place where it is added. The look of the *Gradient* will not change.

The *Stop* (handle) can be dragged to move it. Move it to the center.

Now let's give our can a shiny metallic look. Select the leftmost *Stop* by clicking once on it. Change the color to dark gray by either clicking on the *80% Gray* swatch in the *Palette* (a *tool tip* with the color name will be displayed when the cursor is over a swatch) or by using the *Fill and Stroke* dialog. Both the *Fill* and *Stroke paint* tabs will show the color of the *Stop* and can be used to change the color. With the *RGB* tab; change the values to R: 51, G: 51, B: 51, A: 255.

Select the middle *Stop* and set its color to *White* with the *Palette* or R: 255, G: 255, B: 255, A: 255 with the *Fill and Stroke* dialog. Finally, select the last *Stop* and set its color to match the first *Stop*. You should now have a metallic can with a highlight that is in the center.

After adding a stop to the *Gradient* and changing the colors of all stops.

Let's move the highlight to the side. One way to do this would be to further edit the *Gradient*, changing the position of the middle *Stop* and maybe lightening or darkening the side *Stops*. However, the easier way is to move the *Gradient* handles.

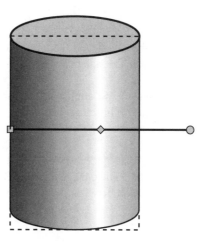

After dragging the right *Gradient* handle to move the highlight.

Before we continue, let's make a couple of quick cosmetic changes: Turn off the *Stroke* of both the can side and top (click on *x* at left end of *Palette* while holding down the **Shift** key). Change the color of the top to *40% Gray* (R: 153, G: 153, B: 153).

A silver can.

4. **Adding a shadow.**

Our can has a light shining on it from the right but no corresponding shadow. We'll fix that now. To do it perfectly is not an easy feat. Inkscape is a 2D drawing program and cannot project shadows for 3D objects (try POV-Ray for that). But we can do a pretty good approximation.

a. **Create the shadow object.**

For the shadow, we need to combine copies of the top and of the side of the can into one object. We'll play a similar game to that used to create the side of the can.

Select the top of the can (an ellipse) and duplicate it. Change its color to make it easier to keep track of. Any color will do. Convert the new ellipse to a path (Path → ⬚ Object to Path (**Shift+Ctrl+C**)). Remove the bottom node (change to the *Node Tool*, ⬚ ). Select the two side nodes and remove the line in between them ( ⬚ ).

Select the side of the can, duplicate it, and change its color. Remove the top three nodes. Select the remaining two side nodes and remove the line in between them.

After creating the top and bottom of what will become the shadow.

Select both new objects. Combine them into one path (Path → 🖻 Combine (**Ctrl+K**)). Select the two nodes on the left side, join them ( ⁚⁚ ), and convert the path in between to a line ( ✐ ). Do the same for the two right nodes.

b.  **Distort the shadow shape.**

Select the three top nodes and move them down and over, as shown below.

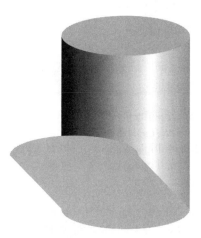

Distorting the shape for the shadow.

It is clear that the side nodes are not properly positioned and the path is distorted. We'll make a few adjustments to set this straight. But first put the shadow object behind the can (Object → 🔽 Lower to Bottom (**End**)).

Node *handles* are used to control the direction and curvature of a path on either side of a node. The handles are the circles attached by straight lines to a node that are displayed when the node is selected. The lines are always tangent to the path at the point the path intersects the node. The distance between the handle and its node controls the curvature of the path—the farther away, the less curved is the path near the node. If no node handles are visible, make them visible by clicking on the ⸢ icon in the *Tool Controls* or if the icon is not visible, check the *Show handles* box in the drop-down menu opened by clicking on the down arrow at the right end of the *Tool Controls*.

The nodes indicated by the arrows in the following figure need to be adjusted. The handle on the leftmost node needs to be rotated a small amount counterclockwise so that the handle line is parallel to the side of the shadow. This produces a smooth transition between the straight side and the curved part of the shadow. To make the rotation, drag the handle while holding down the **Alt** key (which keeps the distance between the handle and node constant).

The other node indicated by the arrow also needs to have its handle adjusted in the same way. In addition, the node should be moved slightly down to the right so that the shadow's straight edge is tangent to the can's bottom.

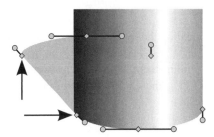

Adjusting the shadow. The two nodes indicated by the arrows have been adjusted by rotating the handles slightly so the handle lines are parallel to the straight side of the shadow. In addition, the lower node has been shifted up slightly (**Alt+Up Arrow**) so the shadow doesn't leak out at the bottom.

Now change the color of the fill to *50% Gray* (R: 127 G: 127 B: 127).

c.  **Soften the shadow's edge.**

The easiest way to soften the shadow's edge is to use the *Blur* slider on the *Fill* tab of the *Fill and Stroke* dialog. A value of 3% gives a nice shadow.

The *Blur* slider uses a *Gaussian Blur* filter. *Filters* are not well supported yet in many web browsers so it might be better to use an alternative method of softening the shadow. One can use the *Inset/Outset Halo* extension. This extension makes multiples copies of an object's path, each time enlarging or shrinking it a small amount. Each copy has a small opacity so the net effect is a blurred object. The copies are placed in a *Group* that acts as a single object.

To use the extension, select the shadow, then call up the extension from the *Generate from Path* sub-menu under the *Extensions* menu. In the dialog that appears, set the *Width* to 5 and the *Number of Steps* to 11. This will produce a blur that is 5 pixels wide with 11 layered objects. The original shadow is still selected. It is no longer needed and can be deleted by using one of the keyboard shortcuts: **Del** or **Ctrl+X**.

Select the new blurred shadow. Move the shadow to the back (Object → ⬛ Lower to Bottom (**End**)).

One problem needs to be taken care of. The shadow leaks out from the bottom of the can in the front. Select the shadow and move it slightly up and to the left. You can do this either by dragging the shadow with the mouse or using the **Arrow** keys. Holding down the **Alt** key while using the **Arrow** keys will allow finer adjustments.

A basic can.

5.  **Add a label.**

The label has the same curvature as the side of the can. To make the label, we'll take a slice from the can side and then decrease its height.

Select the side of the can and duplicate it. Then select the *Rectangle Tool* and draw a rectangle that extends from above the can to below the can and extends from 60 to 140 pixels in the horizontal direction.

Select both the new rectangle and the duplicate of the can side. Use the Path → ⬚ Intersection (**Ctrl+***) command to form the label from the intersection of the two selected objects.

Change the *Fill* of the label to a solid red by clicking the red square in the *Palette* or by first clicking on the *Flat color* (▣) icon in the *Fill* tab of the *Fill and Stroke* dialog and then changing the sliders to red (R: 255: G: 0: B: 0). Change the opacity to 50% using the *0:* entry box in the *Style Indicator* (at the lower-left corner of the Inkscape window) or using the *Opacity* slider in the *Fill and Stroke* dialog. This will allow a bit of the can highlight to leak through. (If you desire a metallic label, just change the color of the gradient.)

With the *Node Tool*, select the three nodes along the top of the label at the same time and move them down 25 pixels. Move the bottom three nodes of the label up 25 pixels.

A can with a label.

6. **Add text to the label.**

To add text to the label, select the *Text Tool*. Click somewhere on the canvas and type in the text "SPLIT PEA SOUP" with a carriage return after each word. To change the size and style of the text, use the drop-down menus in the *Tool Controls*. Pick an appropriate font (I've used Bitstream Vera Sans) and font size (24). Click on the ≡ icon in the *Tool Controls* to center the text. The line spacing may need to be adjusted. This can be done in v0.48 from the *Text Tool-Tool Controls* ( ↕ ). In v0.47 you need to use the *Text and Font* dialog. Call up the dialog by either clicking on the **T** icon in the *Command Bar* or through the menu entry (Text → **T** Text and Font... (**Shift+Ctrl+T**)). Change the line spacing to 100%. Finally, change the text to a nice Split Pea green with the *Fill and Stroke* dialog (R: 63, G: 127: B: 0).

In v0.48, the text can be aligned to the center of the label via dragging with snapping to the grid enabled ( ↖ and ⊞ ) as the snap point for center-aligned text is at the center. In v0.47, the *Align and Distribute* dialog must be used. Bring up the dialog by clicking on the ⊫ icon in the *Command Bar* or through the menu entry Object → ⊫ Align and Distribute... (**Shift+Ctrl+A**). Select both the label and text objects. Set the reference for the alignment by selecting from the *Relative to* drop-down menu *First selected* if you selected the label first or *Last selected* if you selected it last. Then click on both the *Center on vertical axis* ( ⊻ ) and the *Center on horizontal axis* ( ⊪ ) icons.

A can with a label and text.

Now we have flat text on a round can! Inkscape can shift and rotate individual letters of text but it cannot skew the text as is needed for the characters toward the edge of the can. In order to skew the letters, we will convert the text into a path and modify the path. To do this, select the text and then use the Path → Object to Path (**Shift+Ctrl+C**) command. The text has become a *Group* of path objects and can no longer be edited as text. It will be easier to modify the paths if they form just one path. Ungroup the objects using Object → Ungroup (**Shift+Ctrl+G**) and then combine the individual letters into one path using Path → Combine (**Ctrl+K**).

We'll use a couple of very handy *Extensions* to do the hard work for us.

Start by using the *Add Nodes* extension to increase the number of nodes in the path. This will improve the look of the final letters. Select the text path, then select Extensions → Modify Path → Add Nodes... . A small dialog will pop up, allowing you to set the upper limit to the space between nodes. Set the *Maximum segment length* to 5.0 and click the *Apply* button.

Next we'll use the *Pattern along Path* extension to put the text on a path. There is a Text → Put on Path command, but this uses the *SVG textPath* specification, which would result in the letters being rotated to follow the path.

We need a path to put the text on. The path should be an arc with the same shape as the curve of the top ellipse but have the width of the text. Select the top *Ellipse* of the top of the can and duplicate it (Edit → Duplicate (**Ctrl+D**)). Move the *Ellipse* straight down to the center of the can. Remove the *Fill* but add a *Stroke*. Add a *Rectangle* that overlaps the bottom of the *Ellipse*, centered on the can and with the width of the text.

Creating a path for the text from an oval that is a duplicate of the can top and a rectangle with the width of the text.

The *Rectangle* should be on top of the *Ellipse*. Select both and use the Path → ◌ Cut Path (**Ctrl+Alt+/**) command to divide the *Ellipse* into two pieces. The *Rectangle* will disappear. Delete the top piece of the *Ellipse*.

The extension requires that the *Pattern* (text in this case) be above the path in *z-order* (that is, on top of the path). You can move the pattern to the top by selecting it and then clicking on the *Raise to Top* (Object → ▤ Raise to Top (**Home**)) icon.

Next, select the text and the path. Call up the *Pattern Along Path* extension (Extensions → Generate from Path → Pattern along Path). This will open a dialog. In the dialog, select *Single* in the *Copies of the pattern* menu and *Ribbon* in the *Deformation type* menu. All the entry boxes should be 0.0 and none of the boxes should be checked. Click the *Apply* button. The text will probably be backward. Flip it with the Object → ◭ Flip Horizontal (**H**) command. Finally, delete the small arc.

A can with a label and wrapped text.

7. **Spiff up the can top.**

There is no stopping at the level of detail you can add. In the final figure, a series of ovals of different sizes, positions, and gradients have been used to give the top of the can more realism. These ovals are shown in an expanded view in the next figure.

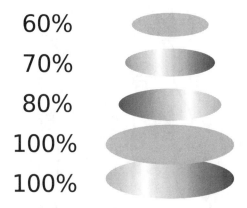

60%

70%

80%

100%

100%

The ellipses that make up the can top in an expanded view with the relative sizes indicated.

All the ellipses were created by taking the original can top, duplicating it, and then using the *Scale* tab of the *Transform* dialog. The fill was then changed to either a flat fill or a linear gradient with the same colors as used for the rest of the can.

# A Vine Design—A Tiling Example

Inkscape has a *Create Tiled Clones* dialog that can be used to produce complex tilings. This tutorial covers preparing a base tile that can be used for such tilings. The objects in the base tile can overlap the tile boundaries to produce continuous designs, as shown below.

A 3 × 3 tiling of a base tile.✪

The steps to produce a repeated tiling are:

* Start Inkscape and set the drawing size.

* Create a tile prototype.

* Clone tile.

* Decorate tile.

* Use base tile for tiling.

## Procedure 1.7. Creating a Tile Pattern

1. **Set up the canvas.**

   To begin, start Inkscape and set the drawing size to a width of 400 and a height of 580 pixels. Create a *Grid* with spacing of 10 pixels. Turn on snapping of nodes to *Grid* (and off snapping of *bounding boxes* to *Grid*). Don't forget to turn the *Grid* on.

2. **Create a tile prototype.**

   We need to create a tile prototype that consists of a rectangle in a *Group*. Having a *Group* will allow adding new objects to the tile.

Using the *Rectangle Tool*, create a rectangle 100 pixels wide by 160 pixels tall with the upper-left corner 50 pixels from the left edge and top. This will be the size of our base tile. Tile spacing will be determined by the *bounding box* of this rectangle. There are two definitions for the *bounding box*. The first, called the *Visual bounding box*, includes the *Stroke* width in the calculation while the second, called the *Geometric bounding box*, is calculated using just the nodes of an object. It will be easier to make tilings without worrying about the *Stroke* width, so select the *Geometric bounding box* in the *Tools* section of the *Inkscape Preferences* dialog (File → ▣ Inkscape Preferences... (**Shift+Ctrl+P**)).

So we can visualize the tiles, give the tiles a *Stroke* by either using the *Fill and Stroke* dialog or by using a **Shift+Left Mouse Click** on one of the color swatches in the *Palette*. You can also give the tile a *Fill* by simply clicking on a swatch.

Now *Group* the tile by selecting the rectangle and using the Object → ▣ Group (**Ctrl+G**) command.

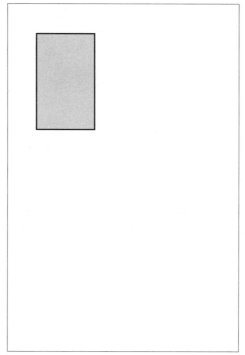

The base tile.

3.  **Clone the tile.**

    The next step is to clone the tile. This will give you a way to visualize the tile as it is decorated, making sure that objects that are near or overlap the boundary fit in properly.

    Bring up the *Create Tiled Clones* dialog (Edit → Clone → ▣ Create Tiled Clones... ).

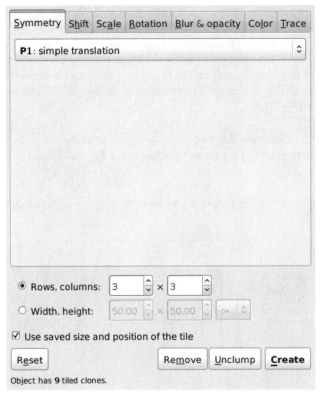

*Tile Clones* dialog.

Select *P1: simple translation* from the drop-down menu on the *Symmetry* tab. This will produce a rectangular array of tiles. Choose the *Rows, columns* option and set the number of columns and rows to three by entering 3 in both entry boxes. Make sure the base tile is selected in the drawing (*Notification Region* should state that a "Group of 1 object" is selected) and click on the *Create* button in the dialog.

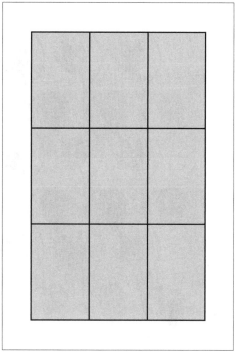

A 3 × 3 array of the base tile.

4.  **Decorate the tile.**

It is time to draw the design on the base tile. Nine copies (clones) of the base tile have been created, including one on top of the original tile. It is necessary to modify the original tile if the copies are also to be modified. Select the original tile by clicking on any of the clones (*Notification Region* will indicate a clone is selected) and using Edit → Clone → ▣ Select Original (**Shift+D**). The *Notification Region* should now say "Group of 1 object." The original tile is below a clone. Bring it to the top by using Object → ▥ Raise to Top (**Home**) (click on the ▥ in the *Tool Controls* bar).

"Enter" the *Group* by either double-clicking on the base tile or selecting *Enter group #xxxx* from the menu that pops up when you **Right Mouse Click** the base tile. The *Layer* name displayed in the *Status Bar* will start with "#g" indicating that a *Group* is open for editing (the *Group* has been temporarily been promoted to a *Layer*). While the *Group* is open, any object added to the drawing will be a member of the *Group*.

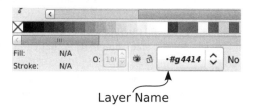

Layer Name

The *Layer* name in the *Status Bar* showing that a *Group* is open for editing.

Now that the *Group* is open, add any details you want to the tile. Any detail you add to the base tile is automatically included in the cloned tiles. Our example has a continuous grapevine pattern. The main vine is a single line with the place and angle of the ends carefully adjusted for continuity at the base tile boundary. The *Fill* and *Stroke* of the base rectangle have been removed (the rectangle, itself, has not been deleted as it will be useful in the next step).

A 3 × 3 array of the decorated base tile. Note how some of the decoration extends outside the base tile (indicated by the black rectangle).

5. **Use the base tile for tiling.**

The newly created base tile can be used in several ways to decorate the *Fill* of another object. The easiest way is to use the base tile with the *Create Tiled Clones* dialog to create a simple tiling that is then clipped with the path of the object.

a.  Delete all the clones of the base tile. This can be done by either selecting each clone and deleting it or, quicker, by selecting the base tile and clicking on the *Remove* button at the bottom of the *Create Tiled Clones* dialog. (Note, the *Remove* button will only be enabled if you have selected the base tile.)

b.  Select base tile (if not already selected).

c.  With *Create Tiled Clones* dialog, create a tiling large enough to fill the object you wish to fill. Make sure *Use saved size and position of the tile* box is checked. The tiling will then use the saved dimensions of the base tile before it was decorated (the dimensions when the first tiling was made) rather than the current *bounding box*, which may include objects that extend outside the border. (Once an object has been tile cloned, Inkscape keeps a private record of the original tile size and position that can be used for later recloning.)

d.  If one of the base tile objects has partial transparency it may be necessary to delete (or move) the base tile. If the base tile is deleted, the links to the cloned tiles are broken but the cloned tiles remain.

e.  *Group* the tiled clones. Move the object to be filled above the grouped clones in *z-order*. Select both the object and the grouped clones and use the Object → Clip → Set command to make the clipping.

An oval path has been used to clip the tiling. To get the oval border, the oval path was duplicated prior to making the clipping. The duplicated oval was then given a black *Stroke* and no *Fill*.

The base tile can be used for a *Pattern* by selecting it and using the command Object → Pattern → Objects to Pattern (**Alt+I**). When the *Pattern* is first used, you will notice that the spacing is wrong if some of the objects extended outside the borders of the base tile. This can be corrected by using the *XML Editor*. In the *svg:defs* section, select the *svg:pattern* item that corresponds to the object with the pattern fill. This entry may be linked to another pattern. Follow the links until you find the entry with *height* and *width* attributes (and no other pattern links). Change the *height* and *width* attributes to the height and width of the base tile. Note that most *SVG* renderers will not draw areas that are outside the nominal area of the pattern (defined by the *height* and *width* attributes) despite setting the *style* attribute to "overflow:visible". Batik (which is used for the PDF version of this book) has rendering problems with this type of pattern. Evince, a popular Linux PDF displayer, also has a different bug rendering *Patterns*. Acroread will display *Patterns* correctly.

The base tile has been converted to a *Pattern* that has been used to fill the oval. The pattern's internal height and width attributes have been adjusted to match that of the base tile.

For some purposes, it may be preferred to have the entire design within the edges of the base tile. This is a bit tricky.

a.   Unlink all the clones by selecting the clones and using Edit → Clone → Unlink Clone (**Shift+Alt+D**).

b.   Delete the center clone of the 3 × 3 clone array.

c.   Select base tile and move it to the center (it may be under a clone). Use the *Move* tab of the *Transform* dialog to precisely move the base tile (by its width and height). The internal information about the position and size of the base tile that is used for cloning is preserved.

d.   For each object that overlaps the base tile but is not part of it, enter the *Group* it belongs to (double-click on the *Group*), cut the object (Edit → Cut (**Ctrl+X**)), enter the *Group* of the base tile, and paste the object in place (Edit → Paste In Place (**Ctrl+Alt+V**)). Pay careful attention to the *Notification Region* to keep track of what is selected and the *Layer* information in the *Status Bar* to see which *Group* is open.

e.   Delete the clones with the leftover objects.

The base tile with all the necessary decorations, before clipping.

At this point, one could convert the base tile to a *Pattern* (see above). There are still problems with some *SVG* renderers that can be worked around by modifying the *transform* attribute with a negative translation in $x$ and $y$ for the *Group* in the *Pattern*. Note that Inkscape ignores this *transform* attribute.

f. In the opened base tile group, select the rectangle and cut it. Exit the group and paste it in place. Select both the base tile group and the rectangle and then use the Object → Clip → Set command. The base tile is now finished. You can translate it back to its original position using the *Transform* dialog.

The base tile, clipped and moved back to its original position.

g.   The base tile can now be used in a tiling.

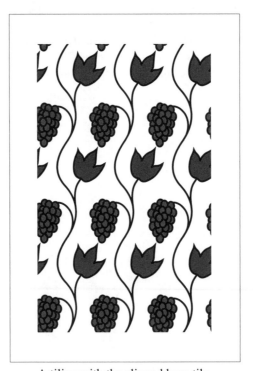

A tiling with the clipped base tile.

Using the clipped base tile has one main drawback. There may be drawing artifacts where tiles abut. This is due to weaknesses in the drawing algorithms that don't properly handle cases where the tile's edge doesn't align with a screen pixel or other display quanta.

Note that the clipped tile cannot be used directly as a *Pattern*. To create a pattern, first convert the tile into a bitmap (Edit → 📷 Make a Bitmap Copy (**Alt+B**)), then use that bitmap for the pattern. This method may also create drawing artifacts.

An oval filled with a bitmap pattern. The pattern was created by first turning the base tile into a bitmap. Note the drawing artifacts between the tiles (e.g., *PNG* web version).

This tutorial has covered creating the most simple base tile. More complex base tiles with different symmetries can be just as easily created, as shown next.

A tiling with the "P31M" symmetry.

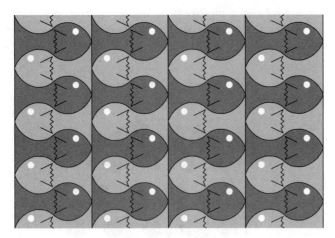

A "P1" tiling with a base tile created by the "CMM" tiling of a smaller base tile.

# An SVG Button—SVG and the Web

In building web pages it is often necessary to add some sort of button. What better way of doing so than with an *SVG* button? This tutorial guides you through drawing a simple SVG button and then adding some functionality to it.

An *SVG* button.

The steps are:

- Draw a simple button with 3D shading.

- Use the button in an *HTML* page to access another web page.

- Animate the button using *SMIL*.

- Use JavaScript (ECMAScript) to create a two-state button with accessibility features.

- Add *CSS* styling to the button.

 ## SVG in HTML5

*SVG* in *HTML5* is a work in progress. The *HTML5* standardization process in not complete. The are major inconsistencies in how different browsers handle *SVG* content in *HTML*. Work is being done to make the integration of *SVG* into *HTML* easier for the web designer.

### Procedure 1.8. Creating an *SVG* Button

1. **Drawing a Button.**

   There are countless ways to draw buttons as one can see by searching for button images on the web. This example uses a rather simple style that allows the button color to be defined by a *CSS* style sheet. The button's color will be the color of a base rectangle. 3D effects will be added using semi-transparent overlays.

a. **Set up the drawing.**

With the *Document Properties* dialog (File →  Document Properties... (**Shift+Ctrl+D**)), set the drawing size to 240 × 100 pixels. Create a *Grid* with spacing of 10 pixels and turn snapping nodes to the *Grid* on ( ▦ in *Snap Bar*).

b. **Draw the base rectangle.**

Draw a rectangle 220 × 80 pixels centered on the page (upper-left corner at 20, 90 pixels). Drag the *Corner Shape* handle (circle at upper-right corner of rectangle) down as far as it will go to round the corners. Give the rectangle a red (or other color) *Fill*.

The base of the button.

It is useful to change the *id* (the internal label) of the rectangle to "ButtonBase". This will allow us to easily reference the rectangle to change its color via *CSS* style sheets or JavaScript.

The *id* of the rectangle can be changed using the *Object Properties* dialog (Object → ⬚ Object Properties... (**Shift+Ctrl+O**)) or the *XML Editor* dialog (Edit → ⊡ XML Editor... (**Shift+Ctrl+X**)). We'll use the latter as we'll have one case later where the former won't work. Open the *XML Editor* dialog. Select the rectangle in drawing. The *XML* entry for the rectangle will be highlighted on the left side of the *XML Editor* dialog. The attributes for the rectangle are shown on the upper right. Click on the *id* attribute on the right. This selects the attribute for editing in the entry area on the lower right. Change the *id* value to "ButtonBase". Either click the *Set* button or use **Ctrl+Enter** to finalize the change. While looking at the dialog, note that the corner radius *ry* is set to 40, half the height of the rectangle.

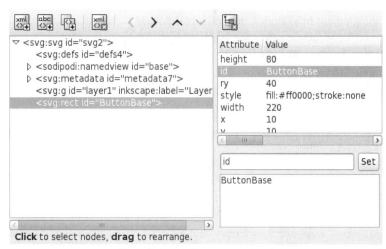

*XML Editor* dialog (after rectangle relabeled).

c. **Add a highlight.**

Now we'll add some 3D effects. First we'll add a reflection off the top. First draw a rectangle with a size of 180 × 40 pixels and with the top 10 pixels below the top of the base rectangle (upper-left corner at 30, 85 pixels). Change the *Fill* to white so that the rectangle can be seen. Make sure that the *Corner Shape* handle is half-way down the right side. If you have trouble moving the handle, try resetting the handle by clicking on the ⌐ icon in the *Tool Controls*.

The next step is to convert the rectangle to a path via Path → ⬚ Object to Path (**Shift+Ctrl+C**). Then, with the *Node Tool*, select the two (possibly four) side nodes and convert then to *Auto-smooth Nodes* by clicking on the *Make selected nodes auto-smooth* ( ◡ ) icon in the *Tool Controls*. Next move the bottom two nodes up 15 pixels.

Use the *Gradient Tool* to add a *Gradient* to the highlight. First select a linear *Gradient* by clicking on the *Create linear gradient* ( ▢ ) icon in the *Tool Controls*. Next, click-drag from the top of the base rectangle down to its center. This should create a gradient that is solid at the top and transparent at the bottom. If the top color is not white, click on the top *Gradient* handle (a square) and click on the white square in the *Palette*. You may also need to set the bottom handle (a circle) to white but with an *Alpha* of zero. To do this you must either use the *Gradient Editor* dialog or the *Fill and Stroke* dialog.

Finally, with the *XML Editor* dialog, change the *id* of the path to "ButtonHighlight".

After adding the highlight.

d. **Add a glow.**

Now we'll make the button glow a little bit by adding a rectangle with a radial gradient. The gradient will have a transparent center and darken toward the edges. First, select the base rectangle and duplicate it (Edit → ▢ Duplicate (**Ctrl+D**)). Change the *Fill* to black. Now use the *Gradient Tool* to create a *Radial Gradient* by clicking on the ▢ icon in the *Tool Controls* and then click-dragging from the bottom center of the rectangle upward. This creates a radial gradient that is black in the center and transparent on the edges. Swap the center and edge colors by using **Shift+R**. Set the *opacity* of the rectangle to 50% by selecting *50%* in the menu that pops-up when **Right Mouse** clicking on the *Opacity* indicator (O:) at the lower left of the Inkscape window. Stretch the gradient by dragging the horizontal *handle* to the left about 50 pixels past the left edge of the page. Move the rectangle below the highlight by clicking on the ⬓ icon in the *Tool Controls* of the *Select Tool* or using the shortcut **Page Down**.

With the *XML Editor* dialog, change the *id* of the glow rectangle to "ButtonGlow".

After adding the glow.

There are endless ways to enhance the visual effect of the button by adding shadows, more highlights, etc., but for the moment we'll stop here.

e. **Add some text.**

Add some text to the button using the *Text Tool*. Choosing center-aligned text via the *Align center* icon in the *Tool Controls* makes it easier to keep text centered in the button. In v0.48, the snapping point for center-aligned text is in the center. In v0.47 one can use the *Align and Distribute* dialog to center the text. Give the text a white fill. Change the *id* of the `<tspan>` element to "Text" with the *XML Editor* dialog.

To access the `<tspan>` object, you may need to click on the little triangle at the left of the `<text>` entry in the dialog.

To help with a 3D effect, a copy of the text with a black fill can be placed behind the original text and shifted down one pixel. The text can also be moved behind the highlight to make the text look like it is inside the button. If you have added a copy of the text, change the new <tspan> *id* to "TextShadow" with the *XML Editor* dialog.

After adding some text.

Finally, save the button as `button.svg`.

2. **Use the button in an HTML web page.**

In this step we'll use the button in an HTML web page. We'll first use the button as a static object as one would use a *PNG* button. The advantage of using an *SVG* button, of course, is that is scalable.

Here is a simple *HTML5* web page to test our button (it uses *XHTML* so save the file as `test.xhtml` and in the same directory as the *SVG* file):

```
<!DOCTYPE html>          ❶
<html xmlns="http://www.w3.org/1999/xhtml">          ❷
  <head>

    <meta charset="UTF-8"/>          ❸

    <title>Sample use of an SVG Button</title>

  </head>
  <body>

    <h1>An SVG button</h1>

    <a href="http://tavmjong.free.fr/INKSCAPE/">
      <img src="button.svg" alt="A sample button."/>          ❹
    </a>

  </body>
</html>
```

❶   *HTML* declaration. (With *HTML5* no "dtd" is required.)
❷   *HTML Name Space* declaration. The *XML* syntax is specified here.
❸   The character encoding of the file (normally `UTF-8`).
❹   Inclusion of the *SVG* file via the `<img>` tag.

The *SVG* button has been included via the `<img>` tag. Unfortunately, this tag does not have a simple means of providing a *PNG* backup. The more useful `<object>` tag, which does have that ability will not pass mouse pointer events from the *SVG* to the *HTML* (i.e. to the `<a>` tag) in most browsers.

3. **Animate the button using *SMIL***

The next step is to give our button a little pizazz. We'll do this via *SMIL* animation. We could also use JavaScript (ECMAScript) but *SMIL* animation has the advantages of being simpler and also working inside the <img> tag where scripting won't work. Unfortunately, *SMIL* animation will not be supported in Internet Explorer 9 (*SMIL* also appears to be a bit of a resource hog).

You can do a lot of things with *SMIL* animation such as shifting or scaling parts of the button. We'll simply make the button "throb" by animating the "glow" rectangle. This will be done by varying the *opacity* of one of the *Stops* of the "glow" *Gradient*. To make the necessary changes, the *SVG* file must be edited using a text editor that can save the file as plain text.

Open the *SVG* button file in the text editor. Look for the rectangle with the *id* "ButtonGlow". Note the name (*id*) of the referenced gradient. This will be the value of the "url" for the "fill". It will be something like "radial-Gradient3165" (the '#' is not part of the name). Now go to the <defs> section near the top of the file at find the radial gradient with the same *id*. This "radialGradient" will reference a "linearGradient" where the *Stops* are defined. The name of this "linearGradient" will be found in the "xlink:href" line. Find the "linearGradient" in the <defs> section.

Now that we have found where the *Stops* are defined, we can edit the file. Find the *Stop* with the *stop-opacity* value of '0'. Change this "stop" from a self-closing tag to an opening tag. That is change: <stop ... /> to <stop ... >. Next, add a "stop" closing tag: </stop> after the opening tag. Then insert the following lines between the "stop" opening tag and the "stop" closing tag:

```
<animate attributeName="stop-opacity" values="0;0.5;0"
   dur="2s" repeatCount="indefinite"/>
```

The "stop" should look something like this:

```
<stop
   id="stop3163"
   style="stop-color:#000000;stop-opacity:0"
   offset="0">
  <animate attributeName="stop-opacity" values="0;0.5;0"
     dur="2s" repeatCount="indefinite"/>
</stop>
```

The button should now slowly throb when viewed in a browser that supports *SMIL* (not Inkscape!). The first part of the <animate> tag defines which attribute is being animated; most attributes can be, although colors may need a special <animateColor> tag. The next part gives a list of values that should be interpolated between. In this case, *stop-opacity* begins with a value of zero which is ramped up to 0.5 and then back down to zero. The *dur* parameter gives the time the animation should take to go through one cycle. The *repeatCount* defines the number of times the animation should be repeated, in this case indefinitely. There are many more options but a full discussion of *SMIL* is outside the scope of this book.

4. **A two-state button with accessibility features.**

We'll now modify the button to have two states. This will necessitate using JavaScript (ECMAScript) which means that the button will not work on a web page if embedded using the <img> tag. We'll keep track of the two states by using the value of the attribute *aria-pressed*. We could use any JavaScript variable to keep track of the state but by using this attribute, which is defined in the WAI-ARIA [http://www.w3.org/TR/wai-aria/] specification, the state of the button can be monitored by accessibility programs such as screen readers.

The first step is to add a couple attributes to the opening <svg> tag. The first is the *role* attribute. This attribute, necessary for *ARIA*, defines the purpose of the *SVG* file. In this case, the *SVG* is being used as a button so set the value to "button". The second attribute to add is *aria-pressed*. This attribute, also required by *ARIA*, can have the values: "true", "false", or "mixed" (we'll use only the first two). It keeps track of the button state. Set the value to "false" to begin with.

```
<svg
  ...
  role="button"
  aria-pressed="false"
  ... />
```

Next, in the <g> tag add the two attributes: *onkeydown* and *onclick* to specify actions to be taken when a user activates the button. In both cases, the same JavaScript function, buttonEvent(evt), is called. The *onkeydown* attribute is not yet part of the *SVG* standard but is supported by many browsers. It is required for accessibility to allow a person to activate the button using the keyboard. The attributes are added here rather than in the <svg> tag to ensure that the button is active only when the mouse is over the visible parts of the button (which are all contained inside the <g> tag).

```
<g id="layer1"
  onkeydown="return buttonEvent(evt);"
  onclick="return buttonEvent(evt);">
```

The final step is to add the JavaScript just after the "defs" section (after </defs>). This is the script:

```
<script type="text/ecmascript">          ❶
  function buttonEvent(event) {           ❷
    if ((event.type == "click" &amp;&amp; event.button == 0) ||
        (event.type == "keydown" &amp;&amp;
   (event.keyCode == 32 || event.keyCode ==13))) {        ❸

      var SVGDocument = event.target.ownerDocument;       ❹
      var SVGRoot     = SVGDocument.documentElement;
      var ButtonBase  = SVGDocument.getElementById("ButtonBase");
      var Text        = SVGDocument.getElementById("Text");
      var TextShadow  = SVGDocument.getElementById("TextShadow");

      var pressed = false;        ❺
      var fill = "red";
      var text = "OFF";

      if ("false" == SVGRoot.getAttribute("aria-pressed")) {        ❻
        pressed = true;
fill = "green";
text = "ON";
      }

      SVGRoot.setAttribute("aria-pressed", pressed);        ❼
      ButtonBase.style.setProperty("fill", fill, "");
      Text.firstChild.nodeValue = text;        ❽
      TextShadow.firstChild.nodeValue = text;
    }
  }
</script>
```

❶    Start of script section. The "type" must be declared as text/ecmascript.

❷ Start of function called when the button is clicked (or when activated by a key press). A pointer to an "event" structure is passed to the function.

❸ The event is checked to make sure it is of a type we are interested in.

❹ References are obtained to the relevant *SVG* objects.

❺ Initial variable values. They should match what is declared in the body of the *SVG*. (This is not the most optimal way to structure the *SVG* as the same values are defined twice. One could add an initiation function to set the values once.)

❻ Variables are toggled if necessary.

❺ The necessary attributes and properties are set.

❽ The text is changed. Note that the text is stored in a child node of the `<tspan>` object.

A two state button.

Our two state button is self-contained and would be useful, for example, in turning on and off an animation inside the same *SVG* file. To make it useful to control something external to the *SVG* file one just needs to call a function in the parent *HTML* document with the value of the current state. This is as simple as adding `top.status(text);` at the end of the "buttonEvent" function, where `status` is a function defined in the parent *HTML*. Inside the `<head>` section of the *HTML* add:

```
<script type="text/ecmascript">

  function status(text) {
    document.getElementById("status").innerHTML = text;
  }

</script>
```

And in the `<body>` of the *HTML* add something like:

```
<p>The button is <b id="status">OFF</b>.</p>
```

If you would like to use the button several times on one web page you'll need to know which button has been pressed. You can find the *id* of the object that wraps the *SVG* by adding `var frameId = window.frameElement.id;` in the script inside the *SVG* file and then passing `frameId` as an argument in the call to the *HTML* funciton (i.e., `top.status( text, frameId );`).

5. **CSS styling.**

This section will demonstrate how to style *SVG* with both internal and external style sheets. This section provides only an introduction into style sheets. A full discussion of *CSS* is outside the scope of this book.

The first step is to remove the "fill" entry in "ButtonBase" rectangle's style attribute. Delete: `fill:#ff0000;`. If this is not removed, it will override any *CSS* style attribute. All lines referencing "ButtonBase" or "fill" should be deleted in the script as the style sheet will replace their functionality.

For an internal style sheet, add a style section before the `<defs>` section in the *SVG* file as shown below. Keeping it at the top makes the style sheet easy to find. The style sheet sets the color of the base rectangle with both a default value and an override value when the button is in a pressed state. As a bonus, the style sheet also dictates that when the mouse cursor is over the button the cursor should be changed to a pointer and that the button should be highlighted.

```
<style type="text/css">        ❶
  rect[id="ButtonBase"] { fill: red; }        ❷
  svg[aria-pressed="true"] rect[id="ButtonBase"] { fill: green; }        ❸
  g:hover {cursor: pointer}        ❹
  g:hover rect[id="ButtonGlow"] {opacity: 0; }        ❺
</style>
```

❶   `<style>` start tag with type declaration.
❷   This selector matches the rectangle with *id* of "ButtonBase" and assigns a "fill" value of "red" to it.
❸   This selector matches the rectangle with the *id* of "ButtonBase" but only when the "svg" attribute *aria-pressed* is "true". It overrides the previously line as it follows it in the style sheet.
❹   This selector matches the `<g>` object, but only when the cursor is above the *Group*. When the selector matches, the cursor is changed to a "pointer".
❺   This selector matches the "ButtonGlow" rectangle when the cursor is above the `<g>` object. When the selector matches, the *opacity* of the "ButtonGlow" rectangle is set to zero, thereby highlighting the button (as the rectangle normally darkens the button).

That completes styling the *SVG* with an internal *CSS* style sheet. To use an external style sheet, remove the `<style>` section from the *SVG* file and paste it into a separate style file, removing the opening and closing `<style>` tags. Add at the top of the *SVG* file, just after the *XML* version and encoding line (if present):

```
<?xml-stylesheet type="text/css" href="button.css" ?>
```

where the "href" value is the style-sheet file name. This file can be shared between the *HTML* and *SVG*, allowing one to keep all the styling in one place.

# A Neon Sign—Animation

While Inkscape cannot directly handle animation, it is possible to use Inkscape drawings as a starting point for creating animation. This tutorial demonstrates two techniques for creating an animated neon sign. It also discusses a number of issues the artist must consider in creating the animations.

An animated neon sign (*GIF* and *SVG* versions on web).⊗

Several things must be considered in planning an animation. The most critical is how will the animation be displayed? The *SVG* standard includes provisions for natively incorporating animation via *SMIL*. Until recently, support by *SVG* viewers was limited. It will not be included in Internet Explorer 9. JavaScript [http://en.wikipedia.org/wiki/JavaScript] or ECMAScript [http://en.wikipedia.org/wiki/ECMAScript] can also be used for animations. This is more widely supported. Most web browsers support JavaScript but the speed of JavaScript in older browsers is poor, especially for complicated drawings. The most recent browsers have vastly improved speed. An alternative method to using JavaScript is to use an external program such as Gimp to create an animated *GIF*.[1] In this case, performance is more than adequate but one loses several advantages of using *SVG*, such as scalability.

This tutorial is divided into two parts. The first part covers the creation of an unanimated neon sign and the second part covers animating the sign both via an animated *GIF* and by using JavaScript. Attention is paid to the first part to facilitate the animation. Heavy use of the *XML Editor* is made to give the various drawing objects names useful in the animation as well as to adjust some object parameters.

The steps are:

- Draw an unanimated neon sign.

    - Set up the drawing.

    - Draw Saturn and the rings.

    - Draw the sign board.

    - Draw the arrow.

    - Add finishing touches.

- Animate the sign.

    - Via an animated *GIF*.

    - Via JavaScript.

Before we begin the illustration, let's discuss neon lights. A neon light is made from a glass tube with a noble gas inside and electrodes on both ends. The gas will glow when an alternating high voltage is applied to the electrodes. The two main gases used are neon and argon. Neon produces orange light, while argon produces blue light. Adding a small amount of mercury to a tube filled with argon produces ultraviolet light that can be used to produce a wide spectrum of colors via coating the glass with phosphors. An example of the possible colors can be found in color charts [http://www.egl-neon.com/chart3.html] from EGL, a neon light parts manufacturer.

When viewed from a distance a neon light produces a sharp bright line of light. If the neon tube is placed in front of a mat background material, a diffused light will be reflected, producing a soft glow around the line. A close-up of a neon tube will show a bright center (the glowing gas) and a more diffused border (the glass). A photograph of a neon light may show a blurred region around the light if the photograph is overexposed. In many cases, the color of the tube will be over-saturated. One must decide which effects the drawing will show, keeping in mind that using the *Gaussian Blur* filter is CPU intensive. Perhaps the best way to obtain the colors you want is to grab the colors using the *Dropper Tool* from a photograph imported into Inkscape (search for "neon sign" with Google Images).

---

[1] It is normally recommended to save drawings in the *PNG* format rather than the *GIF* format. Unfortunately, the animated versions of the *PNG* format, *MNG* and *APNG*, have limited support. This leaves the *GIF* format the only real option for animation.

A section of a neon sign showing orange and blue tubes.

## Procedure 1.9. Creating a Neon Sign

1. **Drawing an unanimated neon sign.**

   a. **Set up the drawing.**

   With the *Document Properties* dialog (File → ⬚ Document Properties... (**Shift+Ctrl+D**)), set the drawing size to 300 × 300 pixels. Create a *Grid* with spacing of 5 pixels and turn snapping nodes to the *Grid* on.

   Our sign is depicted at night. We'll need a black background. Use the *Rectangle Tool* to draw a rectangle that covers the page. Give it a black *Fill* and remove any *Stroke*. For the moment, change the *Opacity* to 50%. This will make it easier to see other objects as they are drawn (such as black text). We'll change the *opacity* back to 100% at the end.

   We don't want the background to move so use the *Object Properties* dialog (Object → ▨ Object Properties... (**Shift+Ctrl+O**)) to lock the rectangle (normally it is recommended to lock objects indirectly by using a locked *Layer*, but in this case, we need to keep all of the sign parts on the same *Layer* if we want to animate the sign using an animated *GIF*). While we're at it, in the dialog, change the *Id* to "Background" to make it easier to find the *Rectangle* later.

   b. **Draw Saturn and the rings.**

   Saturn will consist of a yellow plastic orb surrounded by three neon rings. The neon rings will be tilted and the whole mechanism will rotate in the *SVG* animated version. For animation purposes, it is easier to draw the orb and rings centered around the *SVG* coordinate origin (upper-left page corner) and then group the parts and translate the group into place.

   Using the *Ellipse Tool*, draw a circle with radius 30 pixels and origin at the upper-left corner of the page. If the **Shift** key is held down while using the *Ellipse Tool*, the center of the circle will be at the start of the drag. Holding the **Ctrl** key down also, will force the ellipse to be a circle (or have an integer height/width or width/height ratio). Set the *Fill* color to light yellow (RGB: 252, 249, 63) and turn off any *Stroke*. A slight *Blur* of a few percent gives the globe a soft glow, but at the cost of more CPU usage. For the moment, leave the blur set to zero.

   If you plan to animate the sign, it is very useful to have each object labeled with an appropriate name. One could use the *Object Properties* dialog for this (as we did for the background rectangle), but it is probably more useful to use the *XML Editor* dialog (Edit → ▨ XML Editor... (**Shift+Ctrl+X**)). The *XML Editor* dialog allows you to easily move objects up and down in *z-order* and into and out of *Groups* as well as change various object properties. Open the *XML Editor*. When the orb is selected on the main Inkscape window, its *XML* entry will be highlighted in blue on the left side of the *XML Editor* dialog. You can also select a single object or *Group* by clicking on its entry in the *XML Editor*. Click on the *id* line on the left side of the dialog. This selects the *id* attribute for editing in the lower-right side of the dialog. The orb will have an id of the form "path####". Change this to "Orb" and use **Ctrl+Enter** to register the new name. While you have the dialog open, note the Sodipodi parameters *cx*, *cy*, *rx*, and *ry*. These attributes mark the center and radius of the arc. Inkscape automatically calculates the *SVG* path from these parameters.

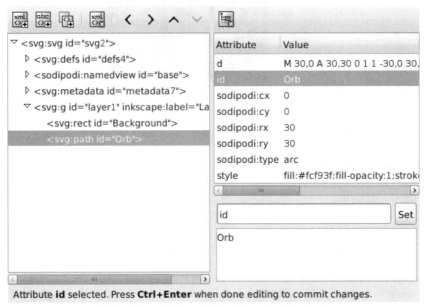

*XML Editor* dialog (after orb path relabeled).

Now add the rings by using the *Ellipse Tool*. Holding the **Shift** key down, create an arc with an *x* radius of 50 and a *y* radius of 10. Turn off the *Fill* and add a 2-pixel wide red *Stroke* (RGB: 255, 34, 34). Create a second arc with *x* radius of 55 and *y* of 15. Set the color to orange (RGB: 255, 144, 6). Finally, create a third ring with *x* radius of 60 and *y* radius of 20. Set the color to the same red as the first ring. Using the *XML Editor* dialog, change the *id* names to "Ring1", "Ring2", and "Ring3", respectively.

The rings don't look right. There are two problems. The first is the shape of the larger rings. The *y* radius is too large. This resulted from snapping to the grid not allowing the correct *y* radius. Use the *XML Editor* to set the *y* radius (*ry*) of "Ring2" and "Ring3" to 12 and 14 pixels, respectively.

The second problem is that both the top (front) and bottom (back) of the rings are in front of the orb. We could just open the arc using the *Start* and *End* entry boxes in the *Ellipse Tool Tool Controls* but this will run into problems when we animate the drawing as the start and end angles of the arcs will change with the rotation of the rings. The best solution is to move the rings behind the orb and create three new half rings in front of the orb.

Duplicate each ring in turn. Name the new rings "Ring1-Front", and so forth. Rename the old rings "Ring1-Back", and so forth. Rearrange the rings so that the three "Back" rings are behind the orb. This is easy to do by selecting each of the rings on the left side of the *XML Editor* and clicking on the ^ and ˅ icons in the *XML Editor* to move the rings up or down in *z-order*.

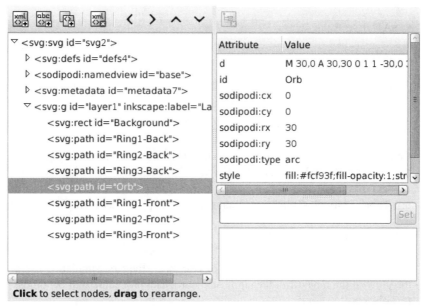

*XML Editor* dialog after labeling the rings and adjusting their *z-order*.

Now take each of the "Front" rings and with the *Ellipse Tool-Tool Controls* set the *End* of each ring to 180° and toggle on the *Open arc* option (　). 

Group the orb and rings together and label the new *Group* "Saturn-Group". Your drawing should look like the one below.

Saturn group before the move.

Finally move the "Saturn" *Group* 150 pixels to the left and 80 pixels down. Our Saturn is complete.

c.  **Draw the sign board.**

We will start with the text before adding the neon sign border.

i.  **Add the text.**

Start by adding the required text as shown in the first figure of this section. The text for the list of items (Hamburger, etc.) need to be center justified. Select this option by clicking the *Center* icon ( 　 ) in the *Text Tool-Tool Controls*. (Note: The "SATURN" text should *not* be center justified if animation is planned.) Add the following using a sans-serif font:

- SATURN: Bold, 36 pt
- DRIVE IN: 28 pt
- Hamburgers
  Root Beer Floats
  Shakes--Fries: Italic, 14 pt

Center the text under Saturn by using the *Align and Distribute* dialog (Object → Align and Distribute... (**Shift+Ctrl+A**)). Set *Relative to* to *Page* and after selecting the text objects, use the *Center on vertical axis* icon ( ). With the *XML Editor* dialog, change the *id* attribute of the text objects to "Saturn-Tube", "DriveIn-Tube", and "Items-Tube" as appropriate. This should be done before the next step.

ii. **Add neon effect to the text.**

The neon effect for the text consists of two parts, the first simulating the neon tube and the second the glow of the tube off of the sign backboard. The procedure will be almost the same for each of the text objects.

Start with the "SATURN" text. We'll simulate using a neon tube to outline each letter. Select the text object and give the *Stroke* a width of 2 pixels and an orange-neon color of RGB: 255, 191, 127. Remove the *Fill*.

To add the neon glow, use the Path → Linked Offset (**Ctrl+Alt+J**) command to duplicate the path. This command produces a copy of an object that is linked to the original so that any change to the original object will be reflected in the duplicate. In addition, there is a handle that one can use to enlarge or shrink the duplicate relative to the original. The *inkscape:radius* parameter controls the offset. You can precisely set it by using the *XML Editor*. Set it to 5.

With the *Fill and Stroke* dialog give the new path a *Fill* of RGB: 255, 31, 31; remove the *Stroke* and add a blur of 7.5%. If necessary (it shouldn't be), move it below the original path via the Object → Lower (**Page Down**) command. Label the path "Saturn-Glow" and *Group* it with the original path. Give the *Group* the name "Saturn-Text".

Repeat the above process for the "DRIVE IN" text but with the following changes: Instead of removing the *Fill* of the text, change it to RGB: 207, 228, 241;. Also remove any *Stroke*. For the neon glow, use a *Fill* color of RGB: 0, 127, 189. Name the objects as before, substituting "DriveIn" in place of "Saturn".

One problem with the "DRIVE IN" text is that the font is too thick to approximate the neon tube. This can be remedied by selecting the text ("DriveIn-Tube") and using the Path → Dynamic Offset (**Ctrl+J**) command. This command will convert the text to a path with a handle that can be used to expand or shrink the path. Unlike a *Linked Offset*, no new path is created. With the *XML Editor* dialog, precisely set the offset by changing the *inkscape.radius* parameter to −0.2. As a last step, you'll need to change the *id* attribute back to "DriveIn-Tube".

For the "Items" text, again follow the procedure for the "SATURN" text, but use a *Fill* rather than a *Stroke* for the neon tube text and substitute "Items" for "Saturn" in the labels.

Sign board text completed.

### iii. Create the sign shape.

Inkscape and *SVG* support *Rectangles* with rounded corners. Our 1950s style sign, though, has a trapezoid shape. How can we get uniform rounded corners in this case? The easiest way is to create a trapezoid *Path* smaller than our desired sign and then give it a wide *Stroke* with a *Round* join. Then we can use the Inkscape *Stroke to Path* command to convert the outer edge of the stroke to a new path with beautifully rounded corners.

Using the *Bezier Tool*, draw a trapezoid a bit smaller than the text. With the *Stroke style* tab of the *Fill and Stroke* dialog, set the *Stroke Width* to 40 pixels. Click on the *Round join* icon ( ) to round the corners. Remove any *Fill*, and set the *Stroke* color to black and the *Opacity* to 50% (to better view the text with the trapezoid). Use the *Node Tool* to make adjustments to the corners of the trapezoid so that the trapezoid encloses the text with a margin wide enough to account for the glow of the neon border light. You can also tweak the text positions if desired.

Sign board prior to converting *Stroke* to *Path*.✪

Select the signboard and use the Path → ☞ Stroke to Path (**Ctrl+Alt+C**) command to convert the *Stroke* of the trapezoid to a *Path*. The signboard *Path* now consists of two separate sections. Remove the inner section by using the Path → ◔ Break Apart (**Shift+Ctrl+K**) command and deleting the inner *Path*. The outer section will be our neon tube. Change the *id* attribute to "Border-Tube" and give it a neon-orange *Stroke* color (RGB: 255, 231, 110) and a *Stroke* width of 2 pixels. Remove the *Fill* and set the *Opacity* to 100%.

Now we will add the glow to the border neon light. Use the Path →  Linked Offset (**Ctrl+Alt+J**) command to duplicate the tube path. In this case, we will not use an offset. Change the *Stroke* color to RGB: 255, 32, 32 and the width to 10 pixels. Give the path a blur of 3%. Finally, change the *id* attribute to "Border-Glow".

The glow of the border neon light needs to be clipped to the size of the sign backboard (no backboard, no light reflected). Select the "Border-Tube" path and duplicate it with the Path → Linked Offset (**Ctrl+Alt+J**) command. Set the offset to 4 pixels with the *XML Editor* dialog by changing the *inkscape-radius* attribute to 4. Finally, add the "Border-Glow" path to the selection (**Shift+Alt+Left Mouse** maybe useful for adding the path to the selection) and use the Object → Clip → Set command to execute the clipping.

As a final step, select both the "Border-Tube" and "Border-Glow" paths and *Group* them, labeling the *Group* "Border".

The sign border neon light completed.

d. **Draw the arrow.**

i. **Create the tail.**

The simplest way to add the arrow is to use the *Bezier Tool*. I prefer to create the arrow with a bit more precision by using the *Stroke-to-Path* trick.

- Select the "Border-Tube" path and copy it to the *clipboard* (Edit → Copy (**Ctrl+C**)). Leave the "Border" group (double-click on the canvas where there is no object). Put a copy in the drawing using the Edit → Paste In Place (**Ctrl+Alt+V**) command.

- Set the *Stroke* width to 50 pixels and use the Path → Stroke to Path (**Ctrl+Alt+C**) command to convert the *Stroke* to a path. Remove the inner path as done previously.

- Remove the *Fill* and add a *Stroke* with a width of 20 pixels.

- With the *Node Tool*, remove the nodes on the top and left (select the nodes, then click on the *Delete Selected Nodes* icon ( ). If necessary, remove the extra node at the top right. Select the bottom-left and top-right nodes. Open the path with the *Delete segment between two non-endpoint nodes* command in the *Node ToolTool Controls* ( ). You should have four nodes left, as follows.

Arrow tail showing the four *Path* nodes.

ii. **Create the arrow head.**

In principle one could use one of the arrow *Markers* for the arrow head but none of the default markers is quite the right shape. Creating an appropriate arrow head is trivial with the *Node Tool* so we will go that route.

First convert the *Stroke* to a *Path* with the Path → ✿ Stroke to Path (**Ctrl+Alt+C**) command. Next, with the *Node Tool* select the two leftmost nodes and drag them left 30 pixels. They should snap to the grid.

Next, double-click on the *Path* between the two leftmost nodes. This will create a new node. Drag the new node left 40 pixels. This will be the tip of the arrow. Double-click on the path between the tip and the top-left node, and drag the new node above the top-left node 10 pixels. Mirror that node with a new node on the bottom.

Arrow ready for adding color.

iii. **Lighting up the arrow.**

We'll follow the same procedure we used for the sign border to add the neon effects to the arrow. First set the *Stroke* color to RGB: 160, 255, 255, the *Stroke* width to 2 px, and the *Stroke Join* style to *Miter join* ( ▥ ). Remove the fill and label the arrow "Arrow-Tube".

Next create the neon glow by using the Path → ▨ Linked Offset (**Ctrl+Alt+J**) command to duplicate the path. Change the *Stroke* color to RGB: 0, 127, 255; and the width to 10 px. Set the blur to 3%. Name the path "Arrow-Glow".

To clip the glow, we could use the same trick we used for the neon border but this would give us rounded corners for the backboard of the arrow. Instead we'll again use the *Stroke-to-Path* trick. Select the "Arrow-Tube" path and duplicate it. Set the width of the *Stroke* to 8 pixels and then use the Path → 🖈 Stroke to Path (**Ctrl+Alt+C**) command. Remove the inner path. The outer path will be our clip-path. Select both the clip-path and the "Arrow-Glow" path. You may have to use the *XML Editor* dialog to select the "Arrow-Glow" path first before adding the clipping path to the selection. Apply the clip with the Object → Clip → Set command. Finally group the two "Arrow" paths into a *Group* with the label "Arrow".

Finally, add the "ENTER" text to the arrow following the instructions for the "Items" text. Use a 12-point font. Center it between the top and bottom of the arrow's tail as show in the figure below. Use the **Alt+Arrow** keys to move the text up and down.

Arrow with neon.

e.   **Add finishing touches.**

Most of the finishing touches described here should be applied at the end of the drawing process. If you wish to animate the sign, skip ahead to the animation section and return here at the end.

• Change the background to black: Select the background rectangle with the *XML Editor* dialog. Remember that the rectangle has been locked and normal methods of selection will not work. Set the color to black.

• Convert the text objects to paths: The "glow" of the text is defined as a path linked by Inkscape to the original text. This linkage is only used by Inkscape. The program recalculates a normal *SVG* path every time the original object is changed. Other *SVG* browsers will use the *SVG* path in their display. If the original font is missing, browsers will substitute a different font, which is unlikely to match the style and spacing of the original and thus the glow will not match the text. This can be avoided by applying the Path → 🖳 Object to Path (**Shift+Ctrl+C**) command to all of the text objects. Inkscape supports the *Morphology* filter that could handle the offset needed for the glow. But we'll not use it here as it is a bit complicated and there are still some problems with web-browser filter support.

• Add more detail: The amount of detail one could add is limitless. A structural support for the sign would be one idea of a detail to add. Blurring the Saturn globe would be another.

Finished unanimated sign.

2. **Animate the sign.**

We will demonstrate two ways of animating the sign. The first is to use an animated *GIF*. The second is to use JavaScript. In both cases, we will need to make six versions of the "SATURN" text with the following combinations of letters: "S", "SA", "SAT", "SATU", "SATUR", and "SATURN"; saving each version on a different layer. It would be ideal if we could just add one letter at a time to the sign but if we did that the glow of each new letter would cover the tube of the previous letter.

Start by deleting the "SATURN" *Group* ("Saturn-Text") by selecting and then using the Edit → ✂ Cut (**Ctrl+X**) command. Check the *XML Editor* to verify you have selected the right thing. The group will be stored in the Inkscape *clipboard*.

Next, create a new *Layer* above the base *Layer* by using the Layer → ☝ Add Layer... (**Shift+Ctrl+N**) command or through the *Layer* dialog (Layer → ▤ Layers... (**Shift+Ctrl+L**)). Give the *Layer* the title "Saturn1". The new *Layer* will be automatically selected. The drop-down menu in the *Status Bar* shows the currently selected *Layer*. Paste a copy of the "SATURN" *Group*, previously stored on the *clipboard*, using the Edit → ▤ Paste In Place (**Ctrl+Alt+V**) command. This command puts the copy in the exact position of the original. Repeat the *Layer* creation process to add five more *Layers* named "Saturn2" through "Saturn6", each with a copy of the "SATURN" *Group*.

Now we can work our way backward through the *Layers*, removing one additional letter on each *Layer*. So the "Satellite6" *Layer* has all the letters in "SATURN" while the "Satellite1" *Layer* has only the "S".

There is one problem with removing letters: the copy of "Saturn-Glow" in each *Layer* is linked to the original text object "Saturn-Tube" (now in the *Layer* "Saturn1"). The "glow" in each *Layer* won't be properly updated as letters are removed. This can be changed by systematically changing the attributes *inkscape:href* and *xlink:href* using the *XML Editor* dialog.

Starting with *Layer* "Saturn6", change the *Group id* to "Saturn-Text-N", the text *id* to "Saturn-Tube-N", and the path *id* to "Saturn-Glow-N". Then in the path change *xlink:href* to "#Saturn-Tube-N" (*inkscape:href* will update automatically).

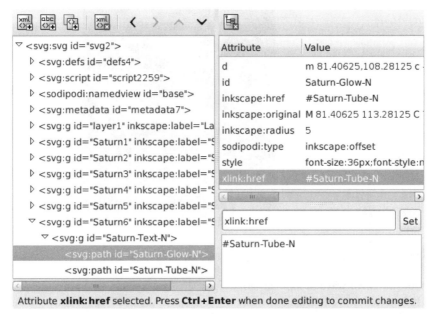

*XML Editor* dialog after changing the *xlink:href* attribute.

Now continue on to *Layer* "Saturn5". To make it easier to select objects in this *Layer* it is easiest to hide *Layer* "Saturn6" by using the *Toggle current* Layer *visibility* icon in the *Status Bar*. After hiding "Saturn6", select the text object and remove the N. Follow the instructions in the paragraph above to relabel and to relink the objects, substituting R for N.

Before proceeding to the actual animation, complete the "finishing touches" listed previously.

a.   **Produce an animated *GIF*.**

We will need to use an external program to create an animated *GIF*. There are a number of programs that have the ability to animate bitmaps. We'll use Gimp. Inkscape has the ability to save drawings in the native Gimp file format but unfortunately, the export does not yet properly handle objects using the *Gaussian Blur* filter. If it did, then we could just save the drawing in that Gimp format, open the file in Gimp, and export as a *GIF*. The Gimp export dialog would ask us if we wanted to use the *Layers* as overlays for the animation. (We would have to take care of one other issue with overlapping letters, but that's an issue we'll leave for a different time.)

Since we cannot export to the Gimp format, we will save each time step as an individual *PNG* and then import each *PNG* into Gimp as a *Layer*. We can then save the whole thing as an animated *GIF*.

Start by hiding all the *Layers* but "Layer 1". Export to a *PNG* using the *Export Bitmap* dialog (File → 
Export Bitmap... (**Shift+Ctrl+E**)). Make sure you export the *Page*. At this point, you will need to decide the size in pixels of the final drawing. Give the *PNG* the name "Saturn_00.png".

Next, turn on *Layer* "Saturn1" and export the drawing as "Saturn_01.png". Then hide *Layer* "Saturn1" and show "Saturn2", exporting as "Saturn_02.png". Continue through all the *Layers*. We'll add an extra flash with all the letters turn on. Hide *Layer* "Saturn6" and export the drawing as "Saturn_07.png". Redisplay *Layer* "Saturn6" and export as "Saturn_08.png" and "Saturn_09.png".

Now start up Gimp. Open "Saturn_00.png". Next add all the other *PNG* files, in order, using the *Open as Layer* command under the *File* menu. You can check your work by looking at the *Layers* dialog (open with **Ctrl**+L). Once all the drawings are imported, save the file as a *GIF* using the *Save as* command under the *File* menu. Give the *GIF* file the name "Saturn.gif". Using the *.gif* filename tag will automatically set the file type to *GIF*. Hit the *Save* button. A dialog will pop up. Select the *Save as Animation* option. Click the *Export* button. Another dialog will pop up. Set the *Delay between frames* to 1000 milliseconds and then hit the *OK* button. The animation is finished! You can view the author's version on the book's website [http://tavmjong.free.fr/INKSCAPE/].

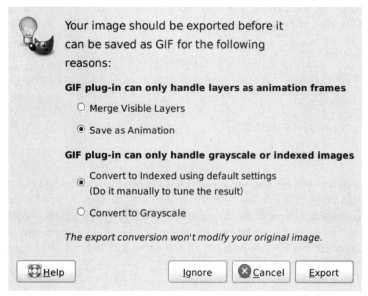

Gimp *GIF* Export dialog.

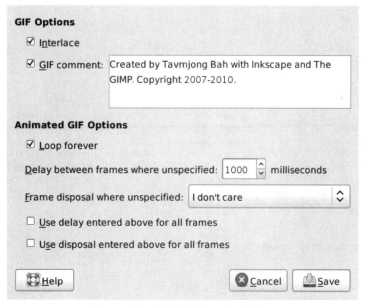

Gimp animated *GIF* Save As dialog.

b.   **Produce an animated *SVG*.**

We will use JavaScript to animate the *SVG* version of the sign. It will be necessary to save the file as plain text; that is, without special formatting characters. Most text editors have a "Save as Plain Text" option. It would be helpful to look at the the section called *Simple Animation* for an introduction to animating an *SVG*.

# Debugging

Most browsers contain an *Error Console* or its equivalent that can help in debugging your script. Look under *Tools* in Firefox and Chrome, and under *Tools→Advanced* in Opera.

Open the drawing in the editor. The first step is to add an instruction to start the JavaScript program to run. In the *SVG* header, add "onload="Start(evt)"".

```
...
   width="300"
   height="300"
   onload="Start(evt)"
   id="svg2122"
   sodipodi:version="0.32"
...
```

The next step is to add the JavaScript itself. A good place to add it is just after the <defs> section. The script must include the type. If you don't add the *id* attribute, Inkscape will add it the next time you open and save the file with Inkscape. Note that you cannot use > and < symbols unless you embed the script in a "CDATA" block. However, Inkscape will remove the "CDATA" block if you open and save the file. It will also change all double quote marks (") to &quot; and all < and > to &lt; and &gt;, respectively. The script will still work.

```
...
  <script                          ❶
    type="text/ecmascript"
    id="script2259">

    /* SATURN layers */
    var nlayers = 6;    /* Number of layers */
    var tlayer  = 0;    /* Time for layers */
    var layer = new Array( nlayers );  ❷

    function Start(evt) {  ❸

      layer[ 0 ]  = evt.target.ownerDocument.getElementById(&quot;Saturn1&quot;);  ❹
      layer[ 1 ]  = evt.target.ownerDocument.getElementById(&quot;Saturn2&quot;);
      layer[ 2 ]  = evt.target.ownerDocument.getElementById(&quot;Saturn3&quot;);
      layer[ 3 ]  = evt.target.ownerDocument.getElementById(&quot;Saturn4&quot;);
      layer[ 4 ]  = evt.target.ownerDocument.getElementById(&quot;Saturn5&quot;);
      layer[ 5 ]  = evt.target.ownerDocument.getElementById(&quot;Saturn6&quot;);

      Run();  ❺
    }

    function Run() {  ❻

      /* Select only one 'layer', turn off others. */
      for( var i = 0; i &lt; nlayers; ++i ) {
        if( i == tlayer-1 ) {
          layer[i].setAttribute( &quot;style&quot;, &quot;opacity:1&quot; );
        } else {
          layer[i].setAttribute( &quot;style&quot;, &quot;opacity:0&quot; );
        }
      }
      /* Flash all letters */
      if( tlayer == 7 || tlayer == 9 )
        layer[ nlayers-1 ].setAttribute( &quot;style&quot;, &quot;opacity:1&quot; );

      tlayer++;
```

```
        if( tlayer &gt; 10 ) tlayer = 0; /* Reset every 10 seconds */

        setTimeout(&quot;Run()&quot;, 1000) ❼

    }

</script>
```

❶     Declaration and start of script.
❷     Array to store pointers to objects, in this case *Layers*.
❸     Start function, called on loading file.
❹     Find pointer to specified object using *id* tag.
❺     Call to run function.
❻     Function that is repeatedly called.
❼     Set a timeout to call the "Run" function every second.

We now have the *SVG* equivalent of the *GIF* animation, except that the *SVG* can be rescaled without losing sharpness. But we can do even more by animating the Saturn sphere and rings and by making the "Enter" neon tube flaky.

The first step is to change the time interval between redrawing to 0.2 seconds. This requires a few modifications but will result in a smoother animation.

The next step is to animate the rings. The animation is composed of two parts. The first is to change the tilt of the rings by adding a transformation attribute with a rotation. The second is to change the *y* radii (or height) of the rings by modifying the path attribute.

The last step is to create a flaky "ENTER" neon tube by randomly changing the opacity of the "ENTER" group.

Here is the full script:

```
<script
  type="text/ecmascript"
  id="script2259">

  /* Time (frame) */
  var time  = 0;      /* Time in seconds */

  /* SATURN layers */
  var nlayers = 6;    /* Number of layers */
  var layer = new Array( nlayers );

  /* Saturn's rings */
  var nrings = 3;     /* Number of rings */
  var ring_front = new Array( nrings );
  var ring_back  = new Array( nrings );
  var angle = 90;     /* Angle of rings with respect to Saturn */
  var ring_width  = new Array( 50, 60, 70 );
  var ring_height = new Array( 10, 12, 14 ); /* 1/5 of width */

  /* ENTER neon tube */
  var enter;

  function Start(evt) {

    layer[ 0 ]  = evt.target.ownerDocument.getElementById(&quot;Saturn1&quot;);
    layer[ 1 ]  = evt.target.ownerDocument.getElementById(&quot;Saturn2&quot;);
    layer[ 2 ]  = evt.target.ownerDocument.getElementById(&quot;Saturn3&quot;);
```

```
layer[ 3 ]   = evt.target.ownerDocument.getElementById("Saturn4");
layer[ 4 ]   = evt.target.ownerDocument.getElementById("Saturn5");
layer[ 5 ]   = evt.target.ownerDocument.getElementById("Saturn6");

enter        = evt.target.ownerDocument.getElementById("Enter-Text");

ring_front[0] = evt.target.ownerDocument.getElementById("Ring1-Front");
ring_front[1] = evt.target.ownerDocument.getElementById("Ring2-Front");
ring_front[2] = evt.target.ownerDocument.getElementById("Ring3-Front");

ring_back[ 0 ] = evt.target.ownerDocument.getElementById("Ring1-Back");
ring_back[ 1 ] = evt.target.ownerDocument.getElementById("Ring2-Back");
ring_back[ 2 ] = evt.target.ownerDocument.getElementById("Ring3-Back");

Run();

}

function Run() {

  /* SATURN Text */

  /* Select only one 'layer', turn off others. */
  var t = Math.floor( time );
  for( var i = 0; i < nlayers; ++i ) {
    if( i == t-1 ) {
      layer[i].setAttribute( "style", "opacity:1" );
    } else {
      layer[i].setAttribute( "style", "opacity:0" );
    }
  }
  /* Flash all letters */
  if( t == 7 || t == 9 )
    layer[ nlayers-1 ].setAttribute( "style", "opacity:1" );


  /* Animate Saturn's rings */

  /*
   * Rotation is composed of two parts:
   *  Changing the y radius of the ellipses.
   *  Changing the incline angle of the ellipses.
   */

  /* Update angle */
  angle += 3; /* Rotate rings */
  if( angle > 360 ) angle = 0;

  var angle_radians = angle * 3.141592653/180.0;

  /* Change incline */
  var incline = 10 * Math.cos( angle_radians );
  var transform = "rotate(" +incline+ ")" ;

  for( var i = 0; i < nrings; ++i ) {

    /* Change incline */
    ring_front[ i ].setAttribute( "transform", transform );
    ring_back[  i ].setAttribute( "transform", transform );

    /* Change y radius */
    var height = ring_height[i] * Math.sin( angle_radians );
    /* This little do da is necessary as an arc must have a positive radius. */
    var df = 1;
    var db = 0;
    if( height < 0 ) {
      height = - height;
```

```
        df = 0;
        db = 1;
    }
    var path_front = &quot;M &quot; + ring_width[i] +&quot;, 0 A &quot; +
            ring_width[i] + &quot;,&quot; + height + &quot; 0 1 &quot; +
            df + &quot; &quot; +
            -ring_width[i] + &quot;, 0&quot; ;
    var path_back  = &quot;M &quot; + ring_width[i] +&quot;, 0 A &quot; +
            ring_width[i] + &quot;,&quot; + height + &quot; 0 1 &quot; +
            db + &quot; &quot; +
            -ring_width[i] + &quot;, 0&quot; ;

    ring_front[ i ].setAttribute( &quot;d&quot;, path_front );
    ring_back[  i ].setAttribute( &quot;d&quot;, path_back  );
}

/* Create flaky ENTER sign by randomly changing opacity */
var enter_opacity = Math.round( 10.0 * Math.random() )/10.0;
if( enter_opacity &lt; 0.2 ) enter_opacity = 0.2; /* Minimum glow */
enter.setAttribute( &quot;style&quot;, &quot;opacity:&quot; +enter_opacity );

time += 0.2;
if( time &gt;= 10 ) time = 0.0; /* Reset every 10 seconds */

setTimeout(&quot;Run()&quot;, 200)


    }
</script>
```

# A Bank Note—Security Features

Bank notes are known for their various security features. Most notes include the heavy use of intaglio printing where the design is composed of complicated patterns of fine lines. Inkscape has many features that allow one to design attractive bank notes complete with a variety of security features. In this tutorial, we explore some of the tricks while creating a "50 Inkies" bank note.

The bank note is composed of a variety of different types of objects. Most of these objects are independent of each other. Unlike the other tutorials, there is no natural order in creating the drawing. Just pick and choose which features you want and how and where they are placed.

A 50 Inkies bank note.✪

The steps are:

- Set up the drawing and block out note.

- Add text with pattern fill.

- Add security designs via:

  - Tiling

  - Star tool

  - Spirograph Extension

  - Function Plotter Extension

  - Function Plotter Extension (Seal)

- Add Pen.

## Procedure 1.10. Drawing a Bank Note

1. **Set up the drawing and block out note.**

   Open a new Inkscape window and set the drawing size to an appropriate size for a bank note. The example uses a size of 450 by 250 pixels. Create a *Grid* with $x$ and $y$ spacing of 5 pixels. Enable snapping of nodes to the *Grid*.

   We'll divide the bank note into two parts. On the left will be a small part that will be kept simple, allowing for a watermark and the note's value to be written in a large, easy-to-read font. On the right will be a larger area that will be filled with the intricate designs typical of bank notes. To mark the right region, draw a rectangle from 125 to 450 px in the horizontal direction and from the top to the bottom of the note in the vertical direction. Remove any *Fill* and add a *Stroke* if none is present. We will use this rectangle to clip the intricate designs.

   With the *Text Tool*, add the main text features as shown in the example or as you desire. The upper-left note value is in large print for easy reading by the visually impaired. The note values are written in the bold variant of different fonts to make them stand out and to give adequate space for the *Pattern Fills*.

   Here are the values I have used (clockwise from upper left):

   - Bitstream Vera Sans Bold (64/32 pt)

   - Times New Roman Bold (48 pt)

   - Nimbus Sans L (48 pt)

   - Impact (28 pt)

   The "Bank of Inkscape" font is Nimbus Roman 9 (14 pt) and the "Draw Freely" font is URW Chancery L (32 pt).

Next, add large circles with the *Ellipse Tool* (hold down the **Ctrl** to force a circle). It is not important to place or size the circle exactly. It is more important to try to achieve a pleasing balance. The two circles on the right will eventually be centered on the numbers. Set the *Fill* to a gray with an *opacity* of 50%. Group the circles together (Object → ✐ Group (**Ctrl+G**)) and move the group to the bottom in *z-order*. Add the clip rectangle to the selection and apply the clipping with Object → Clip → Set. We will be able to move or resize the circles without having to undo the clipping.

Finally, block out the pen place with a rectangle that has been rotated. The pen is placed to cover the point where the two largest circles meet. The bank note should look like the following figure:

The bank note blocked out.

2. **Add *Pattern Fills* to numbers.**

Each of the numbers will be filled with a small *Pattern* to make counterfeiting difficult. We'll use a different *Pattern* for each number. The choice of pattern size should be determined by the use of the drawing. If the note will be viewed on a screen or reproduced at a small size, it may even be better to skip this step as the patterns will not be visible or result in an interference pattern when it is digitized.

Now is the time to pick a color theme for the note. To give our note a sense of cohesiveness, we'll use dark red as the base color.

Start with the number of the upper left. This number should stand out for the visually impaired. Set the *Stroke* color to dark red (with the number selected, hold the **Shift** key down while clicking on the dark red square in the default *Palette*). Set the *Stroke* thickness to 2 px (using the *Stroke style* tab of the *Fill and Stroke* dialog or the menu that pops up when you **Right Mouse Click** on the *Stroke* thickness in the *Style Indicator*). While you are at it, change the "Fifty" text to have a *Fill* of the same color.

Next we'll create a *Pattern* to fill the number. Since this number is meant to be easily read, we'll make it visually dark. With the *Bezier Tool* draw a "squiggle" above the bank note as shown below. Use the *Grid* to help place the nodes. The center node is 5 px above and 50 px to the left and right of the end nodes. Set the *Stroke* width to 10 px and the color to dark red. The *Stroke* covers two-thirds of the *bounding box* area.

The squiggle for the first *Pattern*. The nodes, handles, and *bounding box* are shown.

Convert the squiggle to a *Pattern* by selecting it and using the Object → Pattern → Objects to Pattern (**Alt+I**) command. Three handles appear that allow one to move, scale, and rotate the *Pattern*. Leave these alone for now. The *Pattern* uses the *Visual bounding box* for the tile size. Note that the *Visual bounding box* assumes that the *Cap* style is *Square*.

Select the number text object. Then, on the *Fill* tab of the *Fill and Stroke* dialog select a *Pattern Fill* by clicking on the pattern icon ( ⊞ ). Since this is the first *Pattern* defined, it is not necessary to select the *Pattern* with the drop-down menu.

With the number selected and the *Node Tool* in use, the *Pattern* handles should be displayed near the original *Pattern*. Drag the square handle to the left to reduce the scale of the pattern tile. A reasonable size pattern is produced if the square handle is dragged to be about 5 px from the cross handle. As of v0.47 one can independently scale in *x* and *y*. Hold the **Ctrl** down while dragging the node to keep the proportion fixed.

Fine tuning: Inkscape and some other *SVG* viewers may have problems with discontinuities at a tile's border when the border doesn't align with a pixel boundary. Creating a slight overlap between the tiles reduces this possible problem. To create an overlap for the "squiggle" *Pattern*, use the *XML Editor* dialog. Find the *Pattern* in the <defs> section by using the name given in the *Fill and Stroke* dialog. Change the *width* attribute from 110 (100 pixels between nodes plus 10 pixels for the square *Cap* style) to 100. This will result in a 10-pixel overlap.

The upper-left number with *Pattern Fill*.

Now move on to the number in the upper-right corner. We'll use the text "Draw Freely" to fill the number. It will look better if the text is offset a bit from line to line. For this reason the pattern will consist of two text lines with the word order swapped. To ensure uniform line spacing and interword spacing, each word will first be grouped with and then centered horizontally in a rectangular box.

Select the *Text Tool*; set the font to "Times New Roman", bold, and 12 points. Above the bank note, add the text "Draw". Draw a *Rectangle* around the text. To the right, add the text "Freely" and draw a *Rectangle* around this text also, with the same height as the previous rectangle. If the baselines of the two words are not aligned horizontally, select both words and align them by clicking on the ᵧᵃ icon in the *Align and Distribute* dialog.

Temporarily group the two words and center them vertically inside the two boxes by selecting the boxes and text, and clicking on the ▦ (set the *Relative to* drop-down menu to *Selection*). Ungroup the two words. Center each word in its box by selecting the word and box and clicking on the ♛ icon. Now, duplicate each word and box pair and drag them to new positions as shown below. Select the four boxes and make them invisible by removing their *Stroke* and *Fill*. Finally, convert the text and boxes into a pattern by selecting the text and invisible boxes (use a *rubber-band* selection) and using the Object → Pattern → Objects to Pattern (**Alt+I**) command.

The "Draw Freely" design before the *Stroke* of the boxes is removed and the *Pattern* is created.

Now select the number in the upper-right corner. Give the text a dark red *Stroke* with a width of 1 px. With the *Fill and Stroke* dialog, give the number a *Pattern Fill*. Select the correct *Pattern* from the drop-down menu if not already correct. Again the text must be converted to a path before the *Pattern* handles are shown. Adjust the pattern as desired.

The upper-right number with *Pattern Fill*.

Move onto the lower-right corner. This number will get a simple diagonal line *Fill*. Below the bank note, draw a long horizontal *Rectangle*. Give it a dark red *Fill* and remove any *Stroke*. Duplicate the *Rectangle* and move the copy directly below the original. Remove the *Fill* to make it invisible. Select both *Rectangles*, *Group*, and convert to a *Pattern*. Reduce the width of the *Pattern* tile as in the first *Pattern* to create a small overlap.

A simple line pattern. The dotted line is the *bounding box* of the *Group*.

Again, convert the text to a path and adjust the scale with the square *Pattern* handle. Then rotate the *Pattern* 45° with the circle handle, holding the **Ctrl** key down to restrain the rotation to a multiple of the *Rotation snap angle* (normally 15°).

Note: One could eliminate the tiling-edge problem by making the *Rectangles* in the *Pattern* long enough to cover the entire number with one tile width.

The lower-right number with *Pattern Fill*.

For the last number, let's do something different. Instead of using a *Pattern*, we'll create a *Fill* by using a *Spiral* and *clipping* it. First, give the text a dark red *Stroke* with a width of 1 px. Remove any *Fill*. Next use the *Spiral Tool* to create a *Spiral* that covers the text. Change the *Stroke* to a dark red with a width of 0.25 px. Set the number of turns to 100. Now, select the text and duplicate it. Convert the duplicate text to a path. Select both the text and the spiral and use the Object → Clip → Set command to clip the spiral with the text outline. Move the clipped spiral behind the original text with the Object → ⬛ Lower to Bottom (**End**) command. While we are at it, give the "Bank of Inkscape" text a dark-red *Fill*.

**Bank of Inkscape**

**50 Inkies**

The lower-left number with a *Spiral Fill* created by clipping a *Spiral* with a text path.

The bank note with the text *Fill* added.

3.   **Add security designs.**

Now it is time to turn to adding the background designs on the right side of the bank note. Each area will utilize a different Inkscape tool or function. Two of the designs are centered on numbers.

In many cases, it may be easier to prototype your designs in a new window and then copy and paste the design into the bank note. In any case, make sure the *Group* with the four gray circles is open when you add the security designs so that the designs are clipped.

a.   **Via Tile Clones**

The design in the upper-left corner of the right section is created using the *Create Tiled Clones* dialog. A simple circle has been cloned 36 times, each time rotated 10° around a point on the circle's radius.

The first step is to draw a circle using the *Ellipse Tool* with radius of 75 px and center at 200 px in *x* and 100 px in *y*. Remove any *Fill* from the circle and give it a dark red *Stroke* of width 0.25 px.

In the *Create Tiled Clones* dialog (Edit → Clone → 🖼 Create Tiled Clones... ), set the *Symmetry* to *P1* and the number of *Rows, columns* to 1 and 36 respectively. Click the *Reset* button to clear any previously set options. Under the *Shift* tab, check the *Exclude tile* box. This will place each clone on top of the previous; we'll change this in a moment.

Under the *Rotation* tab set the *Angle* to 10° per column. The reference point for the rotation needs to be set to the top of the circle. The *Rotation center* is used as the reference point. This can be set by dragging the + handle when the *Select Tool* is in use and the rotation handles are shown (click the object twice). Click the *Create* button to generate the tiling.

To generate a "checkerboard" *Fill*, the clones need to be combined into one path. First, unlink the clones from the original (Edit → Clone → 🖼 Unlink Clone (**Shift+Alt+D**)). Second, delete the original circle (or the clone on top of it). Select all the clones (can be done with *Touch Selection*) and merge them into one path (Path → 🖉 Combine (**Ctrl+K**)). Give the object a light-red *Fill*. Set the *Fill Rule* to *Even-Odd* by clicking on the ↻ icon in the *Fill* tab of the *Fill and Stroke* dialog. Lastly, remove the gray prototype circle from behind the design.

Addition of a pattern created by tiling a circle to the bank note.

b.  **Via Star tool**

The *Star Tool* can be used in a variety of non-star-like ways. By using a large number of *Corners*, a large value of *Rounded*, and putting the *Tip* handle on the other side from the *Base* handle, an intricate pattern can be created.

For our "Star", draw a *Star* centered on the upper-right number with the same radius as the template circle. Set the *Star* parameters to:

• *Corners*: 36

• *Spoke ratio*: 1.000

• *Rounded*: 0.210

You could drag the *Base* handle to the other side but getting the loops evenly spaced is difficult. Instead use the *XML Editor* to set *sodipodi:arg1* (*Tip* handle) to π (3.1415927) and *sodipodi:arg2* (*Base* handle) to π/36 (0.08726).

Set the *Stroke* color to dark red and the width to 0.25 px. With the *Fill and Stroke* dialog, set the *Fill Rule* to *Even-Odd* and set the *Fill* color to a light red.

For a more interesting pattern, add a background circle slightly smaller than the "star" with a radial *Gradient Fill* (you can use the gray prototype circle). To make the number stand out, add a second, white circle with the radius of the inner "circle" created by the "star". This circle should be above the "star" and larger circle but below the number in *z-order*. Hints: Use the *Align and Distribute* dialog to make the "star" and circles concentric, and adjust the size of the circles with the *Ellipse Tool* while holding the **Ctrl** key down to keep the *x* and *y* radii the same.

Addition of "Star" to the bank note.

c.  **Via Spirograph Extension**

We'll use the *Spirograph* to produce the complex circular pattern around the number at the lower right. Select the extension (Extensions → Render → Spirograph). Enter the following values in the dialog:

• *R*: 30.0

• *r*: 56.0

• *d*: 50.0

- *Gear Placement*: Outside

- *Rotation*: 0.0

- *Quality*: 16

Set the *Stroke* color to dark red, the width to 0.25 px, and set the *Fill* color to light red, the *Fill Alpha* (A) to 191, and the *Fill Rule* to *Even-Odd*. Center the design on the number at the lower right. Remove the temporary gray circle. Push the design behind the "Star" design in *z-order*. Remove the gray prototype circle behind the design.

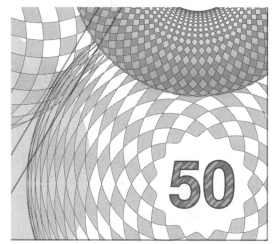

Addition of a "Spirograph" design to the bank note.

d. **Via Function Plotter Extension**

The lower-left design will be created using the *Function Plotter* extension to plot a function in polar coordinates. The extension uses a *Rectangle* to set the scale in the horizontal and vertical directions. Draw a *Rectangle* centered below the "Draw Freely" text with width and height of 100 pixels. With the rectangle selected, call up the extension. Use the following values:

- *Start x-value*: 0.0

- *End x-value*: 20.0

- *Multiply x-range by 2\*pi*: Checked

- *y-value at rectangle's bottom*: −1.0

- *y-value at rectangle's top*: 1.0

- *Samples*: 1000

- *Isotropic scaling*: Not Checked

- *Use polar coordinates*: Checked

- *Function*: 0.02\*x + 0.25\* sin(20.25\*x)

- *Calculate first derivative numerically*: Checked

- *First derivative*: Not Used

- *Remove rectangle*: Checked

- *Draw Axes*: Not Checked

The *x* (theta) domain corresponds to 20 rotations around a circle. The *x* range is set so that the left edge of the *Rectangle* is at −1 and the right side at +1. The *Function* consists of several parts. The first part, "0.2*x", by itself would give a spiral increasing by a small amount each loop. The next part, "0.25*sin(20.25*x)", adds a sinusoidal wave to the spiral with an amplitude of 0.25 (center to peak).

Set the *Fill Rule* to *Even-Odd*. Use a red radial *Gradient* for the *Fill*. Set the *Stroke* to dark red with a width of 0.25 px. You may notice some irregularities in coloring where a line connects the first and last nodes on the right of the design. You can make these less obvious by rotating the design 90° in the clockwise direction.

For the background to the design: duplicate the design, change the *Fill Rule* to *Non-Zero*, use Path → 📄 Union (**Ctrl++**) to simplify the shape. Give it a light-red color and move it behind the original design.

Add a white ellipse with a dark-red *Stroke* on top to bring out the text. Center the ellipse on the text.

Addition of *Function Plotter Extension* design to the bank note.

e.   **Via Function Plotter Extension (Seal)**

Off to the left is a silver security seal. The seal was also created using the *Function Plotter* extension to plot a function in polar coordinates.

To set the scale for the extension, draw a *Rectangle* centered below the upper-left number 55 pixels wide and 45 pixels high. With the rectangle selected, call up the extension. Use the following values:

- *Start x-value*: 0.0

- *End x-value*: 8.0

- *Multiply x-range by 2*pi*: Checked

- *y-value at rectangle's bottom*: −1.0

- *y-value at rectangle's top*: 1.0

- *Samples*: 1000

- *Isotropic scaling*: Not Checked

- *Use polar coordinates*: Checked

- *Function*: 1.0 + 0.3*sin(3*x)*sin(20.125*x)

- *Calculate first derivative numerically*: Checked

- *First derivative*: Not Used

- *Remove rectangle*: Checked

- *Draw Axes*: Not Checked

The *x* (theta) domain corresponds to eight rotations around a circle. The *Function* consists of several parts. The first part, "1.0", by itself would give a circle at radius 1.0. The next part, "0.3*sin(3*x)", adds a sinusoidal envelope to the radius with an amplitude of 0.3 (center to peak) and with six "pulses". The last part, "sin(20.125*x)", fills the "pulses" with a rapidly varying sine wave, offset by 0.125 parts of the period of the sine wave each rotation around the circle. The path closes on itself since the total offset is one period after eight rotations.

Give the seal a *Fill* color of light silver (gray). Set the *Fill Rule* to *Non-zero*. Add a *Stroke* color of a darker silver and a *Stroke* thickness of 0.25.

One can give a hint of a 3D embossing by duplicating the pattern, removing the *Fill*, lightening and thinning the *Stroke*, and shifting the duplicate pattern a small amount.

Lastly, add a silver number 50 centered in the seal.

Addition of "Silver Seal" to the bank note.

The bank note with security features added.

## 4.  Add Pen

It is easiest to draw the pen off to the side of the note with the pen in a vertical or horizontal position. This allows using the *Grid* to place nodes and handles symmetrically. Once the pen is drawn, the parts can be put in a *Group* and then moved and rotated into place.

The body of the pen consists of just four nodes, drawn using the *Bezier Tool*. The nib is also drawn with the *Bezier Tool*. One can search the Internet for a photograph of a pen nib to use for tracing. The body has a simple white to black gradient *Fill* while the nib has a black-white-black gradient *Fill*.

The bank note pen.

To make the shadow for the pen: duplicate the pen, ungroup the pieces, remove the detail (slot and circle) from the nib, with the nib outline and pen outline selected, and create a union (Path → ◯ Union (**Ctrl++**)) of the pieces. Remove the *Stroke* and give the shadow a gradient *Fill* from black to black with zero *Alpha*. Rotate the shadow into place and move behind the pen in *z-order*.

Inkscape has a nifty mode for using the *Calligraphy Tool* to create engravings. The pen would be an ideal place to use this feature instead of using *Gradients*.

# A Bottle—Photorealism

Inkscape can be used to produce photo-realistic drawings. Inkscape features that are useful for this include: *Gradients*, the *Gaussian Blur* filter, and *Bitmap Tracing*. This tutorial uses all of these to produce a realistic drawing of an old seltzer bottle. The source photograph is available on the book's website [http://tavmjong.free.fr/INKSCAPE/].

Our goal is to capture the essence of an antique bottle, not to copy all the fine detail (use a photograph for that). The hand-blown glass is irregular, something that would be hard to reproduce by hand drawing, even with gradients and blurring. To simulate the glass, we'll use the auto-tracing routines built into Inkscape. Tracing has its flaws, though, which we'll need to work around. The handle and background, on the other hand, are prime candidates for *Gradients* and *Blurs*.

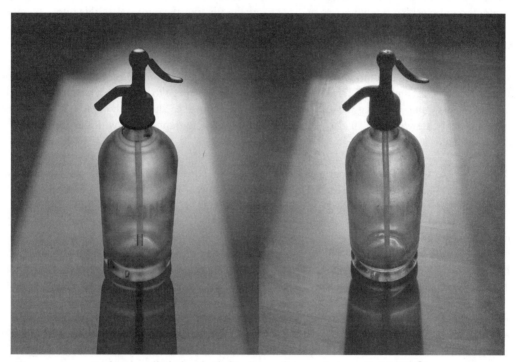

A photo-realistic bottle (left), drawn from a photograph (right).✪

The steps are:

• Set up the drawing.

• Draw the background.

• Draw the handle.

• Trace and draw the bottle.

## Procedure 1.11. Drawing a Bottle

1. **Set up the drawing.**

   The first thing to do is to determine how much detail is required in the drawing. The actual drawing size is of little relevance as *SVG* drawings are scalable without loss of detail. What is more important is the size of the starting *bitmap* image. The larger that image is, the more detail will be included, and the more complex (and accurate) the paths created by tracing will be. But too much detail will result in large paths that will tax computer resources. A *bitmap* size of 768 by 1024 pixels seem a reasonable compromise between detail and path size. We'll set the drawing (page) size to half the bitmap size, or 384 by 512 pixels.

## Gaussian Blur and Speed

This tutorial makes heavy use of the *Gaussian Blur* filter. The filter is CPU intensive. One can reduce the CPU use at the cost of image quality by going to the *Inkscape Preferences* dialog (File → Inkscape Preferences... (**Shift+Ctrl+P**)) and setting *Gaussian blur quality for display* to *Lowest quality* in the *Filters* section. Export to a *bitmap* will still be done with the highest quality.

After creating a new drawing and setting the size, import the *bitmap* using File → Import... (**Ctrl+I**). In v0.48 a dialog will pop-up asking if you wish to *embed* or *link* the file. For the purposes of this tutorial, embedding the photo is not needed so selecting *link* will keep the *SVG* file size down. Fit the photograph to the page by enabling snapping to the page ( ) and dragging opposite corners of the photograph to the page corners.

A second copy of the photograph is useful for comparing our drawing to the original. Select the photograph, duplicate it (Edit → Duplicate (**Ctrl+D**)), and move it just off the page to the right. The duplicate can be aligned to the page by snapping. Clicking the **4** key will set the *zoom* level to show both copies. When working close-up, a second duplicate window can also be used to show the photograph. Open with the View → Duplicate Window command.

It will be easier to work if the photographs are on their own *Layer*, which can be locked and hidden at will. Change the *Layer* name to "Photo" (Layer → Rename Layer... ) and click on the icon in the *Status Bar* to lock the *Layer*.

2. **Draw the background.**

The background will be created with some simple shapes using *Gradients* and the *Gaussian Blur* filter. Create a new *Layer* by using Layer → Add Layer... (**Shift+Ctrl+N**). Give it the name "Background".

It is easiest to start with the smallest detail, which in this case is the white glow behind the bottle's handle. In this way, already drawn objects don't obscure the photograph in the area where new objects are being drawn. The white glow can be drawn with a blurred *Ellipse*. Draw the *Ellipse* a bit smaller than the size of the glowing region. Give the ellipse a white *Fill* and turn of the *Stroke*. Use the *Select Tool* to adjust the position and to rotate the ellipse slightly clockwise. With the *Fill and Stroke* dialog, add a 30% *Blur*. We can make finer adjustments later.

Next, add the light from the window (outside the drawing) by drawing a quadrilateral using the *Bezier Tool*. The quadrilateral should extend off the page at the bottom as it will be blurred. A blur allows some of the background to leak through at an object's edge but the bottom of the quadrilateral should be solid. Add a linear *Gradient* using the *Gradient Tool* by selecting the (*Create linear gradient*) and the (*Create gradient in the fill*) icons in the *Gradient Tool-Tool Controls*, and click-dragging from the top to bottom of the quadrilateral. With the *Fill and Stroke* dialog, temporarily set the *Opacity* to 1%. This will allow us to "pick" the *Gradient Fill* colors from the photograph using the *Dropper Tool* while still being able to use the *Select Tool* to select the quadrilateral.

With the *Dropper Tool*, select the top *Gradient* handle. Then click near the top-left corner of the quadrilateral, where the white from the *Ellipse* is minimal. This will copy the color to the *Gradient*, although you won't be able to see it in the drawing since the opacity is almost zero. The *Fill and Stroke* dialog as well as the *Style Indicator* will show the change. Make sure that *Alpha* is set to 255. Select the bottom *Gradient* handle, then click near the bottom of the drawing on the wood to set the color of the bottom handle. Change the *Master Opacity* back to 100%. Remove any *Stroke* and give the object a "Blur" of about 2%. Move the object behind the white *Ellipse* in *z-order* (Object → Lower (**Page Down**)).

Now add a *Rectangle* the same size as the *page*. Duplicate the *Rectangle*. Use one copy to clip the light from the window (select both the copy and the window light object, clip with Object → Clip → Set). Give the other

*Rectangle* a gradient the same way as that given for the previous quadrilateral. Move this *Rectangle* behind the other objects.

The wood is missing some texture. This could be added but the background is not the focus of the tutorial. There is a bit of light "glow" behind the bottle on the right that is easy to add. A second white *Ellipse* with a *Master Opacity* of 50% and a *Blur* of 40% takes care of that.

The bottle's background. Objects without blurring (left) and with blurring (right).

3. **Draw the handle.**

We'll create the handle by using the *Bezier Tool* (and one *Ellipse*). It is relatively easy to sketch the outline of the handle with the tool, while it is difficult to use the built-in tracing routines to isolate the handle from the similarly colored background.

First hide the "Background" layer by clicking the 👁 icon in the *Status Bar* when the "Background" *Layer* is selected. Create a new *Layer* for the handle by using the Layer → 🗐 Add Layer... (**Shift+Ctrl+N**) command. Name the *Layer* "Handle".

After a rough outline is drawn with the *Bezier Tool*, use the *Node Tool* to refine the path. Some hints on using the *Bezier Tool* and the *Node Tool*:

• Use a thin *Stroke* with no *Fill* to better see the photograph.

• Put a node at every extreme (top, bottom, left, right). You can then constrain the node handles to be perpendicular or horizontal by holding down the **CTRL** key while dragging the handles.

• Put a node every place where there is a significant change of curvature or where a straight line changes to a curved line.

• With the *Node Tool*, you can drag the line itself.

• Double-clicking on the line with the *Node Tool* will add a new node where you clicked.

- Holding down the **Shift** key while dragging on a node will drag out a node handle if the handle is not already out.

- If the node handles are not shown with the *Node Tool*, enable them by clicking on the ⟋ icon in the *Tool Controls*.

As can be seen next, the main part of the handle has been enclosed by a path. An *Ellipse* has been used for a small part. This will help in re-creating the discontinuity in light on the sides of the rim.

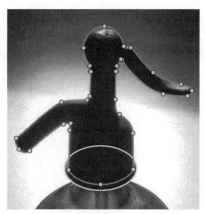

The outline of the bottle's handle. The main path (with nodes) is
shown in red. The green path was drawn with the *Ellipse Tool*.✪

Now that we have the handle outlined, begin to add highlights starting with the smallest regions. Outline each region using the *Bezier Tool*. The *Bezier Tool* normally draws a *Path* without *Fill*. Once the *Path* is drawn and adjusted, remove the *Stroke* and use the *Dropper Tool* to give the *Path* a *Fill* that matches the color of the highlight. To sample a larger area, you can click-drag the *Dropper Tool*. Add some blur with the *Fill and Stroke* dialog. Also give the *Ellipse* a *Gradient* to match the photograph.

Handle with highlights outlined (for visibility).

Once all the highlights are drawn, select the handle outline. Use the *Dropper Tool* to set the *Fill* color. You can go back and adjust the highlights, using the copy of the photograph as a reference.

There is one last detail for the handle. The blurs may leak outside the handle area. Fix this by *Clipping* the handle with a copy of the handle outline. Select all the highlights and the handle outline and put them in a *Group*. Enter the *Group* (double-click on it), select the handle outline, and make a copy of it on the *clipboard* (Edit → 📋 Copy (**Ctrl+C**)). Exit the *Group* (double-click outside the *Group*), and then paste the copy in place (Edit → 📋 Paste In Place (**Ctrl+Alt+V**)). Now select both the copy and the *Group* and use Object → Clip → Set to execute the clipping (the *Ellipse* has been left out of the clipping).

The finished handle.✪

4. **Trace and draw bottle.**

The glass is the trickiest part to draw. We'll use the built-in tracing routines to capture the irregularities of the glass. Tracing is not without its problems, two of which are:

• The paths are monochrome. We'll need to add *Blur* to blend the paths together. Blurring introduces its own problems: unwanted blurring at the edges the bottle (the blur leaks outside the bottle's edge while the background leaks in) and loss of detail.

• The paths are not perfect. If we trace with the option *Stack scans*, we end up with paths that stick out where they should not. If we trace without this option, we end up with gaps between the paths where the background leaks through.

Our solution is to create a stack of sub-layers. The bottom layer will be a base consisting of simple shapes with *Gradient Fills*. This base will minimize the effect of the background leaking through the blurred paths. The next layer will be the blurred paths from the tracing, clipped by the outline of the bottle. The top layer will be hand-drawn details.

a. **Create the bottle base.**

To begin the bottle, first hide the "Background" and "Handle" layers to reveal the photograph. Create a new *Layer* with the name "Bottle-Base" just above the "Background" *Layer* and below the "Handle" *Layer*.

Use the *Ellipse Tool* to draw an *Ellipse* to match the top of the bottle. Draw two more to match the bottom of the bottle (see figure that follows). Draw a quadrilateral between the edges of the top and middle ellipses (it can be done easily by enabling node snapping in the *Document Properties* dialog). Use the *Bezier Tool* to draw the outline of the bottle's shadow. The line between the shadow and bottle can be duplicated accurately by using a copy of the bottom *Ellipse* to "subtract" a bit from a slightly too large shadow path (Path → ⌕ Difference (**Ctrl+-**)).

The "base" layer for the bottle. Left: outlines of the objects for the base. Right: the objects with *Gradient Fills*.✪

Now it is time to give the objects *Gradient Fills*. We don't need to be very precise as the base layer will be mostly hidden. The base will only leak through at the edges of the bottle and between traced paths.

Give the top *Ellipse* a radial *Gradient* by selecting the *Ellipse* and clicking on the ☐ icon on the *Fill* tab of the *Fill and Stroke* dialog. Set the *Opacity* to 1% so we can grab the colors with the *Dropper Tool*. Switch to the *Dropper Tool*. The *Gradient* handles should still be visible. Select the center handle with the *Dropper Tool* and then click on the photograph just beside the handle. Select one of the outer handles and click on the photograph near the left or right edge of the bottle. Now return the *Master Opacity* to 100%. Select the *Gradient Tool* and use the handles to stretch the *Gradient* in the vertical direction.

Give the quadrilateral a horizontal linear *Gradient*. Use the *Dropper Tool* as above to set the colors of the *Gradient* handles. We'll need to add a new *Gradient Stop* in the middle of the *Gradient*. You can edit *Gradients* onscreen. With the *Gradient Tool* active and the quadrilateral selected, double-click at the center of the *Gradient* line. This will add the required *Stop*. Select the *Stop* and the use the *Dropper Tool* to set the color (sample a color just outside the center stem of the bottle). Set the *Opacity* back to 100%.

Add *Gradients* to the rest of the base objects in the same manner.

b.   **Bottle tracing.**

Create a new *Layer* above the "Bottle-Base" layer with the name "Bottle-Trace". Open up the *Trace Bitmap* dialog (Path → ◐ Trace Bitmap... (**Shift+Alt+B**)).

Since we are only interested in the blue glass at this point, we can limit the tracing region by using SIOX foreground selection, enabled by checking the *SIOX foreground selection* in the dialog. We'll need a path with *Fill* to define what is foreground and what is background. The SIOX routine will use the area outside the path to characterize the background. Since the bottle's shadow includes some blue, we'll include it inside the path.

We can use the previously drawn "Bottle Base" objects to create the selection path. Return to the "Bottle-Base" *Layer*. Select and duplicate (Edit → ▢ Duplicate (**Ctrl+D**)) all the bottle-base objects including the shadow. Merge the duplicated objects by using the Path → ⬭ Union (**Ctrl++**) command. Set the *Fill* to red with an *opacity* of 50%. You may notice some tiny sub-paths at the border between the shadow and the bottle. These can be deleted after using the Path → ◕ Break Apart (**Shift+Ctrl+K**) command. Move the path to the "Bottle-Trace" *Layer* by using the Layer → ⬚ Move Selection to Layer Above (**Shift+Page Up**) command. Finally, lock and hide the "Bottle-Base" *Layer*.

Left: The path defining the foreground region for SIOX. Right: The results of tracing the photograph. The white background has been left so the tracing can be easier seen. The red specs indicate gaps between the paths where the background leaks through.✪

Now select the both the path and the photograph (you will have to unlock the "Photo" *Layer* to select it). Use the following settings in the *Trace Bitmap* dialog:

- Set the *Mode* to *Colors*.

- Uncheck *Stack Scans*. With *Stack Scans*, the lighter paths enclose all the darker paths. This can lead to the lighter areas "leaking" out from under the darker areas.

- Check *Remove background*. We don't need the solid white background.

- Set the number of *Scans* to 16. This is a balance between detail and file size.

- Enable *Suppress speckles* (*Options Tab*) with a *Size* threshold of 10 (px). This will remove the smallest sub-paths, reducing file size.

- Enable *Smooth corners* with a *Threshold* of 1.00 to minimize file size.

- Enable *Optimize paths* with a *Tolerance* of 1.00, again to minimize file size.

Clicking on the *Update* button will update the *Preview*. Click on the *OK* button in the dialog to initiate the tracing. Be prepared to wait a few minutes for the results.

The tracing will consist of 15 paths (the *Background* path has been removed) in a *Group*. The tracing is on the "Photo" *Layer*. Select the tracing and move it to the "Bottle-Trace" *Layer* by multiple use of the Layer → ⬚ Move Selection to Layer Above (**Shift+Page Up**) command. Delete or hide the foreground path. Lock the "Photograph" *Layer*. Unhide the "Bottle-Base" *Layer*.

You'll notice that the blocky nature of the traced paths. We can eliminate this by blurring the paths. Select the path *Group* and with the *Fill and Stroke* dialog set the *Blur* to 2%. This, unfortunately, also blurs much of the detail. We'll add some back in the last step.

The blurred paths leak outside the bottle's edge. This can be resolved by clipping. Return to the "Bottle-Base" layer, unlock the layer, and select all the bottle objects (but this time not the shadow object). Duplicate and combine into a single path. For clarity, give the path a red *Stroke* and remove the *Fill*. Move the path to the "Bottle-Trace" *Layer*. Select both the tracing *Group* and the outline path. Use the Object → Clip → Set command to perform the clipping.

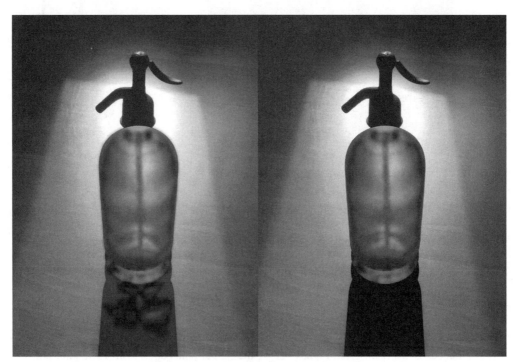

Left: Bottle with blur added but before clipping. Right: Bottle after clipping.

c. **Bottle details.**

Now it is time to add back some of the detail that went missing with the blurring of the traced paths. It is easiest to do this by using the *Bezier Tool* to draw paths on top of the copy of the photograph (on the right). Setting the *Stroke* color to red and the width to 0.25 px makes drawing the outlines easier. Then one can use the *Dropper Tool* to set the *Fill* color. Add a bit of blur and then use the the *Transform* dialog to move the the blurred paths 384 px to the right so that they are correctly positioned on top of the actual drawing.

Left: Bottle with added details. Right: Added details on a white background to show what has been added.

The last step is to unhide all the *Layers*. The final drawing is at the beginning of this section.

# Chapter 2. Files

This section covers the manipulation of the files that are used by Inkscape. This includes the files for storing your drawings in the Inkscape format, and for importing and exporting drawings in other formats. All the commands to manipulate files can be found under the File menu. Several of the commands can also be found in the *Command Bar* (New-default, Open, Save, Print, Import, and Export Bitmap).

# Opening and Saving Files

Inkscape drawings are stored in *SVG* files. Upon starting, Inkscape normally creates a new blank drawing. The parameters used for this drawing can be changed by altering the file `inkscape/templates/default.svg`; see the section called *Custom Templates* in Chapter 24, *Customization*. You can also add your own templates to the template directory.

Depending on how your operating system is set up, a preexisting Inkscape drawing may be opened by clicking on the drawing's icon or by giving the drawing's filename as a command-line argument. Drawings in other formats may be opened the same way if Inkscape supports the format (see next section).

The following commands for working with files are found under the *File* menu:

• File → New: Create a new drawing after Inkscape has been started. The submenu allows you to choose between various sized drawings. Inkscape will automatically give your new drawing a temporary name. The keyboard shortcut **Ctrl+N** will open a new file with the default size (template), as will clicking on the ▨ icon in the *Command Bar*.

The drawing (page) size can be changed at anytime by going to the *Page* tab of the *Document Properties* dialog. You can choose a predefined *Page size* such as A4 or US Letter, or you can set a custom size. The *Resize page to content...* option allows you to automatically set the size of the drawing to the *bounding box* of the drawing or a selection within the drawing, and with or without margins. (*Margin option added in v0.48.*)

### Sizing an *SVG* for the Web

If you plan on using an *SVG* in a Web page, see the section called *Positioning SVG*.

You can add *Metadata* to a drawing via the *Document Metadata* dialog (File → ▤ Document Metadata... ). This includes fields such as author, copyright date, and license information.

• File → ▥ Open... (**Ctrl+O**): Open an existing file. Multiple files can be opened at the same time by using **Shift+Left Mouse Click** to select more than one file from the file opening dialog. This command can also be used to create a new Inkscape drawing from a file with a non-Inkscape format. The file types that can be opened are the same as those listed in the *Importing Files* section below.

The *Open* dialog includes a folder of Inkscape example drawings under the name *examples*.

• File → Open Recent: Open a recently used file. Choose file from list in submenu. The *Recent* menu list may include system-wide recently used files. This list can be cleared in the *Interface* section of the *Inkscape Preferences* dialog. As of v0.48, hovering over a filename will show the entire path to the file.

• File → ▤ Revert: Revert a file to remove all changes made in the current Inkscape session.

• File → ▤ Save (**Ctrl+S**): Save your drawing to a file.

• File → ▥ Save As... (**Shift+Ctrl+S**): Save your drawing to a file with a new name.

The *Save As* dialog includes a folder for Inkscape templates under the name *templates*. Saving a drawing with the name `default.svg` in this directory will replace the default template (the file opened when **Ctrl+N** is used). Saving in this directory under a different name will add the file as a template under the new name in the File → New submenu.

An option under the *Save* tab of the *Inkscape Preferences* dialog allows one to choose between opening the *Save As* dialog with the directory set to the same directory as that for the current open document or to the last directory where a file was saved using the dialog.

- File → Save a Copy... (**Shift+Ctrl+Alt+S**): Save your drawing to a file with a new name but keep the old file name (and type) for future saves.

Inkscape will autosave backups if desired. The feature can be toggled on in the *Autosave* section of the *Inkscape Preferences* dialog. The interval between saves, the maximum of saves to keep, and the directory where the saves are placed can also be set here.

# Importing Files

Inkscape is capable of importing many types of *vector* and *bitmap* graphics files. It can also import text. Some types are handled internally by *GDK* (ani, bmp, gif, ico, icns, jpeg, pcx, png, pnm, ras, tga, tiff, wbmp, xbm, xpm). Other types require additional programs, listed under the relevant entries as listed. One special feature allows importing images from the Open Clip Art Library [http://www.openclipart.org/], a free source of clip art. This is discussed at the end of this section.

Two methods exist for importing files into an already open document. The first is to use your window manager to drag a file and drop it onto an open Inkscape window. The second is to use the File → ⬀ Import... (**Ctrl+I**) dialog. These work for both *bitmap* and *SVG* files.

## Embedding versus Linking

*New in v0.48:*

When bitmap files are imported, a dialog will open up asking if you wish to *embed* or *link* the file. Embedding a file will cause the *SVG* file to be larger (sometimes significantly) but the *SVG* file will be stand alone as a copy of the bitmap is encoded inside the file. If you link to the bitmap, you will need to move the *SVG* file and bitmap file together. If at a later time you change your mind, you can use the *Embed Images* or the *Extract Image* extensions to embed or extract images. See the section called *Images* in Chapter 22, *Extensions*. Note that prior to v0.48, by default, *bitmap* images are linked.

## Bitmap Editing

You can edit linked *bitmap* images with an external program by doing a **Right Mouse Click** on the image and selecting the *Edit Externally...* option. The external program specified in the *Bitmap* section of the *Inkscape Preferences* dialog will open with the image loaded. Inkscape will update the image if any changes are saved (updates will happen any time the linked *bitmap* file changes, not just when the editing was initiated from Inkscape). Note, you cannot edit an embedded image file with an external program.

## *SVG* Bitmap Support

The *SVG* standard only requires renderers to support *PNG*, *JPEG*, and *SVG* formats. The other formats that Inkscape supports internally due to GDK (ani, bmp, ico, pcx, pnm, ras, tga, tiff, wbmp, xbm, xpm) render fine in Inkscape. Other renderers, however, will most likely not support external files of these types referenced from within an *SVG* file. When you select the embed option, Inkscape will convert the file first to a *PNG*. Your safest bet is to either embed them or use another program such as Gimp to convert these formats to *JPEG* or *PNG*.

## UniConvertor

A number of import types (CDR, PLT, SK1, and WMF) use the program UniConverter [http://www.sk1project.org/modules.php?name=Products&product=uniconvertor]. As of UniConvertor version 1.1.4 text is not imported. It is planned that UniConvertor version 1.1.5 will handle text.

**Windows.** UniConvertor 1.1.3 is included in v0.47, 1.1.5 in v0.48.

**Macintosh.** UniConvertor is not included with Inkscape. Installation is not trivial.

**Fedora Users.** The executable `uniconv` was renamed to `uniconvertor` to avoid a naming conflict. This is accounted for in v0.48. For v0.47, you can add a "symbolic link" from `/usr/bin/uniconv` to `/usr/bin/uniconvertor` (if you don't already have a binary with that name) or you can edit files such as `cdr_input.inx` and `cdr2svg.sh` in the `share/inkscape/extensions` directory.

## In Case of Failure

If importing fails to work, check the file `extension-errors.log` located on Linux at `~/.config/inkscape/` and on Windows at `%userprofile%\Application Data\Inkscape\`. Any missing programs (dependencies) will be listed.

File types supported (a * indicates the author has not tested the file import):

- *Updated for v0.48:*

  .ai (Adobe Illustrator) Opens version 9.0 and later files (based on PDF). See PDF entry below. In v0.47, older versions (based on PostScript) can be opened by selecting the PostScript or EPS file type from the drop-down menu. On Linux, you can use the **file** command to check the version. In v0.48, older versions can be opened via Uni-Converter [http://www.sk1project.org/modules.php?name=Products&product=uniconvertor] if you explicitly select *Adobe Illustrator 8.0 and below (*.ai)* in the file-type menu.

- .ai.svg (Adobe Illustrator *SVG*) Strips the input of everything in Adobe Illustrator *Name Spaces*, leaving the file as pure *SVG*.

- .ani (Animation Cursor)

- .bmp (Windows Bitmap)

- .cdr, .ccx, .cdt, .cmx (CorelDRAW) Requires UniConverter [http://www.sk1project.org/modules.php?name=Products&product=uniconvertor]. File versions 7 to X4 supported by UniConverter 1.1.1 and later.

- .cgm (Computer Graphics Metafile)* Requires UniConverter [http://www.sk1project.org/modules.php?name=Products&product=uniconvertor].

- .cur (Windows cursor)

- .dia (Dia) Requires Dia [http://www.gnome.org/projects/dia/] to be installed.

- .dxf (AutoCAD) Imported via internal script. The import is geared for AutoCAD release 13 and newer files (use QCad to update older files). Note that the imported objects may be very small, use **4** to zoom in on them.

- .eps (Encapsulated PostScript) Requires Ghostscript [http://www.ghostscript.com] with the utility `ps2pdf` in your "PATH". The EPS file is converted to PDF first and then imported. Versions prior to v0.47 require pstoedit [http://www.pstoedit.net/]. The same options as for PDF import are available.

- .fig (XFig) Requires xfig [http://www.xfig.org/] (fig2dev) to be installed.

- .ggr (Gimp gradient) Requires Gimp. Imported *Gradients* will appear in the *Gradients* menu. Works only for linear *Gradients*.

- .gif (GIF: Graphic Interchange Format)

- .icns (Apple Icon Image icon icon)

- .ico (Windows icon)

- .jpg, .jpe, .jpeg, jp2, .jpc, .jpx, .j2k, .jpf (JPEG and JPEG2000: Joint Photographic Experts Group)

- .pbm, .pgm, .pnm, .ppm (PNM, Portable Anymap)

- .pcx (PC Paintbrush Bitmap Format)

- .pdf (Adobe Portable Document Format) Supported natively through the *poppler* [http://poppler.freedesktop.org/] library. Also supports .ai (Adobe Illustrator) version 9.0 and later files. A dialog will appear in which you can specify which page of a multipage file should be imported as well as a clip region. *Gradient meshes* are converted to groups of small tiles. Text is imported with manual kerning. To make editing easier, manual kerning can be removed via the Text → ⬛ Remove Manual Kerns command. One can select if Inkscape should attempt to replace font names with the most similarly named fonts installed on your system and if images should be embedded. A preview is shown in v0.48.

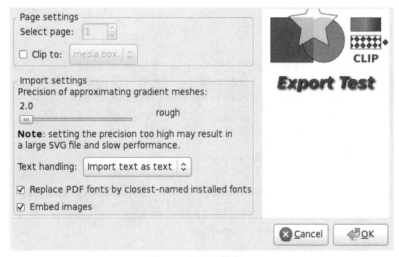

*Import PDF* dialog.

Importing PDF files can be done from the command line.

- .plt (HPGL File for desktop cutters) Requires UniConverter [http://www.sk1project.org/modules.php?name=Products&product=uniconvertor], version 1.1.4 or later.

- .png (PNG: Portable Network Graphic)

- .ps (PostScript) Requires Ghostscript [http://www.ghostscript.com] with the utility `ps2pdf` in your "PATH". The EPS file is converted to PDF first and then imported. Versions prior to v0.47 require pstoedit [http://www.pstoedit.net/]. The same options as for PDF import are available.

- .ras (Sun Raster)*

- .sk (Sketch/Skencil) Requires Skencil [http://www.nongnu.org/skencil/] to be installed. Special shape information (e.g., rectangles) is not preserved.

- .sk1 (sK1, fork of Sketch) Requires UniConverter [http://www.sk1project.org/modules.php?name=Products&product=uniconvertor].

- .svg (SVG)

- .svgz (SVG Compressed)

- .tga, .targa (Truevision Advanced Raster Graphics Adapter) Common in video games.

- .tif, tiff (TIFF: Tagged Image Format)

- .txt (Text), Requires Perl SVG.pm [http://search.cpan.org/~ronan/] module. Text is imported as a group of regular text objects, one for each line.

- .wbmp (Wireless Application Protocol Bitmap Format)

- .wmf (Windows Meta File) Requires UniConverter [http://www.sk1project.org/modules.php?name=Products&product=uniconvertor].

- .wpg (WordPerfect Graphics)*

- .xaml (Microsoft Application eXtensible Markup Language).*

- .xbm (X-BitMap).

- .xpm (X-Pixmap)

## Open Clip Art Library

The command File → ✥ Import From Open Clip Art Library opens a search dialog that connects to the Open Clip Art Library [http://www.openclipart.org/] website, a source of free clip art. The dialog allows searching for drawings that match descriptive words. Previews of files are shown in a window on the right side of the dialog.

*Import From Open Clip Art Library* dialog. An example of searching for a butterfly is shown.

You may have to set the server name (`openclipart.org`) in the *Import/Export* section of the *Inkscape Preferences* dialog. In the future, export to the library will also be supported.

# Exporting Files

Inkscape is capable of exporting drawings to various types of *vector* and *bitmap* graphics files. Exporting methods are divided between exporting *PNG* (Portable Network Graphics) files and exporting to all other file formats. The *PNG* graphics standard is a patent unencumbered standard that is supported natively by all major web browsers and graphics programs.

### Setting Page Size to Drawing Size

You can set the page size to match the *bounding box* of a selection by clicking on the *Fit page to selection* button (v0.47) or opening the *Resize page to content...* section and clicking on *Resize page to drawing or selection* button (v0.48) in the *Document Properties* dialog. This is useful for setting the page size *after* creating an illustration. Margins can be set in v0.48.

# Exporting PNG (Portable Network Graphic) Files

Exporting a *PNG* file is done through the *Export Bitmap* dialog (File → ⬧ Export Bitmap... (**Shift+Ctrl+E**)).

### Note

This dialog *ONLY* exports *PNG* files, regardless of what file extension you use.

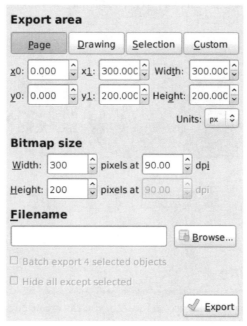

*Export Bitmap* dialog.

At the top of the dialog are four buttons that give an initial setting as to what area of the drawing should be exported (except for the *Custom* button, which does nothing). Once given an initial setting, the area can be adjusted.

- *Page*: Export the area enclosed by the page. The default filename is the *SVG* filename with the "svg" extension replaced by "png".

- *Drawing*: Export all objects in drawing (including those outside the page). The initial export area is the *bounding box* of all the objects. The default filename is the *SVG* filename with the "svg" extension replaced by "png".

- *Selection*: Export the region enclosed by the *bounding box* surrounding the selected objects. The default filename is the internal name of the last object selected.

- *Custom*: Export the area defined in the entry boxes.

The area to be exported can be modified by the entry boxes in the *Export area* part of the dialog. The units can be changed in the *Units* pull-down menu.

In the *Bitmap size* section of the dialog, the size of the exported bitmap can be defined. Inkscape uses a default conversion of 90 *dpi*. The *Width*, *Height*, or width *dpi* can be changed; changing one will change the others, preserving the height to width aspect ratio of the drawing.

In the *Filename* section, a filename can be entered or one can open a dialog to browse for a filename.

There are two options at the bottom of the dialog. The first one, *Batch export n selected objects*, is available if more than one object is selected. If checked, each of the selected objects will be exported into its own file. The name of the file will be the *id* name for the object (see *XML Editor* dialog) unless an object has been previously saved with a specific filename, in which case the previous filename will be used (the filename is stored under the *export-filename* attribute). The resolution will be 90 *dpi* unless previously saved with a different *dpi*. Note: Batch export will overwrite files without warning.

The second option, *Hide all except selected*, is available if one or more objects are selected. If checked all unselected objects will be hidden during export.

The following figure shows a test file exported to a *PNG*. The file includes basic shapes, a linear *Gradient*, a *Pattern*, a *Clipping*, and a blur *Filter* applied to text.

Export test: PNG.

## Slicing a Drawing

To slice a drawing into pieces for use on the web, you can create an array of hidden rectangles (no *Stroke* or *Fill*) in a separate "export" *Layer*. Save each rectangle one time to define the export filename (or change each rectangle "Id" with the *Export Bitmap* dialog prior to any exporting). Then when it is time to export the drawing, go to the "export" layer, use the command Edit → ◎ Select All (**Ctrl+A**) to select all the rectangles in the *Layer*, then do a batch export.

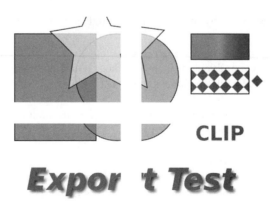

Four slices created using batch export.

*New in v0.48*: The *Slicer* extension facilitates creating slices and producing the necessary *CSS* and *HTML* for their use.

### Tip

The default window size for the dialog may be too narrow to view the output filename including the directory path. Just widen the window to see the entire path.

### Rendering Errors

Inkscape v0.47 has rendering problems when two objects touch each other along a common border. This is often seen when a *Pattern* is used for a *Fill*. This has been significantly improved in v0.48. Firefox, Opera, and Batik do not have this problem. Batik can be used to produce a high-quality *PNG*, *JPEG*, or *TIFF* file.

Inkscape saves metadata, if included in the *SVG* file. Author, Copyright, Creation Time, Description, and Title fields are some of the fields saved. *PNG* metadata can be viewed using the ImageMagick `identify` command.

# Exporting Other File Types

Exporting to a type other than a *PNG* is done through the *Save As* dialog (File → 🖫 Save As... (**Shift+Ctrl+S**)). The file type is chosen from a pull-down menu. Additional programs are required for many of the file exports. Required programs are mentioned under each file type entry.

### UniConvertor

A number of export types (PLT, SK1, and WMF) use the program UniConverter [http://www.sk1project.org/modules.php?name=Products&product=uniconvertor]. Inkscape includes this program in the Windows build. As of UniConvertor version 1.1.4 text is not exported. References to text in the drawing may prevent proper file conversion (even if converted to a path). The work-around is to convert text to path and then search the *SVG* file to remove references to fonts. It is planned that UniConvertor version 1.1.5 will handle text.

Note for Fedora Users: The executable `uniconv` was renamed to `uniconvertor` to avoid a naming conflict. You can add a "symbolic link" from `/usr/bin/uniconv` to `/usr/bin/uniconvertor` (if you don't already have a binary with that name) or you can edit files like `cdr_input.inx` and `cdr2svg.sh` in the `share/inkscape/extensions` directory.

### In Case of Failure

If exporting fails to work, check the file `extension-errors.log` located on Linux at `~/.config/inkscape/` and on Windows at `%userprofile%\Application Data\Inkscape\`. Any missing programs (dependencies) will be listed.

File types supported (a * indicates the author has not tested the file export):

- .ai (Adobe Illustrator). Inkscape v0.46 and earlier supported export to the Adobe Illustrator version 8.0 file format which is a modified form of the EPS level 2 format. This support has been removed since Adobe Illustrator versions 10 (2001) and later can directly import *SVG* files. This is a better solution as the quality of the AI export was poor.

- .dxf (AutoCAD, Desktop Cutting Plotters). Inkscape provides two distinct DXF export routines. The first is geared toward CAD uses and the second toward desktop cutting plotters.

  - *AutoCAD DXF*: This routine uses Pstoedit with Ghostscript to produce a DXF file compatible with AutoCAD release 12. This is a rather ancient file format (1992!). QCad can be used to translate the file into a more recent format. There has been a slight improvement in export in v0.48. The options available are the same as for PostScript output.

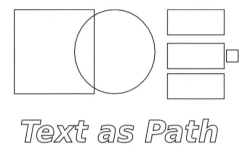

Export test: DXF, AutoCAD. As read in by QCad.

- *Desktop Cutting Plotter*: A built-in routine is used to output files directed at desktop plotters like Wishblade and Craft ROBO. The file format is a simplified form compatible with AutoCAD release version 13 or later. One option targets Craft ROBO Desktop plotters that require an even simpler file format. Another option, added for v0.48, toggles on/off *LWPOLYLINE* use.

The packages *python-lxml* and *numpy* are required.

DXF output dialog for Desktop Cutting Plotter routine.

Export test: DXF, Desktop Cutting Plotter. As read in by QCad.

Note that there is a *Convert to Dashes* extension that turns a *Path* with *Dashes* to an identical-looking *Path* composed of individual sub-paths.

- .emf (Enhanced Meta File)*. Only works with Windows. Only exports *Strokes* and *Fills* with solid colors.

- .eps (Encapsulated PostScript). With just a few minor differences, the generation of an EPS file is identical to a PostScript file. See .ps section below details of options in the export dialog

The major difference from an artist's perspective is that the *bounding box* of the EPS file is set to the smallest rectangle that fully encloses all drawn objects as per the EPS specification [http://www.adobe.com/devnet/postscript/pdfs/5002.EPSF_Spec.pdf]. Selecting *Export area is page*: does not change this. This unfortunate "limitation" is encoded in the Cairo graphics package used for PostScript, EPS, and PDF output. If you want the bounding box to match the page, you can use one of the following:

- Include a white rectangle covering the page in the background.

- Save as a PostScript file, changing the file extension to .eps (this should work in most cases; see following paragraph).

- Hand-edit the %%BoundingBox line near the top of the EPS file.

There are a couple more differences between Cairo-generated EPS and PostScript files that mostly concern experts: Both file types include a *%%BoundingBox* line and a *showpage* command. The *showpage* command should be ignored when an EPS file is embedded in a PostScript file. A Cairo-generated EPS file includes code to clean up after itself if it has left junk on the dictionary stack or operand stack. A Cairo-generated PS file includes an error message if the printer supports a lower PostScript level than specified in the file.

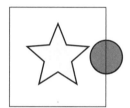

A comparison of export areas. Left: An *SVG* drawing showing the page boundary. Note the circle is half off the page. Middle: The exported EPS file with the *Export area is drawing* option selected (this is the default when exporting from the command line). The *bounding box* is shown. Right: The exported EPS file with the *Export area is drawing* option not selected (this is the default when exporting from the *GUI*). The *bounding box* is shown.

- .fx (JavaFX). Saves file in the JavaFX [http://en.wikipedia.org/wiki/JavaFX] format via an internal Inkscape routine. No options are available. Only paths and shapes are supported. *Gradients* are partially supported (endpoints of *Gradient* are not defined). *Patterns* are not supported and references to them will need to be hand-edited from the FX file.

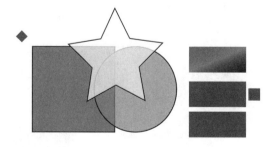

Export test: JavaFX.

- .gpl (Gimp Palette). Saves a list of colors used in the drawing to a Gimp Palette file. The file can then be moved to the Inkscape palette directory (`share/inkscape/palettes/`) and the palette can be selected in the *Palette* bar or the *Swatches* dialog. Requires PyXML module.

- .hpgl (Hewlett-Packard Graphics Language). See also .plt format that follows. Saves file in the HPGL [http://en.wikipedia.org/wiki/HPGL] format, useful with various plotters and cutters. An Inkscape-supplied export routine is used. The *Mirror Y-axis* box should be checked to preserve the same orientation as shown in the Inkscape program.

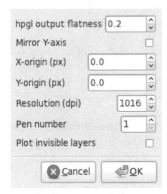

*HPGL output* dialog.

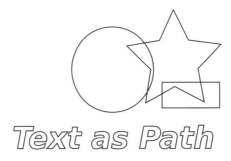

Export test: HPGL.

- .odg (Open Document Graphic). Limited support, better support planned. Currently only export of paths, shapes, and text is supported. Text and paths may initially be invisible. You can select them and change the *Stroke* style from "Invisible" to "Continuous". Some objects may be shifted.

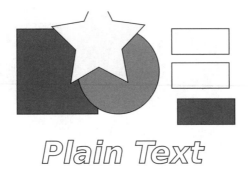

Export test: ODG. The text was initially invisible.

- .pdf (PDF). Inkscape uses a Cairo-based [http://cairographics.org/] exporter. It is recommended that at least *cairo 1.5.2* be used. Note, a pattern that consists of a *Group* created off the page may not work. Note also that the *Print* dialog can also be used to produce a PDF file.

# Evince and Acroread

Older versions of Evince, a popular Linux PostScript and PDF viewer, do not show gradients with *transparency* nor handle *Patterns* properly. Try Acroread instead.

The *Portable Document Format* dialog offers a variety of options:

- *PDF Version*: Only one option: PDF 1.4.

- *Convert text to paths*: Characters in text strings are converted to paths. Fonts are normally subsetted and saved in the file.

- *New in v0.48:*

  *PDF+LaTeX: Omit text in PDF, and create LaTeX file*: Creates a PDF file with text excluded and a LaTeX file with text to overlay the PDF file so that the text font matches that of the LaTeX document and LaTeX math equations in the drawing can be typeset by LaTeX. Supports text alignment and text color (with transparency). See PDF, PostScript, or EPS with LaTeX Overlay entry in this section.

- *Rasterized filter effects*: Converts filter effects to bitmaps. If not enabled, objects with filters are not drawn.

- *Resolution for rasterization*: Sets *dpi* for rasterized filter effects.

- *Export area is drawing*: Sets the area for the PDF to the area that includes all the drawing elements, even if out of the *Page* area.

- *Export area is page*: Export only objects in *Page*. Useful with following option.(Default when not exporting one object.)

- *Limit export to object with ID*: Limits export to only the object listed. If you want to select more than one object, use a *Group*.

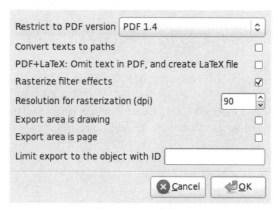

*PDF output* dialog.

Export test: PDF.

- .plt (HPGL File for desktop cutters) Saves file in a form of the HPGL [http://en.wikipedia.org/wiki/HPGL] format, useful with various plotters and cutters. Requires UniConverter 1.1.4 [http://www.sk1project.org/modules.php?name=Products&product=uniconvertor]. No options available.

### Uniconverter Failure

If you have a version of UniConvertor older than 1.1.4, conversion will silently fail, producing an *SVG* file instead. You can examine the file with a text editor. An *SVG* file will include an *<?xml version...>* declaration on the first line, while a PLT file will be a solid mass of letters and numbers without spaces.

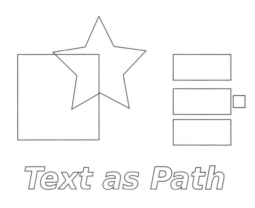

Export test: PLT (HPGL).

- .png (PNG via Cairo) Saves file as a *PNG* via Cairo. Better export is performed using the File → ⬚ Export Bitmap... (**Shift+Ctrl+E**) command. This routine is mainly for testing Cairo-based export. It always adds a non-transparent white background.

### Note

You will probably have much better results in exporting to a *PNG* if you use the *Export Bitmap* dialog.

- .pov (POV-Ray). Saves shapes and paths, with color and transparency, as *prism* objects. Stroke is not saved. To render a drawing, a camera with lights, and so forth, must be defined. See share/inkscape/examples/istest.pov for an example.

Export test: POV.

- .ps (PostScript). Inkscape uses a Cairo-based [http://cairographics.org/] exporter. It is recommended that at least *cairo 1.5.2* be used. Note, a pattern that consists of a *Group* created off the page may not work. Note also that the *Print* dialog can also be used to produce a PostScript file. PostScript output relies on bitmap fallbacks more than PDF output. This includes any place transparency is used. Finally, the *bounding box* of the PostScript file will by default be scaled by 80% from the %bbox_nl; of the *SVG* file. This is the ratio of the PostScript standard 72 points per inch to the 90 pixels per inch default of Inkscape.

The *PostScript* dialog offers a variety of options:

- *Restrict to PS level*: Either PostScript level 2 or PostScript level 3.

- *Convert texts to paths*: Characters in text strings are converted to paths. Fonts are normally subsetted and saved in the file.

- *New in v0.48:*

  *PS+LaTeX: Omit text in PS, and create LaTeX file*: Creates a PostScript file with text excluded and a LaTeX file with text to overlay the PostScript file so that the text font matches that of the LaTeX document and LaTeX math equations in the drawing can be typeset by LaTeX. Supports text alignment and text color (but not transparency). See PDF, PostScript, or EPS with LaTeX Overlay entry in this section.

- *Rasterized filter effects*: Converts filter effects to bitmaps. If not enabled, objects with filters are not drawn.

- *Resolution for rasterization*: Sets *dpi* for rasterized filter effects.

- *Export area is drawing*: Sets the area for the PostScript file to the area that includes all the drawing elements, even if out of the *Page* area.

- *Export area is whole page*: Export only objects in *Page*. Sets *BoundingBox* to page size. This option is useful if exporting only one object.

- *Limit export to object with ID*: Limits export to only the object listed. If you want more than one object exported, use a *Group*.

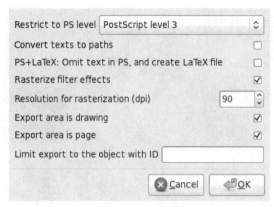

PostScript output dialog.

Export test: PS.

- .sk1 (sK1, fork of Sketch)*. Requires UniConverter 1.1.4 [http://www.sk1project.org/modules.php?name=Products&product=uniconvertor]. No options available.

- .tex (LaTeX) *Updated for v0.48.*

There are a number of ways to use Inkscape with LaTeX. The first is to export as a LaTeX file with *PSTricks* macros. The second is to export as a PDF, PostScript, or EPS file with the text moved to a LaTeX overlay; this allows LaTeX to typeset the text. The third is to export as an EPS file and have LaTeX use the *psfrag* package to replace text labels with text defined inside LaTeX. A fourth is to use the *Latex Formula* extension that uses LaTeX to typeset an equation and re-import it into Inkscape as a path. And a fifth is to Inkscape to design LaTeX presentations; see Latex Presentation Designer [http://jedidiah.stuff.gen.nz/lpd.html]. The first three will be discussed here in turn.

- **LaTeX with PSTricks Macros.** In the method, Inkscape exports the drawing as series of PSTricks macros. This requires that PSTricks package to be installed, which is normally included with LaTeX.

  Here is an example of a LaTeX file to use with Inkscapes tex output saved in the file `FileExportTest.tex`.

```
\documentclass[12pt]{article}
\usepackage{pstricks}
\begin{document}

Test of PSTricks with Inkscape.

\input{FileExportTest.tex}

\end{document}
```

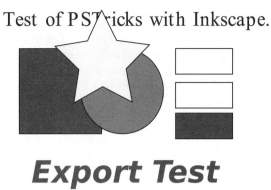

Export test: LaTeX (with PSTricks).

- **PDF, PostScript, or EPS with LaTeX Overlay.** In the method, you insert LaTeX text strings into your drawing. On export to PDF, PostScript, or EPS, check the *PDF+LaTeX: Omit text in PDF, and create LaTeX file* (or equivalent box for PostScript or EPS); the text will be excluded on export and instead be inserted into a LaTeX file that can be overlayed on the figure inside LaTeX. This has the advantage that the text font matches between the drawing and the rest of the document as well as the ability to typeset LaTeX math equations. This method supports text alignment and text color (transparency is supported in PDF export but not PostScript or EPS as the latter formats do not support transparency). See svg-inkscape [http://tug.ctan.org/tex-archive/info/svg-inkscape/] on CTAN for more details.

  Here is an example of its use:

  ```
  \documentclass[12pt]{article}
  \usepackage{graphicx}
  \usepackage{color}
  \begin{document}

  \Huge
  \def\svgwidth{3.333in}
  \input{FileExportText_LaTeX.pdf_tex}

  \end{document}
  ```

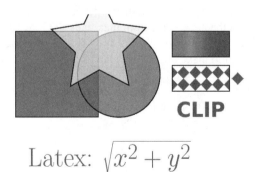

$$\text{Latex: } \sqrt{x^2 + y^2}$$

Export test: PDF with LaTeX overlay. The phrase "Export Test" has been replaced by a LaTeX expression in the Inkscape file.

- **LaTeX with psfrag LaTeX Package.** In the method, you put text tags as placeholders inside of Inkscape. You then export the file to EPS (without converting the text to a path and without manual kerning!). The *psfrag* package then finds the tags and replaces them with LaTeX expressions.

Here is an example of a LaTeX file to use with Inkscapes tex output saved in the file `FileExportTest.tex`.

As of v0.47, this method will fail as the Cairo-based export uses font subsetting (storing only the characters actually used and then using an index to reference these characters) to save space thus your strings can't be found. A work-around is to search the PostScript file for strings of the form *<01020304>Tj* or *[<010203>-1<0405>-1<06>-1<07>1<08>129<090a06>]TJ* and replace them by strings of the form *(Export Test)Tj*. It is probably better just to use the previous method of saving a PDF, PostScript, or EPS file with a LaTeX overlay.

Here is an example of its use:

```
\documentclass[12pt]{article}
\usepackage{graphicx}
\usepackage{psfrag}
\begin{document}

\Huge
\psfrag{Export Test}{PSFrag: $\sqrt{x^2+y^2}$}
\includegraphics{FileExportTest_PlainText.eps}

\end{document}
```

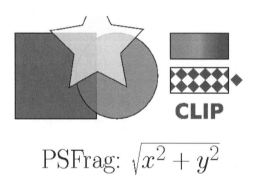

PSFrag: $\sqrt{x^2 + y^2}$

Export test: LaTeX using an EPS file with simple text with psfrag.
The phrase "Export Test" has been replaced by a LaTeX expression.

- .svg, .svgz (*SVG*, *SVG* compressed). Several options are available: Plain *SVG* and *SVG* with Inkscape extensions (for storage of Inkscape meta data). In theory, any program that reads *SVG* files should ignore the Inkscape extensions. One additional option is to save an "Optimized" *SVG* file. This file has been passed through the *Scour* [http://www.codedread.com/scour/] script to make the file as small as possible.

- .wmf (Windows Metafiles)*. Requires UniConverter 1.1.4 [http://www.sk1project.org/modules.php?name=Products&product=uniconvertor]. No options available.

Export test: WMF (As re-imported into Inkscape).

- *Updated for v0.48*

.xaml (Microsoft Application eXtensible Markup Language) Supports gradients and transparency. In v0.47 some objects may end up translated to the wrong place. In addition to fixing translations, v0.48 adds support for blurs and opacity.

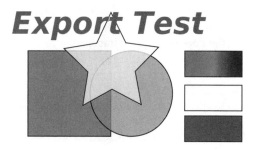

Export test: XAML (As re-imported into Inkscape).

- .xcf (Gimp). All top-level layers and objects are exported as separate layers in the *PNG* format and then inserted as layers into the Gimp native *XCF* format. Export resolution is fixed at one Inkscape pixel to one Gimp pixel. Requires Python, PyXML, and Gimp 2.2 or higher. Both Gimp and Inkscape must be in the executable path.

In the export dialog for XCF one can choose whether the *Grid* and *Guide Lines* should be saved. If saved, they can be viewed in Gimp by toggling them on under the View → Show Grid and View → Show Guides menu items. Only rectangular *Grids*, and vertical and horizontal *Guide Lines* will be saved.

XCF output dialog.

Export test: XCF.

- .zip (Compressed Inkscape *SVG* with Media). This option will save the drawing as an Inkscape *SVG* file and then package that along with all included (linked) graphics files as a *zip* package. The resulting file cannot be read directly by Inkscape. However, when the file is uncompressed, all the included graphics should be placed where Inkscape can find them when the *SVG* file is opened.

# Printing Files

Printing your drawing can be done through the File → 🖨 Print... (**Ctrl+P**) dialog. The standard GTK print dialog is used. This allows printing to any PostScript-capable printer as well as to either a PostScript or PDF file. Printing uses Cairo-based [http://cairographics.org/] routines. The PostScript back-end makes heavy use of rasterizing the image. This is partly due to the fact that PostScript does not support transparency.

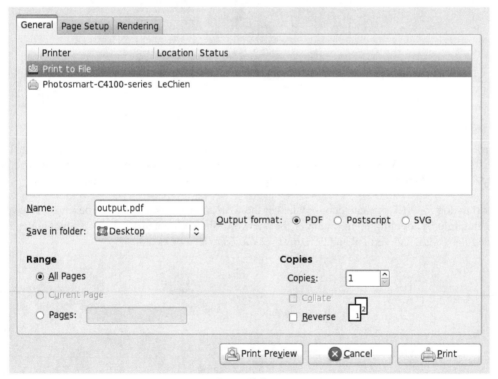

*Print* dialog.

There are two options for rendering output found under the *Rendering* tab. The first *Vector* uses vector operators. The drawing is scalable.

The second option is *Bitmap*, which rasterizes the output. There is an option to set the DPI for the output.

### Using a PS File as an EPS File

An Inkscape PostScript file can be normally be used as an Encapsulated PostScript file (EPS) as it already has a "BoundingBox" line. You may need to change the first line from `%!PS-Adobe-3.0` to `%!PS-Adobe-3.0 EPSF-3.0` and delete the "showpage" at the end of the file.

# Vacuuming Files

The command File → ⛲ Vacuum Defs removes unused definitions from the *<defs>* section of the *SVG* file. This includes things like unused gradients, patterns, markers, and filters.

### Note

Due to the mechanism that Inkscape uses to keep track of which definitions are in use, it may be necessary to close a file and reopen it before this command will remove *all* unused items.

# Chapter 3. Changing the View

The view presented by the Inkscape window can be changed in many ways. The changes can be divided into two types: those that change the way drawings appear and those that change how the Inkscape interface appears. A few of the latter type of changes are covered in other chapters such as Chapter 5, *Positioning and Transforming*, for *Grids* and *Guide Lines*, and Chapter 24, *Customization*, for changing parts of the *GUI*.

An Inkscape drawing can be viewed in many different ways. The view can be changed by panning and by zooming the canvas. The Inkscape window can be made full screen. Multiple views of the same canvas are possible. An *Outline* or *Wire-frame* mode is available as well as an *Icon Preview* window.

## Panning the Canvas

The region of the canvas that is visible can be changed via

- *Scroll Bars*: Perhaps the easiest method. The visibility of the scroll bars can be toggled using **Ctrl+B**.

- **Mouse Wheel**: pan up and down. **Shift**+**Mouse Wheel**: pan sideways.

  By checking the *Mouse wheel zooms by default* button under the *Scrolling* section of the *Inkscape Preferences* dialog, the function of the **Mouse Wheel** changes to zooming while the normal **Ctrl**+**Mouse Wheel** changes to panning up and down. This is the normal behavior in CorelDRAW and AutoCAD.

- **Middle Mouse Drag**. With a two-button mouse, use **Shift**+**Right Mouse Drag** or **Ctrl**+**Right Mouse Drag**.

- **Ctrl**+**Arrow** keys.

- **Space Bar**+**Left Mouse Drag** will pan the canvas if the *Left mouse button pans when Space is pressed* option is checked in the *Scrolling* section of the *Inkscape Preferences* dialog. Turning this option on prevents using the **Space Bar** to toggle between tools.

## Zooming the Canvas

The canvas can be zoomed in and out in many ways. For many of the options, the zoom changes by a default factor of 1.41 (repeat twice to zoom by a factor two). This factor can be changed in the *Steps* section of the *Inkscape Preferences* dialog.

By default, a zoom of "1" corresponds to one Inkscape pixel per screen pixel. If you would like to calibrate the zoom to a real physical measurement unit (like inches or centimeters), you can do so under the *Interface* section of the *Inkscape Preferences* dialog. You will find there a slider that can be dragged to set a *Zoom correction factor*. Simply hold up your ruler to the screen and drag until the onscreen ruler matches.

- + or = keys to zoom in, - key to zoom out. Zoom is around center of viewable canvas.

- **Ctrl**+**Middle Mouse Click** or **Ctrl**+**Right Mouse Click** to zoom in, **Shift**+**Middle Mouse Click** or **Shift**+**Right Mouse Click** to zoom out. Zoom in is around cursor position.

- **Shift**+**Middle Mouse Drag** to zoom in on area within *rubber-band*.

- **Ctrl**+**Mouse Wheel** to zoom in and out. Very convenient. The cursor position is the center of the zoom.

  By checking the *Mouse wheel zooms by default* button under the *Scrolling* section of the *Inkscape Preferences* dialog the function of the **Mouse Wheel** changes to zooming while the normal **Ctrl**+**Mouse Wheel** changes to panning up and down. This is the normal behavior in CorelDRAW and AutoCAD.

- Zoom section of the *Status Bar*. This is the best way to select a precise zoom level. One can activate the entry box via the keyboard shortcut **Alt+Z**.

- *Zoom Tool* 🔍 (**F3**) from the *Tool Box*. Click on the canvas with the *Zoom Tool* to zoom in around the cursor. Use **Shift** click or click with the **Right Mouse** button to zoom out.

- *Zoom Tool*: *Tool Controls* and under the View → Zoom menu. When the *Zoom Tool* is selected, the *Tool Controls* will show a series of icons representing different zoom options. The View → Zoom menu has the same options.

The *Zoom Tool-Tool Controls*.

- ⊕ (+): Zoom in.

- ⊖ (-): Zoom out.

- 🔍 (**1**): Zoom to 1:1 (100% of drawing size, one drawing pixel equal one screen pixel).

- 🔍 (**2**): Zoom to 1:2 (50% of drawing size).

- 🔍 Zoom to 2:1 (200% of drawing size).

- 🔍 (**3**): Zoom to fit selection in window.

- 🔍 (**4**): Zoom to fit drawing in window (show all the drawn objects, which may be smaller or larger than the page).

- 🔍 (**5**): Zoom to fit page in window.

- 🔍 (**6** or **Ctrl+E**): Zoom to fit page width in window.

- 🔍 (`` ` ``): Previous zoom (from the history of zooms). A history of zoom levels is stored in a list, see below.

- 🔍 (**Shift**+`` ` ``): Next zoom (from the history of zooms).

Note the two commands ( 🔍 and 🔍 ) that allow one to traverse backward and forward through a list of the previously used zoom levels.

- Holding down the **Q** key (Q for quick) will temporarily zoom in on selected items making it easier to make a small tweak. Releasing the key restores the previous zoom.

# Miscellaneous View Commands

## Hide/Show

The *Hide/Show* submenu can be used to toggle on and off various parts of the graphical user interface, including the *Palette*. **Shift+F11** hides/shows all parts of the graphical user interface, including the main menu bar.

## Hide/Show Dialogs

Inkscape dialogs can be hidden and unhidden with the View → 📄 Show/Hide Dialogs (**F12**) command.

# Outline Mode

Inkscape has an *Outline* or *Wire-frame* mode. In this mode, all paths and shapes are drawn as outlines with a one screen-pixel-wide stroke and no fill, regardless of zoom level. Text is drawn with an inverse fill and no stroke. Images are outlined in red, clip paths in green, and masks in blue.

The *Outline* mode is useful for seeing the overall structure of a drawing, precise node editing, and for finding and selecting those pesky, hidden objects that may have been created by accident. The mode is marginally faster than the normal mode. It can be turned on via View → DisplayMode → Outline, turned off by View → DisplayMode → Normal, and toggled via View → DisplayMode → Toggle (**Ctrl+Keypad 5**).

The same drawing shown in the normal view on the left and the wire-frame view on the right (the text has been converted to a path).

The colors used by the *Outline* mode can be changed by editing the *wireframecolors* group in the preferences file (Linux: `~/.config/inkscape/preferences.xml` for v0.47, `~/.inkscape/preferences.xml` for v0.46). Inkscape can be forced to start up in *Outline* mode by adding <group id="startmode" outline="1"/> to the preferences file inside the *options* group.

# No Filters Mode

Inkscape also has an *No Filters* mode where the rendering of *Filters* is turned off. This is useful for working on complicated drawings where the use of *Filters* causes the rendering to be too slow. It can be selected via View → DisplayMode → No Filters, turned off by View → DisplayMode → Normal, and toggled on/off via View → DisplayMode → Toggle (**Ctrl+Keypad 5**).

# Full Screen Mode

The Inkscape window can be made to cover the full screen with the View → ⊕ Full Screen (**F11**) command. A second use of the same command returns the window to its original size and position.

# Switch Windows

Each new drawing is created in a separate window. To move between these windows, you can use the method provided by your operating system (try **Alt+Tab**) or the methods provided by Inkscape View → ▣ Next Window (**Ctrl+Tab**) and View → ▣ Previous Window (**Shift+Ctrl+Tab**).

# Duplicate Window

A duplicate Inkscape window can be created with the View → ▤ Duplicate Window command. Both the original and new window refer to the same drawing. Thus, one can use one window for detailed work while keeping watch over how the work affects a larger region of a drawing.

# Icon Preview

*Updated for v0.48.*

An *Icon Preview* window can be created with the View → 🔲 Icon Preview command. This allows one to see what a drawing (or selection) will look like as icons of different sizes. In v0.47 one needs to click on the *Refresh* button to update the previews. In v0.48 the update is automatic. One can choose between viewing the whole drawing or a selected object by clicking the *Selection* button in v0.47 or by checking the *Selection* box in v0.48. In v0.48, by default, the previews are "locked" to the initial selected object's region. To change the region, uncheck and recheck the *Selection* box while a different object is selected.

Which sizes are displayed can be specified in the preferences file (Linux: `~/.config/inkscape/preferences.xml`) under the *iconpreview* group. In v0.48, you can also toggle on/off the automatic refresh of the previews, change the arrangement of the icons from compact to stacked (as in v0.47), change the previews to not follow the selected object, or to remove the frame around the icon previews.

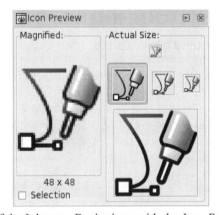

A preview of the Inkscape Bezier icon with the *Icon Preview* dialog.

# Chapter 4. Editing Basics

We discuss here some of the basic editing concepts of Inkscape, including: undoing and redoing changes, selecting objects, copying and deleting objects, and grouping objects. It is assumed that you have some familiarity with Inkscape by having worked through some of the examples in Chapter 1, *Quick Start*, or through the tutorials included with Inkscape (Help → ▣ Tutorials).

## Undo and Redo

One can undo and redo changes made to your drawing in the current Inkscape session. The *Undo* and *Redo* commands can be repeated to undo or redo multiple changes. These commands can be accessed both in the *Command Bar* and under the *Edit* menu in the *Menu Bar*. When accessed through the *Edit* menu, a description of the change that would happen if the command is selected is given.

- Edit → ↺ Undo (**Ctrl+Z**) (or **Shift+Ctrl+Y**): Undo change.

- Edit → ↻ Redo (**Ctrl+Y**) (or **Shift+Ctrl+Z**): Redo change.

Multiple changes can also be undone or redone in one step by using the *Undo History* dialog (Edit → ⟲ Undo History... (**Shift+Ctrl+H**)).

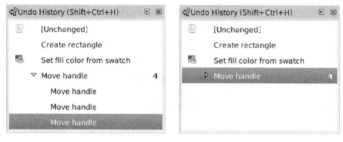

Two views of the *Undo History* dialog, both showing the drawing of a rectangle followed by changing the color and and four resizings. Clicking on any line returns the drawing to the state when the change described on the line was completed. Consecutive changes of the same type may be collapsed to one line to improve readability; the number of such changes is given on the top line of the group. Clicking on the triangle collapses (left) or uncollapses (right) the list.

All changes to a file can be undone with the File → ▤ Revert command.

## Selecting Objects

Before objects can be manipulated, they must be selected. This section covers the myriad of ways selection can be done.

Normally, the *Select Tool* is used for selecting objects. To activate, click on the ▸ icon in the *Tool Box* or use the keyboard shortcut (**F1**). One can toggle between another tool (except the *Text Tool* when in *text enter* mode) and the *Select Tool* by using the **Space Bar** if that other tool was selected first.

Some objects can be directly selected by other tools. For example, shapes (e.g., *Rectangles*) can be directly selected with any of the *shape tools*.

Rapid double-clicking on an object when the *Select Tool* is active will select an object and change the tool to a tool appropriate for editing that object. For example, double-clicking on a rectangle will select the rectangle and change the tool to the *Rectangle Tool*.

Multiple objects can be selected at the same time. The *Notification Region* lists the number and type of objects selected. This is especially useful when objects overlap and it isn't clear which are selected. By default, a box is drawn around each selected object. This can be changed to a small diamond *Selection Cue* under the *Tools-Selector* tab of the *Inkscape Preferences* dialog (File → ▦ Inkscape Preferences... (**Shift+Ctrl+P**)).

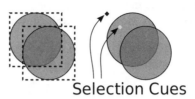

**Selection Cues**

Selection indicated by dashed boxes (on left) and by small diamonds
(on right). Only one of these two methods can be active at a time.

The *Find* dialog (Edit → ↶ Find... (**Ctrl+F**)) discussed at the end of this section, is another way of selecting objects.

## Locked Objects

If an object cannot be selected, it may be *locked*. Objects can be locked against modification in the *Object Properties* dialog (Object → ▣ Object Properties... (**Shift+Ctrl+O**)). Unlocking individual objects requires use of the *XML Editor* (look for the locked object and then either delete the "sodipidi:insensitive" attribute or uncheck the *Lock* box in the *Object Properties* dialog; see Chapter 18, *XML Editor*). One can unlock all objects with the command Object → Unlock All. Objects may also be in a locked *Layer* (see the section called *Layers*).

## Hidden Objects

It is possible to "hide" an object by checking the *Hide* box in the *Object Properties* dialog. This raises the question: How do you select a hidden object? There are several ways. One is to use the *Find* dialog (Edit → ↶ Find... (**Ctrl+F**)); search for the Style *display:none* with the *Include hidden* box checked. A second way is to look for it with the *XML Editor* (see Chapter 18, *XML Editor*). A third way is to enable the selection of hidden objects using the **Tab** key in the *Inkscape Preferences* dialog's *Selecting* tab. A fourth way is to unhide all hidden objects using the Object → Unhide All command. While these are solutions, the ultimate solution is just to not hide objects. Instead put them on a separate *Layer* and hide the *Layer* (see the section called *Layers*).

# Selecting with the Mouse

This section covers selecting objects with a mouse. By adding **Ctrl** to many of the commands below, objects within a *Group* can be selected (see the section called *Groups*).

- **Left Mouse Click**: Select Object: Select an object by clicking on it.

- **Shift+Left Mouse Click**: Toggle Selection: Add or subtract an object to or from a selection. This allows multiple objects to be selected. If the object clicked on is not already selected, it will be. If it is already selected, it will be deselected.

- **Alt+Left Mouse Click**: Select Under: Select next object below the currently selected object under the pointer. This allows one to select objects covered by others. Repeat to move downward in *z-order*. If the bottommost object is already selected, this will select the topmost object.

- **Left Mouse Drag**: Select Multiple Objects: When started from empty space, this will select all objects that are completely within the rectangle that is formed by the start and stop points of the drag. This is often referred to as *rubber-band* selecting. The *rubber band* is the temporary line drawn while dragging.

- **Shift+Left Mouse Drag**: Add Objects to Collection: Add objects within the *rubber band* to a preexisting selection. Also inhibits selection of an object under the start of the drag (without the shift, an object under the start of a drag is selected *and* moved). Selected objects within the *rubber band* are *not* deselected.

- **Alt+Left Mouse Drag**: Touch Select Multiple Objects: This will select all objects that the mouse cursor touches while being dragged. A red line will indicate the path the cursor took. This is *very* useful when needing to select multiple paths as found in engravings or hair. Holding the **Shift** down will prevent dragging an already selected object if the drag begins over that object.

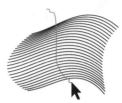

Using **Alt+Left Mouse Drag** to "touch" select the individual paths.

- **Shift+Alt+Left Mouse Drag**: Touch-Add Multiple Objects to Collection: This will add all objects touched to a selection. It can also be used when the drag begins over an already selected object.

# Selecting with the Keyboard

Most selecting of objects is done with the mouse. However, there are a few handy keyboard shortcuts.

- **Tab**: Select next object in *z-order*, that is the next object above the previous selected object. If no object is selected, it will select the lowest object. Works for objects in current *Layer*.

- **Shift+Tab**: Select previous object in *z-order*, that is the next object below the previous selected object. If no object is selected, it will select the highest object, which is normally the last object created. Works for objects in current *Layer*.

- **Ctrl+A**: Select All: Selects all objects in current *Layer*.

- **Ctrl+Alt+A**: Select All in All Layers: Selects all objects in all visible and unlocked *Layers*.

- **!**: Invert Selection: Invert selection in current *Layer*. That is, all selected objects are deselected and all unselected objects are selected.

- **Alt+!**: Invert selection in all visible and unlocked *Layers*. That is, all selected objects are deselected and all unselected objects are selected.

- **Esc**: Deselect: Deselect all selected objects.

Select All, Select All in All Layers, Invert Selection, and Deselect are also available under the *Edit* menu.

# Selecting with the Find Dialog

The *Find* dialog (Edit → ✎ Find... (**Ctrl+F**)) is another way to select objects with common features. A search is made through the *SVG* file and the found objects are selected on the Inkscape canvas.

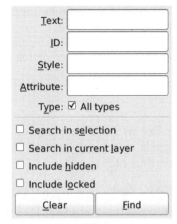

*Find* dialog.

The *Find* dialog has two parts. The top part defines what is searched for, while the bottom part defines where to search.

You can specify a *Text* string (in a text object), *ID* name (e.g., "rect1314"), *Style* feature (e.g., "fill-opacity"), or an *Attribute* type (e.g., "width") for the search. The matches can be full or partial (i.e., "rect" would match "rect1314" and "rect1316").

With the check boxes, you can specify where to search. If the *All types* box is checked, the search will take place in all objects (shapes, paths, text strings, etc.). If the box is not checked, a list of object types is presented that can be individually included or excluded from the search.

The *Search in selection* box determines if the search is limited to the currently selected objects. The *Search in current layer* box determines if the search is limited to the currently selected layer. The *Include hidden* box determines if hidden objects are included in the search, while the *Include locked* box determines if locked objects are included in the search.

At the very bottom of the dialog are two buttons: the first, *Clear*, to clear the search entry boxes and the second, *Find*, to perform the actual search. All objects that are found to match the search criteria are selected.

# Copying, Pasting, and Deleting Objects

Inkscape includes commands to copy, paste, and delete objects. Commands of this type can be found in three places: Under the *Edit* menu (see below), in the *Command Bar* (Cut, Copy, Paste, and Duplicate), and in the pop-up menu when you **Right Mouse Click** over the canvas (Cut, Copy, Paste, Duplicate, and Delete).

**Clipboard:** Inkscape uses the system-wide *clipboard* (a place where a description of one or more objects is stored temporarily in memory). You can copy and paste between different instances of Inkscape and other applications that support *SVG*. Adding an object or group of objects (a selection) to the *clipboard* removes any previous selection stored in the *clipboard*.

The commands available under the *Edit* menu are:

- Edit → ✄ Cut (**Ctrl+X**): Selection is removed from drawing, but stored in *clipboard*.

- Edit → ▦ Copy (**Ctrl+C**): Copy of selection is stored in *clipboard*.

- Edit → ▦ Paste (**Ctrl+V**): A copy of objects stored in *clipboard* is placed in the drawing at the location of the cursor.

- Edit → ▦ Paste In Place (**Ctrl+Alt+V**): Objects are copied from *clipboard* to original location of objects. This is very useful in copying a selection from one drawing to the corresponding spot in another drawing.

- Edit → 📋 Paste Style (**Shift+Ctrl+V**): The style (fill and stroke attributes or for text the font, size, and style) of the object in the *clipboard* are given to the selected object(s).

- Edit → 📋 Duplicate (**Ctrl+D**): An object is copied and placed on top of the original object. The copied object is left selected.

- *Modified for v0.48:*

  Edit → 📷 Make a Bitmap Copy (**Alt+B**): The selection is exported as a bitmap then pasted back into the drawing at the same place. The original objects remain unchanged. In v0.47 the exported bitmap is *not* stored in the *SVG* file. In v0.48 the bitmap is embedded in the *SVG* file.

  The bitmap will have a resolution specified by the *Resolution for Crate Bitmap Copy* entry in the *Bitmaps* section of the *Inkscape Preferences* dialog. If the resolution is specified to be 90 *dpi* (the default) the pixels will be snapped to the pixel grid.

- Edit → 🗑 Delete (**Delete or Backspace**): Selection is removed from drawing and *not* stored in *clipboard*.

Hitting the **Space Bar** while dragging or transforming an object with the mouse will "drop" a copy of the object at the current point.

Another method for copying objects, *cloning*, is discussed in the next section.

# Clones

Cloning is a special way to copy an object. The cloned copy retains a link to the original object so if that object is changed, the clone will change in the same way. The copies, however, can be *transformed* (moved, scaled, rotated, and skewed) independently. Technically, the cloning is achieved through the use of the *SVG >use< object type.

The style (color, fill pattern, etc.) of the clones can be changed independently but only if the style of the cloned object is *Unset*. See the section called *Fill and Stroke Paint* in Chapter 10, *Attributes*.

Only a single object can be cloned at a time. If more than one object needs to be cloned, then those objects can be placed into a *Group*.

The original may be cloned any number of times. It is also possible to clone a clone. In this case, changing the original will change both clones, while changing the first clone will only change the second clone. It is not possible, however, to set the *Attributes* independently with multiple layers of cloning.

Inkscape has the ability to "relink" clones to a another object. To do this, copy the new "original" to the clipboard. Select all the clones to be *relinked* and then use the Edit → Clone → Relink to Copied command. The clones will probably shift in place. In practice, this just changes the *xlink:href* attribute of the clones to point to the new "original".

Inkscape also has the ability to "relink" clones when the original and clones are copied. Normally, the duplicated clones are linked to the original object, and the duplicate of the original object is not linked to anything. The behavior can be changed by enabling the *Relink duplicated clones* option in the *Clones* section of the *Inkscape Preferences* dialog so that new copies are linked to the copy of the original object.

Inkscape includes the *Create Tiled Clones* dialog for creating a set of cloned objects that are automatically placed via tiling algorithms. This dialog is very powerful and is sufficiently complex that it deserves its own chapter. See Chapter 19, *Tiling*, for more information.

The following commands are available for working with clones (*Clone* and *Unlink Clone* are also located in the *Command Bar*).

- Edit → Clone → 📋 Create Clone (**Alt+D**): Clone object. Clone is placed exactly over original.

- Edit → Clone → 🖾 Create Tiled Clones... : Opens up *Create Tiled Clones* dialog.

- Edit → Clone → 🖾 Unlink Clone (**Shift+Alt+D**): Remove link between clone and original object. Clone will no longer update when original object is modified.

- Edit → Clone → Relink to Copied: Link any clone of an object to a duplicate (not clone) of the original object. To use, first copy the duplicate to the clipboard (Edit → ▸ Copy (**Ctrl+C**)). Next, select the clones to be relinked and then use this command.

- Edit → Clone → 🖾 Select Original (**Shift+D**): Select original of clone. Use to find the original of a cloned object. Select clone before using. Use multiple times to find original if starting with a clone of a clone. A line is drawn between the clone and the original for one second.

What happens when you move a cloned object? By default, the clones don't move. This is because if you select an object that was cloned and one of its clones, the two will move together as expected. In the *Inkscape Preferences* dialog under the *Clone* section, you can change this behavior so that if a cloned object is moved, its clones also move. But in this case, if you select a cloned object and one of its clones, then move them, the clone will move "twice" as far— once because the cloned object moved and once because the clone itself was moved. Things can get really strange if you move a cloned object that has been cloned and that clone has been cloned!

# Ordering Objects (Z-Order)

The *z-order* determines the order in which objects are drawn on the canvas. Those object with high *z-order* are drawn last and therefore drawn on top of objects with lower *z-order*. The order is determined by the order that the objects are listed in the *SVG* file.

The yellow star has the highest *z-order* on the left but the lowest on the right.

Inkscape has a number of commands to change *z-order*. The commands are available from the Menu and via Keyboard Shortcuts. They are also available in the *Tool Controls* when the *Select Tool* is active.

- Object → 🖾 Raise (**Page Up**): Move selected object(s) up one step.

- Object → 🖾 Lower (**Page Down**): Move selected object(s) down one step.

- Object → 🖾 Raise to Top (**Home**): Move selected object(s) to top.

- Object → 🖾 Lower to Bottom (**End**): Move selected object(s) to bottom.

The *XML Editor* dialog can also be used to change *z-order*. There is also a *Restack* extension that can reorder arrays of objects.

# Groups

A set of objects can be collected into a *Group*. Once placed in a *Group*, the objects can be manipulated together, the *Group* acting as a single object. *Groups* can be nested; that is, a *Group* can be combined with other *Groups* or objects to make a higher level *Group*.

The following commands, found both in the *Command Bar* and under the *Edit* menu, can be used to make and break up groups:

- Object → ⬚ Group (**Ctrl+G**): Group selected items.

- Object → ⬚ Ungroup (**Shift+Ctrl+G**)(**Ctrl+U**): Ungroup selected *Group*. Ungroups one level.

An alternative method to break up a *Group* is to select the *Ungroup* command from the menu that pops up when you **Right Mouse Click** over a *Group*.

Objects within *Groups* can be edited and manipulated without breaking up the *Group*. The following commands select objects within *Groups*:

- **Ctrl+Left Mouse Click**: Select Within Group. Select an object within a *Group*. This command selects objects regardless of how many levels of *Groups* they are buried in.

- **Ctrl+Alt+Left Mouse Click**: Select Under Within Group. Select an object within a *Group* that is under the cursor and that is next lower in *z-order* than the currently selected object. If the currently selected object is at the bottom in *z-order*, the top object is selected. This command selects objects regardless of how many levels of *Groups* they are buried in.

- **Shift+Ctrl+Alt+Left Mouse Click**: Toggle Under in Groups. Add an unselected object or remove a selected object within a *Group* to or from a selection.

A *Group* can be *entered* or turned into a temporary *Layer* for editing. Two ways to *Enter a Group* and *Exit a Group* are available:

- **Double+Left Mouse Click** on a *Group* to enter a *Group*. Click an object outside the *Group* to exit.

- **Ctrl+Enter** on a *Group* to enter a *Group*. **Ctrl+Backspace** to leave a *Group*. This will take you up one group level.

- **Right Mouse Click** over *Group* to pop up a menu. Select the *Enter group* command to enter the *Group*. The command line included the name of the *Group* that will be entered. Once in a *Group*, the menu option *Go to parent* will exit the *Group* (although there is no visible feedback).

## Tip

To add an existing object to an existing *Group*, cut the object (Edit → ✂ Cut (**Ctrl+X**)), enter the *Group* (**Double+Left Mouse Click**), and then paste in place (Edit → 📋 Paste In Place (**Ctrl+Alt+V**)).

## Tip

The *XML Editor* dialog can be very useful in rearranging objects between *Groups*.

# Layers

One can think of *Layers* as the acetate sheets that were once used to make animated cartoons. Each *Layer* can contain one or more objects. The final image is made up of all the (visible) *Layers* stacked on top of each other. *Layers* can be made visible or invisible, given an opacity, moved up or down relative to other *Layers*, locked, deleted, and named.

Internally, *Layers* are just *SVG Groups* with a few extra Inkscape specific parameters that Inkscape uses to control the *Layer* interface. Like *Groups*, *Layers* can contain sub-*Layers*.

*Layers* can be manipulated by using the *Layers* dialog, through commands in the *Layers* menu, or through items in the *Status Bar*. The *Layers* dialog can also be used to quickly blend a *Layer* with the background. See the next section for details.

# Layers Dialog

The *Layers* dialog is the easiest way to manipulate *Layers*. Call up the dialog via the Layer → ◄ Layers... (**Shift+Ctrl+L**) command.

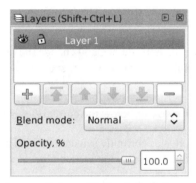

*Layers* dialog with the default *Layer*.

The dialog will list all the *Layers* in the document. The currently selected *Layer* is highlighted. Selecting an object in a different *Layer* will select the *Layer* that object is in. One can also click on a *Layer* name to select that *Layer*. Only one *Layer* can be selected at a time.

In front of the *Layer* names are two icons that show if a *Layer* is visible ( 👁 ) or not ( 👁 ) and if a *Layer* is locked ( 🔒 ) or unlocked ( 🔓 ). Clicking on one of the icons toggles the state of that icon. A *Layer* need not be selected in order to toggle its states. Objects in locked or invisible *Layers* cannot be selected or changed.

A **Right Mouse Click** on any *Layer* name will pop up a small and rather useless menu where you can access the rename, duplicate, and add *Layer* functions. The only really interesting thing in this menu is the ability to toggle on and off at the same time all other *Layers* than the one clicked on. This is done by clicking on the *Show/hide other layers* item.

The buttons below the *Layer* list can be used to add or delete a *Layer* and to move the selected *Layer* up or down relative to other *Layers*. A sub-*Layer* cannot be moved outside of the *Layer* it is under; you can use the *XML Editor* to do this.

- ✛ : Add a new *Layer*. A dialog will pop up allowing input of the *Layer* name. A drop-down menu allows you to add the new *Layer* above, below, or as a sub-*Layer* of the currently selected *Layer*.

- ⬆ : Move selected *Layer* to top.

- ⬆ : Move selected *Layer* up one step.

- ⬇ : Move selected *Layer* down one step.

- ⬇ : Move selected *Layer* to bottom.

- − : Delete selected *Layer*.

Beneath the row of buttons is a drop-down menu for the *Blend mode*. This is a short cut to applying the *Blend* filter to the entire *Layer*. The *Normal* entry corresponds to no *Filter*. Selecting one of the other entries creates a *Blend* filter with the selected mode. The first input to the filter is the *Layer* (recall that a *Layer* is just a *Group*) and the second input is the *Background Image*. If the menu is returned to the *Normal* setting, the *Blend* filter is automatically deleted.

A demonstration of using *Layer* blending. The two texts are in different *Layers* with
"Layer 1" beneath "Layer 2." The *Blend mode* is set to *Screen* for the upper *Layer.*✪

At the bottom of the dialog is a slider and an entry box that can be used to change the opacity of the *Layer*.

## Layers Menu

The *Layers* menu has commands to create, rename, delete, and change the order of *Layers*. There are also commands to move objects between *Layers*. The commands in the *Layers* menu are

- Layer → ⬛ Add Layer... (**Shift+Ctrl+N**): Add a new *Layer*. A simple dialog opens up where the *Layer* can be named and you choose to add the *Layer* above or below the current *Layer* or as sub-*Layers*.

- Layer → Duplicate Current Layer: Duplicates currently selected *Layer* The new *Layer* will have the same name as the old one but with the word "copy" added. Hidden and locked objects will also be copied as well as sub-*Layers*.

- Layer → ⬛ Rename Layer... : Rename selected *Layer*. A simple dialog opens up where the *Layer* can be renamed. *Layer* names do not need to be unique.

- Layer → ⬛ Switch to Layer Above (**Ctrl+Page Up**): Select *Layer* above current *Layer*.

- Layer → ⬛ Switch to Layer Below (**Ctrl+Page Down**): Select *Layer* below current *Layer*.

- Layer → ⬛ Move Selection to Layer Above (**Shift+Page Up**): Move selected object(s) to *Layer* above current *Layer*.

- Layer → ⬛ Move Selection to Layer Below (**Shift+Page Down**): Move selected object(s) to *Layer* below current *Layer*.

- Layer → ⬛ Raise Layer (**Shift+Ctrl+Page Up**): Move current *Layer* above *Layer* above.

- Layer → ⬛ Lower Layer (**Shift+Ctrl+Page Down**): Move current *Layer* under *Layer* below.

- Layer → ⬛ Layer to Top (**Shift+Ctrl+Home**): Move current *Layer* to top of *Layer* stack.

- Layer → ⬛ Layer to Bottom (**Shift+Ctrl+End**): Move current *Layer* to bottom of *Layer* stack.

- Layer → ⬛ Delete Current Layer: Delete current *Layer*.

- Layer → ⬛ Layers... (**Shift+Ctrl+L**): Open *Layers* dialog.

## Status Bar

The *Status Bar* includes a pull-down menu to select the current *Layer*. The icons in front of the menu indicate whether the *Layer* is visible or hidden and whether it is locked or unlocked (see the section called *Layers Dialog*). Clicking on an icon toggles the state.

# Chapter 5. Positioning and Transforming

Inkscape has a variety of ways to position objects as precisely as required. These include onscreen *Grids* and *Guide Lines* where objects "snap" into alignment, dialogs for moving individual objects or for aligning multiple objects, and the *Create Tiled Clones* dialog for placing multiple clones of an object. Additional features allow you to scale, skew, or rotate an object. This section will begin with a discussion of the coordinate system of Inkscape followed by a discussion of the way Inkscape describes object transformations. Then the commands and dialogs for transforming objects are discussed.

One key thing to know is that transforming a *Regular Shape* object or a *Group* of objects by the methods described in this chapter does not (usually) change the underlying description of the object(s). For example, suppose you have an ellipse that is 100 pixels wide but you need it to have a width of 50 pixels. There are two different ways to achieve the required width. The first is to scale the object by 50% in the horizontal (*x*) direction. The underlying definition of the ellipse width remains 100 pixels but when the ellipse is drawn a scale factor of 50% is applied in the horizontal direction. The second way to change the ellipse is to use the *Ellipse Tool* to resize the ellipse. In this case, the underlying description of the ellipse changes and no scale factor is applied.

An exception to this rule is for *Rectangle* objects. Inkscape will attempt to change the description of the rectangle itself when a simple transformation is applied. This behavior can be changed under the *Transforms* tab in the *Inkscape Preferences* dialog (File → ▦ Inkscape Preferences... (**Shift+Ctrl+P**)). Change the *Store transformation* parameter to *Preserved*.

Note that in *Paths*, the individual points are transformed (unless the *Store transformation* parameter has been changed as above).

## Inkscape Coordinates

Understanding the way Inkscape handles coordinates is necessary to be able to fully take advantage of the tools Inkscape has for positioning objects. When you open the main Inkscape window, *Rulers* are drawn by default at the top and left edges of the canvas (see the section called *The Anatomy of the Inkscape Window*). The units of the *Rulers* are the same as the default units of the canvas. If you hover the pointer over a *Ruler*, a *tool tip* will show the current unit. The default unit can be changed via the *Document Properties* dialog (File → ▦ Document Properties... (**Shift+Ctrl+D**)). Options for the coordinates system units are:

| | |
|---|---|
| cm | Centimeters |
| ft | Feet |
| in | Inches |
| m | Meters |
| mm | Millimeters |
| pc | Picas |
| pt | Points |
| px | Pixels |

Conversion between the units is fairly straightforward: 1 inch = 1/12 ft = 2.54 cm = 25.4 mm = 0.0254 m = 6 pc = 72 pt. The pixel (px) unit is adjustable in the *Inkscape Preferences* dialog (File → Inkscape Preferences... (**Shift+Ctrl+P**)) under the *Import/Export* tab (Default export resolution). It is also equivalent to the *User Unit* in the *SVG* specification. Inkscape takes care of conversions when changing units. Note: Feet and meters are not *SVG* or *CSS* defined units.

Various Inkscape parameters can be set using independent units. For example, the default *x* scale can be set to millimeters, while the alignment *Grid* can be defined in inches.

One confusing aspect is that Inkscape uses a different scale internally. On the canvas, the *x* and *y* coordinates increase as one moves right or up. Internally the *y* coordinate is flipped as per the *SVG* standard. Thus, (0, 0) is defined from the upper-left corner of the page region internally but at the bottom-left corner in the canvas window. The internal scale is fixed (by default) to 90 *dpi*. The internal scale is important if you wish to edit by hand an object using the *XML Editor*.

There are two competing camps for how angles should be defined. Fortunately for the peace, Inkscape supports both through the *Compass-like display of angles* option under the *Steps* tab in the *Inkscape Preferences* dialog (File → Inkscape Preferences... (**Shift+Ctrl+P**)).

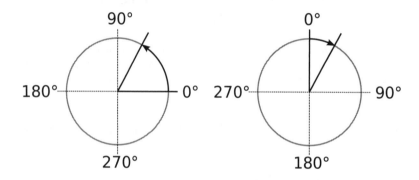

Definition of angles. Left: The mathematician's view (default). Right: The geographer's view.

# Transformations

Objects can be moved, scaled, rotated, skewed, and flipped. Inkscape provides a variety of ways to make these transformations. These include: using the *mouse*, the *keyboard*, items in the *Tool Controls bar*, the *Object menu*, the *Transform dialog*, the *Paste Size commands*, and the *XML Editor dialog*. Each method will be discussed in turn. Each method begins by selecting an object or group of objects to be transformed. The *Select Tool* must be active for making transformations with the mouse or keyboard. To activate, click on the ↖ icon in the *Tool Box* or use the keyboard shortcut (**F1**).

There are a couple of things to note:

First, some operations use *SVG* pixels while some use *Screen pixels*. The former is the scale used in the *SVG* file. It is fixed (by default) to 90 *dpi*. The latter refers to a pixel on the screen and changes as the zoom level changes.

Second, positions and dimensions are often with reference to the *bounding box*. One can choose between two definitions for the *bounding box* in the *Tools* section of the *Inkscape Preferences* dialog (File → Inkscape Preferences... (**Shift+Ctrl+P**)). The *Visual bounding box* includes the stroke width if the stroke is visible. For example, a square 100 pixels to one side (between corner nodes) will have a width of 102 pixels if the stroke width is 2 pixels. The *Visual bounding box* also includes any *Markers* and both the *Stroke Join* and *Cap* styles are assumed to be *Round*. The *Geometric bounding box* mode uses only the nodes to determine the *bounding box*.

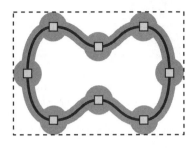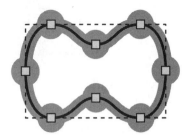

The dashed lines are *bounding boxes* for the same path with *Markers*. Left: *Visual bounding box*. Right: *Geometric bounding box*.

Third, transformations do *not* change the underlying definition of regular shape objects or grouped objects, as discussed in the introduction of this chapter (an exception being simple transformations of *Rectangle* objects when the *Store transformation* parameter is set to *Optimized*).

Fourth, there are a number of options that can be toggled on and off in the *Tool Controls* when the *Select Tool* is being used. The following are active when the icon is highlighted:

- ⛶ When scaling objects, scale the stroke width by the same proportion.

- ⛶ When scaling rectangles, scale the radii of rounded corners.

- ⛶ Move gradients (in fill or stroke) along with the objects.

- ⛶ Move patterns (in fill or stroke) along with the objects.

Fifth, rotation and skewing take place around a *Rotation center* point. The point is indicated by a draggable "plus"-shaped handle that is viewable when using the *Select Tool* in rotation or skewing mode. See the next section for details.

# Transforms with the Mouse

## Translations

The **Shift**, **Ctrl**, and **Alt** keys can be used in combination:

- **Left Mouse Drag**: Select (if not selected) and move object. Move selected object(s) if drag starts on any selected object.

- **Alt+Left Mouse Drag**: Move selected object(s) regardless of where drag starts. Don't select object where drag began.

- **Ctrl+Left Mouse Drag**: Move selected object(s) constrained to horizontal or vertical directions.

- **Shift+Left Mouse Drag**: Temporarily disable snapping to *Grids* or *Guide Lines*.

## Scaling, Rotating, and Skewing

When an object or objects are first selected, eight double-headed arrows will appear.
A **Left Mouse Drag** of any handle will rescale the selection. The corner arrows will
and vertical (*y*) directions. The side arrows will scale in only one direction.

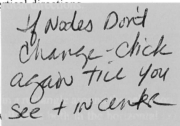

*If Nodes Don't Change-Click again till you see + in center*

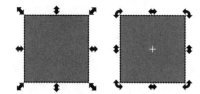

Scaling arrows (left). Rotation arrows on corners, skewing arrows on sides (right).
The "plus" in the center of the square on the right is the *Rotation center* handle.

Clicking a second time on a selected object or using the keyboard shortcut **Shift+S** will change the direction of the double-headed arrows. Now, a **Left Mouse Drag** of a handle will rotate the selection if used on a corner arrow, or skew the selection if used on a side arrow. Click again to revert to the scaling mode.

**Rotation Center.** Rotation takes place around the *Rotation center* indicated by a "plus"-shaped handle. The handle (and thus the center of rotation) can be dragged. Dragging while holding the **Ctrl** down will restrict movement to the horizontal and vertical directions. The handle will snap to the edge of the *bounding box* or the center axis of the selection's *bounding box*. It will also snap to a *Grid* or *Guide Lines* if snapping of nodes to those items is turned on. The movement of the *Rotation center* handle can be undone (**Ctrl+Z**). Holding the **Shift** key down while clicking on the *Rotation center* handle will restore the handle to the center of the *bounding box*. The *Rotation center* is preserved when an object is moved, scaled, duplicated, cloned, or converted to a path. It is also preserved between editing sessions.

When multiple objects are selected, the *Rotation center* of the first selected object will be used if it has been moved from its default position. Otherwise, the center of the *bounding box* of all selected objects will be used.

The **Shift**, **Ctrl**, and **Alt** keys can be used with the **Left Mouse Drag**. They can be used in combination when scaling, rotating, or skewing.

## Scaling

- **Ctrl**: Preserve width to height ratio.

- **Shift**: Rescale symmetrically, around center of selection.

- **Alt**: Restrict scaling up to an integer factor (2, 3, 4, ...) or down to a simple fraction (1/2, 1/3, 1/4, ...). Negative values are also allowed (i.e., mirroring object around *bounding box* edge).

## Rotating and Skewing

- **Ctrl**: Constrain a rotation or skew to a multiple of the *Rotation snap angle*. Allows stretching in the orthogonal direction to a skew by a multiple of the width or height of the *bounding box*.

- **Shift**: Keep opposite corner fixed for rotation or opposite side fixed for skew. (This is opposite of what happens for scaling.)

# Transforms with the Keyboard

A selection may be moved, scaled, rotated, or flipped (but not skewed) with the keyboard. For some key combinations, the size of the transformation is determined by parameters (e.g., *Nudge factor*) that can be set in the *Inkscape Preferences* dialog (File → ⊞ Inkscape Preferences... (**Shift+Ctrl+P**)) under the *Steps* tab.

# Translations

- **Arrow**: Move selection by *Nudge factor* (2 *SVG* pixels by default).

- **Shift+Arrow**: Move selection by 10 times the *Nudge factor*.

- **Alt+Arrow**: Move the selection 1 *Screen pixel*.

- **Alt+Shift+Arrow**: Move the selection 10 *Screen pixels*.

## Scaling

Scaling is around the center point of the *bounding box*.

- **.**, **>**: Scale up by *Scale step* (2 *SVG* pixels by default).

- **,**, **<**: Scale down by *Scale step* (2 *SVG* pixels by default).

- **Ctrl+.**, **Ctrl+>**: Scale up to 200%.

- **Ctrl+,**, **Ctrl+<**: Scale down to 50%.

- **Alt+.**, **Alt+>**: Scale up by 1 *Screen pixel*. Scale factor = 1 screen pixel/distance from center of *bounding box* to farthest edge.

- **Alt+,**, **Alt+<**: Scale down by 1 *Screen pixel*.

## Rotation

Rotation is around the *Rotation center*.

- **[**: Rotate counterclockwise by *Rotation snap angle* (15 degrees by default).

- **]**: Rotate clockwise by *Rotation snap angle* (15 degrees by default).

- **Ctrl+[**: Rotate counterclockwise by 90 degrees.

- **Ctrl+]**: Rotate clockwise by 90 degrees.

- **Alt+[**: Rotate counterclockwise by 1 *Screen pixel* (angle = arctan [1 *Screen pixel* divided by the distance from the center to the corner point of the *bounding box*]).

- **Alt+]**: Rotate clockwise by 1 *Screen pixel*.

## Flipping

Flip around center point of *bounding box* if in *scaling* mode or around horizontal/vertical line passing through *Rotation center* if in *rotation*/*skewing* mode. These keys work when any tool is active.

- **H**: Flip horizontally.

- **V**: Flip vertically.

# Transforms with the Tool Controls Bar

The *Tool Controls* contains a number of items for transforming an object when the *Select Tool* is in use. An object can be translated using the X and Y entry boxes. An object can be stretched by using the width (W) and height (H) entry boxes. These quantities are specified in a unit of length determined by a selection box just to the right of the entry boxes. The ratio of the height and width can be locked by clicking on the lock icon so that changing one dimension automatically changes the other. There are also icons for rotating and flipping objects.

# Transforms with the Object Drop-Down Menu

The *Object* drop-down menu contains four entries for rotating and flipping objects:

- Object → ⤵ Rotate 90° CW

- Object → ⤴ Rotate 90° CCW

- Object → ◭ Flip Horizontal (**H**)

- Object → ◮ Flip Vertical (**V**)

# Transforms with the Transform Dialog

Objects can be moved, scaled, rotated, and skewed using the *Transform* dialog (Object → ◌ Transform... (**Shift+Ctrl+M**)). There is a different tab in the dialog for each of these transforms. In addition, there is a *Matrix* tab that allows the application of a *Transformation Matrix* to a selection.

The *Transform* dialog contains an option to apply the chosen transformation to a selection as a group or to the individual objects within the selection. (This option has no effect for the *Matrix* tab.) The dialog also has a *Clear* button to reset the entered values to their default values.

Two squares (Left) are transformed as a group (Center) or separately (Right).

## Move Tab

Using the *Move* tab, you can translate an object.

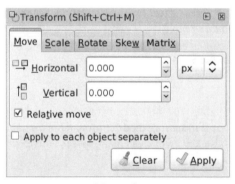

*Move* tab.

An object will be translated relative to its current position if the *Relative move* box is checked. If the box is not checked, the lower-left corner of the objects *bounding box* will be moved to the given coordinate.

Enabling the *Apply to each object separately* option causes objects to move so that they are more spread out (with a positive displacement) and closer together with a (negative displacement). For example, in displacing objects horizontally, the leftmost object moves the specified amount, the next leftmost moves twice as much, and the third leftmost three times as much. The algorithm uses the left edges of the *bounding boxes* for horizontal movement and the bottom edges of the *bounding boxes* for vertical movement. If two objects have the same left position, they will still move different amounts.

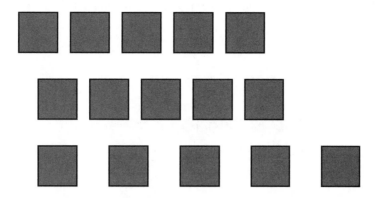

An example of specifying a positive horizontal move of half a square width with and without the *Apply to each object separately* option. From top to bottom: Original placement of squares. With the option not enabled. With the option enabled.

## Scale Tab

Using the *Scale* tab, you can scale an object.

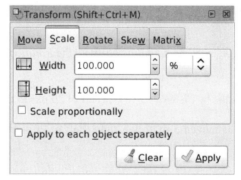

*Scale* tab.

An object will be scaled relative to the center of its *bounding box*. The *Scale proportionally* option forces the width and height to scale by the same percentage. Note that a scale factor of 100% corresponds to leaving an object unchanged.

## Rotate Tab

Using the *Rotate* tab, you can rotate an object.

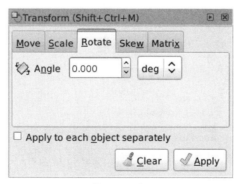

*Rotate* tab.

An object will be rotated relative to *Rotation center*. The direction of the rotation is positive in the counterclockwise direction.

## Skew Tab

Using the *Skew* tab, you can skew an object.

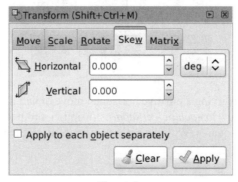

*Skew* tab.

You can skew in the horizontal and vertical directions separately. The skewing is relative to the center of the *bounding box*. The magnitude of the skew can be specified as a distance, percentage, or angle. In all cases, the skew is relative to the size of the *bounding box*.

Examples for a horizontal skew of a 100 by 50 px *bounding box* with the *Rotation center* in the middle of the *bounding box*:

- Distance of 20 px: The top edge of the box is moved 10 px (half of 20 px) to the right, the bottom 10 px to the left.

- Percentage of 20%: The top edge is moved 5 px to the right (half of 20% of the height) to the right, the bottom 5 px to the left.

- Angle of 30°: The top edge of the box is moved 14.4 px (tan(30°) × 50 px × 0.5) to the *left* (angles are defined to be positive in the counterclockwise direction), the bottom 14.4 px to the right.

Note: The center of the new *bounding box* is not necessarily at the center of the original *bounding box* if the skewed object was not a rectangle.

## Matrix Tab

Using the *Matrix* tab, you can apply a generic transformation to an object.

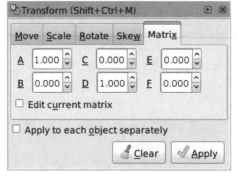

*Matrix* tab.

The transformation is described by a 3 × 3 *Transformation Matrix* of which only the upper two rows are displayed and modifiable. The upper-left 2 × 2 submatrix (A, B, C, and D) controls scaling, rotating, and skewing, while the upper-right 1 × 2 submatrix (E and F) controls translations.

The tab includes the option *Edit current matrix* to select if the entered matrix should post-multiply the existing transformation matrix (option not selected) or if it should replace the current matrix (option selected).

There are two important points to note. First, the transformation matrix is with respect to the point (0, 0) in *screen* coordinates if not editing the current matrix. If editing the current matrix, the transformation is with respect to the *User Coordinate System* which, if an object is not in a *Group*, is equivalent to the *SVG* coordinate system (*Initial View Port*) where the origin is at the top-left corner of the page. See the SVG standard [http://www.w3.org/TR/SVG/coords.html] for more details.

Second, Inkscape will modify the matrix and other parameters of an object internally so that the internal E and F terms are zero if the *Store transformation* parameter under the *Transforms* section in the *Inkscape Preferences* dialog is set to *Optimized*. This means, for example, that for a horizontal skew of a rectangle, the internal height parameter may change. The displayed object will still look correct.

# Transforms with Paste Size Commands

The commands in the Edit → Paste Size submenu can be used to scale a selection or the objects in a selection to match the width and/or height of a selection that is stored in the *clipboard*. To use the commands, first copy (or cut) a selection with the desired dimension(s) to load the selection into the *clipboard*. Then select the target object or objects and use one of the commands below.

The first three commands scale a selection as a whole to match the clipboard while the last three commands scale each object to match the clipboard. Dimensions are determined by *bounding boxes*. The *Scale ratio lock* ( 🔒 / 🔓 ) located in the *Select Tool-Tool Controls* controls how the width and height transform in some cases.

- Edit → Paste Size → Paste Size: The selection is scaled so its *bounding box* matches that of the selection in the *clipboard*. Scaling is around the center of the selection's *bounding box*.

- Edit → Paste Size → Paste Width: The selection is scaled so the width of its *bounding box* matches that of the width of selection in the *clipboard*. The height is left alone if the *Scale ratio lock* is off; otherwise, the height is scaled in the same proportion as the width.

- Edit → Paste Size → Paste Height: The selection is scaled so the height of its *bounding box* matches that of the height of selection in the *clipboard*. The width is left alone if the *Scale ratio lock* is off; otherwise, the width is scaled in the same proportion as the height.

- Edit → Paste Size → Paste Size Separately: Each object in the selection is scaled so its *bounding box* matches that of the selection in the *clipboard*. Scaling is around the center of each object's *bounding box*.

- Edit → Paste Size → Paste Width Separately: Each object in the selection is scaled so the width of its *bounding box* matches the width of the selection in the *clipboard*. The heights are left alone if the *Scale ratio lock* is off; otherwise, the heights are scaled in the same proportion as the widths.

- Edit → Paste Size → Paste Height Separately: Each object in the selection is scaled so the height of its *bounding box* matches the height of the selection in the *clipboard*. The widths are left alone if the *Scale ratio lock* is off; otherwise, the widths are scaled in the same proportion as the heights.

# Transforms with the XML Editor

Full control over the transformation of an object is available through the *XML Editor* dialog (Edit → 🖾 XML Editor... (**Shift+Ctrl+X**)). Selecting an object in the document window will bring up the object's attributes in the *XML Editor* dialog. Any transform an object is subject to is described by the *transform* attribute. A transform can be of type "translate", "scale", "rotate", "skewX", "skewY", or "matrix". In most cases, the transform will be of the "matrix" type. A *matrix* entry contains the *Transformation Matrix* in the order (A, B, C, D, E, F) where (ACE) is the first row of the matrix.

One thing to note is that the matrix describes a transformation with respect to the *User Coordinate System* which, if an object is not in a *Group*, is equivalent to the *SVG* coordinate system (*Initial View Port*) where the origin is at the top-left corner of the page (in contrast to the screen coordinate system where the origin is at the bottom-left of the page). See the SVG standard [http://www.w3.org/TR/SVG/coords.html] for more details.

# Snapping

To help precisely place objects on the canvas, an object can be made to *snap* to a target. The target can be a points on another object, the page boundary, a *Grid* line, or a *Guide Line*. Snapping takes place when some defined point on an object, a snapping point, is near a target. *Snapping* can be divide into two parts: defining snapping points and setting targets. This is mostly done with the *Snap Bar*. Snapping was introduced in the tutorials at the beginning of the book.

Snapping can be set to always happen or only happen when a snapping point is within a set distance (the *Snap Distance*) from a target. Setting *Snap Distance* is made under the *Snap* tab of the *Document Properties* dialog.

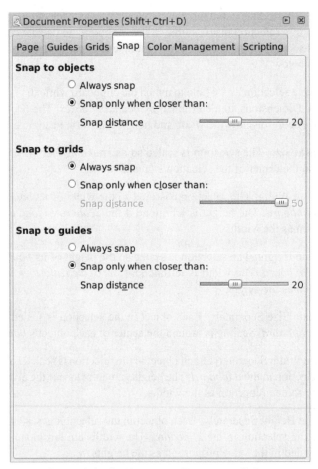

*Snap* tab in the *Document Properties* dialog.

When a snapping point is snapped to a target, a small cross will flash at the snapping site. Next to this indicator, a message indicates what snapping point and snapping target were used. In v0.48, a *bounding box* will also flash when it is a target of snapping. The indicator can be disabled in the *Snapping* section of the *Inkscape Preferences* dialog by unchecking the *Enable snap indicator* option.

A few other options can be found under the *Snapping* section of the *Inkscape Preferences* dialog:

- *Delay (in ms):* Sets the delay between the time the cursor stops moving and snapping is attempted. Useful if there are many snapping targets (e.g., with a *Grid*).

- *Only snap the node closest to pointer*: If this option is enabled, only one node is used as a snapping point on a target. This node will be highlighted as an object is dragged. Useful if an object has many snapping points. Note: if an object has too many nodes, and this option is disabled, a "convex hull" is used for snapping.

- *Weight factor:* If multiple snapping possibilities exist, the value of this parameter determines if the smallest distance between a snap point and snap target is favored (0.0) or if a snap using the closest snap point to the cursor is preferred (1.0).

# Snapping Objects

This section covers defining snapping points and targets associated with objects. Defining *Guide Lines* and *Grids* as targets is covered in following sections.

The *Snap Bar* includes a variety of clickable icons that toggle various snap points and targets on and off. It is divided into a number of sections. The first section has one icon ( ⬏ ) for globally toggling on or off snapping (this includes snapping to *Guide Lines* and *Grids*). The second section concerns snapping to and from points defined by objects' *bounding boxes*. The third section covers options for snapping to and from nodes and handles. The last section has icons for toggling on and off snapping to the page boundary, *Guide Lines*, and *Grids*. Note that snapping of *bounding boxes* is independent of snapping of nodes (i.e., a node cannot be directly snapped to a point on a *bounding box* and vice versa). Both *bounding boxes* and nodes, however, can be snapped to the page boundary, *Guide Lines* and *Grids*.

The section for snapping *bounding box* items includes the icons for enabling and disabling:

- ⌐ : Snap *bounding box* corners. Global control for *bounding box* snapping. If enabled, *bounding box* corners are always snap points.

- ⌐ : Snap to edges of a *bounding box*. Note that edges are never snap points.

- ⌐ : Snap to *bounding box* corners.

- ⌐ : Snap from and to midpoints of *bounding box* edges.

- ⌐ : Snapping from and to centers of *bounding boxes*.

Most types of nodes and handles can be snap points and/or targets. These include path nodes, regular *Shape* nodes and handles, *Rectangle* round-corner handles, and *Rotation center* handles. The options in the *Snap Bar* section for nodes and handles includes icons for enabling and disabling:

- ⌐ : Snap nodes or handles. If enabled, selected nodes are always snap points.

- ⌐ : Snap to paths.

- ⌐ : Snap to path intersections. Snap to paths must be enabled for this option to be enabled.

- ⌐ : Snap to cusp nodes. nodes.

- ⌐ : Snap to smooth nodes.

- ⌐ : Snap from and to midpoints of line segments. This includes straight line segments on either *Shapes* or paths).

- ⌐ : Snap from or to centers of objects. (The same point as the center of the *bounding box*.)

- ⌐ : Snap from an to an item's *Rotation center*.

Snapping can be globally toggled on/off via View → Snap (%).

# Guides

*Guide Lines* are individual lines that can be arbitrarily placed. They are defined by an *x-y anchor* (origin point) through which the line passes and an angle. The *anchor* is shown as a small circle on the line.

*Guide Lines* can be hidden or unhidden by using View → └ Guides (|). To be active, a *Guide Line* must be visible. Snapping to *Guide Lines* can be enabled or disabled by clicking on the |/| icon in the *Snap Bar*.

The color of *Guide Lines* can be changed under the *Guides* tab in the *Document Properties* dialog. Snapping of *Guide Lines* to other objects can be enabled or disabled also under this tab.

## Guide Creation

To create a *Guide Line*, **Left Mouse Drag** from the left *Ruler* onto the canvas for a vertical *Guide Line* or from the top *Ruler* for a horizontal *Guide Line*. An angled *Guide Line* can be created by dragging from the end of a *Ruler*. By default, the angle is set to 45° if a rectangular *Grid* is displayed or parallel to the angled lines if an axonometric *Grid* is displayed.

*Guide Lines* can also be automatically created at the edges of the *Page* by using the Edit → Guides Around Page command. They can also be created around objects as discussed in a following section.

## Guide Adjustment

*Guide Lines* can be translated and rotated using the mouse:

- **Left Mouse Drag**: Translate *Guide Line*. Both the *Guide Line* and *anchor* are moved. If dragged off the page, the *Guide Line* is deleted.

- **Shift+Left Mouse Drag**: Rotate *Guide Line*. Rotation is around the *anchor*. You must be a small distance away from the *anchor* for rotation to be enabled.

- **Ctrl+Left Mouse Drag**: Move the *anchor*, constrained to the *Guide Line*.

- **Ctrl+Shift+Left Mouse Drag**: Rotate *Guide Line* with constraint. Angle snaps to multiples of the *Rotation snap angle*, (15 degrees, by default).

- **Del**: While over a *Guide Line*, delete the *Guide Line*.

*Guide Lines* can be precisely placed by using the *Guide Line* dialog, called up by double-clicking on a *Guide Line*. A check box toggles between absolute and relative placement.

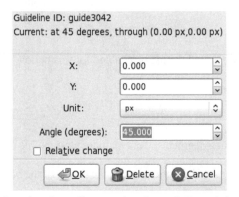

*Guide Line* dialog showing a line passing through the origin at a 45° angle.

## Guides Created from Objects

*Guide Lines* can be created from objects using the Object → Object to Guides (**Shift+G**) command. The keyboard shortcut works with the *Select Tool*, *shape tools*, *Bezier Tool*, and *Pencil Tool*. Different objects are converted in different ways. In each case, the selected objects are deleted unless the *Keep objects after conversion to guides* entry is checked in the *Tools* section of the *Inkscape Preferences* dialog.

- *Rectangles* and *Boxes*: *Guide Lines* are drawn along edges, even when rotated, if the *Conversion to guides uses edges instead of bounding box* box is checked under the *Rectangle* or *3D Box* sections in the *Inkscape Preferences* dialog. Otherwise the *bounding box* is used.

- Paths: A *Guide Line* is drawn along each straight line segment.

- Other objects: *Guide Lines* are drawn along *bounding box*. The *Geometric* or *Visual bounding box* is used depending on which is selected in the *Tools* section of the *Inkscape Preferences* dialog.

If a *Group* is selected, *Guide Lines* are drawn for each object in the *Group*, unless the *Treat groups as a single object* entry is checked in the *Tools* section of the *Inkscape Preferences* dialog.

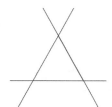
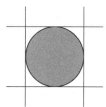

*Guide Lines* from a rotated *Rectangle*.

*Guide Lines* from a triangular path, one line for each straight path.

*Guide Lines* from a circle, lines determined from the *bounding box*.

# Grid

A *Grid* is composed of two or three sets of evenly spaced parallel lines. A *Rectangular Grid* consists of horizontal and vertical lines, much like a sheet of ordinary graph paper. An *Axonometric Grid* consists of three sets of parallel lines, typically one vertical and two at 30° angles from the horizontal. It is often used to draw three-dimensional objects.

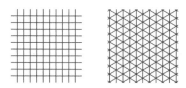

Examples of a *Rectangular Grid* (left) and *Axonometric Grid* (right).

*Grids* can be created and edited on the *Grids* tab of the *Document Properties* dialog. To create a *Grid*, select the type (*Rectangular* or *Axonometric*) from the drop-down menu at the top of the dialog and then click on the *New* button. The parameters for the new *Grid* will then be editable under a tab in the bottom of the dialog. It is possible to have more than one *Grid* defined (and in use). Each *Grid* will have a tab entry.

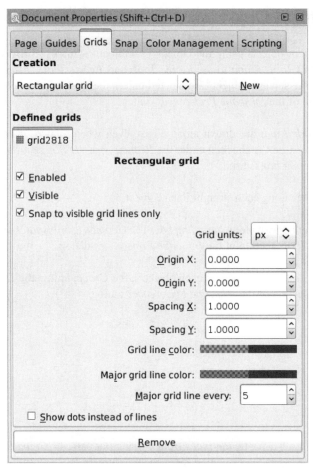

*Grids* tab in *Document Properties* dialog showing the parameters for a *Rectangular Grid* with the default parameters.

Each *Grid* can individually be *Enabled* and made *Visible* by the check boxes on the *Defined Grid* tabs. If a *Grid* is not enabled, it will not be visible. However a *Grid* can be enabled and not visible. All *Grids* can be enabled or disabled by clicking on the ▦ in the *Snap Bar* or by using the global command View → ▦ Grid (#). This setting overrides the settings on the individual *Grid* tabs. Note: There is no visual indication whether this overall setting is on or off if the visibility of the individual *Grids* are all set off. Note also that, depending on the zoom scale, not all *Grid* lines are shown. "Missing" lines will not be snapped to if the *Snap to visible grid lines only* box is checked under the *Grids* tab.

For both types of *Grids*, the *Grid unit* can be selected from a drop-down menu and the *Grid* origin can also be specified. For *Rectangular Grids*, the $x$ and $y$ spacing can be set independently. For *Axonometric Grids* the $x$ and $z$ spacings are derived from the $y$ spacing and the angle settings. In both cases the color of the lines can be set by clicking on the color box and making changes in the dialog that pops up.

The default *Grid* parameters can be modified in the *Grids* section of the *Inkscape Preferences* dialog.

Different "views" of the same drawing share the same *Grids* but the *Grids* can be enabled or made visible independently for each view.

# Alignment and Distribution of Objects

This section describes the *Align and Distribute* dialog (Object → 🗐 Align and Distribute... (**Shift+Ctrl+A**)) which allows the positioning of objects with respect to other objects or to the selection, drawing, or page. Two types of positioning are available: *alignment* where the centers or edges of objects are aligned to one another, and *distributing* where objects are distributed in some direction based on their centers or edges.

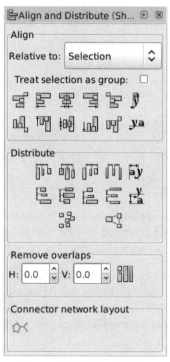

*Align and Distribute* dialog.

# Align

The alignment of objects is with respect to an *anchor*. The anchor can be an object or be defined by the selection, drawing, or page; the choice of what is used is set in the pull-down menu *Relative to*. The object may be specified to be the first or last object selected. If multiple objects are selected at the same time, this is equivalent to the top or bottom object in *z-order*. Alternatively, the object can be specified to be the biggest or smallest item, where size is determined by the size of the *bounding box*, the width for vertical alignment and the height for horizontal alignment. The *bounding box* sides are used as the reference points for alignment except for text, where the *baseline* is used.

When the *Treat selection as group:* box is checked, all selected objects are treated as if they were in a *Group*. This saves on having to group and ungroup the selected objects when you wish to align them together to the *Page* or to the drawing. Alignment relative to other criteria is unpredictable.

The various alignment options are:

- Horizontal:

  - 🗐 Align right sides to left side of anchor.

  - 🗐 Align right sides to right side of anchor.

  - 🗐 Align horizontal centers to center of anchor.

- ⯁ Align left sides to left side of anchor.

- ⯁ Align left sides to right side of anchor.

- ⯁ Align baselines of text to anchor, horizontally. As of v0.48, text anchor position depends on alignment and orientation of text (e.g. the anchor box will be on the right for right-aligned text).

- Vertical:

  - ⯁ Align top sides to bottom side of anchor.

  - ⯁ Align top sides to top side of anchor.

  - ⯁ Align vertical centers to center of anchor.

  - ⯁ Align bottom sides to bottom side of anchor.

  - ⯁ Align bottom sides to top side of anchor.

  - ⯁ Align baselines of text to anchor, vertically.

# Distribute: Uniform

The distribute part of the *Align and Distribute* dialog allows objects to be evenly spaced in the horizontal or vertical direction based on some criteria. Two options are included in this part of the dialog, which perhaps should be included separately: randomizing the center of objects and unclumping. They will be considered in the next section.

The distribution of objects is between the two objects at the extremes (i.e., the leftmost and rightmost objects for horizontal distribution). The definition of which is the leftmost and rightmost object is made using the objects' *bounding boxes*, and it may depend on the type of distribution selected. For example, if a distribution is based on the rightmost edge of the objects, then the objects rightmost edge will be used to determine which objects are at the extremes.

The various distribution options are:

- Horizontal:

  - ⯁ Distribute left sides evenly.

  - ⯁ Distribute centers evenly.

  - ⯁ Distribute right sides evenly.

  - ⯁ Distribute with uniform gaps between objects.

  - ⯁ Distribute baseline anchors evenly.

- Vertical

  - ⯁ Distribute left sides evenly.

  - ⯁ Distribute centers evenly.

  - ⯁ Distribute top sides evenly.

  - ⯁ Distribute with uniform gaps between objects.

  - ⯁ Distribute baseline anchors evenly.

# Distribute: Non-Uniform

The distribute part of the *Align and Distribute* dialog has two options that modify the distribution of objects in a non-uniform way. Both affect the horizontal and vertical distributions at the same time.

The two options are:

- ⊞ Randomize the center of objects.

- ⊟ *Unclump* objects (i.e., move objects to more evenly space the edge-to-edge distances). Repeated application approaches the use of the *Distribute with uniform gaps* commands described previously.

# Distribute: Remove Overlaps

Another section of the *Align and Distribute* dialog allows one to move objects just enough that they don't overlap. Two entry boxes, one for the horizontal direction and the other for the vertical direction, allow the addition of a minimum space between adjacent objects.

# Rows and Columns

The *Rows and Columns* dialog (Object → ⊞ Rows and Columns... ) can be used to arrange an arbitrary number of objects into a two-dimensional grid.

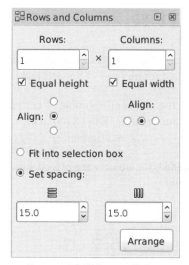

*Rows and Columns* dialog.

To use the dialog, first select all the objects you wish to arrange into a grid. The dialog will default to a one-dimensional array. You can use the *Row* and *Column* entry boxes to change the number of rows and columns. If you use the up or down arrow to change the number of rows, the number of columns will change to give you the minimum number required to include all the objects in the selection. A similar change to the number of rows will happen if you change the number of columns. The maximum number of rows or columns is 100.

The algorithm for determining the *order* the objects are placed in the array attempts to preserve any existing rows. For this algorithm, the *bounding box* of each object is used. Technically, the objects are first sorted by their vertical positions. Then objects that overlap vertically are sorted by their horizontal positions. Finally, the objects are placed from left to right and from top to bottom in the array. The algorithm works pretty well but cannot handle all situations since determining what objects are in a row is objective. (If in the vertical direction A overlaps B and B overlaps C but A does not overlap C, are A and C in the same row?)

$$
\begin{array}{llll}
1 & 2 & 3 & 4 \\
 & 6 & & \\
5 & & 7 & 89 \\
10 & 11 & 12 &
\end{array}
\qquad
\begin{array}{lll}
1 & 2 & 3 \\
4 & 5 & 6 \\
7 & 8 & 9 \\
10 & 11 & 12
\end{array}
$$

Twelve object before (left) and after (right) aligning with a 3 by 4 grid.

For placing objects, the grid is divided into cells. First, the cell size and placement is determined and then the objects are positioned inside the cells, one object to one cell.

Cells are given the height of the tallest object if the *Equal height* box is checked; otherwise, they are given the height of the tallest object in their row. A similar policy is followed for width.

$$
\begin{array}{lll}
1 & 2 & 3 \\
4 & 5 & 6 \\
7 & 8 & 9 \\
10 & 11 & 12
\end{array}
\qquad
\begin{array}{lll}
1 & 2 & 3 \\
4 & 5 & 6 \\
7 & 8 & 9 \\
10 & 11 & 12
\end{array}
$$

Alignment with the *Equal height* box checked (left) and unchecked (right). Note how the height of the "8" has been used for all rows on the left and just its own row on the right.

If the *Fit into selection* option is selected, the rows and columns of cells are evenly spaced with the edge rows and columns flush against the bounding box of the selection. If the *Set spacing* option is selected, the rows and columns are separated by the amount entered in the *Row spacing* and *Column spacing* entry boxes. The spacing can be negative.

Once the cell positions have been determined, the objects are placed inside the cell according to the selected *Align* options (top, middle, bottom; left, center, right).

$$
\begin{array}{lll}
1 & 2 & 3 \\
4 & 5 & 6 \\
7 & 8 & 9 \\
10 & 11 & 12
\end{array}
\qquad
\begin{array}{lll}
1 & 2 & 3 \\
4 & 5 & 6 \\
7 & 8 & 9 \\
10 & 11 & 12
\end{array}
\qquad
\begin{array}{lll}
1 & 2 & 3 \\
4 & 5 & 6 \\
7 & 8 & 9 \\
10 & 11 & 12
\end{array}
$$

Grid alignment with alignment to top (left), center (middle), and bottom (right) of cell.

Note that the *bounding box* of all the objects after alignment may not be the same as the *bounding box* of the selection prior to alignment even though the *Fit to selection* option has been chosen. This is because the selection *bounding box* has been used to place the *cells*. The objects within the cells may not touch the cell walls. (There also appears sometimes to be a gratuitous shift: Bug?)

# Chapter 6. Geometric Shapes

Inkscape provides a number of tools for drawing geometric shapes. The tools for drawing regular[1] geometric shapes (rectangles, boxes, ellipses, regular polygons, stars, and spirals) are covered here. Path (pencil and pen) tools, discussed in the next section, may be used to draw arbitrary shapes.

**Current Style:** The style of an object includes attributes that determine how the inside of the shape (*fill*) and how the boundary path (*stroke*) are drawn. It also includes shape-specific attributes such as the number of points in a star. New objects are drawn with the *Current style*. Some components of the *Current style* are displayed (e.g. *Fill* color) or changed (e.g. number of points in a star) in the *Tool Controls* of a relevant tool.

The *Rectangle Tool-Tool Controls* showing the current *Fill* color (blue) and *Stroke* color (black), as well as the *Stroke* width (1 px).

A component of the *Current style* is changed when that component is modified through, for example, an entry in the *Tool Controls* or the *Fill and Stroke* dialog (Object → ✏ Fill and Stroke... (**Shift+Ctrl+F**)) discussed in Chapter 10, *Attributes*. Note that if in the *Current style*, a star has five points, just selecting a star with six points (and even modifying its color) is not enough to change the number of points in the *Current style*. The number of points must be explicitly changed.

By default, the *shape tools* (except the *Spiral Tool* and *Box Tool*) as well as the *Calligraphy Tool* are drawn with a global *Current style*. Changing the style for one of these tools, changes the style for all. Control over which tools use the global *Current style* and setting a default *Current style* can be done on each tool's entry in the *Inkscape Preferences* dialog (File → ▦ Inkscape Preferences... (**Shift+Ctrl+P**)).

Each of the shape tools can be given a fixed style by selecting the *This tool's own style* option under the tool's entry in the *Inkscape Preferences* dialog (File → ▦ Inkscape Preferences... (**Shift+Ctrl+P**)). Clicking on the *Current style* color swatches will open the correct section of the *Inkscape Preferences* dialog. Set the style by selecting an object with the desired style and click on the *Take from selection* button. The *Box Tool* style cannot be changed. (However the *Box Tool* with the *Last used style* option will remember its own style.)

While drawing some objects (arcs, stars, regular polygons, and spirals), some features (such as the orientation of a polygon) can be constrained to specific angles with respect to the center of the shape and the horizontal axis. These angles are multiples of the *Rotation snap angle*. The default snap angle is 15°. It can be set under the *Steps* entry in the *Inkscape Preferences* dialog.

Shapes can be scaled, rotated, and skewed. (See Chapter 5, *Positioning and Transforming*.) When doing so, a transformation is applied to the shape. The internal parameters defining the shape (such as the width and height of an ellipse) remain *unchanged*.[2] This is important to remember if you later modify a shape, for example, by editing the *XML* file directly.

# Rectangles and Squares

The *Rectangle Tool* allows one to draw rectangles and squares. Basic use of the tool is introduced in Chapter 1, *Quick Start*. To draw a rectangle or square, select the tool by clicking on the ▢ icon (**F4** or **r**) in the *Tool Box*. To draw a

---

[1] The *Star Tool* includes a randomization feature so that the resulting shapes are not regular. The underlying description is still based on a regular shape.

[2] This is not always true for rectangles. If the option *Optimized* is selected in the *Store transformation* section of the *Transforms* entry of the *Inkscape Preferences* dialog, the *x*, *y*, *width*, and *height* attributes will change rather than adding a *transformation matrix* for simple translating and scaling operations.

rectangle, use a **Left Mouse Drag** from one corner to the opposite corner. To force a square to be drawn, hold down the **Ctrl** while dragging the mouse. This also allows rectangles with an integer height to width or width to height ratio to be drawn. As a special case, rectangles with sides constrained to the "Golden Ratio" [http://en.wikipedia.org/wiki/Golden_ratio] are also allowed with the **Ctrl** key. Holding the **Shift** key down while dragging will create a rectangle centered around the starting point.

The size of a preexisting rectangle can be changed by selecting the rectangle via a **Left Mouse Click** on the rectangle with the *Rectangle Tool*. Once the rectangle is selected, handles (small squares and circles) will appear at some of the rectangle's corners. **Left Mouse Drag** the handle (square) at the top left or bottom right to change the size of the rectangle.

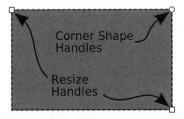

A rectangle showing the *Resize* (square) and *Corner Shape* (circle) handles.

A rectangle can be given rounded corners. There are two ways to do this. The first is to use the handle(s) at the top-right corner of the rectangle. Initially, only one handle is visible. If this handle is dragged down, a rounded corner in the shape of a quarter circle is created. A second handle is now visible. Dragging this second handle to the left will create an elliptical rounded corner. Upon dragging the second handle, the radii of curvature in the horizontal ($x$) and vertical ($y$) directions are independent.

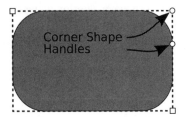 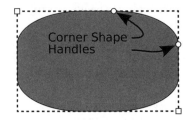

A rectangle with circular rounded corners.    A rectangle with elliptical rounded corners (different x and y corner radii).

A second way to set the radius of curvature of a rectangle is to use the settings *Rx* and *Ry* in the *Tool Controls* when the *Rectangle Tool* is selected. The settings will affect any selected rectangle as well as rectangles that are drawn afterward. Rounded corners can be removed from a rectangle by using the *Make corners sharp* button ( ⌐ ). The width and height of a rectangle can also be set using entry boxes in the *Tool Controls*.

The *Rectangle Tool-Tool Controls*.

## Note

If you want the rounded corners to scale with the rectangle object, you must toggle on this option using the ⇗ icon that is in the *Tool Controls* when the *Select Tool* is in use.

# 3D Boxes

The *Box Tool* allows you to draw three-dimensional boxes that remain editable in Inkscape but display normally in other *SVG* renderers. A box is composed of an *SVG Group* of six paths. Information about the vanishing points, and so forth are stored in the Inkscape *Name Space*. This extra information is only used by the *Box Tool*. All other tools treat the box as a normal *Group*. The sides of the box can be styled independently (or even deleted).

To draw a 3D box select the *Box Tool* by clicking on the 🔖 icon (**Shift+F4**) in the *Tool Box*. Use a **Left Mouse Drag** to draw the left side of the box (in the *x-y* plane). The start of the drag sets one corner while the end of the drag sets the opposite corner. The other sides of the box are automatically drawn with the right side of the box set to a default width. Pressing the **Shift** while creating the box changes the function of the cursor to defining the depth (width of the right side or *z* dimension) of the box.

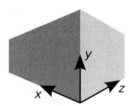

A simple 3D box showing two sides and the box coordinate system. There are an additional four hidden sides.

When a box is selected and the *Box Tool* active, a variety of handles are displayed. The eight handles at the corners of the box are used to adjust the size of the box. The four in front (see figure below) change the size of the left box face in the *x-y* plane. The other four change the depth (*z*) of the box. Holding the **Shift** down swaps the functions of the handles. With the **Ctrl** down, the handles are restricted in movement to lines along the box edges or to a box diagonal. This allows adjusting one dimension of a box face while keeping the other fixed in the first case or keeping the aspect ratio fixed in the latter case.

Dragging the *Cross* handle moves the box while keeping the same perspective. Without a modifier key, the box is kept in the *x-y* plane. Holding the **Ctrl** down while dragging limits movement to lines along the box edge or along the box diagonal. Holding down the **Shift** while dragging moves the box in the *z* direction.

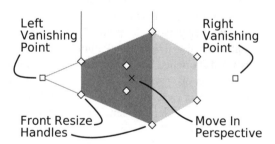

A simple 3D box showing showing its handles. Two of the *Front Resize* handles are labeled. The other two are directly above those. The four remaining handles at the corners of the box are the *Back Resize* handles. The cross in the middle is use to move the box while keeping the same perspective.

By default, a box is drawn with two vanishing points, one each on the left (*x*) and right (*z*) sides. The vanishing points are initially placed at the edge of the page, halfway between the top and bottom. These points are determined when the *SVG* drawing is first created so resizing the page does not move them. The vanishing points can be dragged to new locations. Dragging the points a ways off the page will probably give you a more satisfactory perspective than the default.

All boxes that share the same vanishing points will change together. If you wish to change the vanishing points of just selected boxes, hold down the **Shift** while dragging. If multiple boxes are selected with different vanishing points, dragging a vanishing point for one box near that of another box will "merge" the points together.

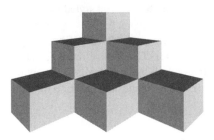

All the boxes share the same vanishing points. The "stack" was created by duplicating the bottom-center box and then dragging the *Move In Perspective* handle with the **Shift** key or **Ctrl** key. Two moves were required for each box.

The same boxes as in the previous figure but with both the *x* and *z* vanishing points moved up and right.

# Perspectives

The *Box Tool* can be used to draw boxes with 1, 2, and 3-point perspectives as well as a box using an isometric projection. The above examples use a 2-point perspective with two vanishing points. The type of perspective is changed via the *Box Tool Tool Controls*. Each of the three perspective points (*x*, *y*, and *z*) can be set to infinity or to a specific point. To set or unset a perspective point to infinity, toggle the "Parallel Lines" button ( ‖ ) in the *Tool Controls* next to the appropriate angle (or use the keyboard shortcuts: **Shift+X**, **Shift+Y**, and **Shift+Z** that are available when using the *Box Tool*). When set to infinity, the direction of a perspective point is set by an *Angle* parameter. The angles can be changed via the entry boxes in the *Tool Controls* or by using the keyboard shortcuts: *x*: [, ]; *y*: (, ); and *z*: {, }. The angles will be changed by the *Rotation snap angle* (15° by default, settable in the *Steps* section of the *Inkscape Preferences* dialog). With the **Alt** key, the angle change will be 0.5°.

The *Box Tool-Tool Controls*, showing the default parameters for a 2-point perspective.

**1-point Perspective:** Set the *x* and *y* vanishing points to infinity by using the *x* and *y* "Parallel Line" buttons ( ‖ ) in the *Tool Controls*. Set *Angle X* to 180° and *Angle Y* to 90°. Toggle off the "Parallel Line" button for *z* and drag the vanishing point to the desired point (typically near the center of the drawing).

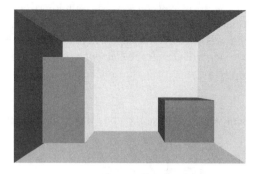

The boxes have been drawn using a 1-point perspective. The front side of the outer box has been made transparent.

**2-point Perspective:** The default perspective. Set the $y$ vanishing point to infinity by toggling on the $y$ "Parallel Line" button ( ‖ ) in the *Tool Controls*. Set *Angle Y* to 90°. Enable the $x$ and $z$ vanishing points by toggling off their "Parallel Line" buttons. Drag the $x$ and $z$ vanishing point to the desired points (typically at the same level on opposite sides of the page).

**3-point Perspective:** Enable the $x$, $y$, and $z$ vanishing points by toggling off their "Parallel Line" buttons ( ‖ ) in the *Tool Controls*. Drag the $x$, $y$, and $z$ vanishing points to the desired places. Typically the $x$ and $z$ vanishing points are at the same level on opposite sides of the page. They are either above or below the page depending on if the observer is looking down or up at the scene. The $y$ vanishing point is then on the opposite side, either below or above the page.

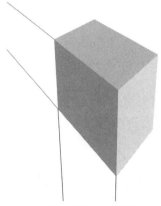

The box has been drawn with a 3-point perspective. The vanishing points have been dragged off the page as indicated by the red, yellow, and blue lines. Dragging the $y$ vanishing point below the others turns the box inside out. The proper perspective can be achieved by changing the *z-order* of the sides or by swapping the $x$ and $z$ vanishing points.

**Isometric Projection:** Boxes can be drawn with an *Isometric Projection* by toggling on all "Parallel Line" buttons in the *Tool Controls* and setting the $x$, $y$, and $z$ angles to be: 150°, 90°, and 30°, respectively.

The perspective information is stored in the *defs* section of the *SVG* file. Look for the "inkscape:perspective" tag. With the *XML Editor* one can precisely place vanishing points. There is a triplet of numbers for each point (e.g., "inkscape:vp_x"). The first two are the $x$ and $y$ coordinates of the vanishing point and the third is a flag to indicate if the perspective lines converge or are parallel.

# Attributes

The attributes of the six sides can be changed independently. To select one of the sides, one must use one of the methods of selecting an object in a *Group*. There is one problem: The common method for entering a *Group*, namely double-clicking on an object with the *Select Tool*, won't work as this enables the *Box Tool* instead. The *Group* can be entered by selecting the box and using **Ctrl+Enter** or by selecting the *Enter group* line from the pop-up menu when you **Right Click** on the box. Using **Ctrl+Left Mouse Click** will select a side of the box without entering the *Group*. Using **Ctrl+Alt+Left Mouse Click** to select a hidden side.

By default, a box will always be drawn with sides of the same default colors (shades of blue), even after editing the attributes for one side. This behavior can be changed by selecting the *Last used style* option on the *3D Box* page in the *Inkscape Preferences* dialog. If this option is selected, Inkscape will remember the *Fill* and *Stroke* colors independently for each side. Changing the color of one side will change the *Current style* for all other shapes but the inverse is not true.

### Nested Boxes

Inkscape does not prevent you from creating a box inside another box *Group*. This can lead to strange behavior.

# Ellipses, Circles, and Arcs

The *Ellipse Tool* allows one to draw ellipses, circles, and arcs. Select the tool by clicking on the ○ icon (**F5** or **e**) in the *Tool Box*. To draw an ellipse or arc, use a **Left Mouse Drag**. An ellipse will be drawn with the sides touching a rectangular box defined by the starting and stopping points of the drag. To force a circle to be drawn, hold down the **Ctrl** while dragging the mouse. This also allows ellipses with a height to width or width to height ratio that is either an integer or in the "Golden Ratio" to be drawn. Holding the **Shift** key down while dragging will create an ellipse centered around the starting point. Holding down the **Alt** key while dragging will create an ellipse with the circumference passing through the start and end points of the drag. Using **Alt+Ctrl** while dragging will create a circle with a diameter defined by the distance between the start and stop point of the drag.

When an ellipse is selected and the *Ellipse Tool* is active, the ellipse will have a set of handles (small squares and circles) that can be used to resize it or convert it to an arc. (The handles are also available if one of other shape *Tools* or the *Node Tool* is active.)

To change the size of the ellipse, drag the handle at the top or left. The **Ctrl** key can be used to force the ellipse to be a circle.

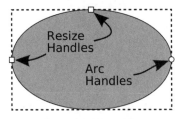

An ellipse showing the *Resize* and *Arc* handles.

To convert an ellipse into an arc, use the two *Arc* handles. Initially both handles are on top of each other. Drag one handle to set one end of the arc, then drag the second handle to set the other end. Holding down the **Ctrl** key while dragging an *Arc* handle will force the angle of the arc to begin or end at a multiple of the *Rotation snap angle* (15° by default).

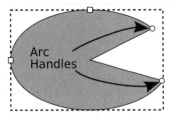

An arc showing the *Resize* and *Arc* handles.The path of the arc is
closed by an extension to the point at the center of the arc's curvature.

If an *Arc* handle is dragged with the pointer outside the curve of the virtual ellipse, the arc will be defined with a closed path that has a wedge that extends to the center of curvature (as shown above). If the *Arc* handle is dragged with the pointer inside the curve, the path defining the arc will start and stop at the two *Arc* handles, as shown below.

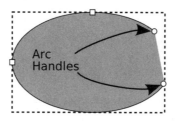

An open arc.

An arc can also be defined using the settings in the *Tool Controls* when the *Ellipse Tool* is selected. The settings will affect any ellipse or arc that is selected as well as any that are drawn afterward. The *Start* and *End* angles are defined in degrees and are measured in the *clockwise* direction starting at the *x*-axis. There are two buttons that toggle arcs between opened ( ⌣ ) and closed ( ⌣ ) (switchable if either angle is not zero). There is also a button to reset an arc to an ellipse ( ◉ ).

The *Ellipse Tool-Tool Controls*.

# Regular Polygons and Stars

The *Star Tool* can be used to draw regular polygons and stars. To draw one of these objects, select the tool by clicking on the ✧ icon (**Shift+F9** or **\***) in the *Tool Box*. To draw a polygon or star, use a **Left Mouse Drag**. A star will be drawn with the center at the starting point of the drag and one vertex at the ending point of the drag. The vertex can be forced to be at a multiple of the *Rotation snap angle* (15 degrees by default) by holding down the **Ctrl** key during the drag.

Stars can be reshaped by either dragging handles (small diamonds) on the star or by using the settings in the *Tool Controls* when the *Star Tool* is selected. Two important parameters can only be changed in the *Tool Controls*. The first is an option to specify that the shape drawn be a star or a polygon. This is controlled by two toggled buttons ( ⬠ and ✩ ). The second is a parameter that controls the number of points in a star or the number of corners of a polygon.

The *Star Tool-Tool Controls*.

There are two handles for stars (one for polygons). The *Tip radius* handle (see the *Notification Region* if in doubt which is which) is used to control the position of the tip of a star or corner vertex of a polygon. This is the handle that was used when first drawing the star or polygon. Using the **Ctrl** key while dragging the handle restricts it to a radial line.

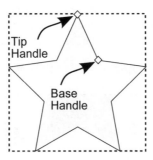

A star showing the *Tip radius* and *Base radius* handles.

The *Base radius* handle controls the position of the "inner" vertex of a star. The *Base radius* handle can be constrained to have an angle halfway between adjacent tips by holding down the **Ctrl** key while dragging it. Note that it is possible that the radius of the *Base* vertex be larger than the *Tip* vertex or it can be *negative* as shown next.

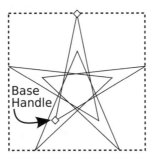

A star with a negative *Base* radius.

Holding the **Shift** key while dragging either handle will round the corners of the star or pentagon.

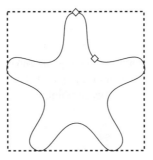

A star with rounded corners.

Holding the **Alt** key while dragging either handle will move all the star's or polygon's vertices independently in a random fashion.

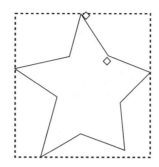

A star with a random factor added.

As mentioned above, the *Tool Controls* area contains entries to determine if a star or regular polygon is drawn and to set the number of points or vertices. For stars, it also contains a box to set the *Spoke ratio*. This is defined as the ratio of the *Base* radius to the *Tip* radius. Useful values are: for a regular 5-pointed star, 0.382; for a regular 6-pointed star, 0.577; and for a regular 8-pointed star, 0.541. Numerical values for *Rounded* and *Randomized* can also be entered (try −10 for *Rounded*!). And lastly, there is a *Defaults* button ( ) to reset all of the settings to their default values.

# Spirals

The *Spiral Tool* can be used to draw Archimedes' spirals [http://en.wikipedia.org/wiki/Archimedean_spiral]. Other types of spirals can be drawn using the *Function Plotter* extension with polar coordinates. Select the tool by clicking on the ⊚ icon (**F9** or **i**) in the *Tool Box*. To draw a spiral, use a **Left Mouse Drag**. The start of the drag will be the spiral's center. Holding down the **Ctrl** key while dragging will constrain the position of the spiral end point to a multiple of the *Rotation snap angle* (default 15 degrees). To reverse the direction of the spiral, flip it (Object → ⩕ Flip Horizontal (**H**) or Object → ◀ Flip Vertical (**V**)).

Spirals can be reshaped by either dragging handles (small diamonds) on the spiral or by using the settings in the *Tool Controls* when the *Spiral Tool* is selected. There are two handles, the *Inner* and *Outer*. Dragging either handle allows *rolling* and *unrolling* the spiral from its respective end (i.e., making the spiral longer or shorter, or changing the radius of the inner and outer ends). Holding down the **Ctrl** key forces the end to be at a multiple of the *Rotation snap angle* with respect to the center. Holding down the **Shift** key while clicking on the *Inner* handle will set the inner radius to zero.

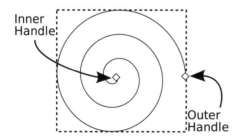
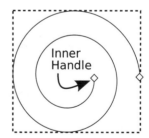

A spiral showing the Inner and Outer handles.      A spiral after unrolling one turn with the Inner handle.

The *Inner* handle can also be used to change the divergence of the spiral by dragging the handle up or down while holding down the **Alt** key. The divergence is a measure of how rapidly the radius changes with respect to the angle as the spiral progresses. A divergence of one gives a spiral where the distance between successive turns remains uniform (an Archimedes' spiral). Divergences smaller (larger) than one give a spiral where the distance between successive turns decreases (increases) moving outward. Mathematically, the radius of a point is proportional to its angle (measured in radians) raised to a power equal to the divergence. Clicking on the *Inner* handle while holding down the **Alt** key will reset the divergence to one.

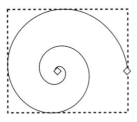
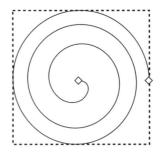

A spiral with a divergence of 2.          A spiral with a divergence of 0.5.

The *Outer* handle can be used to scale and rotate the spiral by dragging it with the **Shift** key pressed. If both the **Shift** and **Alt** keys are held down, then the spiral will only rotate, keeping the radius fixed.

The number of turns, divergence, and inner radius can all be set in the *Tool Controls*. These values can also be reset to their default values by clicking on the *Defaults* button (  ).

The *Spiral Tool-Tool Controls*.

To understand the *Fill* of spiral one must understand how Inkscape calculates *Fill*. This is covered in detail in Chapter 10, *Attributes*. A spiral is basically an open path. The *Fill* is drawn as if the path was closed with a line segment between the path ends (the *Inner* and *Outer* handles). Then the current *Fill Rule* is applied.

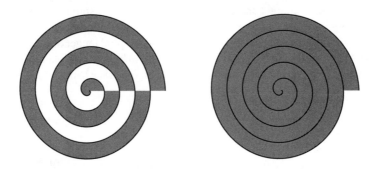

*Even-odd* fill rule (left). *Non-zero* fill rule (right).

How do you completely fill a spiral with the *Even-odd* fill rule? The trick is to use a second duplicate spiral, with one less turn (drag *Outer* handle to unwind the spiral one turn).

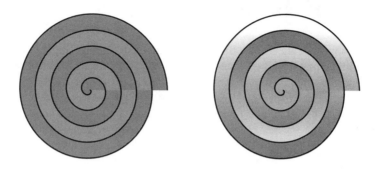

Two overlaid spirals, both with an *Even-odd* fill rule. Solid fill (left), gradient fill (right).

# Chapter 7. Paths

Paths are arbitrary shaped objects. This chapter first covers some path terminology and how paths are described in Inkscape, then moves onto how paths can be created, and finally how paths are edited. Chapter 8, *Live Path Effects (LPEs)*, covers effects that can be applied to paths.

Paths can be *Open* (have two ends) or *Closed* (have no ends). They can also be *Compound* (composed of separate open and/or closed paths).

| An Open path. | A Closed path. | A Compound path. |

Paths differ from *Shapes* in that there is no predefined structure. For example, a *Rectangle* shape is defined in terms of a width and height with an *x* and *y* offset. A corner point cannot be moved independently of at least one other corner point. A path, in the shape of a rectangle, consists of the coordinates of the four corner points. A single corner point can be moved by itself with the resulting shape no longer rectangular.

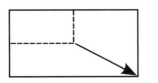

A *Rectangle* shape, shown before (dashed line) and after (solid line) a corner has been dragged.

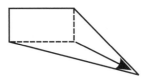

A rectangular path, shown before (dashed line) and after (solid line) a corner has been dragged.

A regular shape can be converted into a path: Path → ⬚ Object to Path (**Shift+Ctrl+C**), but the reverse is not possible.

# Bezier Curves

Most paths are described internally in Inkscape (and in many other drawing programs) as a series of Bezier curves. It is very useful to understand the basic properties of Bezier curves for drawing and manipulating paths. Bezier curves are defined by four points, two of which are the *end* points or *nodes* of the curve. The other two are *control* points or handles, each paired with one of the end points. The control points have the useful property that a line starting at one end of the curve and ending at the corresponding control point is tangent to the curve at the end point. This enables the smooth joining of multiple Bezier curves to form a path.

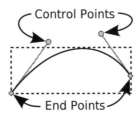

A Bezier curve showing the *end* points (*nodes*) and *control* points (*handles*).

Two or more Bezier curves can be joined to form a more complex path. The node where they are joined may be smooth, indicated by a square (normal) or circle (auto-smooth node, see *Auto-smooth Nodes*).

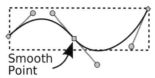

Two Bezier curves joined by a smooth node.

Or the node may be a *corner* node, also referred to as a *cusp* node, indicated by a diamond, where an abrupt change in direction is allowed.

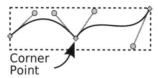

Two Bezier curves joined by a *corner* node.

The segment between two nodes may be a *curve* or a *line*. Note that there are no control points for line segments.

Two segments, one a *curve* and the other a *line*.

# Creating Paths

Paths can be created by the *Pencil* (Freehand), *Bezier* (Pen), and *Calligraphy* drawing tools. They can also be created by conversion from a regular shape or text object.

By default, paths created with the *Pencil* and *Bezier* tools have a black stroke with a width of one pixel while the *Calligraphy* tool will use the *Current style*. These behaviors can be changed in the corresponding sections of the *Inkscape Preferences* dialog. (**Right Mouse Click** on the *Current style* indicator in the *Tool Controls* to open the dialog.)

## The Pencil Tool

The *Pencil (or Freehand) Tool* is perhaps the easiest tool with which to draw a path. Simply click on the ✐ icon (**F6** or **p**) in the *Tool Box* and then click-drag the mouse over the canvas to draw a line. Holding down the **Shift** key while drawing temporary disables nodes snapping to the *Grid* or *Guide Lines*. It also, if a path is selected, add the new sub-path to the selected path.

Holding down the **Alt** key while drawing enables the *Sketch* mode. While in this mode, all strokes are averaged to create a final stroke, temporarily shown as a red path. Releasing the **Alt** key finalizes the path. This feature is considered experimental and does not give the expected result if one strokes a line back and forth. Instead, draw all your strokes in the same direction.

As long as a path is selected, you can extend the path by click-dragging from one of the path's ends. To prevent adding to a path, deselect the path with the **Esc** key.

To delete an unfinished path, use **Esc** or **Ctrl+Z**.

Paths drawn with the *Pencil Tool* tend to be composed of many Bezier curves leading to an erratic-looking path. One can smooth and simplify such curves by using the Path → ≊ Simplify (**Ctrl+L**) command one or more times.

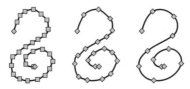

A path drawn with the *Pencil Tool* after zero, one, and multiple applications of the *Path Simplify* command (with nodes shown).

There are two possible modes for the simplify command. The default is to treat all of the selected paths as one object. The second mode is to treat each sub-path separately. To use the second mode, add an entry in the "options" section with "simplifyindividualpaths" set to 1 in the `preferences.xml` file.

A variety of options are available from the *Tool Controls*. These include selecting the drawing mode, the amount of smoothness, and a "brush".

The *Pencil Tool-Tool Controls*.

- Mode:

  - ┌ : Create regular Bezier path.

  - ∾ : Create *Spiro* path. Probably not very useful, especially if *Smoothing* is set to a low value. Use the *Bezier Tool* instead.

- Smoothing: range from 1 (minimum) to 100 (maximum).

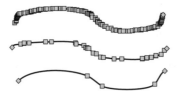

From top to bottom: Paths drawn with smoothing of 5, 20, and 50.

- Shape: Applies a shape to the path after it is drawn. This is equivalent to using the *Pattern Along Path LPE* in *Single, stretched* mode. The same option is available with the *Bezier Tool*; look there for an example of use. Using the *Pencil Tool*, a high *Smoothness* value is more useful. The width can be adjusted by varying the *Width* parameter in the *Path Effect Editor* dialog when the path is selected.

Single dots can be created by using **Ctrl+Left Mouse Click**. The size of the dot can be set in the *Pencil* section of the *Inkscape Preferences* dialog as a multiple of the current *Stroke* width. The dot is represented in *SVG* as a filled path. Adding the **Shift** key doubles the dot size (and prevents snapping) while adding the **Alt** creates a random-size dot. The *Bezier Tool* has the same options.

# The Bezier (Pen) Tool

As mentioned previously, all paths are represented in Inkscape as a series of Bezier curves. The *Bezier (or Pen) Tool* allows you to more directly control the Bezier parameters as you draw a path. To select the tool, click on the 𝒫 icon (**Shift**+**F6** or **b**) in the *Tool Box*.

**Tip**

This is one place where paying attention to the *Notification Region* is especially useful. The region not only lists your options at each step but also gives the distance and angle the cursor is from the last node when placing a new node or dragging a handle.

To begin to draw a curve, click-drag on the canvas. The point where you click becomes the end point or node of the curve. As you drag the cursor, you'll see a gray line between the end point and the cursor. This line is a tangent to your curve at the end point. Release the mouse button to establish the first control point.

Start of drawing Bezier curve.

Move the cursor to the position of the next Bezier curve end point or node. A red line will show you the shape of the curve.

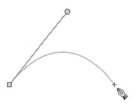

Positioning of next Bezier curve end point (node).

Click-drag from the end point to draw out a handle that allows you to set the second control point. The pointer is actually pointing to the sister of the second control point, which is the initial control point of a second Bezier curve to be attached to the first. The two points are collinear with and the same distance from the Bezier curve end point or node.

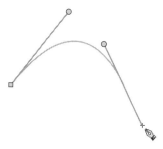

Setting of second Bezier curve control point.

Next, move the cursor to the end point of the second Bezier curve.

Positioning of end point (node) of second Bezier curve.

One can repeat the above steps to add as many Bezier curves to the path as required. To end the path, press **Enter** or do a **Right Mouse Click** after placing the last Bezier curve end point.

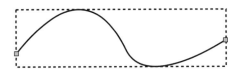

The finished path, composed of two Bezier curves.

Other useful things to know while using the Bezier Tool:

- To create a path of straight lines, click rather than click-drag at each node.

- You can use the **Arrow** keys to move the last node created while drawing a path. **Shift+Arrow** moves the node by ten times the normal step, **Alt+Arrow** will move the node by a screen pixel.

- To set the two control points of a node separately (and force the node to be a *corner* point), first set the control point for the end point of the previous Bezier curve, then without releasing the mouse button hold down the **Shift** key while setting the control point for the next Bezier curve.

- To constrain a node to be at a multiple of the *Rotation snap angle* with respect to the previous node, hold down the **Ctrl** key while setting it.

- To constrain a control point to be at a multiple of the of the *Rotation snap angle* with respect to a node, hold down the **Ctrl** key while setting it. (Can be used in conjunction with the **Shift** key.)

- To delete the last node drawn, use the **Backspace** key or the **Del** key.

- To delete an unfinished path, use **Esc** or **Ctrl+Z**.

- To change an unfinished segment (the red line) from a curve to a line, use **Shift+L**. To change an unfinished segment from a line to a curve, use **Shift+U**.

- To extend a previously drawn path, select the path, then click or click-drag on an end point.

- To close a path, click on the first endpoint when placing the last endpoint.

Two options are available from the *Tool Controls*. They are selecting the drawing mode and selecting a "brush".

The *Bezier Tool-Tool Controls*.

- Mode:

  - ⌐ : Create regular Bezier path.

  - ∿ : Create *Spiro* path.

  - ⚡ : Create a sequence of straight line segments.

  - ⊕ : Create a sequence of paraxial line segments. (Line segments are created parallel to the coordinate axes.) Each line segment is normally drawn perpendicular to the previous segment. Holding the **Shift** key down allows drawing a segment collinear to the previous segment. A path is closed with an L-shaped section, the direction can be changed by holding down the **Shift** key.

- Shape: Applies a shape to the path after it is drawn. This is equivalent to using the *Pattern Along Path* effect in *Single, stretched* mode.

From top to bottom: Paths drawn with a *Shape* of: *None, Triangle in, Triangle out, Ellipse*, and *From clipboard*. In the last case, the diamond path was copied to the clipboard before the path was drawn.

A drawing created with the *Bezier Tool* and the *Ellipse* shape.

Single dots can be created by using **Ctrl+Left Mouse Click**. This works only when in one of the straight line modes. The size of the dot can be set in the *Pen* section of the *Inkscape Preferences* dialog as a multiple of the current *Stroke* width. The dot is represented in *SVG* as a filled path. Adding the **Shift** key doubles the dot size (and prevents snapping) while adding the **Alt** creates a random-size dot. The *Pencil Tool* has the same options.

# The Calligraphy Tool

As the name suggests, the *Calligraphy Tool* can be used to draw calligraphic lines. The resulting paths are different than those drawn with the *Pencil* and *Bezier* tools in that they are composed of two parallel (or almost parallel) sub-paths, allowing the resulting line to have a variable width. The path is not stroked, but the *Fill* is solid (see Chapter 10, *Attributes*).

*p.227*

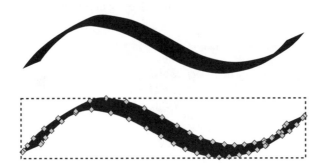

A path drawn with the *Calligraphy Tool*. The bottom path shows how the nodes are placed.

To begin drawing a Calligraphy path, select the tool by clicking on the ✒ icon (**Ctrl+F6** or **c**) in the *Tool Box* and then click-drag the mouse over the canvas to draw a line. The line will have by default the *Current style*. You can choose to draw all lines with a fixed style by selecting the *This tool's own style* option under the Calligraphy section in the *Inkscape Preferences* dialog. If you turn off the *Select new path* option in the dialog, a newly drawn object will not remain selected; you can then choose a color from the *Palette* for the next calligraphic stroke without changing the color of the previously drawn stroke.

The Calligraphy Tutorial (Help → Tutorials → Inkscape: Calligraphy) has many ideas on how to use the *Calligraphy Tool*.

The *Calligraphy Tool* has many options, several accessible from the keyboard and the rest from the *Tool Controls*. It is best just to try changing the various option settings to get the feel for them. With so many options, it is desirable to be able to save the settings for future use. You can create and access "Presets" from the drop-down menu at the left side of the *Tool Controls*.

Options with keyboard:

- To change the pen width while drawing: **Left Arrow** and **Right Arrow**. The **Home** key sets the width to the minimum while the **End** key sets the width to the maximum. Typing **Alt+X** will enable the *Width* entry box in the *Tool Controls*; enter a number and then hit **Enter** to set an exact width while drawing.

- To change the pen angle while drawing: **Up Arrow** and **Down Arrow**.

- To add to an existing (selected) path (form a union), hold the **Shift** down while drawing. *Shapes* are automatically converted to paths.

- To subtract from an existing (selected) path, hold the **Alt** down while drawing. *Shapes* are automatically converted to paths.

- To delete an unfinished path, use **Esc** or **Ctrl+Z**.

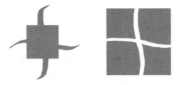

Left: Adding calligraphic paths to a square. Right: Subtracting calligraphic paths from a square.

The *Tool Controls* contains too many options to all be shown at the default Inkscape window width. To access all the options, widen the Inkscape window or click on the "v" near the right of the bar, which will show a drop-down menu with the missing options.

The *Calligraphy Tool-Tool Controls*, split to fit page.

- Predefined and custom presets: There are six predefined presets as shown in the figure below. You can add your own custom presets by selecting *Save...* in the *Preset* menu. A window will pop up where you can enter a name for your preset. The presets are stored in your preference file so they are available for future drawing sessions.

Paths drawn with *Calligraphy Tool* presets. From top to bottom: Dip pen, Marker, Brush, Wiggley, Splotchy, Tracing.

- Pen width (1 to 100): number is tenths of percent of canvas width (i.e., 15 is 1.5% of canvas width). Note that if you change the zoom level, the effective pen width will change. To keep the pen width constant, check the *Width is in absolute units* box under the *Tools-Calligraphy* page in the *Inkscape Preferences* dialog. The pen width will then be in units of *px*.

- ⊥ : On/Off button: Use tablet pressure for width (requires tablet input device).

- ◢ : Trace background: Vary the width of the pen as a function of the background. A dark background yields a wider pen.

- Thinning (−100 to 100): How the width change depends on the speed of the drawing stroke:

  - \> 0: Line width decreases with speed.

  - = 0: Line width independent of speed.

  - < 0: Line width increases with speed.

- Angle (−90 to 90 degrees): Angle of pen relative to horizontal axis.

- ∠ : On/Off button: Use tablet tilt for pen orientation (requires tablet input device).

- Fixation (0 to 100): How the angle of the pen follows the direction of the pen.

  - 0: Angle follows pen direction (always perpendicular to motion).

  - 100: Angle fixed to angle defined in *Angle* entry.

- Caps (0.0 to 5.0): How round is the end of the stroke. This can be used to produce round end-caps when the fixation is small (i.e., simulating a round brush). Note that the cap extends beyond where the stroke would normally end.

- 0.0: Flat end.

- 1.0: Approximately semicircular.

- 5.0: Elliptical, approximately five times longer than wide.

- Tremor (0 to 100): How much random shake should the stroke have. This parameter can be used to create a more realistic looking calligraphic stroke by adding some randomness to the thickness of the stroke. It works by adding randomness to the node handle orientations.

  - 0: Smooth

  - 100: Chaotic.

- Wiggle (0 to 100): How resistant the pen is to movement. With a value of 100, the pen will *wiggle* all over the paper.

- Mass (0 to 100): How the line follows pen movement. The more *massive* the pen, the smoother the stroke but the less responsive the pen will be. Try a value of 10 for a good compromise between smoothness and responsiveness.

Two options require the use a tablet (e.g., Wacom): using tablet pressure to control the width of a stroke and using tablet tilt to control the orientation of the pen's nib. This is discussed in the next section.

# Using a Tablet

*Updated for v0.48 and v0.48.1*

Inkscape can make good use of a tablet for input. This is especially true with the *Calligraphy Tool* where stroke width and nib orientation can be controlled directly with a pen. Before using the special features of a tablet, the *extended input devices* must be configured and enabled with the *Input Devices* dialog (File → ⬛ Input Devices... ). The dialog received a major change between v0.47 and v0.48. and a minor update between v0.48 and v0.48.1.

For each device (or pseudo device) there are three possible modes:

- Disabled: Special features of extended input device disabled. Treat as a regular mouse.

- Screen: Special features of extended input device enabled. Note that device will work as regular mouse outside of Canvas region.

- Window: Extended input device works only in Canvas region. Normally, this mode is not needed and has been eliminated in v0.48.1.

**0.47 Dialog.** To enable pressure and tilt control, select the device to be used from the pull-down menu at the top left then set the mode using the drop-down menu on the top right.

The *Axes* tab allows you to swap input assignments; that is, the *x*-axis for the *y*-axis if you rotate the tablet by 90 degrees (although the axis are backward).

The *Keys* tab allows you to assign key combinations to the macro keys, if any, on the tablet.

Pressure and tilt do not work properly on OS X due to problems with the X11 implementation.

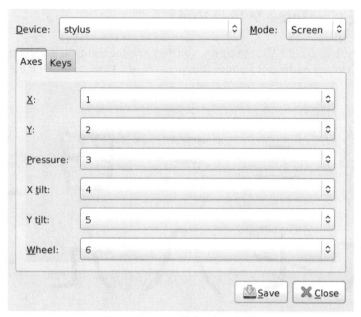

*Input Devices* dialog in v0.47.

**0.48 Dialog.** To enable pressure and tilt control, select the device to be used from the tree menu in the *Configuration* tab. In v0.48, click on the entry at the right (Disabled/Screen/Window) to open a pop-up menu to set the mode (you may have to hold the button down for a bit to open the menu). If you don't see the entries on the right, widen the dialog window. In v0.48.1, check box at the far left of each line to switch to *Screen* mode.

The *Hardware* tab allows you to test an input device. If a device has been set in *Screen* mode, then with the cursor in the test area, the little circles will change color in response to button events while the rectangles will change color in response to motion events (*x* position, *y* position, pressure, tilt left/right, tilt forward/back, wheel). An icon in the center of the test area shows the type of device in use (mouse, pen, eraser, pad). An addition, if the device you are testing is selected in the tree menu, the incoming data will be displayed numerically and graphically in the lower right.

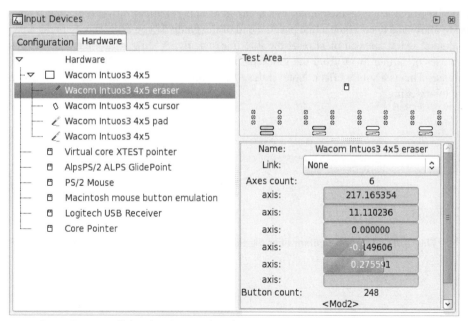

*Input Devices* dialog in v0.48.1 showing test data for a Wacom tablet eraser.

## Panning via Mouse Wheel Bug

In v0.48, if you enable the Wacom cursor, you may lose the ability to pan the canvas by using the mouse wheel. As there are no special features (tilt, pressure, etc.) associated with the cursor, it is best to leave it disabled.

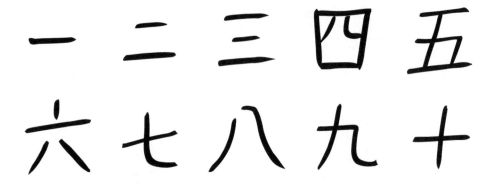

An example of calligraphy using a Wacom tablet. The figures are the numbers 1 through 10 written (poorly) in the characters common to Chinese, Japanese, and Korean. The tablet pressure was used to control the stroke width.

# Hatchings

The *Calligraphy Tool* has an option that allows parallel lines (hatchings), as found in engravings, to be easily drawn. To use this option, first select a guide path. Any path, *Shape* or text can be used as a guide. Then with the **Ctrl** key held down, drag the pointer along a line parallel to the guide path. The closest distance between the start of the drag and the guide path determines the distance the new line will be away from the guide. This is indicated by the gray circle around the pointer. As you begin to drag, the circle turns green. This indicates that the cursor is tracking the guide. When you finish drawing a line, don't release the **Ctrl**! Just start drawing (**Left Mouse Drag**) another line. As long as you hold the **Ctrl** key down, each new line will use the last drawn line as a guide and the spacing will remain the same.

If you deviate too far from the guide, the pointer will break free. This is indicated by a red circle. This is an intentional design decision to allow one to continue a line past the end of the guide. If you accidentally break free, you can delete the last path and start again; but you must reset the interline spacing. A slow steady hand works best. If the cursor is consistently closer or farther away from the guide path than the set spacing, the interline spacing will gradually decrease or increase. This is a subtle effect. Note: if the *Mass* value is zero, you may get small discontinuities in the path that disrupt the tracking.

The *Calligraphy Tool* cursor near a guide path when the **Ctrl** key is held down.

A series of "engraved" lines created with the *Calligraphy Tool*
while holding down the **Ctrl** key. The red line is the guide path.

The *Trace Background* (  ) option can be used to generate hatchings with pen width reflecting the background darkness as shown below.

A tracing of the shadow on the left is shown on the right. The *Tweak Tool* was used to clean up the ends.

By default, each new line uses the previous line as its guide path. To use the original guide path for each line, turn off the option *Select new path* found under the *Calligraphy Tool* section in the *Inkscape Preferences* dialog. The author finds it easier to make hatchings with this option turned off.

 **Tip**

Use *Touch selection* to select the lines in the hatchings. It is often easier to keep hatchings in a separate *Layer*.

# Paths from Other Objects

There are several ways to generate paths indirectly. One is to *convert* a regular shape or text object into a path. Another is to use *Stroke to Path*, which converts a path into a closed path with two parallel sub-paths. A third way to generate a path is to trace a bitmap image. This method is considered in Chapter 20, *Tracing Bitmaps*.

## Object to Path

To convert a regular shape or text object to a path, use Path → ⬛ Object to Path (**Shift+Ctrl+C**). Once an object is converted, the object loses any special knowledge associated with its previous existence. For example, the text font cannot be changed. But once an object is converted to a path, it can be modified in any arbitrary way, as shown in the section called *A Hiking Club Logo—An Exercise in Paths*.

Converting text to path produces a *Group* of paths with one path for each glyph. This allows the resulting characters to be manipulated easier as well as preserves any custom attributes (i.e., color) that individual glyphs might have had.

## Stroke to Path

A stroked path can be converted to a filled object consisting of two parallel sub-paths using Path → ✐ Stroke to Path (**Ctrl+Alt+C**). The path should have a non-zero thickness. The before and after objects look the same but have different structure and behavior. See the difference in the nodes in the figures that follow.

A stroked path consisting of three nodes.

A filled path made from the stroked path by using the *Stroke to Path* command. It consists of ten nodes.

The *Stroke to Path* command can be used to make a sets of parallel lines. Simply draw the path you desire, setting the width to the desired gap plus the desired final stroke width. Convert the stroke to path, remove the fill, and add the stroke paint. The line segments at the ends can be removed if desired by selecting each pair of end nodes and using the *Delete segment between two non-endpoint nodes* ⁝⁞ command in the *Node Tool-Tool Controls* (see next section). The *Path Offset* commands (for closed paths) or *Complex Strokes* are alternative ways of creating parallel lines.

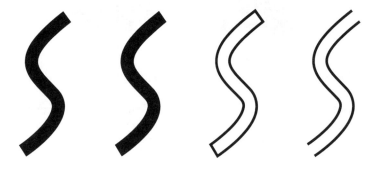

Creating parallel lines. From left to right: Single line, Filled path after *Stroke to Path* command, Fill removed — Stroke painted, Paths at ends removed.

The *Stroke to Path* command can also be used to make polygons with uniformly rounded corners, as shown below. The trick is to use a wide *Stroke* and set the *Join* style to *Round*.

From left to right: A simple triangle; the triangle with a wide *Stroke* (the *opacity* of the *Stroke* has been set to 50% to allow the triangle shape to be seen); the finished triangle with rounded corners after using the *Stroke to Path* command and after removing the inner triangle.

# Editing Paths

*Updated for v0.48.*

The primary means for editing paths is to use the *Node Tool* to modify one or more path nodes. A few exceptions are covered at the end of this section (simplifying, reversing, and offsetting paths) and in Chapter 11, *Tweak Tool*.

## Using the Node Tool

Paths are normally edited using the *Node Tool*. This flexible tool enables the addition, deletion, and movement of nodes. A *Sculpting* mode allows easy fine tuning of paths with many nodes. *Auto-smooth* nodes enable nodes to be moved while maintaining smooth curves.

Select the *Node Tool* by clicking on the ⬃ icon (**F2** or **n**) in the *Tool Box*. Then click on the path you wish to edit. All of the path's nodes will be shown. *New in 0.48:* Additional paths can be added (or removed) from the selection with **Shift+Left Mouse Click**.

When the *Node Tool* is over a path, the path's outline will briefly be displayed. The duration and color of this outline can be altered under the *Node* entry in the *Inkscape Preferences* dialog (double-click on the ⬃ in the *Tool Box* or call up the *Inkscape Preferences* dialog via File → ⬚ Inkscape Preferences... (**Shift+Ctrl+P**)). *New in v0.48:* If you are editing a complex drawing, you can improve performance by disabling updating of the path outline while dragging nodes. You can also disable updating the path itself while dragging nodes.

### Parallels in Node and Object Editing

Many of the things you can do with objects, you can do with nodes using the same methods. This is especially true for selecting and moving nodes. For example, the **Arrow** keys move selected objects by the *Nudge factor* when the *Select Tool* is active; they move selected nodes by the *Nudge factor* when the *Node Tool* is active. (The *Nudge factor* is a parameter that can be set in *Inkscape Preferences* dialog (File → ⬚ Inkscape Preferences... (**Shift+Ctrl+P**)) dialog under the *Steps* tab.) Knowing this should make learning to use the *Node Tool* quicker.

## Selecting Nodes

Nodes must be selected before they can be edited (with one exception, click-dragging a path will move the path by adjusting the handles on the nearest nodes). Selected nodes are indicated by a change in color as well as a slight enlargement in size. *New in v0.48:* Nodes from different paths can be selected at the same time if the paths are selected.

By default, the handles of the selected nodes are shown, as are the handles for adjacent nodes. If the handles get in the way of selecting nodes, they can be toggled off by clicking on the *Hide Handles* icon ⌐ in the *Tool Controls*. Clicking the icon a second time toggles the handles back on.

Nodes can be selected for editing a number of ways:

- **Left Mouse Click** on a node to select that node. A node turns red when the pointer hovers over it and it can be selected (or deselected). Note that a node can be selected and moved in one step by click-dragging on the node.

- **Left Mouse Click** on the path to select the nearest node on each side of the place where you clicked. The hand symbol is added to the pointer when hovering over a clickable path. Note that the path can be adjusted by click-dragging on the path. In this case, nearest nodes are not selected.

- **Left Mouse Drag** will select all nodes within the rubber-band box. The drag must not begin on a path unless the **Shift** is used. Using the **Shift** key allows the drag to begin on a path except over a node (broken in v0.48).

Nodes can be added (or removed) from the selection by holding down the **Shift** key while using one of the previous methods.

Nodes can also be added to or removed from the selection by hovering the cursor over a node and using the **Mouse Wheel**, moving "up" to add nodes and "down" to remove nodes. The **Page Up** and **Page Down** keys can be used in place of the **Mouse Wheel** (broken on v0.48, fixed in v0.48.1). This selection technique is especially useful in conjunction with *node sculpting*.

Two modes are possible: The default mode adds nodes based on the *spatial* distance from the cursor. If the **Ctrl** key is held down, the nodes are selected based on the *linear* distance measured *along the path* (swapped in v0.48, fixed in v0.48.1). In this latter case, only nodes in the same sub-path can be selected.

**Tab** selects the *next* node in a path if one is already selected. This is usually the adjacent node in the direction the path was drawn. If no node is selected, it will select the first node. **Shift+Tab** will select the *previous* node in a path. **Ctrl+A** selects *all* nodes in a selected path. **!** inverts the node selection for any sub-path with at least one node selected. **Alt+!** inverts the node selection for the entire path (or paths).

# Editing Nodes with the Mouse

The mouse can be used to move nodes and handles by dragging them. It can also be used to alter the shape of a path between two nodes by dragging the path. And finally, nodes can be inserted anywhere along a path by double-clicking the path or by clicking the path while holding down the **Ctrl+Alt** keys.

## Nodes

- **Left Mouse Drag**: Move selected nodes: If the pointer starts over a selected node, all selected nodes will move. If the pointer starts over an unselected node, that node will be selected and moved.

- **Ctrl+Left Mouse Drag**: Move selected nodes in either the horizontal or vertical direction.

- **Ctrl+Alt+Left Mouse Drag**: Move selected nodes along a line collinear with a node handle or to its perpendicular (passing through the node). The handles used are those belonging to the node where the pointer begins the drag.

- **Shift+Left Mouse Drag**: Temporarily disable snapping nodes to the *Grid* or to *Guide Lines* (if snapping of nodes enabled). Broken in v0.48, fixed in v0.48.1.

- **Left Mouse Drag+Space**: While dragging, drop an unlinked copy of the nodes. The copy is of the entire path even if only a few nodes are selected. Broken on v0.48.

## Handles

A handle becomes active when the mouse hovers over its control point. The control point will turn red. The **Shift**, **Ctrl**, and **Alt** keys can be used in combination for the options listed below.

- **Left Mouse Drag**: Move handle.

- **Shift+Left Mouse Drag**: Rotate both handles of a node together (useful for corner nodes).

- **Ctrl+Left Mouse Drag**: Snap handle to either a multiple of the *Rotation snap angle* (15 degrees by default), a line collinear with or orthogonal to the original handle position, a line collinear with the opposite handle (if it exists), or a line collinear with the opposite straight line segment (if it exists).

- **Alt+Left Mouse Drag**: Allow only angle and not length to change as handle is dragged.

## Transforms

*New in v0.48.*

A group of selected nodes can be transformed exactly like an object. Clicking on the ⨉ icon in the *Node Tool-Tool Controls* (or checking/unchecking *Show Transform Handles* from drop-down menu if icon not displayed) toggles on and off transformation handles that have the same functions as described in the section called *Transforms with the Mouse* in Chapter 5, *Positioning and Transforming*. **Shift+H** toggles between Scaling and Rotating/Skewing modes (this does not work with the *Select Tool*).

# Editing Nodes with the Keyboard

This section covers using the keyboard to move nodes and to adjust their handles. The keyboard can also be used to add and delete nodes, change the type of node, and to join or break paths. For these latter uses, see the keyboard shortcuts in the following section on the *Node Tool-Tool Controls*.

In this section, **Left-** and **Right-** applied to the **Ctrl** and **Alt** modifying keys refers to the keys on the left and right side of the **Space** bar. Using a left modifying key causes the left handle of a node to be modified; using a right modifying key modifies the rightmost handle. The definition of which handle is left or right is not always completely obvious as when one handle is directly above the other or when the leftmost handle is moved to the right of the former rightmost handle.

## Multinode Operations

The scaling and rotating operations described below are different if one node is selected as compared to two or more nodes. If two or more nodes are selected, the nodes act like an object and scale or rotate around the center of the selection, as described in the section called *Transforms with the Keyboard* in Chapter 5, *Positioning and Transforming*. If the mouse is over a node, then that node is used as the center of rotation. It is also possible to flip the nodes horizontally and vertically by using keyboard shortcuts.

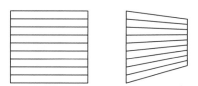

An example of editing multiple nodes. The rectangles on the right are formed by one path. By selecting all the nodes on the right side of the path and using the normal transformation commands a perspective effect can be achieved. Use < to move the nodes closer together and the **Arrow** keys to move the nodes to the left and up.

## Translations

Same as for translating objects.

- **Arrow**: Move selected nodes by the *Nudge factor* (2 *SVG* pixels by default).

- **Shift+Arrow**: Move selected nodes by ten times the *Nudge factor*.

- **Alt+Arrow**: Move selected nodes one *Screen pixel*.

- **Alt+Shift+Arrow**: Move selected nodes ten *Screen pixels*.

## Scaling Handles

Scaling applies to the the node handles and is not directly mappable to scaling objects. These items only apply when *one* node is selected.

- **.** or **>**: Expand handles on both sides of selected node by *Scale step* (2 *SVG* pixels by default).

- **,** or **<**: Shorten handles on both sides of selected node by *Scale step* (2 *SVG* pixels by default).

- **Left-Ctrl+.** , **Left-Ctrl+>** , **Right-Ctrl+.** , **Right-Ctrl+>** : Expand handle on one side of selected node by *Scale step*. **Left-Ctrl** selects the leftmost handle while **Right-Ctrl** selects the rightmost handle.

- **Left-Ctrl+,** , **Left-Ctrl+<** , **Right-Ctrl+,** , **Right-Ctrl+<** : Shorten handles on one side of selected nodes by *Scale step*. See above for usage of Left versus Right **Ctrl** keys.

- **Left-Alt+.** , **Left-Alt+>** , **Right-Alt+.** , **Right-Alt+>** : Expand handle on one side of selected node by one *Screen pixel*. See above for usage of Left versus Right **Alt** keys.

- **Left-Alt+,** , **Left-Alt+<** , **Right-Alt+,** , **Right-Alt+<** : Shorten handle on one side of selected node by one *Screen pixel*. See above for usage of Left versus Right **Alt** keys.

## Rotating Handles

Rotating applies to the the node handles and is not directly mappable to rotating objects. These items only apply when *one* node is selected.

- **[** : Rotate handles of selected node counterclockwise by the *Rotation snap angle* (15 degrees by default).

- **]** : Rotate handles of selected node clockwise by the *Rotation snap angle* (15 degrees by default).

- **Left-Ctrl+[, Right-Ctrl+[**: Rotate handle on one side of selected node counterclockwise by the *Rotation snap angle*. **Left-Ctrl** selects the leftmost handle while **Right-Ctrl** selects the rightmost handle, as described earlier. Only works with corner nodes.

- **Left-Ctrl+], Right-Ctrl+]**: Rotate handle on one side of selected node clockwise by the *Rotation snap angle*. See above for usage of Left versus Right **Ctrl** keys. Only works with corner nodes.

- **Left-Alt+[, Right-Alt+[**: Rotate handle on one side of selected node counterclockwise by one *Screen pixel*. See above for usage of Left versus Right **Alt** keys. Only works with corner nodes.

- **Left-Alt+], Right-Alt+]**: Rotate handle on one side of selected node clockwise by one *Screen pixel*. See above for usage of Left versus Right **Alt** keys. Only works with corner nodes.

# Using the Node Tool-Tool Controls

The *Node Tool-Tool Controls* provides an easy way to access many of the methods of editing nodes.

The *Node Tool-Tool Controls*.

- ⯊ (**Insert**): Insert new nodes into selected segments. (Note: Clicking on the path will select the nearest node on both sides of the point where the path was clicked. Double-clicking on the path or clicking the path once using the **Ctrl**+**Alt** keys will also insert a node, in this case under the pointer. Inkscape will try to add the node without changing the shape of the path by adjusting the handles of the nodes adjacent to the new node.)

- ⚏ (**Backspace**, **Delete**, or **Ctrl**+**Alt**+**Left Mouse Click**): Delete selected nodes. Inkscape will attempt to preserve the shape of the path when nodes are removed by adjusting the handles of adjacent nodes. If you wish to remove a node and *not* change the handles of adjacent nodes use **Ctrl**+**Backspace** or **Ctrl**+**Delete**.

- ⚎ (**Shift**+**J**): Join (merge) selected endnodes. Normally the merged node is placed at the midpoint between the end nodes. With the keyboard shortcut, hovering the mouse over one of the end nodes will result in the merged node being placed at the position of that end node. *New in v0.48:* If more than two end nodes are selected, pairs of end nodes will be merged, starting with the end nodes closest to each other until either zero or one end nodes are selected. If zero or one end node is selected at the start, then any adjacent stretches of selected nodes (including non-end nodes), will be merged into one node.

- ⚏ (**Shift**+**B**): Break path at selected nodes. Each selected node is converted into two end nodes.

- ⚎ : Join selected endnodes with a new segment. *New in v0.48:* If more than two end nodes are selected, pairs of end nodes will be joined with a segment, starting with the end nodes closest to each other until either zero or one end nodes are selected. If zero or one end node is selected at the start, then any adjacent stretches of selected nodes (including non-end nodes), will have their middle nodes removed, leaving one segment between outermost selected nodes.

- ⚎ : Delete segment between two non-endpoint nodes.

- ⋎ (**Shift**+**C**): Make selected nodes corner (or cusp). If the nodes are already cusp, both handles are retracted.

- ⌣ (**Shift**+**S**): Make selected nodes smooth. When the keyboard shortcut is used, placing the mouse over a handle will preserve the position of that handle, rotating the partner handle, if extended, to be collinear. If the partner handle is not extended, the partner handle will be extended so that it is collinear and of the same length as the preserved handle. If the node is next to one straight line segment (the other segment being curved) and the opposite handle is not collinear with the segment, the keyboard shortcut will rotate it to be collinear, extending the handle if necessary. A second application will extend out the second handle.

- ⌣ (**Shift**+**Y**): Make selected nodes symmetric (and smooth).

- ⌣ (**Shift**+**A**): Make selected nodes *auto-smooth* nodes.

- ⟋ (**Shift**+**L**): Make selected segments (straight) lines. One or more segments must be selected (by selecting nodes on both ends of the segment). Handles that are extended are retracted.

- ⟋ (**Shift**+**U**): Make selected segments curves. One or more segments must be selected. Segments remain straight lines but handles are extended that can be used to change the curvature.

- ⬚ (**Shift**+**Ctrl**+**C**): Convert selected object(s) to path(s).

- ✦ (**Ctrl**+**Alt**+**C**): Convert selected object's stroke to paths.

- Entry box for *x* coordinate of selected nodes.

- Entry box for *y* coordinate of selected nodes.

- Units for *x* and *y* coordinates.

- ⟋ Enable editing of a clip path. Path shown in green by default. *New in v0.48:* The clip path and object can be edited at the same time. (This only works if the clip path is an actual path and not a shape.) See the section called *Clipping* for more details.

- ✐ Enable editing of a mask path. Path shown in blue by default. *New in v0.48:* The mask path and object can be edited at the same time. (This only works if the mask path is an actual path and not a shape.) See the section called *Masking* for more details.

- ⚙: Toggle through parameter list for an *LPE*.

- ⚲ : Toggle on/off display of handles.

- ⵔ Show outline of path. Useful if part of the path is clipped or masked (green path by default), or if an *LPE* is applied to the path (red path by default).

## Editing Nodes with the Align and Distribute Dialog

The *Align and Distribute* dialog (Object → ⧉ Align and Distribute... (**Shift+Ctrl+A**)) has special commands for editing nodes when the *Node Tool* is in use.

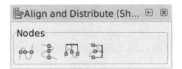

*Align and Distribute* dialog when *Node Tool* is active.

The commands will align or distribute selected nodes and can be useful to evenly place markers on a straight line (as shown in the figure below).

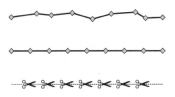

A path composed of nodes connected by straight line segments as drawn (top), aligned and distributed (middle), and with scissor markers (bottom). (*Markers* can be added by using the *Stroke style* tab of the *Fill and Stroke* dialog (Object → ⧉ Fill and Stroke... (**Shift+Ctrl+F**)). See the section called *Markers* in Chapter 10, *Attributes*.

The commands available are:

- ⤢ Align selected nodes along a horizontal line.

- ⤡ Align selected nodes along a vertical line.

- ⤤ Distribute selected nodes horizontally.

- ⤥ Distribute selected nodes vertically.

## Auto-Smooth Nodes

An *auto-smooth* node is a special node that will automatically adjust to maintain a smooth path when it or one of its neighboring nodes are moved. To create *auto-smooth* nodes, select the nodes and either use the keyboard shortcut **Shift**+**A** or click on the ⌣ in the *Tool Controls*. *Auto-smooth* nodes revert to normal smooth nodes if their handles are explicitly adjusted or if the path is dragged on either side of the node.

A demonstration of using *auto-smooth* nodes. From left to right: A path with *corner* nodes. The path after converting the nodes to *auto-smooth*. The path after moving the two lower nodes.

*Auto-smooth* nodes work by adjustments to the length and direction of the node's handles. The length of the handles are kept about one-third of the distance to the neighboring nodes, and the change in direction is a function of the relative position of the neighboring nodes.

## Sculpting Nodes

The *Sculpting* mode of the *Node Tool* allows one to easily manipulate a complex path, adjusting multiple nodes at the same time. The basic use is to select a group of nodes and then drag one of the selected nodes with the mouse while holding down the **Alt** key. Only the dragged node moves the full amount. The selected nodes at the end remain fixed, and all the other selected nodes will move a distance that is a function of how far they are from the dragged node. The function takes the form of a *Bell Curve* distribution. This is best illustrated by the following diagram.

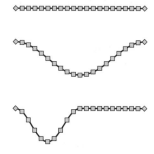

Adjusting a group of nodes using the *Sculpting* mode. Top: A straight line with many nodes. Middle: The line after selecting all nodes and dragging the middlemost node with the mouse while holding down the **Alt** key. Bottom: The line after selecting only the leftmost nodes and dragging the center of the selected nodes down while holding down the **Alt** key.

As usual with the *Node Tool*, only paths may be sculpted. Any other objects must be converted to a path first. In the following illustration, a star has been converted to a path and then the innermost nodes were selected and one was dragged.

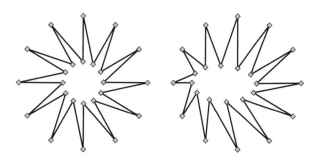

Sculpting a star. Left: A star converted to a path. Right: After selecting the center nodes and dragging one node to the left while holding down the **Alt** key.

The uses of *Sculpting* are endless. One can easily manipulate text into interesting shapes. In the following example, the text is sculpted in two different ways.

Top: Regular text. Middle: Text converted to a path with additional nodes added. First the leftmost characters were selected and one of the middle nodes dragged upward. This was repeated twice for each three letter group on the right. Bottom: The same text as above, but this time the bottommost nodes of each letter were excluded from the selection.

With a tablet, pressure sensitivity can be used to control the extent to which neighbor points are dragged. Neighbor nodes will move farther if the pressure used is greater. The tablet input device must be enabled; see the *Calligraphy Tool* section. Broken in v0.48.

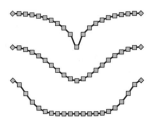

Sculpting of a straight line using the pressure sensitivity of a tablet. Applied pressure increases from top to bottom.

A number of different "profiles" are available. As of now, it is not possible to switch between the profiles using the GUI. You can switch by editing the *sculpting_profile* parameter in the file `preferences.xml` in your Inkscape profile directory. Broken in v0.48.

Available profiles for *Sculpting*. Top to bottom: 0, 1 (default), 2.

# Path Offset Commands

There are four commands grouped under this category, although one of them might be better thought of as a cloning tool. Each allows a path to be enlarged or reduced by moving each point perpendicular to a line tangent to the path at that point. A regular shape or text object is converted to a path automatically, except for the *Linked offset* command. The new paths are all closed, even if the original is open.

- Path → ✎ Inset (**Ctrl+( )** Inset path: Moves path inward by the *Inset/Outset* step (default 2 px).

- Path → ✎ Outset (**Ctrl+) )** Outset path: Moves path outward by the *Inset/Outset* step (default 2 px).

A star with an inset and an outset. The original star is red.

- Path → ✎ Dynamic Offset (**Ctrl+J**) Dynamic offset: Moves path inward or outward. A handle (viewable when *Node Tool* selected) controls the magnitude of the offset. The original path is stored so that further changes in the offset do not degrade the path. The original path is not editable after conversion. To edit, convert the dynamic offset path to a normal path with the Path → ⬚ Object to Path (**Shift+Ctrl+C**) command.

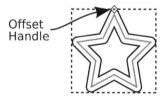

A star with both a dynamic inset and a dynamic outset. The original star is red. Note
that the shape of the outset star is different than in the simple outset example above.

- Path → ✎ Linked Offset (**Ctrl+Alt+J**) Linked offset: Makes a copy of a path that can then be enlarged or shrunk. A handle controls the magnitude of the offset. The original object is *not* converted to a path and remains editable, and the changes are reflected in linked copies. More than one link can be made.

A star with both a linked inset and a linked outset. The original star (red) was modified after the creation of the linked paths.

## Miscellaneous Path Commands

The commands have in common that they act on the entire path, and not on a subset of a path's nodes.

- Path → ⬚ Combine (**Ctrl+K**) Combine paths: Combine selected paths into a compound path. This will work for any set of paths regardless of how the paths are arranged in *Groups*.

- Path → ⬚ Break Apart (**Shift+Ctrl+K**) Break apart paths: Break selected compound path(s) into simple paths.

- Path → ⤺ Reverse (**Shift+R**) (keyboard shortcut only works with *Node Tool*): Reverse path: Reversing the direction of a path will affect things like the order in which nodes are selected by **Tab** and in the direction of *Markers* (e.g., arrows). *New in v0.48:* It is possible to display "harpoons" indicating path direction by selecting *Show path direction on outlines* in the *Inkscape Preferences* dialog. The outline must be visible (toggle on either by selecting *Always show outline* in the dialog or clicking the ⬚ icon in the *Tool Controls*).

- Path → ≈ Simplify (**Ctrl+L**) Simplify path: This command reduces the number of nodes in a path while keeping the shape of the path almost the same. The larger the selection, the more aggressive the simplification. The command may be repeated. If repeated within a set time period (0.5 seconds), the simplification also becomes more aggressive. The *Simplification threshold* can be changed under the *Misc* tab in the *Inkscape Preferences* dialog (File → ⬚ Inkscape Preferences... (**Shift+Ctrl+P**)).

# Path Operations

Inkscape has a number of commands to form new paths from two or more preexisting paths. The *z-order* (see the section called *Ordering Objects (Z-Order)*) of the paths is important. In all cases except for the *Cut Path* command, the *Fill and Stroke* of the new path is inherited from the *bottom* path. For some operations, the *top* path can be thought of as operating on the *bottom* path; that is, part of the *bottom* path remains and the *top* path is thrown away. This is explained in more detail for each operation that it applies to below. All commands are accessible under the *Path* menu.

Any open paths are, for the purpose of these commands, closed by a line between the path's end points. Shape objects and text objects are automatically converted to paths.

- ⬚ Union (**Ctrl++**): Union of one or more paths. One new path is created, containing all the areas of the original paths. A union of one path removes self-intersections, creating individual sub-paths for each section. Note that this is different from the *Path Combine* command where no nodes are lost or created.

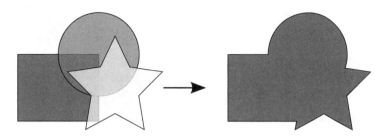

The path *Union* operation.

- ◌ Difference (**Ctrl**+-): Difference of two paths. The area of the top path is removed from the bottom path.

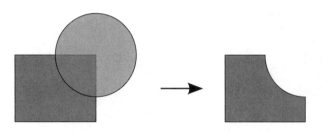

The path *Difference* operation.

- ◌ Intersection (**Ctrl**+*): Intersection of two or more paths. The new path encloses the common area of the original paths.

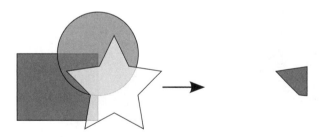

The path *Intersection* operation.

- ◌ Exclusion (**Ctrl**+^): Exclusion of two or more paths. One new path consisting of multiple sub-paths is created according to an *Even-Odd Fill* rule. Inkscape v0.46 and earlier allowed only two paths to be used.

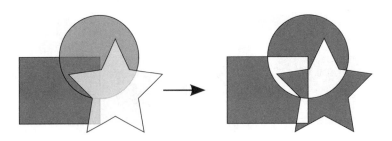

The path *Exclusion* operation.

- ⬚ Division (**Ctrl**+/): Division of two paths. The first path is split by the second path. Two or more new paths are created.

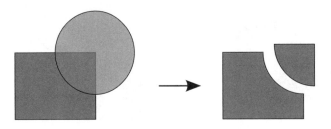

The path *Division* operation. The upper-right corner of the "After" illustration has been shifted to show the two new paths clearly.

- ⬚ Cut Path (**Ctrl**+**Alt**+/): Cutting by two paths. The first path is cut by the second path. Two or more new paths are created. The new paths do not have any *Fill*.

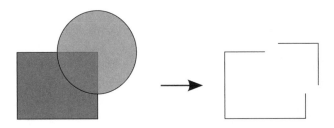

The path *Cut Path* operation. The path in the upper-right corner of the "After" illustration has been shifted to show the two new paths clearly.

# Chapter 8. Live Path Effects (LPEs)

*Live Path Effects*, or *LPEs* for short, is a system for applying some kind of effect to a path. Inkscape stores the original path data in the Inkscape *Name Space* so that it can be modified at a later time (it will not be displayed by other *SVG* renderers). If the original path is modified, the *LPE* will be regenerated. The resulting path is stored as a normal *SVG* path.

Inkscape includes a handful of *LPEs*. With a solid framework in place, it is planned to migrate most of the path effects found under the *Extensions* menu to *LPEs*. This has two advantages: The effects will be faster to render and the original path is stored for future editing. *LPEs* also work with *Groups* of paths. Regular *Shapes* are converted to paths automatically.

To use an *LPE*, select a path (the *skeleton* path), call up the *Path Effect Editor* dialog (Path → Path Effect Editor... (**Shift+Ctrl+7**)), select the desired effect from the drop-down menu in the dialog, and then click the *Add* button. Multiple effects can be chained (stacked) together. The order in which each effect is applied can be changed using the arrow icons. Each effect can be temporarily "turned off" by clicking on the 🐾 icon next to the effect name. This is handy if you want to edit the *skeleton* path (or a *Group* of *skeleton* paths).

*Path Effect Editor* dialog with a path selected.

When an object is selected that was generated by an *LPE* and the *Node Tool* is enabled, the original *skeleton* path nodes are displayed. In addition the path itself may be displayed in red. Visibility of the path is controlled by the ✎ icon located in the *Node Tool-Tool Controls*. This path can be edited like any other path.

Several of the effects require one or more additional *control* paths. In this case, the needed paths are automatically generated (straight green lines). To see these paths, either click on the node editing icon ( ↖ ) in the dialog or press **7** while the object is selected and the *Node Tool* is active. A *control* path is fully editable like any other path. The path can be replaced by another through pasting from the *clipboard* using the paste icon ( 📋 ) in the dialog. You may need to translate the *control* path (select all nodes then drag with the *Node Tool*). The path can also be copied to the *clipboard* by using the copy icon ( 📋 ) in the dialog.

An existing path can be used as a control path through linking. To create a link, first copy the path (Edit → 📋 Copy (**Ctrl+C**)) to the *clipboard* and then click the link icon ( 📇 ). Note that the linked path must be copied and not cut. Linking can be used with *Shapes* and Text without converting them to paths first.

*LPEs* are normally applied recursively to all objects in a *Group*. The *Bend* and *Deformation LPEs*, however, are applied to the whole *Group* once.

An *LPE* can be converted to a regular path(s) by using the Path → ⬚ Object to Path (**Shift+Ctrl+C**) command. An *LPE* can be removed using the Path → Remove Path Effect command. An *LPE* can be copied from one object to another using the Path → Paste Path Effect (**Ctrl+7**) command. To do so, first copy the object with the *LPE* you wish to paste using the Edit → ❧ Copy (**Ctrl+C**) command.

## Warning

The implementation of *LPEs* has many bugs, especially if removing effects from a path or chaining *LPEs*. Paths can be left with *LPE* cruft in their attributes and without a valid *SVG* path. You can always check objects with the *XML Editor* dialog. It may be useful to vacuum the file (File → ❧ Vacuum Defs) to remove unused *LPE* definitions. Save work often!

# Bend

This effect takes an existing path (*skeleton*) and allows one to "bend" it in a well-defined way via a *control* path. The *control* path is automatically created. The style of the bent path is taken from the style of the original path.

To apply the effect, with the source path selected, and using the *Node Tool* select the *Bend* option from the drop-down menu in the *Path Effect Editor* dialog. Click on the *Add* button. The path will turn red. A red path always corresponds to the original source or *skeleton* path. Next, click on the node icon ( ↖ ) in the *Path Effect Editor* dialog. A green, horizontal path will appear in place of the red path. This path controls the bending. It can be manipulated in all the ways that a regular path can be including adding new nodes and dragging the path.

The effect assumes that the *skeleton* path is orientated in the horizontal direction. If it is in the vertical orientation, one can check the *Original path is vertical* box. This distorts the aspect ratio. Restore the aspect ratio by checking the *Width in units of length* box. The size of the bent path can be changed by changing the size of the *control* path.

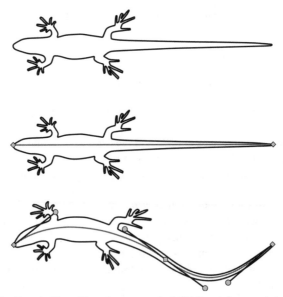

Demonstration of the *Bend* effect. Top: Source path. Middle: After applying the effect and enabling editing of the control path. Bottom: After adding a node and adjusting the control path.

The width of the bent path can be altered with the *Width* entry box.

# Construct Grid

This effect uses the first three nodes of a path to define a two dimension grid. The center node defines the origin, the first and third nodes define the direction and length of the two adjacent sides of the first cell. If a path has more than three nodes, the other nodes are ignored. One can select the number of cells in the two orthogonal directions.

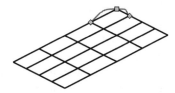

Demonstration of the *Construct Grid* effect. A three node path (red line) determines the grid. The *X* and *Y* sizes have been set to four.

# Envelope Deformation

This effect deforms a path by using four *control* paths, one for each side of the *bounding box*. Each *control* path can be edited individually by clicking on the corresponding ↖ icon. When editing of one *control* path is enabled, that path will be shown in bold green; the other *control* paths will be shown with thinner green lines in v0.47 (not shown in v0.48). Note that the when copying, pasting, or linking a *control* path, the *control* path is referenced from the bottom left corner of the page.

There are options to enabling and disabling the top and bottom paths separately from the left and right paths.

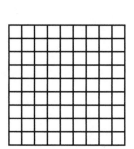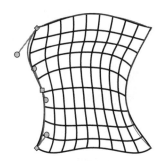

Demonstration of the *Envelope Deformation* effect. Left: A grid created with the *Construct Grid* LPE. Middle: The grid deformed by adding the *Envelope Deformation* LPE. The top *control* path has been altered and the left and right *control* paths have been disabled. Right: The grid deformed by *control* paths on the top, left, and right. The left *control* path is shown being edited.

# Gears

This effect draws a series of intermeshed gears. It is more of a toy effect, designed to demonstrate the possibilities of *LPEs*. The *Gear* extension can also be used to draw gears with a bit more control.

The effect uses the nodes of a path to determine how the gears are drawn. At least three nodes are needed to specify the first gear. Additional gears require one additional node each. Some nodes may be skipped if they would result in impractical gears.

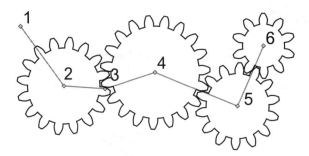

An example of using the *Gear* LPE. The original path is shown in red. Point 1 defines the orientation of the first gear. Point 2 defines the center of the first gear. Point 3 defines the radius of the first gear. Points 4, 5, and 6 determine the centers of additional gears. The radius of the second gear is determined by subtracting the radius of the first gear from the distance between the centers of the first and second gears.

Two parameters are available: *Teeth* determines the number of teeth on the first gear. *Phi* determines the *Pressure Angle* of the gears. For real gears the *Pressure Angle* is typically 14.5, 20, or 25 degrees. Note: The default angle is 5 degrees, not a very realistic value.

# Hatches (Rough)

This effect fills the area inside a path with a squiggly line that simulates quick, hand-drawn shading. Shapes are automatically converted to paths. Note: the squiggly line is constructed like a calligraphic stroke, that is by two almost parallel lines. This allows for variations in line thickness. You may get better results by adding a *Fill* and removing the *Stroke* (not automatically done by the effect). Warning: this effect appears to make heavy demands on the CPU.

There are a great many options to control the way the hatches are drawn. The spacing, direction, and amount of *bend* are determined by on-canvas nodes, visible when the *Node Tool* is in use. The other options are controlled in the *Path Effect Editor* dialog. Many of the options have a random factor. One can "re-roll the dice" by clicking on the *randomize* ( ⚅ ) icon.

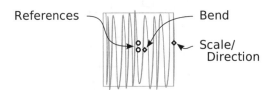

Definition of the nodes used to control the spacing, direction, and amount of bend of the hatches. The circle nodes are reference points. The distance and direction the diamond nodes are displaced from the circle nodes determines the applicable parameters.

Left: Default hatching for the shown rectangle. Middle: After adjusting the *Bend* diamond node. Right: After adjusting the spacing and direction diamond node.

Parameters found in the dialog (see also figure below):

• Frequency randomness: Variation of distance between hatches in percent.

- Growth: The change in spacing between wiggles from right to left. The last wiggle will be about a factor of the *Growth* term times wider than the first wiggle.

- Bend hatches: Determines if the hatches should be bent.

- Magnitude jitter: 1st side: Magnitude of randomness of hatch bottom extents (in pixels).

- Magnitude jitter: 2nd side: Magnitude of randomness of hatch top extents (in pixels).

- Parallelism jitter: 1st side: Magnitude of randomness of hatch bottom positions left to right (in pixels).

- Parallelism jitter: 2nd side: Magnitude of randomness of hatch top positions left to right (in pixels).

- Half-turns smoothness: 1st side, in: How straight or curved are the right side of the hatch bottoms (zero is straight).

- Half-turns smoothness: 1st side, out: How straight or curved are the left side of the hatch bottoms (zero is straight).

- Half-turns smoothness: 2nd side, in: How straight or curved are the left side of the hatch tops (zero is straight).

- Half-turns smoothness: 2nd side, out: How straight or curved are the right side of the hatch tops (zero is straight).

- Variance: 1st side: Variation in how curved are the hatch bottoms.

- Variance: 2nd side: Variation in how curved are the hatch tops.

- Generate thick/thin path: Should the path vary in thickness?

- Thickness: at 1st side: The vertical thickness of the hatch bottom (in pixels).

- Thickness: at 2nd side: The vertical thickness of the hatch top (in pixels).

- Thickness: from 2nd to 1st side: The horizontal thickness of the hatch going from top to bottom (in pixels).

- Thickness: from 1st to 2nd side: The horizontal thickness of the hatch going from bottom to top (in pixels).

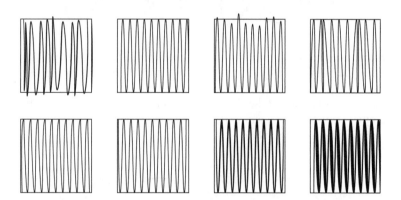

Demonstration of the different *Hatches* effect parameters. Except as noted, all options are removed or set to their neutral values. Top row, from left to right: Default settings; All options/setting removed; Magnitude jitter: 2nd side set to 20; Parallelism jitter: 2nd side set to 10. Bottom row, from left to right: Half turns smoothness 2nd side: in set to 0, out set to 2; Variance 2nd side set to 10 (Bug? Doesn't seem to do anything.); Thickness: at 2nd side set to 10. Thickness: from 1st to 2nd side set to 5.

# Interpolate Sub-Paths

This effect creates additional paths by interpolating between two sub-paths. A *Trajectory* (*control*) path dictates where the additional paths are placed. Note: Only the first and last sub-paths are used.

The total number of paths (including the two sub-paths) can be specified by the *Steps* parameter. An additional option *Equidistant spacing* determines if the nodes of the *Trajectory* path are used in the interpolation. If the option *Equidistant spacing* is checked, the additional paths are spaced evenly along the *Trajectory* path. If it is not checked, the additional paths are divided between the intermediate nodes (see following figure).

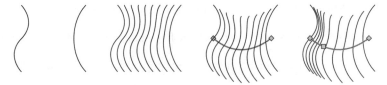

From left to right: Two sub-paths of the same path. After adding the Interpolated Sub-Paths effect with 10 *Steps*. After bending the *Trajectory* path by dragging the
middle down. After adding an intermediate node to the *Trajectory* on the left side.

# Knot

This effect attempts to turn a path into a knot. That is, at each point where the path crosses itself, part of the path is hidden so it appears that that part is below the other part. As one follows the path, the effect attempts to alternate between going above and below.

Left: A path created by the *Parametric Curves* extension. Right: After applying the *Knot*
LPE. (Note: the path was closed by merging the first and last nodes before applying the LPE.)

The gap (length of hidden path) is the sum of the: *Fixed width* (in terms of *stroke width* if the *In units of stroke width* box is checked or pixels otherwise), the stroke width (if the *Stroke width* box is checked), and the crossing stroke width (if the *Crossing path stroke width* box is checked).

Two circular paths in a *Group*. From left to right: Default values. Unchecking *In units of stroke width*. Unchecking *In units of stroke width* and *Stroke width*. Unchecking *In unit of stroke width* and *Crossing path stroke width*.

You can set which path crosses the other or remove the gap completely by using the *Switcher*. The *Switcher* is visible when the *Node Tool* is active. It consists of a circular arrow centered around the crossing point. Clicking on the diamond node at the crossing point toggles between the three states. To change another crossing, drag the diamond node to that crossing; the *Switcher* will follow. Note: as of now, the *Switcher* does not work when paths are in a *Group*.

A path showing the *Switcher* in its three different states.

# Pattern Along Path (LPE)

This effect puts one or more copies of one path (*pattern*) along a second, *control* or *skeleton* path. The resulting object takes the attributes (*Fill*, etc.) of the *skeleton* path.

This *LPE* duplicates much of the functionality of the *Pattern along Path* extension. The advantage of using the *LPE* version is that both the pattern and the *skeleton* path can be edited at a later time. The disadvantages are that only paths can be used for the pattern and that there are fewer options. One subtle difference is that the *LPE* version will bend straight lines drawn with two nodes while the extension version leaves them straight.

 **Note**

Only a path can be used as a pattern. Many objects such as *Rectangles*, *Ellipses* and text must first be converted to a path (Path → ⬚ Object to Path (**Shift+Ctrl+C**)).

To put a pattern on a path:

1. **Copy the pattern:** Select the pattern and copy it to the *clipboard* (Edit → ▓ Copy (**Ctrl+C**)). The pattern must be a single path.

2. **Select the skeleton path:** Only one can be selected.

3. **Apply the effect to skeleton path:** In the *Path Effect Editor* dialog, select *Pattern Along Path* and click on the *Add* button.

4. **Paste pattern:** Click on the *Paste* ( 📋 ) icon in dialog.

The *bounding box* of the pattern is used for placing the pattern along the path, with the *bounding box* of one pattern copy touching the *bounding box* of the next copy (if no additional spacing is specified).

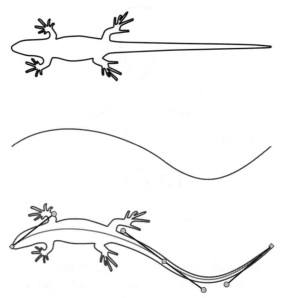

Demonstration of the *Pattern Along Path* effect. Top: Pattern path. Middle: Skeleton
or control path. Bottom: After pasting pattern to skeleton path and enabling editing of
the skeleton path. Note that the created object takes the attributes of the skeleton path.

To edit the pattern, click on the node editing icon ( ) in the dialog. A temporary green copy of the pattern will appear
at the pattern's original location. Any edit to this copy will be reflected in the final object.

To edit the *skeleton* path, select the object with the *Node Tool*. A temporary red copy of the *skeleton* path will appear.
This can be edited as any other path.

A different pattern can be applied to the *skeleton* path by copying the pattern to the *clipboard* ((Edit → Cut (**Ctrl+X**)
or Edit → Copy (**Ctrl+C**)) and then clicking on the *Paste* ( ) button in the dialog.

A copy of the original pattern can be placed on the *clipboard* by clicking on the *Copy* ( ) button in the dialog. The
copy will have all attributes unset.

The *Pattern copies* drop-down menu has options to stretch the pattern to the path length and/or to put multiple copies
along the *skeleton* path.

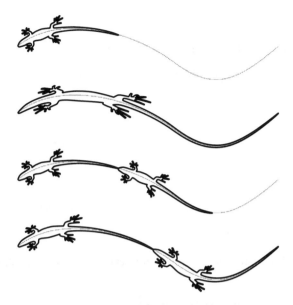

A small lizard is put on a path with *Pattern copies* set to, from top
to bottom: *Single*; *Single, stretched*; *Repeated*; *Repeated, stretched*.

The *LPE* assumes that the pattern is drawn horizontally. This can be changed to vertical by checking the *Pattern is vertical* box.

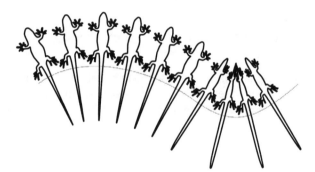

A small lizard is put on a path with the *Pattern is vertical* box checked.

You can specify the spacing between each copy of the pattern with the *Spacing* parameter. You can also specify a transverse (*Normal offset*) and/or a tangential (*Tangential offset*) for each copy. The spacing and offsets are specified in pixels by default. Checking the *Offsets in units of pattern size* will use units of the pattern size (width for spacing and transverse offset, height for tangential offset).

From left to right: A blue square pattern is placed along the the path indicated by the arrowed
line. *Spacing* set to 10 pixels. *Normal offset* set to 10 pixels. *Tangential offset* set to 10 pixels.

One last option, *Fuse nearby ends*, joins copies of the pattern into a continuous path. It is similar to using the *Join selected endnodes* ( ⁙ ) option of the *Node Tool* to connect sub-paths.

# Ruler

This effect turns a path into a ruler. The following options are available:

- Unit. All the following options are based on this unit.

- Mark distance: Distance between adjacent ticks.

- Major length: Length of major ticks.

- Minor length: Length of minor ticks.

- Major steps: Number of intervals between major ticks.

- Shift marks by: The number of intervals the marks are shift. Affects the placement of major ticks.

- Offset: Offset of first tick from path start.

- Mark direction: On which side of path ticks are drawn, referenced from path direction. Choosing *Both* places ticks on both sides of path.

- Border marks: Adds major ticks at start and/or end of path.

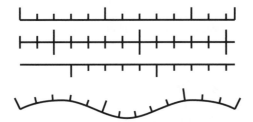

The *Ruler* LPE applied to a number of paths. Top to bottom: Default parameters. *Shift marks by* set to 2, *Mark direction* set to *Both*, *Border marks* set to *None*. *Offset* set to 60 px, *Mark direction* set to *Right*, *Border marks* set to *None*. Default parameters on curved path.

# Sketch

This effect simulates sketching a path. There are two different kinds of lines drawn: The first are *Strokes* that follow the curvature of the path. The second are *Construction lines* that are straight and tangent to the path.

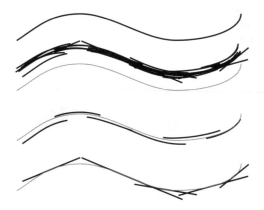

Top to bottom: The *skeleton* path. The resulting path when the Sketch effect is applied with default values. After setting *Strokes* to 1 and *Construction lines* to 0. After setting *Strokes* to 0 and *Construction lines* to 5.

The following parameters are available for *Strokes*:

- Strokes: the average number of strokes along any point on the line (not counting overlaps).

- Max stroke length: maximum stroke length in pixels.

- Stroke length variation: random variation in stroke length in units of *Max stroke length*.

- Max. overlap: maximum amount strokes overlap in units of *Max stroke length*.

- Overlap variation: random variation in stroke overlap relative to *Max. overlap*.

- Max. end tolerance: random variation in position of outermost stroke ends relative to *Max stroke length*. A non-zero value effectively shortens the length of the sketched path relative to the original path.

- Average offset: average displacement of strokes from *skeleton* path in pixels. Strokes follow a uniform distribution between twice this distance on either side of the *skeleton* path.

- Max. tremble: maximum fluctuation of a stroke from its nominal position.

- Tremble frequency: roughly the number of intermediate nodes in a stroke used to create the tremble.

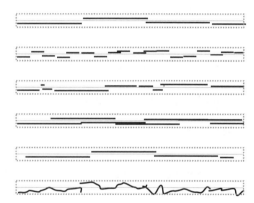

Stroke parameters. All figures with *Strokes* set to 1, *Max stroke length* set to 100.00, and *Average offset* set to 5. All other parameters are set to zero unless otherwise noted. The dashed box shows the length of the *skeleton* path and the maximum offsets (twice *Average offset*). From top to bottom: All parameters as above. *Max stroke length* set to 20. *Stroke length variation* set to 1.00. *Max. overlap* set to 0.50. *Max. end tolerance* set to 0.20; note that the ends are only shortened and never lengthened. *Max. tremble* set to 10.00 and *Tremble frequency* set to 10.00.

The following parameters are available for *Construction lines*:

- Construction lines: number of lines to draw.

- Placement randomness: How lines should be distributed: 0.0 for even spacing, 1.0 for maximum randomness.

- Scale: factor correlating curvature to length of lines. The effect attempts to keep the distance at the end of the lines equal distance from the path (given smooth curvature).

- Max. length: maximum length of construction lines. Lines will be shorter if the *Scale* factor requires them to be so that their ends are not too far from curve.

- Length variation: random variation on line lengths. Always smaller.

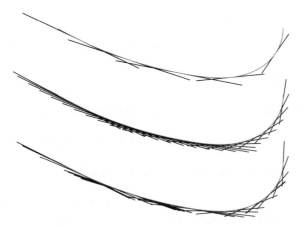

Construction line parameters. From top to bottom: *Construction lines* set to 5, *Placement randomness* and *Variation length* set to 0.00, *Scale* set to 10.00, and *Maximum length* set to 100.00. The same as above but *Construction lines* set to 20. The same as above but *Placement randomness* set to 1.00 and *Length variation* set to 0.30.

# Spiro Spline

This effect turns a series of nodes into a silky-smooth path defined entirely by the position of the nodes. The method was devised by Raph Levien for use in designing fonts. *Spiro* [http://www.levien.com/spiro/] curves have splines that are joined together smoothly.

The *Spiro Spline LPE* can be enabled two different ways. The first is to use the *Path Effect Editor* dialog like for any other *LPE*. The second is to enable the *Spiro* path option in the *Pencil Tool* or *Bezier Tool Tool Controls* by selecting the ∾ icon. Note that the *Spiro* path will not be shown until the *skeleton* path is completed. Using the *Spiro Spline LPE* is probably not so useful with the *Pencil Tool* unless *Smoothing* is set to a moderate value.

The *Spiro Spline LPE* uses the following node types:

- Smooth node: curve smooth at node and rate of curvature continuous. This is indicated by either a square or diamond node with both handles collinear. To convert a node to a smooth node, select it and either click on the ⌣ icon or use **Shift+S**.

- Corner node: connects two different curved splines at a corner. This is indicated by a node with either one or both handles being retracted or the handles being noncollinear. To convert a node to a corner node either retract a handle (**Ctrl+Left mouse click** on handle), or change to a corner (diamond) node ( ⌄ , **Shift+C**) and move one or retract one of the handles so the handles are no longer collinear (using **Shift+C** a second time will retract both handles).

- Tangent node (also called a left or right node): connects a straight line segment smoothly to a curve. To make a tangent node, ensure one side of the node consists of a straight line (select both nodes on either side of the segment and either click on the ⟋ icon or use (**Shift+L**).

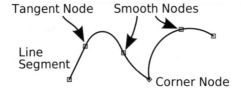

A path composed of a line and two *Spiro* splines (separated by a *Corner* node).

Visualization of the *skeleton* path is probably not very useful. It can be toggled off by clicking on the ✐ icon in the *Tool Controls*. It is sometimes useful to see the node handles. They can be toggled on by clicking on the ⟋ icon. They are only shown for selected nodes and nodes adjacent to selected nodes. Bug: If the handles are not visible when they should be, toggle off, then back on the node handles.

The same path as in the previous figure, but showing the *skeleton* path with node handles. Note that what is important for a *Spiro* spline is the collinearity of the handles with each other (smooth vs. corner node) or with a line segment (corner vs. tangent node). The actual directions of the handles for a smooth or corner node are irrelevant.

The algorithm for generating *Spiro* splines is not particularly robust and sometimes yields wild curves. You can always return to a sane point by undoing the edit that caused the curves to go berserk.

For the technically inclined, in a Spiro curve, splines are joined such that the curve is smooth and the curvature is continuous. Although the *Spiro* package allows for *G4* nodes (continuous to the fourth derivative), Inkscape uses only *G2* nodes (continuous to the second derivative).

*Spiro Spline* paths are also implemented in the font editing program *FontForge* [http://fontforge.sourceforge.net/editspiro.html]. Unfortunately, there is currently no way to share *Spiro Spline* paths between the two without first converting to Bezier splines.

# Stitch Sub-Paths

This effect draws a series of *Stroke paths* between points on sub-paths. Some of the things it is useful for are drawing hatched shading and for drawing hair.

To stitch a sub-path:

1. **Draw the sub-paths:** Draw two simple paths. Combine into a compound path consisting of two sub-paths using Path → 🔗 Combine (**Ctrl+K**). The two sub-paths should be drawn in the same direction. If not, use the Path → ⇄ Reverse (**Shift+R**) command on one of the sub-paths (prior to combining) to reverse its direction.

2. **Apply the effect to compound path:** In the *Path Effect Editor* dialog, select *Stitch Sub-Paths* from the *Apply new effect* menu and click on the *Add* button.

3. **Adjust *Stroke path*:** Click on the node editing icon ( ↖ ) to edit the *Stroke path*.

 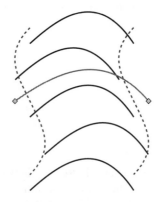

A basic example of using the *Stitch Sub-Paths* LPE. Left: A simple path was drawn and duplicated. The two paths were then combined into a compound path (Path → Combine (**Ctrl+K**)). The effect was then applied. The red lines are shown when the LPE object is selected with the *Node Tool* enabled. Right: The *Stroke path* (green) has been enabled via clicking on the node-editing icon ( ) and the path adjusted. The original sub-paths (not normally visible) are shown by blue-dashed lines. Note how the ends of the *Stroke path* are no longer on the original sub-paths. This is because Inkscape uses the center on the left and right of the *bounding box* to place the *Stroke path*.

The *Stitch Sub-Paths* effect can be used to create the hatchings typically used in engravings as shown in the following example. While the *Interpolate Extensions* could be used to created some of the shadings, it cannot create the horizontal shadings on the cylinder below (likewise, the *Stitch Sub-Paths* effect cannot easily create the precise circular hatching inside the cylinder).

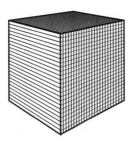 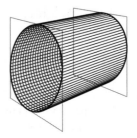

A simple example of using the effect for hatchings. Left: The *Box Tool* was used to draw a box. Then the *Bezier Tool* was used with snapping to draw paths on both sides of a box face. The paths were combined and the effect applied. For the right side of the box, the effect was used twice, once for the horizontal lines and once for the vertical lines. Right: Two ovals were drawn to fit in two opposite side of a box. The ovals were converted to paths and split into two sections. The left sections were used for the inside hatching and the right sections for the outside. The circular hatching inside the cylinder was done by using the *Interpolate* extension.

By varying both the sub-paths and the *Stroke path* quite complicated hatchings can be created. The hatchings can be clipped to limit their range. The *Tweak Tool* could also be used to refine the hatchings if the hatchings are converted to stroked paths (see Chapter 11, *Tweak Tool*).

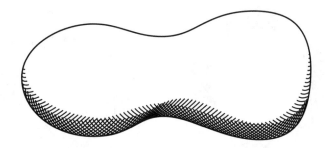

Hatching created by: 1. Copying the bottom half of the object's path. 2. Duplicating the copy with an offset to the upper left. 3. Applying the *Stitch Sub-Paths* LPE with 50 paths. 4. Adjusting the sub-paths and *Stroke path*. 5. Repeating with the duplicate offset to the upper right. 6. Grouping the hatchings and clipping with a copy of the original path.

The *Stroke Sub-Paths LPE* has options that add random shifts to the start and end of each stitching path. The "variance" options can be used to draw hair as shown below. Each variance has a dice icon ( 🎲 ) next to it which, if clicked, sets a new starting random number seed. This will change the random shifts but keep the average shift the same.

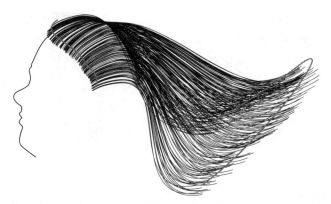

Drawing hair: The sub-paths are shown in red. The number of paths was set to 200 and the following variances were used: Start edge: 0.02, Start spacing: 0.10, End edge: 0.10, End spacing: 0.10.

Interesting geometric patterns can be created with this effect as shown next.

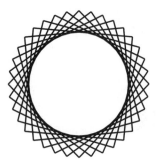

For these designs, a circle was converted to a path and then duplicated. The path copy was rotated and then the two paths combined into a compound path. Left: The duplicate path was rotated 45° and the *Number of paths* was set to 37 (the first and last path are on top of each other). Right: The duplicate path was rotated 150° and the *Number of paths* set to 25. The *Stroke path* was bent until the path ends joined new paths.

What if multiple sub-paths are used? Each sub-path will be connected to every other sub-path by the specified *Number of paths*. This can be used to created some interesting patterns.

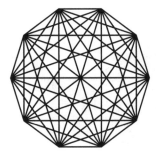

An example of using the multiple sub-paths. A decagon was drawn with the *Star Tool* tool. The decagon was converted to a path (Path → ⊡ Object to Path (**Shift+Ctrl+C**)). The path was broken into 10 sub-paths by using the *Node Tool* (select node, click on ⊹ in *Tool Controls*). Finally, the *Stitch Sub-Paths* LPE was applied. Left: *Number of paths* set to two. Right: *Number of paths* was set to three. Higher numbers yield rendering errors in Inkscape (but display correctly in Firefox 3 and Opera 9.26).

# VonKoch

This effect creates fractals. The most classic fractal is perhaps the Von Koch snowflake. An alternative to using this *LPE* is to use the *L-System* extension.

Applying this effect to a path creates two additional *control* paths: a *Reference segment* and a *Generating path*. The structure of the fractal is completely determined by these *control* paths. The first *generation* is created by placing copies of the *skeleton* path so that the *Reference segment* of each copy lies on top of one of the sub-path segments of the *Generating path*. Each additional generation is created in the same way, using the *Generating path* of each copy of the previous generation.

Left: A *skeleton* path. Center: After applying the *VonKoch* with default parameters. Right: Showing the default *Reference segment* (top line) and *Generating path* (bottom two lines).

When applying the *VonKoch LPE* to a path, the *Reference segment* is created so that it divides the *bounding box* vertically in half. The *Generating path* is initially composed of two single-segment sub-paths, each covering one-third of the lower edge of the *bounding box*. The *Reference segment* and the *Generating path* can be edited just like normal paths by clicking on the ⌢ icon in the *Reference segment* or *Generating path* lines of the *LPE* dialog.

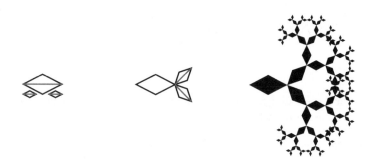

Left: A diamond path with the *VonKoch* LPE applied. The default *control* paths are shown. Center: After moving the *Generating path*s. Right: After increasing the number of generations to six and changing the *Fill* and *Stroke*.

If each sub-path of the *Generating path* consists of a single segment, then each copy of the *skeleton* path is simply scaled and/or rotated. With multiple segments, one can skew each copy. The first path segment controls scaling in the orthogonal direction to the *Reference segment* and it controls skewing. The second path segment is matched to the *Reference segment*. The use of the first segment can be disabled by checking the *Use uniform transforms only* box.

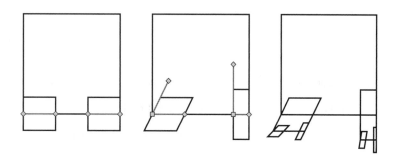

Left: A square path with the *VonKoch* LPE applied. The default *control* paths are shown. Center: After editing the *Generating path* to add a second path segment to each sub-path. Right: After increasing the number of generations to two.

Like all *LPEs*, this one can also be applied to groups.

Left: A fourth generation Sierpinski triangle (triangle with three *Generating paths*).
Right: The same *VonKoch* LPE applied to a group consisting of a triangle and circle.

Here is a short tutorial to create one side of a Von Koch snowflake:

1. Create a regular six-pointed star using the *Star Tool* (set *Spoke ratio* to 0.577).

2. Convert star to a path (Path → ⬚ Object to Path (**Shift+Ctrl+C**)); remove nodes as shown in figure below (use
   ⬚ and ⬚ from the *Node Tool-Tool Controls*).

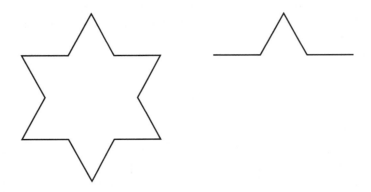

Left: A regular six pointed star. Right: The *skeleton* path after deleting nodes from the star.

3. Make a duplicate of the path as we will need a copy later; move it aside.

4. Apply the *VonKoch* effect to the original path, this will create default *control* paths.

5. We need to edit both *control* paths, it is perhaps slightly easier to start with the *Generating path*. This *control* path,
   by default, consists of two separate path segments. We need four segments exactly like in the *skeleton* path. Select
   the duplicate of the *skeleton* path and use ⬚ on each of the middle three nodes. When you are finished, the *Status
   Bar* should report the path consists of eight nodes.

6. Copy the duplicated path to the *clipboard*; select the original path and in the *Path Effect Editor* dialog click on the
   ⬚ in the *Generating path* line. This will replace the default path. You will probably see the first-generation paths
   jump to the upper-right corner. Don't panic! We'll need to drag the *Generating path* to where it belongs.

7. Click on the ↖ icon in the *Generating path* line of the *LPE* dialog. You should see the *Generating path* as a green path. Select all the nodes and drag them to overlap the *skeleton* path.

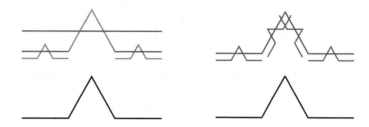

Left: After copying the *skeleton* path and applying the *VonKoch* LPE. Both the *Reference segment* and *Generating path* are shown (the *skeleton* path *Stroke* has been set to gray so it is easier to see the *control paths*). Right: The duplicate of the *skeleton* path has been separated into four sub-paths. It was then pasted into the LPE to replace the *Generating path*. The resulting *Generating path* has been translated as shown.

8. Next we need to edit the *Reference segment*. Click on the ↖ icon in the *Reference segment* line of the *LPE* dialog. Select both nodes and move them down to them to overlap the base of the *skeleton* path.

9. Finally, you can increase the number of generations. If you select four or more generations, you will have to increase the *Max complexity* value. You can also uncheck the *Draw all generations* box.

Left: After the *Reference segment* has been moved. Right: The final result with the number of generations set to 3 and the *Draw all generations* unchecked.

# Chapter 9. Text

Inkscape has a sophisticated system for creating and manipulating text. Text strings can include **Bold** or *Italicized* substrings and changes in font type and size. Text can be justified on the right and/or left. It can be horizontal or vertical. Individual characters can be kerned. Text can be put on a path or flowed into an arbitrarily shaped path.

## This is a text string with **Bold** and *Italicized* text.

Some sample text.

There are three types of text objects in Inkscape. The first is *regular* text. The second is *flowed* text; this is a text object that includes a rectangular frame. The third is *linked-flowed* text. This is a text object where the text is flowed into a separate arbitrary shape or path object(s). It is discussed at the end of this chapter. When a text object is selected, its type is shown in the *Notification Region*.

# Creating Text

Text is created with the *Text Tool*. To add text to a document, select the tool by clicking on the **A** icon (**F8** or **t**) in the *Tool Box*.

### Note

The *Text and Font* dialog has an entry box for entering text on the *Text* tab. This entry box will not be active unless some preexisting text object is selected or at least one character is entered into a new text object using the *Text Tool*. This is because a text object must be created first. Simply clicking on the screen with the *Text Tool* does not create an object.

There are two ways to add text to an Inkscape drawing. The first is as *regular* text. In this case, as text is typed, the *text box* grows to accommodate the text. Line breaks must be manually added.

The second way to enter text is as a *flowed* text object. The text is typed into a presized rectangular *text box*. Line breaks are automatically made. The *flowed* text object includes both the box and text and is thus moved and transformed as such. For a discussion of *flowed* text in an arbitrary shape, see the last section in this chapter.

A few things to note that apply to both entry methods:

- If you click on an already existing text object with the *Text Tool*, the text object will be selected and the cursor will be placed between the letters closest to where you clicked. The text can then be edited.

- Many of the keyboard shortcuts will not work while in the enter text mode. The + and − keys on the numeric keypad will type the corresponding characters if **Num Lock** is on; otherwise, they retain their zoom functions.

- Special characters can be entered by two different methods:

  - **Unicode Mode:** In this method, special characters are entered by typing in *Unicode* values. To toggle between normal and *Unicode* modes use **Ctrl+U**. Once in Unicode mode, type in the two to four digit hexadecimal *Unicode* value followed by the **Space** bar. Repeat to add more characters. Typing any non-hexadecimal character or **Esc** while in Unicode mode will return you to normal mode.

## This is "Japanese" written in Japanese: 日本語.

A sentence with Kanji characters. The characters were entered by typing: **Ctrl+U** 65e5 **Space** 672c **Space** 8a9e **SpaceEsc**. (You must have a Kanji font installed to see the characters.)

- **Glyphs Dialog:** *New in v0.48.* You can use the *Glyphs* dialog to enter special characters. Open the dialog by using the menu entry Text → 🔣 Glyphs.... In the dialog, you can choose in which font family and style you wish to search. Available characters will depend on the font. You can also limit the search to specific *Scripts* or *Unicode Ranges* by using the two drop-down menus. Once you have found the character you want to add, *double*-click on it with the **Left Mouse Button**. This will add the character to the entry box at the bottom left of the dialog. Click the *Append* button to add the characters to a selected text object. Note that you must have already created a text object. A text object is not created until at least one character has been entered (just clicking on the canvas with the *Text Tool* does not create a text object).

  Note that you should use either the *Script* or *Range* menus as they independently limit the list of characters shown. If you select "Latin" in the *Script* menu and "Greek and Coptic" in the *Range* no characters will be shown. The reason for having two different menus is that many scripts have characters in multiple ranges. If you want all "Latin" characters use the *Script* menu. If you already know that the character you want is in the "Latin B" block use the *Range* menu.

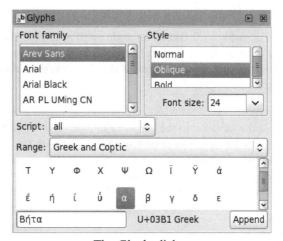

The *Glyphs* dialog.

- One problem you may encounter with saving text in *SVG* files as text objects is that if the font is not available on the computer where the file is to be viewed, it may not be visible. To avoid this problem, you can convert the text to a path. This, though, will prevent the text from being edited as a text object (and it makes your *SVG* less accessible and indexable).

### Tip

Make a duplicate of the text before you convert the text to a path. Put the copy on a separate layer and make that layer invisible. Then if you ever need to edit the text as a text object, you will have a copy available.

- When a text object is selected, a small square is shown at the left of the first line's baseline. This is the *baseline anchor*, which is used for snapping and alignment.

# Entering Regular Text

To add *regular* text, click on the document where you desire the text to start. You should see a cursor (blinking bar) indicating you are in the text enter mode and showing where the text will start. To add text, just start typing. You can enter multiline text by inserting a carriage return. The *text box* will grow as text is entered.

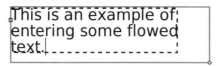

Entering *regular* text.

### *SVG* and Regular Text

*Regular* text created by Inkscape is always inside a <tspan> object that is wrapped by a <text> object. The first <tspan> in a line is marked by a private Inkscape attribute to indicate it is the start of a new line. This is how Inkscape knows how to insert new lines in the middle of a section of text and move the following lines down (*SVG* includes no such mechanism). Text in *SVG* files created not by Inkscape will be missing this attribute and may be structured differently. Inkscape may have problems editing such text.

## Entering Flowed Text

### *SVG* and Flowed Text

*Flowed* text was a draft *SVG* 1.2 specification that will not in the end be adopted. The text is not likely to be viewable by other renderers. In addition, some programs will not render any of a file with *flowed* text (Squiggle, for example). You can convert the *flowed* text to a *regular* text object before saving to avoid this problem.

To add *flowed* text, click-drag on the document with the *Text Tool* to create a blue rectangle box for the text. Once the box is drawn, you can move the cursor into the box area and begin to type. Carriage returns are automatically made. Prior to v0.48, if the text fills the box, you cannot add more text with out enlarging the box. As of v0.48, you can add text but it will not be shown. Instead the rectangle will turn red to indicate that not all the text is displayed. The box can be enlarged or the proportions changed by dragging on the handle at the lower-right side with the *Text Tool*, *Node Tool*, or any of the *shape tools*; however, the *text box* will only be shown when using the *Text Tool*. Use the **Ctrl** key while dragging to constrain the change in box size to a horizontal or vertical direction. The box and text can be moved together.

Entering *flowed* text.

## Selecting Text

Editing and applying attributes to text requires positioning the cursor or selecting text. The following methods are available when using the *Text Tool*:

- Moving text cursor:

  - **Left Mouse Click**: Position cursor under pointer.

  - **Arrows**: Move forward/backward one character, move up/down one line.

  - **Ctrl+Arrows**: Move forward/backward one word, move up/down one line.

  - **Home**: Move to start of line.

  - **End**: Move to end of line.

  - **Ctrl+Up Arrow**: Move up one paragraph.

- **Ctrl+Down Arrow**: Move down one paragraph.

- **Ctrl+Home**: Move to start of text.

- **Ctrl+End**: Move to end of text.

- **Page Up**: Move up one screen worth of text.

- **Page Down**: Move down one screen worth of text.

- Selecting text:

  - **Left Mouse Drag**: Select text under drag.

  - **Double Left Mouse Click**: Select word under pointer.

  - **Triple Left Mouse Click**: Select text line under pointer.

  - **Shift+Arrows**: Move start or end of selection one character in arrow direction.

  - **Shift+Ctrl+Left/Right Arrows**: Move start or end of selection to beginning of word in arrow direction.

  - **Shift+Ctrl+Up/Down Arrows**: Move start or end of selection to character in line above or below current line.

  - **Ctrl+A**: Select all text in current text object.

# Editing Text

Editing text is done with the *Text Tool*. As already mentioned, clicking on existing text will select that text object and enable editing. All the normal text editing keys function as expected: **Backspace**, **Arrows**, **Enter**, and so forth. Cut and paste also work (see above for selecting text): Cut: **Ctrl+X**, Copy: **Ctrl+C**, and Paste: **Ctrl+V**.

An alternative way to edit text is to use the *Text* tab of the *Text and Font* dialog (Text → **T** Text and Font... (**Shift+Ctrl+T**)). Editing text in the tab may be easier, especially for long texts.

## Spell Checking

Inkscape offers on-canvas spell checking. All text is checked, regardless whether or not it is selected. To spell check a document, call up the *Check Spelling* dialog (Text → ⬛ Check Spelling... (**Ctrl+Alt+K**)). When a suspect word is found, it will be highlighted on the canvas by a red box. If using the *Text Tool*, the cursor will be placed at the start of the word. And if the *Text* tab of the *Text and Font* dialog is open, the word will underlined with a red squiggle.

The *Check Spelling* dialog.

A list of suggested corrections will appear in the *Check Spelling* dialog. You can choose to *Accept* (if you have high-lighted the correct spelling in the *Suggestions:* list), *Ignore once*, or *Ignore* (all other similarly spelled words in the document). You can also add the word to a dictionary by clicking the *Add to dictionary:* button. This will cause the spell checker to accept the word as correctly spelled permanently. You can select which language dictionary the word is added by the drop-down menu to the right.

You can select which languages to use (up to three) in the *Inkscape Preferences* dialog in the *Spellcheck* section. At the moment, on Windows, only an English dictionary is included. On Linux, one can install additional dictionaries by installing the *Gnu Aspell* [http://aspell.net/] package with any language packs required.

If no action is taken for a period of time, the spell-checking process will time out. You can restart it by clicking the *Start* button. Spell checking will begin with the text at the top-right and work down the canvas.

# Formatting Text

*Updated for v0.48.*

Text in text objects can be formatted. This section covers changing the font, style, size, justification, letter/word/line spacing, kerning, and orientation. Specifying the fill (color, pattern, etc.) of text is covered in Chapter 10, *Attributes*.

There are three methods to format text. The first is to use the items in the *Text Tool-Tool Controls*, the second is to use keyboard shortcuts, and the third is to use the *Text and Font* dialog (Text → **T** Text and Font... (**Shift+Ctrl+T**)). The *Tool Controls* received a major upgrade in v0.48 of Inkscape.

The *Text Tool-Tool Controls*, v0.47.

The *Text Tool-Tool Controls*, v0.48.

When changing properties of text, if characters within a text object are selected, the changes apply only to those characters. Otherwise, the changes apply to all selected text objects (to select more than one text object, switch temporarily to the *Select Tool*). Changes made when no text object is selected (or a new blank text object is created) change the default style. The default style can also be set with the *Set as Default* button in the *Text and Font* dialog.

# Font Family

The *Font Family* can be changed via the *Tool Controls* or the *Font* tab of the *Text and Font* dialog. The two methods behave slightly different.

**Via *Tool Controls*:** The leftmost drop-down menu selects the font family. When activated, the menu shows samples of the various fonts available to Inkscape. This can be disabled in v0.48 in the *Text* section of the *Inkscape Preferences* dialog if the rendering of the samples takes too much time when starting Inkscape (which can happen if you have a large number of fonts installed on your system). The text used for the sample can be customized by editing your `preferences.xml` file. Use **Alt+X** to access the menu directly. Once accessed, **Alt+Down arrow** will open the drop-down list, **Up arrow** and **Down arrow** move up and down the list as does using the scroll wheel, and **Enter** sets the family. Typing into the font entry box will open a list of all fonts that start with the characters typed. *New in v0.48:* A warning icon will be displayed if the selected font is not available to Inkscape.

***Text and Font* dialog:** The font family can be chosen from a list of all possible font families available to Inkscape on your system. The font is previewed with the text in the bottom of the dialog. Changes are not made to the drawing until the *Apply* button is clicked.

# Font Size

The *Font Size* can be changed via the *Tool Controls* or the *Text and Font* dialog. In both cases, the font size (in pixels) can be selected from a drop-down menu. To select a size that is not in the menu, simply type the number in. The change takes effect upon selection or hitting **Enter** in the case of the *Tool Controls* and upon clicking *Apply* in the case of the *Text and Font* dialog.

# Font Style

*SVG* directly supports **Bold** and *Italic/Oblique* styles.[1] You can toggle on and off these styles (if the font family supports them) by clicking the corresponding buttons in the *Tool Controls* or with keyboard shortcuts:

- **a** (**Ctrl+B**) Toggle **Bold** on/off.

- *a* (**Ctrl+I**) Toggle *Italics* on/off.

A font may have other styles available (e.g. narrow, semi-bold). All possible styles (including Bold, and Italic/Oblique) can be selected in the *Style* section of the *Text and Font* dialog.

# Justification

Text can be justified (aligned) by clicking on the appropriate icons in either the *Tool Controls* or the *Text and Font* dialog. The *Apply* button must be clicked for the change to take place in the latter case.

- ☰ Align left.

- ☰ Center.

- ☰ Align right.

- ☰ Justify (left and right justified).

| Xvnq etuo adgj | Xvnq etuo adgj | Xvnq etuo adgj | Xvnq    etuo    adgj |
| wry i pa zcb rtva | wry i pa zcb rtva | wry i pa zcb rtva | wry i pa zcb rtva |
| zml. Pjvxg ter | zml. Pjvxg ter | zml. Pjvxg ter | zml.   Pjvxg    ter |
| yijlnv, aef. | yijlnv, aef. | yijlnv, aef. | yijlnv, aef. Efabyko |
| Efabyko xoitv hubi | Efabyko xoitv hubi | Efabyko xoitv hubi | xoitv  hubi  aerscf |
| aerscf yhi li. | aerscf yhi li. | aerscf yhi li. | yhi li. |

Left, center, and right aligned text; left and right justified text.

### Note

Only *flowed* text can be both left and right justified at the same time.

---

[1] An *Oblique* font is usually a regular font that has been skewed. A true *Italic* font has several characters (e.g., a and *a*) that have different designs.

# Superscripts and Subscripts

*New in v0.48.*

Superscripts and subscripts can be created by selecting text and clicking on the corresponding icons ( ⌄ , ⌄ ) in the *Tool Controls*. The selected text will be shifted up or down and reduced in size. Superscripts and subscripts can be removed by selecting and then clicking on the same icons. Inkscape implements superscripts and subscripts by setting the *baseline-shift* attribute to either "super" or "sub", and by setting the *font-size* attribute to 65%. Inkscape will only recognize a superscript or subscript if the *baseline-shift* attribute is set in this manner. The font size can be changed after the superscript or subscript is created. The *baseline-shift* attribute is not supported by all browsers (e.g. Firefox 4). As a workaround, one can manually shift the text vertically.

# Line Spacing

Line spacing (the distance between text *baselines*) applies to an entire text object. Note that although Inkscape uses the attribute *line-spacing* to store the line spacing value, it is not part of the *SVG* standard (it is, however, part of the *CSS* standard). Inkscape uses the value to position lines of text. The positions are stored in the *SVG* file and are used by *SVG* renderers to place the text.

Line spacing can be changed by the *Line spacing* entry boxes in both the *Tool Controls* ( ↕ ) (*new in v0.48*) and in the *Text and Font* dialog. It can also be changed by the following keyboard shortcuts (note adjustments are specified in *Screen pixels* and thus depend on the zoom level):

- **Ctrl+Alt+>**: Make text object one *Screen pixel* taller.

- **Ctrl+Alt+<**: Make text object one *Screen pixel* shorter.

- **Shift+Ctrl+Alt+>**: Make text object ten *Screen pixels* taller.

- **Shift+Ctrl+Alt+<**: Make text object ten *Screen pixels* shorter.

# Word Spacing

*New in v0.48.*

Word spacing can be changed via an entry box in the *Tool Controls* ( ⋯ ). Changes apply to selected text if text is selected or to the entire text block if not.

# Letter Spacing

Letter spacing can be changed via an entry box in the *Tool Controls* ( ⋯ ) (*New in v0.48*) or by keyboard shortcuts. Changes apply to selected text if text is selected or the entire text block if not. Note that the keyboard shortcuts are defined in terms of *Screen pixels* and thus depend on the zoom level. Also note that if some text already has letter spacing applied to it, the letter spacing of that text will not be changed if the text cursor is elsewhere.

- **Alt+>**: Expand line (paragraph) or selected text by one *Screen pixel*.

- **Alt+<**: Contract line (paragraph) or selected text by one *Screen pixel*.

- **Shift+Alt+>**: Expand line (paragraph) or selected text by ten *Screen pixels*.

- **Shift+Alt+<**: Contract line (paragraph) or selected text by ten *Screen pixels*.

# Kerning, Shifting, and Rotating Characters

Individual characters in a line of *regular* (but not *flowed*) text may be shifted left or right to change their *kerning*, shifted up or down, or rotated. (Both *regular* and *flowed* text do utilize the internal *kerning* that is included with fonts.)

An example of (badly) kerned, shifted, and rotated text.

Text showing individual character manipulation.

All *manual* kerning/shifts/rotations can be removed with the Text → ⊞ Remove Manual Kerns command.

## Kerning and Shifting

Changing the *kerning* and shifting characters up and down are treated the same in Inkscape. If no characters are selected, all the characters following the cursor are shifted. If some characters are selected, only the selected characters are shifted. Shifts can be made through the *Tool Controls* ( ⬤ , ⬤ ) (*New in v0.48*) or through keyboard shortcuts. Note that shifts via the *Tool Controls* are in pixels while shifts via the keyboard are in *Screen pixels*, thus, in the latter case, the zoom level will affect the magnitude of the shift.

- **Alt+Arrows Key**: Shift character(s) by one *Screen pixel* in arrow direction.

- **Shift+Alt+Arrows Key**: Shift character(s) by ten *Screen pixels* in arrow direction.

## Rotating

If no characters are selected, only the character following the text cursor will be rotated. If characters are selected, all the selected characters will be rotated. Rotations can be made through the *Tool Controls* ( ⬤ ) (*New in v0.48*) or through keyboard shortcuts. Note that rotations via the *Tool Controls* are in degrees while some via the keyboard are in *Screen pixels*, thus, in the latter case, the zoom level will affect the magnitude of the rotation.

- **Alt+[, Alt+]**: Rotate character(s) counterclockwise, clockwise by one *Screen pixel*.

- **Ctrl+[, Ctrl+]**: Rotate character(s) counterclockwise, clockwise by 90 degrees.

# Orientation

The orientation of the text can be chosen by clicking on one of the following icons:

- ⊞ Horizontal text.

- ⊞ Vertical text.

Horizontal (left), vertical (center), and rotated (right) text.

The vertical choice is mostly applicable to languages written from top to bottom and from right to left, such as Chinese, Japanese, or Korean. See the above figure to see the difference between vertical text and text rotated by 90 degrees. A block of text can only have one orientation.

# Text on a Path

Text can be put along an arbitrary path.

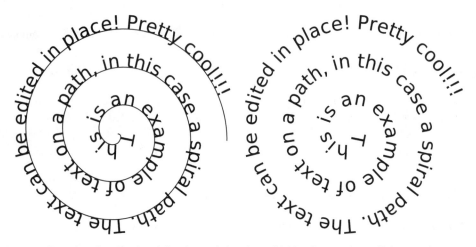

Text on *Spiral* paths. On the right, the path has been hidden by turning off the *Stroke paint*.

To place text on a path, enter the text as a *Regular* text or *Flowed* text. Draw the desired path. Select both text and path, then use the Text → ✎ Put on Path command. The text should now appear along the path. Note that *Shapes* except for *Rectangles* are described internally by Inkscape as paths and thus don't require converting to a path.

Both the text and the path can be edited in place. The text should adjust to any changes in the path. The path can be made invisible by selecting only the path, then removing the *Stroke paint* with the *Fill and Stroke* dialog. To select an invisible path for editing, select the text and use Edit → Clone → ▣ Select Original (**Shift+D**). To remove text from a path, use Text → ✎ Remove from Path.

Parts of the text can be selected and the style, *kerning*, and so forth can be adjusted as for *regular* text. Text can also be moved independently of the path by selecting the text only and using the normal means for moving objects.

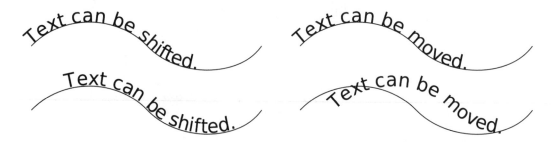

Text can be adjusted or moved relative to the path. Left: the text has been adjusted and kerned with the **Alt+arrow** keys. Placing the cursor at the beginning of the text and using the **Alt+arrow** keys will move the starting position of the text. Right: the text has been moved independent-ly of the path by selecting the text only and dragging it to its new position with the mouse.

Text on a path is initially placed on the "left" side of the path (referenced from the path direction) starting at the beginning of the path. One can change the direction of the text (and the side it is placed on) by reversing the direction of the path (e.g., Path → ⇄ Reverse (**Shift+R**)). If the text is center justified prior to being put on a path, it will centered along the path.

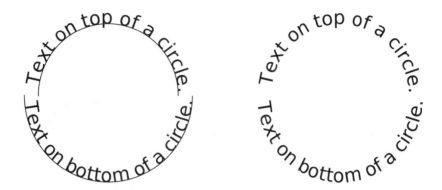

To place text on a circle so that it reads from left to right on both the top and bottom, two circles must be used as seen on the left. The larger circle has been flipped horizontally (Object → ⬛ Flip Horizontal (**H**)) so the text is placed inside the circle starting from the left. The smaller circle has been rotated 180 degrees. (The path of a circle when first drawn starts from the rightmost point. The circle must be rotated or flipped to move the starting point of the path to the left.) By turning the circles into half circles and setting the text to center-justified, the text will automatically be centered at the top or bottom of the circle. Note that *kerning* may be necessary as the characters of text placed on the outside of a curve will be too far apart while those on the inside of a curve will be too close together.

See the *Generate from Path* [371] extension for an alternative way of putting text on a path.

# Text in a Shape

Text can be flowed inside any arbitrary shape by linking a text object to a shape or path. (This "Link Flowed Text" was a draft *SVG* 1.2 specification and will not work with *SVG* 1.1 viewers.)

Text flowed into a path with the shape of an old Chinese coin.
The path consists of both the outer circle and inner square.

To create a linked flowed text object, select a text object and one or more shape/path objects. Then use the Text → ▦ Flow into Frame (**Alt+W**) command. If multiple shape/path objects are selected, the text will flow into the *last* object selected first.

Text flowed into three circles. The circles were selected from
right to left so that the text would flow first in the left hand circle.

Flowed text can be edited in place, including selecting part of the text and changing the style or changing the letter and line spacings. The center circle above has had some adjustments made to the style and the letter spacing. To select all the text, use Edit → ▦ Select All (**Ctrl+A**) command while a text object is selected with the *Text Tool*.

If the flowed text is selected, the Edit → Clone → ▦ Select Original (**Shift+D**) command will select the first shape or path object (especially useful if the path has been made invisible). **Tab** will then rotate the selection one by one through any other shape or path objects that are part of the *linked-flowed* text object, as well as the text itself.

Flowed text can be converted back to a *regular* text object with the Text → ▦ Unflow (**Shift+Alt+W**). The resulting text will be on a single line.

The Text → ▦ Convert to Text command converts *link-flowed* text to a *regular* text object while preserving the appearance of the text. The text is still editable but will no longer reflow inside the shape or path frame. This is necessary for display of the drawing in another *SVG* renderer.

# Chapter 10. Attributes

An object has attributes such as color and line style. An attribute can apply to the *Fill* or to the *Stroke* of the object. The *Fill* refers to how the area inside an object's boundary path is painted while the *Stroke* refers to the path itself. The *Fill* or *Stroke* (*Stroke paint*) can be a single color, a *Gradient* of colors, a *Pattern*, or nothing at all. With the exception of a few small differences, *Fill* and *Stroke paint* have the same properties and are treated together in the following discussion. A *Stroke* can have additional attributes such as width, dash pattern, and marker type (*Stroke style*). These are treated in a separate section.

Text can be given the same attributes as other objects with a few small differences: Individual letters, words, or phrases can be given different solid colors, but *Gradients* and *Patterns* must be assigned to an entire text object.

There are a number of ways to change attributes:

- *Fill and Stroke* dialog (Object → ☑ Fill and Stroke... (**Shift+Ctrl+F**)): Three tabs in the dialog allow the setting of the *Fill*, *Stroke paint*, and *Stroke style*. At the very bottom of the dialog is a slider and entry box for the *Opacity* to set the overall *opacity* (or *transparency*) of an object.

- *Palette*: To change *Fill* and *Stroke paint* colors.

- *Swatches* dialog: To change *Fill* and *Stroke paint* colors (View → ▨ Swatches... (**Shift+Ctrl+W**)).

- *Style Indicator* menu (pops up when a bar in the *Style Indicator* is **Right Mouse Clicked**). An entry box in the *Style Indicator* can be used to set an object's *opacity*.

- *Color Gestures* and *Stroke Width Gestures* where one does a **Left Mouse Drag** from the *Style Indicator*.

- *Dropper Tool*: To select *Fill* and *Stroke paint* colors from another object.

- *Gradient Tool*: To create and modify *Gradients*.

- Edit → ▤ Paste Style (**Shift+Ctrl+V**) command: To copy attributes from one object to another. Copy the source object (Edit → ▨ Copy (**Ctrl+C**)), then select the target object and use the Edit → ▤ Paste Style (**Shift+Ctrl+V**) command.

- *XML Editor*: Useful to access attributes defined in the *SVG* standard but are not yet directly accessible through the Inkscape interface.

# Fill and Stroke Paint

There are a number of different options for the *Fill* and *Stroke paint* of an object. Examples of the different options are shown below. The use of these options for the *Fill* and the *Stroke paint* is basically the same, so we'll use the word *fill* to talk about both at the same time.

Choices for the *Fill* of an object, from left to right: No paint,
Flat color, Linear gradient, Radial gradient, Pattern, Unset paint.

Choices for the *Stroke paint* of an object, from left to right: No paint, Flat color, Linear gradient, Radial gradient, Pattern, Unset paint. The stroke has been widened to make it easier to see the effect of the different options.✪

The fill type can be set using the *Fill and Stroke* dialog (Object → ☑ Fill and Stroke... (**Shift+Ctrl+F**) or click on ☑ in the *Command Bar*) under the *Fill* and *Stroke paint* tabs. The fill type can be one of the following choices (set by clicking an icon):

- × No paint (transparent).

- ■ Flat (solid) color.

- ■ Linear *Gradient* (a smooth transition between two or more colors).

- ■ Radial *Gradient* (a smooth transition between two or more colors in a radial direction).

- ▦ *Pattern* (filled with a repeating pattern).

- □ *Custom Swatch* (document dependent swatch). *New in v0.48.*

- ? Unset (necessary for giving different attributes to cloned copies of an object).

A *Gradient* fill type can also be selected by using the *Gradient Tool*.

Each of the options (except the *No paint* and *Unset* options) is discussed below.

# Flat (Solid) Colors

Color can be the simplest or the most complicated aspect of a drawing depending on your needs. Color is stored internally in Inkscape as a six-digit *hexadecimal* number consisting of three pairs of digits. Each pair of digits corresponds to the amount of Red, Green, Blue (*RGB*). This matches the *SVG* specification for describing color. For example, a color defined as #FF7F00 has red, blue, and green components of 100%, 50%, and 0%, respectively, of the maximum values.

In some cases, a fourth pair of digits is added to describe *Alpha* (*RGBA*). The A or *Alpha* attribute may not be familiar to many people. This attribute specifies how transparent the fill should be. It can range from 0 for complete *transparency* to 255 (*hexadecimal* FF) for complete *opacity*. The term *opacity* is often used in place of *Alpha*. Its value ranges from 0% (0.0) for a transparent object to 100% (1.0) for an opaque object.

In principle, this is a simple description for specifying any color. The complexity comes from assuring that the color reproduced on a display or in printing matches the color the artist envisioned. Various color "systems" have been developed to facilitate this. Inkscape supports base ICC [http://www.color.org] profile functionality through the use of LittleCMS [http://www.littlecms.com/]. Setting up color management can be done under the *Color management* section in the *Inkscape Preferences* dialog. You can declare multiple ICC profiles for a document in the *Color Management* tab of the *Document Properties* dialog. If everything is setup properly the "Color Managed View" can be toggled on/off via View → ▷ Color-managed View or by clicking on the ▷ icon in the lower right corner of the window. This will give a better representation of what you can expect to see in the final rendering of the drawing as well as mark out-of-gamut colors. Note, profiles internal to a *bitmap* are not used. A complete discussion of this topic is beyond the scope of this book.

The fill color of an object can be modified a variety of ways, including using the *Fill and Stroke* dialog, the *Palette*, the *Swatches* dialog, and the *Dropper Tool*. Some of these methods can also be used to change the color of a *Gradient* stop when a *Gradient* handle is selected.

# Fill and Stroke Dialog—Color

When the use of a flat (or solid) color is specified for the *Fill* and *Stroke paint* of an object, the corresponding tab of the *Fill and Stroke* dialog will show five sub-tabs, each one corresponding to a different method of specifying the color plus one for color management. Each method is described next in its own section.

Except for the *Wheel* tab, each color parameter can be set by either dragging a slider (small triangles), typing the desired value into the entry box, using the up/down arrows in the widget (**Right Mouse Click** on an arrow causes the value to change to the minimum or maximum, **Middle Mouse Click** cause the value to increment or decrement by 10), or the **Up/Down Arrow** keys after the entry box is selected. The slider bar shows the current value (triangles) and what the color will look like as that slider is dragged.

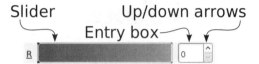

Methods for setting a color parameter.

The A or *Alpha* attribute specifies how transparent the fill should be, 0 for completely transparent and 255 (100) for completely opaque in the case of the *RGB*, *HSL*, and *Wheel* (*CMYK*) methods.

## RGB

*RGB* (Red, Green, Blue) is a method for specifying a color in terms of the three additive primary colors. This is the native method for computer screens. Range of allowed values is from 0 to 255 (0 to FF in *hexadecimal*).

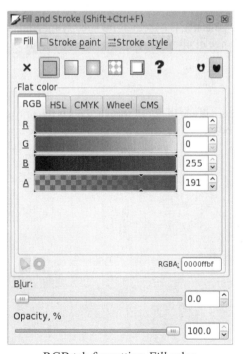

RGB tab for setting *Fill* color.

## HSL

*HSL* (*Hue*, *Saturation*, *Lightness*) is a method for specifying color in terms of hue (color in optical spectrum), saturation (intensity-purity), and lightness. The range for saturation is from a pure color to gray. The range for lightness is from black to pure color to white. Range of allowed values is from 0 to 255 (0 to FF in *hexadecimal*).

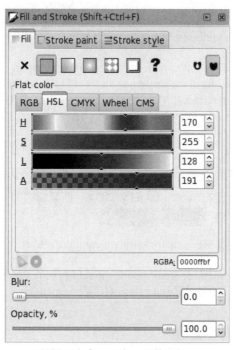

HSL tab for setting *Fill* color.

## CMYK

*CMYK* (Cyan, Magenta, Yellow, Key [Black]), is a method for specifying color in terms of *subtractive* primary colors and is commonly used in printing. Range of allowed values is from 0 to 100.

 **Warning**

Inkscape stores color internally in the *RGB* format. This is the only color specification supported by *SVG*. Furthermore, the entry boxes are set up so that the value in one is always zero. (Any color in *RGB* color space can be defined using only three of the *CMYK* terms. The definition is not unique.) Better support for *CMYK* is planned.

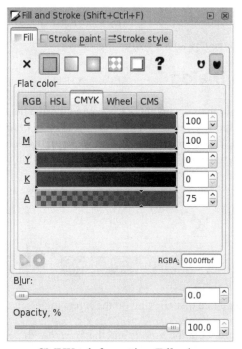

CMYK tab for setting *Fill* color.

## Wheel

The *Wheel* is an alternative way of changing color in the *HSL* paradigm. Dragging the line around the circle changes the *Hue*. Dragging the small circle within the triangle parallel to the edge that varies from white to black changes the *Lightness* and dragging perpendicular to that edge changes the *Saturation*.

Wheel tab for setting *Fill* color.

## CMS

This tab allows editing of colors managed by an *icc profile* if enabled.

# Palette and Swatches Dialog

The color *Palette*, located near the bottom of the main Inkscape window, and the *Swatches* dialog (View → ▣ Swatches... (**Shift+Ctrl+W**)) allows one to quickly set the color of an object's *Fill* or *Stroke* or to set the color of a *Gradient Stop*. They can also be used to set the *Current style*. Their use is essentially identical so they will be treated together. The visibility of the *Palette* can be toggled via a check box in the View → Show/Hide submenu.

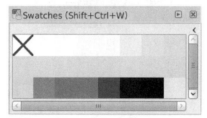

Swatches dialog. Note that clicking on the × rectangle sets the *Fill* to *None*.

The following methods are available for both the *Palette* and the *Swatches* dialog:

- **Left Mouse Click** on a swatch to change the *Fill* of selected objects or the color of selected *Gradient Stops* to the color of the swatch. **Shift+Left Mouse Click** on a swatch to change the *Stroke* of selected objects. The *Current style* will also change (no object need be selected). Note, the *Current style* is not displayed correctly in v0.48 if the *Auto* palette is selected.

- **Left Mouse Drag** from a swatch to an object's *Fill* or *Stroke* or to a *Gradient Stop* to change the corresponding attribute to the swatch's color. **Shift+Left Mouse Drag** to anywhere on an object to set the *Stroke* color (except to a *GradientStop*). The target object need not be selected. The *Current style* will not change.

- **Left Mouse Drag** from a swatch to the *Fill* or *Stroke* part of the *Style Indicator* to change the *Fill* or *Stroke* of selected objects. The *Current style* will also change.

- **Right Mouse Click** on a swatch to open a small dialog which allows you to assign the color to the *Fill* or *Stroke* of selected objects. The *Current style* will also change. In v0.48, one can also edit or delete a *Custom Swatch* through this dialog.

You can also drag colors to or from other applications that support *Drag and Drop*.

Inkscape has a variety of built-in palettes (some copied from Gimp). More palettes can be added by installing palette files in the directory `share/palettes`. The files use the Gimp palette file structure where colors are defined in terms of a triplet of numbers in a *RGB* format. See the section called *Custom Swatches or Palettes* in Chapter 24, *Customization*, for details.

 ## Auto Palette

*New in v0.48.*

An *Auto* palette was added in v0.48. This is the default palette shown in the *Swatches* dialog. Initially it is empty. It will automatically include *Custom Swatches* as they are added to a document. This palette is document dependent.

Both the *Palette* and the *Swatches* dialog have a pull-down menu (far right, small arrow) where you can set the size and shape of the swatches, if the colors should be displayed in one row or in multiple rows, and which palette should be used. Hovering the pointer over a swatch will display a color's name in a *tool tip* and in the *Status Bar*. A scroll bar gives access to colors in a palette that are not displayed when there are too many colors to fit.

# Style Indicator

The *Style Indicator* located on the left side of the *Status Bar* displays information on selected objects, text fragments, or *Gradient* stops. The indicator includes a number of methods to alter style, including: pop-up menus, targets for Drag and Drop colors, and Color Gestures.

## Display

The *Style Indicator* has three parts showing *Fill*, *Stroke paint*, and *opacity* (O), which show attributes for selected objects or text fragments. The *Fill* and *Stroke paint* parts are referred to as the *fill indicators*.

The *Style Indicator* showing the attributes of an object with a red *Fill*, a
blue *Stroke paint*, a *Stroke* width of 10 pixels, and an *Opacity* of 100%.

A displayed *fill attribute* can be one of:

- Color swatch: Shows color with (left) and without (right) *Alpha* (*Alpha* refers to the *Fill* and *Stroke paint* attributes and not the object's *opacity*).

- N/A: Not Applicable (i.e., no object selected).

- None: No fill defined.

- Unset: fill is unset.

- L: fill is a linear *Gradient*.

- R: fill is a radial *Gradient*.

- Pattern: fill is a pattern.

- Different: More than one object selected with different fill.

When multiple objects are selected and all of the selected objects have a color fill, then one of the following letters will be shown:

- m: Selected objects have same fill color.

- a: Selected objects have different fill colors. The color displayed is an average of the colors in the selected objects.

For *Gradient* handles, both parts (*Fill* and *Stroke paint*) show the handle color.

The *Style Indicator* has a number of features that depend on the part.

- Fill/Stroke Paint indicators:

  - A **Left Mouse Click** opens the *Fill and Stroke* dialog with the corresponding tab selected.

  - A **Middle Mouse Click** on a bar removes the fill from the selected objects if a fill is defined. If no fill is defined, it sets the fill to black.

  - A **Right Mouse Click** on a bar opens a pop-up menu as discussed below.

- A color from the *Palette* or *Swatches* dialog can be dragged and dropped onto one of the *fill indicators* to change the fill of all selected objects.

- Stroke indicator:

  - A **Left Mouse Click** opens the *Fill and Stroke* dialog to the *Stroke style* tab.

  - A **Right Mouse Click** opens a pop-up menu that allows the stroke width unit to be changed as well as a preset width to be selected. The stroke can also be removed with this menu.

- Opacity indicator:

  - A **Right Mouse Click** on the numeric field opens up a pop-up menu with preset opacity values.

  - A **Middle Mouse Click** on the "O:" label cycles through the opacity values 0%, 50%, and 100% (0.0, 0.5, and 1.0).

## Fill Indicator Pop-up Menu

A **Right Mouse Click** on either the *Fill* or *Stroke paint* bar opens a pop-up menu with entries that act on the *Fill* or *Stroke paint* of the selected objects or text fragments, depending on which bar was clicked. If a *Gradient* handle is selected, the menu entries apply to that handle.

The *Style Indicator* pop-up menu.

- Edit fill... (Edit stroke...): Opens *Fill and Stroke* dialog. (The dialog can also be opened directly by a **Left Mouse Click** on the *Fill* or *Stroke paint* part of the *Style Indicator*.)

- Last set color: Applies the last *set* color to the *Fill* or *Stroke paint* of selected objects. A color is set when a color is applied to any object or when a color is selected from the *Palette*.

- Last selected color: Applies the last *selected* color to selected objects. The last selected color is the color of the previously selected object(s) prior to selecting the object(s) whose color is to be changed. If the color is to be applied to multiple objects, they must be selected together using a *rubber-band* selection. In v0.48, *Custom Swatches* are ignored in determining last selected color.

- Invert: Inverts the color of the *Fill* or *Stroke paint* of selected objects. If more than one object is selected, the colors of those objects are averaged before the color is inverted. The *opacity* is not changed.

- White: Set *Fill* or *Stroke paint* to white.

- Black: Set *Fill* or *Stroke paint* to black.

- Copy color: Copies color of selected objects to the clipboard in *hexadecimal* format. If more than one object is selected, the colors of those objects are averaged.

- Paste color: Pastes color to selected objects from the clipboard.

- Swap fill and stroke: Exchanges *Fill* and *Stroke paint* colors.

- Make fill (stroke) opaque: Sets *Fill* or *Stroke paint* to full *opacity*. (Does not affect *opacity*.)

- Unset fill (stroke): Unsets the *Fill* or *Stroke paint* of selected objects.

- Remove fill (stroke): Removes the *Fill* or *Stroke paint* of selected objects.

## Color Gestures

*Color Gestures* is the name given to changing the color of a *Fill*, *Stroke*, or *Gradient Stop* by dragging the mouse from a fill indicator into the Inkscape window. The principle is that as you drag the mouse, the color will change proportionally to the distance from a 45° line from the indicator. The farther away you are, the more subtle the changes can be. Changes are made in the *HSL* color space.

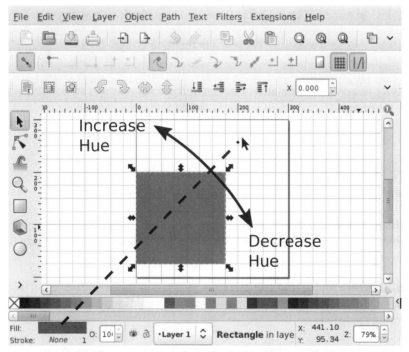

*Color Gestures*: Dragging the cursor away from the *Fill* indicator to the left or up from the dash line increases hue (blue to red) while dragging to the right or down decreases hue (blue to green). Dragging straight up or straight across results in the maximal change possible (blue to yellow).

Without any modifier key, changes are made to hue. With the **Shift** changes are made to saturation while with the **Ctrl** changes are made to lightness. Note that the letter next to the cursor will change to indicate the mode. Key modifiers can be changed while dragging. When a key modifier is changed, the "zero" line (normally at 45°) changes to pass through the current cursor position. This is to avoid abrupt changes in color when changing modifiers. The **Alt** modifier disables changes to the color so that the cursor can be repositioned.

If more than one object or *Gradient Stop* is selected, the starting color will be the average color of the selected items and the final color will be the same. If you wish to shift the color in the same way for a number of objects but preserve the relative differences use the *Tweak Tool*.

Color gestures are very useful once you get the hang of them. It is well worth spending a little time to play with them!

# Dropper Tool

The *Fill* and *Stroke paint* color of an object can be changed by using the *Dropper Tool* to grab an existing color in the drawing. Options allow for grabbing the average color over a circular region, inverting the grabbed color, and saving the grabbed color to the system *clipboard* (as a *RGBA* hexadecimal number).

To use the *Dropper Tool*, first select the object that you want to modify with a tool other than the *Dropper Tool*. Recall that you can switch temporarily to the *Select Tool* by using the **Space Bar**.

Then select the *Dropper Tool* by clicking on the ✐ icon (**F7** or **D**) in the *Tool Controls*. Finally click with the *Dropper Tool* on the desired color. The shortcut **D** will toggle between the *Dropper Tool* and any other tool.

The **Shift** causes the chosen color to be applied to the object's *Stroke paint* rather than the *Fill*. The **Alt** causes the inverse color to be applied. The **Shift** and **Alt** keys can be used in combination. However, neither of the modifier keys are useful when copying a color to the *clipboard*.

- **Left Mouse Click**: Pick *Fill* color.

- **Left Mouse Drag**: Pick average *Fill* color (color is averaged over circle created during drag).

- **Ctrl+C**: Copy color under cursor to system *clipboard* in the form of an 8-digit hexadecimal number (2 digits for each of *RGBA*).

The *Dropper Tool Tool Controls* has two buttons that determine if the *opacity* (*Alpha*) of a color should be *Picked* and/or *Assigned*. These settings affect the way a color is picked if the "Picked" object has an *opacity* different from 100% (or 1.0).

The *Dropper Tool-Tool Controls*.

- **Pick opacity disabled:** The color picked is as shown on the screen. For example, picking the color from an object with a dark blue fill but an opacity of 50% would result in a light blue color with an opacity of 100%. Opacity of set object not changed.

- **Pick opacity enabled, Assign alpha disabled:** The color picked is the color that the object would have if its opacity was 100%. A dark blue object with an opacity of 50% would result in a dark blue color (an opacity of 100%). Opacity of set object not changed.

- **Pick opacity enabled, Assign opacity enabled:** The color and opacity are both copied from the picked object. A dark blue object with an opacity of 59% would result in a light blue color composed of a dark blue fill with an opacity of 50%. Opacity of set object changed. Note: This is only applicable if the color is picked from an object with *transparency* that is not over another object.

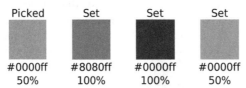

Color squares shown with the numerical values of their color (*hexadecimal*) and opacity. From left to right: Picked color, assign color with *Pick* disabled, assign color with *Pick* enabled but *Assign* disabled, assign color with both *Pick* and *Assign* enabled. In all cases, the original opacity of the "Set" squares was 100%.

# Gradients

*Gradients* are a smooth blending from one color to another. *Gradients* can be used to build up complex shading of an object as shown in the flower petal below. Note: Inkscape supports the *Gaussian Blur* filter, which may be an easier way to produce complex shadings.

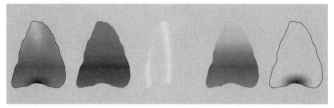

A flower petal consisting of four layers. From left to right: The finished petal. The base layer. A highlight. A duplicate of the base layer with partial transparency to mask part of the highlight layer. Top shadow layer. The background is gray to show the transparency in some layers.✪

In Inkscape, *Gradients* can be *linear* or *radial* and can consist of transitions between two or more well-defined colors referred to as *Stops*.

An example of a linear (left) and a radial *Gradient* (right), both with three defined colors or *Stops*.

Inkscape does not support nonlinear *Gradients*. Nonlinear *Gradients* can be simulated by adding extra *Stops*.

There are three parts to using a *Gradient*; each treated in the next three sections:

1. Attach a *Gradient* to an object.

2. Edit the *Stops*.

3. Adjust the orientation and extent of the *Gradient*.

The use of *linear* and *radial Gradients* is essentially the same and both will be treated together.

 **Note**

If you want a *Gradient* to transform with an object, you must toggle on this option using the ⬚ icon that is in the *Tool Controls* when the *Select Tool* is in use.

## Attaching Gradients to Objects

*Gradients* can be attached to an object either with the *Fill and Stroke* dialog or through the use of the *Gradient Tool*.

To attach a *Gradient* with the *Fill and Stroke* dialog, simply select an object and click on either the linear ⬚ or radial *Gradient* ⬚ icons in the dialog. A *Gradient* with two *Stops* will automatically be created and applied to the object.

The *Stops* will have the color of the previous *Fill* with one *Stop* having full *opacity* and the other full *transparency*. The following figure shows the dialog after attaching a *Gradient* this way.

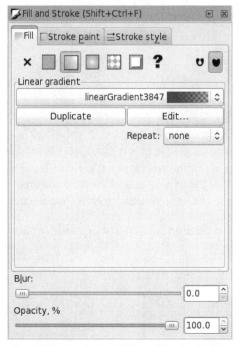

Gradient selected in *Fill and Stroke* dialog.

An already defined *Gradient* can be assigned to the object by selecting the *Gradient* from the drop-down menu under the *Fill* tab of the *Fill and Stroke* dialog. A *Gradient* can also be assigned to the *Stroke* of an object under the *Stroke paint* tab.

To attach a *Gradient* with the *Gradient Tool*, select the tool by clicking on the ▨ icon (**Ctrl+F1 or g**) in the *Tool Box*.

The *Gradient Tool Tool Controls* has options to choose a linear ▢ or a radial ▢ *Gradient* and the application of the *Gradient* to the *Fill* ▨ or *Stroke* ▢ of an object. Once the options are selected, **Left Mouse Drag** across an object to attach a *Gradient*. The start and stop point of the drag will define the range of the *Gradient* (where the start and end *Stops* are placed, see below). If an already defined *Gradient* has been chosen from the drop-down menu in the *Tool Controls* it will be applied to the object. Otherwise a two *Stop Gradient* will automatically be created with both *Stops* the color of the objects existing *Fill* and with one *Stop* full *opacity* and the other with full *transparency*.

The *Gradient Tool-Tool Controls*.

# Editing Stops

*Gradients* can be modified by adding, deleting, moving, or changing the color and *opacity* of *Stops*. They can be edited onscreen. This is much more convenient than using the *Gradient Editor* dialog.

## Onscreen Editing

An object with a *Gradient* displays *Gradient* handles when the *Gradient Tool*, *Node Tool*, or one of the *shape tools* is active (the latter two if enabled in the *Inkscape Preferences* dialog). Some editing actions work when any of these tools is active, others work only with the *Gradient Tool*.

Circle, diamond, and square handles represent start, intermediate, and end *Stops*, respectively. Editing *Stops* has many parallels to editing nodes.

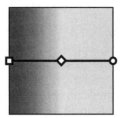 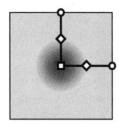

Linear and radial *Gradients* showing the Gradient handles.

*Stops* can be selected by clicking on them with the *Gradient Tool*, the *Node Tool*, or one of the *shape tools*. To select more than one use **Shift+Left Mouse Click**. With the *Gradient Tool* you can use a *rubber-band* selection by using **Shift+Left Mouse Drag** or you can select all the *Stops* by using **Ctrl+A**.

To add a new intermediate *Stop*, with the object selected and the *Gradient Tool* active:

- Double-click on the *Gradient* path. A new *Stop* will be added where you clicked. The *Stop* will take the existing color under the path.

- **Ctrl+Alt+Left Mouse Click** on the *Gradient*. A new *Stop* will be added where you clicked. The *Stop* will take the existing color under the cursor.

- Select two adjacent *Stops* and press **Insert**. A new *Stop* will be added halfway between the selected *Stops* and with a color halfway in-between.

- Drag a color from the *Palette* or the *Swatches* dialog unto the *Gradient* path. A new *Stop* will be created with the dragged color at the point of the drop (drop too far from the path and the *Fill* will be changed to solid with the dragged color). This also works if the *Node Tool* or one of the *shape tools* is active.

To remove an intermediate *Stop*, with the *Gradient Tool* active:

- Click on it using **Ctrl+Alt+Left Mouse Click**. This also works if the *Node Tool* or any of the *shape tools* are active.

- Use the **Del** to remove selected *Stops*. If there is at least one intermediate *Stop*, then deleting the start or end *Stops* will shorten the *Gradient* with the nearest intermediate *Stop* becoming a start or end *Stop*. If there is no intermediate *Stop*, then deleting a start or end *Stop* will replace the *Gradient* with a solid *Fill* of the color of the remaining *Stop*.

- Using **Ctrl+L** will attempt to simplify the *Gradient* over the a region defined by selected *Stops* by adjusting and removing some *Stops*. This is particularly useful for removing redundant *Stops*.

To move an intermediate *Stop*:

- Drag it with the *Gradient Tool*, *Node Tool*, or one of the *shape tools*. If more than one *Stop* is selected, they will all move together. Dragging with the **Ctrl** snaps the *Stops* at points that are multiples of 1/10th of the distance between the nearest neighboring unselected *Stops*. Dragging with the **Alt** moves selected *Stops* according to how far away they are from the dragged *Stop*.

- With one or more *Stops* selected and the *Gradient Tool* active, use the **Arrow** keys. If multiple intermediate *Stops* are selected, they will move together. Using the **Shift** with the **Arrow** keys accelerates the shift by a factor of 10. Using the **Alt** moves the selected *Stops* one screen pixel at a time. Using **Shift+Alt** moves the *Stops* 10 screen pixels at a time.

Note: You cannot move a *Stop* past an adjacent *Stop*.

There are several ways to see and change the style (color and/or *transparency*) of one or more *Stops*. In general, if no *Stop* is selected, indicators and changes apply to the whole object; if one *Stop* is selected, indicators and changes apply to that *Stop*; and if multiple *Stops* are selected, indicators show an average value for the selected *Stops* and changes apply to all selected *Stops*.

• The *Fill and Stroke* dialog: If no *Stop* is selected, the *Gradient* is previewed at the top under the *Fill* or *Stroke* tab. Otherwise the current color and *opacity* values for selected *Stops* are shown. Changes apply to all selected *Stops*.

• The *Style Indicator*: If no *Stop* is selected the indicators show previews of the *Gradients* (*Fill* and *Stroke*). Otherwise the current values for selected *Stops* are shown. Changes apply to all selected *Stops*. See the section called *Style Indicator*, earlier in this chapter for more details.

• Drag-and-Drop: Colors can be dragged from either the *Palette* or from the *Swatches* dialog onto *Stops* (or onto the *Gradient* path to add a new *Stop*).

• Copy-and-Paste: Colors can be copied to and from the *clipboard*. Copying to the *clipboard* (Edit → ▧ Copy (**Ctrl+C**)) will copy a *Stop* color and *opacity* if one *Stop* is selected or the average color if more than one is selected. Pasting the style (Edit → ▧ Paste Style (**Shift+Ctrl+V**)) copies from the *clipboard* the color and *opacity* to all selected *Stops*.

## Using the Gradient Editor Dialog

There is a dedicated *Gradient Editor* dialog for editing *Gradients*. It is envisioned that this dialog be removed as redundant in the future. To call up the dialog, click on the *Edit...* button, either in the *Fill and Stroke* dialog or the *Gradient Tool-Tool Controls*. Note that which *Gradient* is being edited does not change automatically when you select an object with a different *Gradient*.

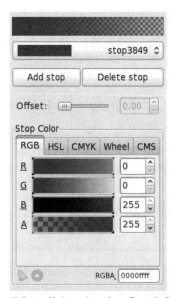

*Gradient Editor* dialog showing first default *Stop*.

In this dialog, the *Gradient* is shown at the very top. Next down is the current *Stop*. You can see that the *Stop* shown above is a solid blue, fully opaque with *Alpha* = 255. You can also see from the *Offset* slider that the *Stop* shown is set all the way to the left (and as the *Stop* is at one limit of the *Gradient*, its position can't be moved). The color and transparency of this *Stop* can be changed in the *Stop Color* section. The tabs work the same as those described in the *Flat Colors* section above. The *Dropper Tool* can also be used to change one of the end *Gradient* colors by first selecting the corresponding *Gradient* handle. (To modify a non-end *Gradient* color, copy the color to the *clipboard* by using **Ctrl+C** with the desired color selected with the *Dropper Tool* and then paste into the *Gradient Editor RGBA* entry box.)

To edit another *Stop*, select that *Stop* in the pull-down menu. In the default case described above, the second *Stop* has the same color as the first but is fully transparent (e.g., *Alpha* = 0). This is shown in the current *Stop* section by the divided box. The left half shows the color with *Alpha* and the right half without *Alpha*. Note also that the *Offset* slider is fully to the right.

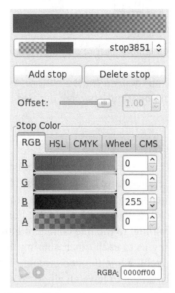

*Gradient Editor* dialog showing second default *Stop*.

To add a *Stop*, click on the *Add stop* button. The new *Stop* will be added to the right of whichever *Stop* was selected, unless that *Stop* was the farthest to the right, in which case the new *Stop* will be added to the left. The position, color, and transparency for the new *Stop* will be set to halfway between its neighbors.

The following figures show a third *Stop* added to a *Gradient* after its color and position have been adjusted.

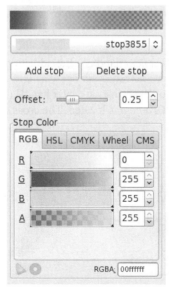

*Gradient Editor* dialog showing added third *Stop*. Note that the new *Stop* has an offset of
0.25, that is the center of the *Stop* will be one quarter of the *Gradient* width from the left.

An example of a *Gradient*, before and after adding a third *Stop*.✪

To delete a *Stop*, select the *Stop*, then click on the *Delete stop* button. As at least two *Stops* are required to define a *Gradient*, you cannot delete a *Stop* via the dialog if only two are defined.

## Adjusting Gradients

Once a *Gradient* has been applied to an object, the orientation and extent of the *Gradient* can be changed via dragging the outer two *Gradient Stops* indicated by the square and circle handles. The handles appear when the *Gradient Tool* is selected. They will also appear by default when many of the other tools are selected (controlled by the *Enable* Gradient *editing* option in the *Inkscape Preferences* dialog under each tool tab). For linear *Gradients*, one set of handles define the range of the *Gradient*. The *Gradient* is parallel to the line connecting the two handles. For radial *Gradients*, there are two sets of handles (or *Stops*) at right angles to each other, sharing the square center handle. The center, handle controls the origin of the *Gradient* (one "edge"), while the two circular handles control the range of the *Gradient* in orthogonal directions. This allows a radial *Gradient* to have an elliptical shape.

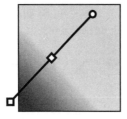
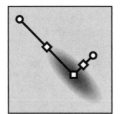

Linear and radial *Gradients* showing the *Gradient* handles after adjusting the orientation and range of the *Gradient*.

A radial *Gradient* can be made asymmetric by dragging the center handle (diamond) while holding down the **Shift** key. A cross will appear where the center of the *Gradient* is located. The cross can be dragged to make further adjustments.

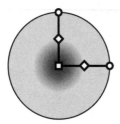
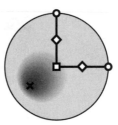

A radial *Gradient* with a symmetric fill (left) and an asymmetric fill (right).

*Gradient* handles from two different objects will snap together if one is placed over the other. This facilitates aligning *Gradients* between different objects. The handles will then move together. If multiple objects are selected when a *Gradient* is created, all the objects will share a common *Gradient*.

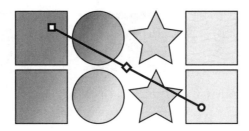

The eight objects share a common *Gradient*.

An option only accessible through the *Gradient* tabs of the *Fill and Stroke* dialog is defining how the area outside the *Gradient* range is filled. The three options are: fill with the solid color of the edge *Stops* (None), fill with a reflection of the same *Gradient* (Reflect), and fill with a translation of the same *Gradient* (Direct). The effect of these three options is shown next.

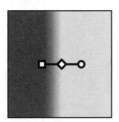  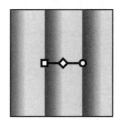

An example of a linear *Gradients* with different repeat options. From left to right: None, Reflected, and Direct.

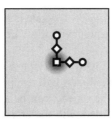 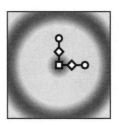 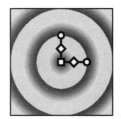

An example of a radial *Gradient* with different repeat options. From left to right: None, Reflected, and Direct.

The keyboard shortcut **Shift+R** reverses the *Gradient* direction when the *Gradient Tool* is active. This is especially useful for radial *Gradients* where one cannot just drag the *Gradient* handles to reverse the *Gradient*.

# Patterns

Any object or set of objects can be turned into a *Pattern* and used in the fill of an object. The *Pattern* can be shifted, rotated, and stretched as necessary. Inkscape includes a set of *Patterns* accessible through the *Fill and Stroke* dialog. The *Vine Design* tutorial covers creating and using *Patterns*.

A few of the *Patterns* included in Inkscape.

## Warning

Check the licenses of the bitmap patterns included with Inkscape to see if they are compatible with your artwork. They are not public domain! (Look inside the *SVG* file or use the *XML Editor* to look in the "defs" section.)

The *Patterns* included with Inkscape are defined in the file `patterns/patterns.svg` located in the Inkscape "share" directory. Edit or replace this file to include your own stock *Patterns*.

To use a *Pattern*, two or three steps are necessary. The first, optional step, is to create a *Pattern*. The second is to apply the newly created *Pattern* or an Inkscape provided *Pattern* to an object. And the third is to adjust the *Pattern* position and scaling as necessary.

## Creating Patterns

*Patterns* are very easy to create. Simply select the object or objects you wish to use as a *Pattern* and then use the Object → Pattern → Objects to Pattern (**Alt+I**) command.

After converting the selection to a *Pattern*, the original selection is replaced by a *Rectangle* shape object filled with the new *Pattern* (and with an invisible stroke). This new object can be deleted but the *Pattern* will remain. *Patterns* have a life of their own.

The "tile" size of the *Pattern* is the total *bounding box* of the objects in the *Pattern*. If space is required around the objects, a non-visible rectangle object can be added or the *Pattern* size can be edited with the *XML Editor* dialog.

The object(s) in any *Pattern* can be edited by selecting an object that is filled with that *Pattern* and then using the Object → Pattern → Pattern to Objects (**Shift+Alt+I**) command. The original objects will reappear in their original place (built-in *Patterns* will appear in the upper-left corner). After editing, the objects can be again turned into a *Pattern*. Both the old and new *Patterns* are available for use. Other objects filled with the original *Pattern* remain unchanged. The new *Pattern* must be "reapplied" to the object the *Pattern* came from.

## Using Patterns

To change the fill of an object to a *Pattern*, simply click on the *Pattern* icon ( ) in the *Fill and Stroke* dialog. Then select the required *Pattern* from the pull-down menu. User created *Patterns* will be listed first.

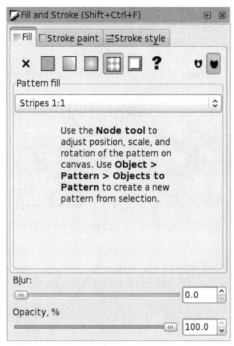

*Pattern* section of *Fill and Stroke* dialog.

Unfortunately, there is no preview of the *Patterns* (as with the *Gradient* tab).

## Note

If you want a *Pattern* to transform with an object, you must toggle on this option using the ⊞ icon that is in the *Tool Controls* when the *Select Tool* is in use.

# Adjusting Patterns

Adjusting *Patterns* is done by a set of handles. The handles will appear when an object with a *Pattern* fill is selected and the node or one of the shape tools is active. The handles will appear on the original objects that defined the *Pattern*, or the former location of those objects if they have been moved or deleted (unless the *Pattern* has been previously adjusted). In the case of built-on *Patterns* they will appear in the upper-left corner of the canvas. The following figure shows the location of the handles for a *Pattern* that has not been adjusted.

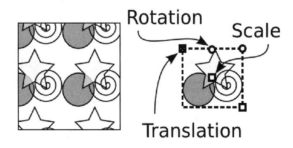

A *Pattern* (right) with an object filled with that *Pattern* (left). The translation handle is a "×" over-laying a *Rectangle* shape handle. The size handle is a square and the rotation handle a circle.

To adjust the origin, scale, and orientation of the *Pattern*, drag the translation handle (×), scale handle (square), and rotation handle (circle). The translation handle can conveniently be dragged over the object with the *Pattern* fill. Holding the **Ctrl** key down while dragging will restrict the movement to the horizontal or vertical direction. The scale is governed by the distance between the translation handle and scale handle, the orientation by the relative position of the rotation handle with the translation handle. The $x$ and $y$ directions can be scaled independently. Hold the **Ctrl** down to force the scaling to be uniform. Handles can be snapped.

The following figure shows how the fill changed after the handles have been adjusted.

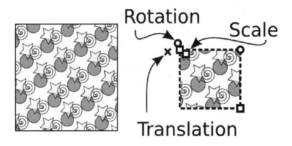

A *Pattern* filled object (left) after adjusting the *Pattern* shown on the right. The *Pattern* was adjusted by dragging the handles shown.

## Tip

For *SVG* viewers that don't support clipping, you can crop a bitmap by turning the bitmap into a *Pattern* and using it to fill an arbitrary path.

A demonstration of cropping a bitmap image. Left: Original image. Center: Image after converting to *Pattern* and using as *Pattern* for circle. Right: Image after enlarging and shifting *Pattern*.

## Hatchings

Inkscape now includes many *Patterns* that can be used as hatchings. If you need to create a new hatching, here is the general procedure. The simplest hatching is to group two rectangular boxes, one with black fill and one with no fill as shown below.

The hatching *Pattern* on the left (surrounded by the dotted line) has been used for the star's *Fill*. The *Pattern* consists of two rectangles in a *Group*.

## Warning

Inkscape has problems properly displaying *Patterns* at the *Pattern* boundaries. Inkscape export to a *PNG* also has problems. To work around this problem, you can make the *Pattern* rectangles wider than the maximum width needed to fill an object. Firefox, Opera, and Batik will display patterns without artifacts. Batik can be used for producing a high-quality *PNG*.

# Custom Swatches

*New in v0.48.*

*Custom Swatches* allow per document palettes with swatches of solid colors and *Gradients*. *Custom Swatches* are automatically added to a special *Auto* palette as they are created (selectable in the *Palette* or *Swatches* dialog). Solid color swatches are implemented as one-stop *Gradients*.

To create a *Custom Swatch*, with an object selected that has the desired solid fill or *Gradient*, click on the ☐ icon in the *Fill and Stroke* dialog (in the *Fill* or *Stroke paint* tab as appropriate). After creation, the color or *Gradient* of a swatch can be edited using the *Swatch fill* section of the *Fill and Stroke* dialog or by using the *Gradient Editor* dialog that is accessed by selecting *Edit...* in the menu that pops up when you **Right Click** on a swatch in the *Palette* or *Swatches* dialog (when the *Auto* palette is displayed). Any change to a swatch affects the fill of all objects that reference that swatch.

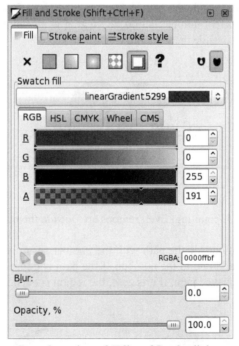

*Swatch* section of *Fill and Stroke* dialog.

To assign a *Custom Swatch* to the fill of an object, either select the desired swatch from the menu in the *Swatch fill* section of the *Fill and Stroke* dialog (if a swatch is already assigned to the fill) or click on the desired swatch in the *Palette* or *Swatches* dialog (if the *Auto* palette is selected).

To delete a swatch, select *Delete* from the menu that pops up when you **Right Click** on the swatch in the *Palette* or *Swatches* dialog (the *Auto* palette must be selected). Note that using File → 🗑 Vacuum Defs will not remove unused swatches.

# Fill Rule

The *Fill Rule* dictates what areas are filled when a path overlaps itself or one part of a complex path surrounds another part. The rule applies only to the *Fill* of an object (and not the *Stroke paint*). One can choose the *Fill Rule* from the two choices:

- ♡ Even-odd.

- ♥ Non-zero.

The difference between these rules is demonstrated in the following figures.

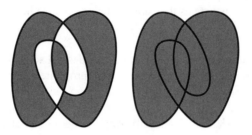

Fill rule: Even-odd vs. Non-zero.

**Even-odd rule.** In this rule, you start outside the path with the number zero. Every time you cross the object's path, you add one to the number. If the current number is odd, the region is inside the path and therefore colored. If the current number is even, the region is outside the path and is not colored.

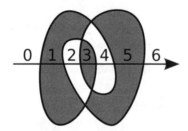

Fill rule: a demonstration of counting. Even regions are *outside* the path, odd regions are *inside*.

**Non-zero rule.** In this rule, you start outside the path with the number zero. Every time you cross the object's path with the path going to the left, you add one to the number. If the path is going to the right, you subtract one. If the number is non-zero, the region is inside the path; if it is zero, the region is outside the path.

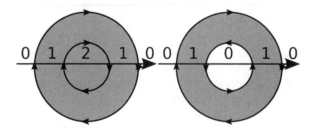

Non-zero fill rule applied to a path consisting of two sub-paths. Zero regions are *outside* the path; non-zero regions are *inside* the path. The arrows on the paths show the paths' direction.

# Stroke Style

In addition to *Stroke paint*, discussed in the previous section, *Stroke* attributes include stroke *Width*, *Join* style, *Cap* style, *Dashes*, and *Markers*. All of these attributes can be set using the *Stroke style* tab in the *Fill and Stroke* dialog. Stroke width can also be set using the *Style Indicator* (see below). The last part of this section is a discussion on how to make complex strokes.

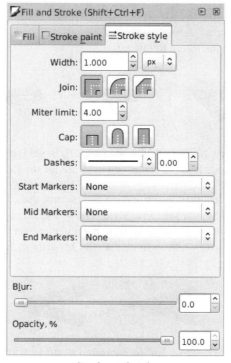

*Stroke style* tab.

# Stroke Width

*Stroke* width can be changed by using the *Stroke style* tab in the *Fill and Stroke* dialog, or by using the *Style Indicator* via a pop-up menu or by *Stroke* gestures.

### Note

If you want the line width to transform with an object, you must toggle on this option using the ⇥ icon that is in the *Tool Controls* when the *Select Tool* is in use.

***Stroke style* tab.** Stroke width can be changed by using the *Width* entry box on the *Stroke style* tab of the *Fill and Stroke* dialog. The units are specified by the drop-down menu on the right.

***Style Indicator.*** A **Right Mouse Click** on the *Stroke* width part of the *Style Indicator* opens a pop-up menu that allows the stroke width unit to be changed as well as a preset width to be selected. The stroke can also be removed with this menu.

***Stroke* Gestures.** *Stroke Gestures* is the name give to changing the *Stroke* width by dragging the mouse from the *Stroke* width section of the *Stroke style* indicator into the Inkscape window. The principle is that as you drag the mouse, the line width will change proportionally to the distance from a 45° line from the indicator. The farther away you are, the more subtle the changes can be. The maximum width increase is a factor of 4 and the minimum width is zero. See *Color Gestures* for more details.

# Join Style

The *Join* style is how two lines meeting at a corner should be joined together. The options are:

-  Miter join.

-  Round join.

-  Bevel join.

The different *Join* styles are shown in the figure following.

*Join* styles: Miter (left), Round (center), Bevel (right). Note
how the node is at the center of curvature for the Round style.

When the *Miter* option is selected, the length of the projection can become quite long if the two lines intersect at a small angle. In this case, it may be preferable to use the *Bevel* style. The *Miter limit* controls the point at which a *Miter* join automatically is converted to a *Bevel* join. If the distance from the inner intersection point to the tip of the triangle ("m" in the following figure) measured in stroke widths is more than the *Miter limit*, the join will be drawn in the *Bevel* style.

On the left is a Miter join. If the distance "m" as measured in stroke widths is more than the Miter limit, the corner will be drawn with a Bevel join as shown on the right. (The nodes are shown as diamonds.)

## Note

The *visual bounding box* is determined by assuming that the *Join* style is *Round*.

# Cap Style

The *Cap* style determines how the end of a line is drawn. The options are:

-  Butt cap.

- Round cap.

- Square cap.

The different *Cap* styles are shown in the figure below.

*Cap* styles: Butt (left), Round (center), Square (right). The nodes are shown as diamonds for reference.

**Note**

The *visual bounding box* is determined by assuming the *Cap* style is *Round*.

# Dashes

A wide selection of *Dash* patterns are available from the drop-down *Dash* menu of the *Stroke style* tab of the *Fill and Stroke* dialog. The patterns scale with the stroke width.

**Note**

Each *Dash* takes on the *Cap* style as shown in the figure below.

The same *Dash* style but with different *Cap* styles: Butt (left), Round (center), Square (right). The nodes are shown as diamonds for reference.

The entry box next to the *Dash* menu is for the *Dash offset*. The offset shifts the *Dash* pattern along the path. The units are in stroke width.

# Markers

*Markers* are objects like arrow heads placed along a path. Different *Markers* can be specified for the start, middle, and end of a path. Middle *Markers* are placed at the location of every non-end node.

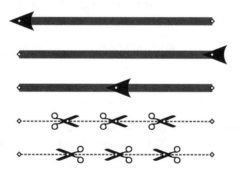

Examples of *Markers*. From the top down: *Start arrow* at the start of a line. *Start arrow* at the end of a line. *Start arrow* in the middle of a line (a node has been added). Scissors at middle nodes. Scissors at middle nodes, path reversed.

A custom *Marker* can be created by selecting the object or objects that you wish to use as a *Marker* and then using the Object → Object to Marker command. The selected objects will disappear and a new entry will appear in the *Marker* pull-down menus of the *Fill and Stroke* dialog. The *Marker* is created assuming a horizontal orientation for the path. The point of attachment to a node is the center of the *bounding box* for the *Marker*. Warning: While the marker will display fine in Inkscape, only a fourth of it will be displayed in most other *SVG* renderers. Adding the attribute *style="overflow:visible"* to the *Marker* definition will fix the problem (Bug). Note, that custom *Markers* can be added to Inkscape; see the section called *Custom Markers* in Chapter 24, *Customization*.

Examples of custom *Markers*. The objects on the left were converted to *Markers* by first duplicating and then using the Object → Object to Marker command. They were then applied to the paths on the right.

Note: The Object → Object to Marker procedure is a bit buggy. The new *Marker* may not show up in the list until another *Marker* is applied to the path. If multiple objects are converted, the *z-order* is reversed. *Group* the objects first to avoid this problem.

Two problems exist with *Markers*. The first is that *Markers* do not take the color of the stroke. This can be worked around by using the *Color Markers to Match Stroke* extension, by editing the *SVG* file with the *XML Editor*, or adding a custom, pre-colored *Marker*. An alternative solution is to convert the path with the *Markers* to a path (Path → Object to Path (**Shift+Ctrl+C**)). This creates a *Group* with the *Markers* converted to separate objects, which can be colored independently.

The second problem is that *Markers* scale with line width. The line width had to be reduced in the above figure for the scissors examples, to give the scissors a reasonable size. Again, one could edit the *SVG* file to adjust the *Marker* size.

**Tip**

To place middle *Markers* evenly along a path you need to have evenly spaced nodes. For straight horizontal and vertical lines, nodes can be distributed evenly using the *Align and Distribute* dialog. To add just one node halfway between two existing nodes click on the *Insert* ⚓ icon in the *Node Tool-Tool Controls*. To add one node anywhere on an existing path, double-click on the path where you want the node (or single click while holding down the **Ctrl+Alt** keys). To add multiple nodes evenly spaced between existing nodes, use the *Add Nodes* extension.

Another thing to note is that *Markers* are included in the *Visual bounding box* calculation.

# Complex Strokes

A complex *Stroke* can be created by overlaying two or more paths with different *Stroke* attributes. The easiest way to make exact copies of a path is to use the Edit → Duplicate (**Ctrl+D**) command.

If one uses *Clones* of a path (Edit → Clone → Create Clone (**Alt+D**)), then one can adjust the original path at a later time and all the *Clones* will change too. This requires unsetting the *Stroke* attributes of the original path (use the *XML* editor to unset the *Stroke* width). Since the original path's attributes are unset, it will not be visible and cannot be used as part of the visible *Stroke*.

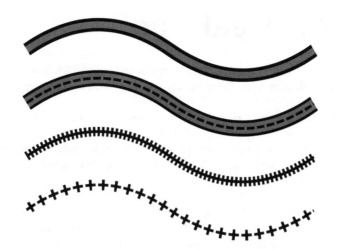

Examples of complex *Strokes*. From top to bottom: Road: consists of a 5 pixel-wide red path over a 10 pixel-wide black path. Divided road: consists of a 2 pixel-wide dashed black path over an 8 pixel-wide red path, over a 12 pixel-wide black path. Railroad tracks: consists of a 7 pixel-wide dashed path, with dash pattern (1.75, 1.75) over a 2 pixel-wide solid path. Border: consists of an 8 pixel-wide dashed path, with dash pattern (2, 8) and an offset of 7 pixels (use *XML* editor to set) over a 2 pixel-wide dashed path with dash pattern (8, 2).

# Chapter 11. Tweak Tool

The *Tweak Tool* is used to make small changes to objects, paths, and colors. While at first objects, paths, and colors may seem to have little to do with each other, the use of *Tweak Tool* to edit them is surprisingly very similar.

To use the *Tweak Tool* select the tool from the *Tool Box* ( ✎ ) or use either of the shortcuts: **W** or **Shift+F2**.

The *Tweak Tool* works like a *brush* that covers a circular part of the screen, indicated by an orange circle. The affect of the brush is strongest in the center and falls off smoothly till the edge. Two parameters, located in the *Tool Controls* affect the "physical" nature of the brush:

- **Width:** Determines the size of the brush. The range is from 1 to 100, where 20 corresponds to a radius of 100 screen pixels. As the brush width is defined in screen pixels, zoom can be used to quickly change the size of the brush relative to the size of an object. The **Left Arrow** and **Right Arrow** keys can be used to decrease and increase the width at anytime. **Home** sets the *Width* to 1, while **End** sets it to 100.

- **Force:** Determines how strongly a movement of the brush affects the objects on the screen. The range is from 1 to 100. If the "Use Pressure" button ( ⬥ ) is toggled on, a pressure-sensitive tablet can be used to control the force; maximum pressure corresponds to the *Force* parameter setting. See the *Calligraphy Tool* section for use of a tablet. The **Up Arrow** and **Down Arrow** keys can be used to decrease and increase the (maximum) *Force*.

The *Tweak Tool* has a number of modes for editing objects, paths and colors. The mode is selected by clicking on the corresponding icon in the *Tool Controls* or using a keyboard shortcut. Many of the modes have their own cursor. The various modes are discussed in the next three sections.

Objects must be selected to be tweaked. Using the **Space Bar** is a quick way to switch back and forth between the *Select Tool* and the *Tweak Tool*. Note that there is no onscreen indication of what objects are selected when the *Tweak Tool* is in use. If no objects are selected, a message to that effect will be displayed in the *Status Bar*.

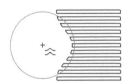

An example of using the *Tweak Tool* on a series of *Rectangles*. The brush size is indicated by the orange circle and the *Mode* by the cursor (in this case *Push*).

# Tweaking Objects

A number of *Tweak Tool* modes modify objects. A typical use would be to create an array of cloned objects using the *Create Tiled Clones* dialog and then use the *Tweak Tool* to move them around.

The following object modes are available:

- **Move.** ▦ (**Shift+M**) Moves objects in direction of drag.

- **Move In/Out.** ▦ (**Shift+I**) Pulls the objects toward the cursor. With the **Shift** held down, pushes the objects away from the cursor.

- **Move Jitter.** ▦ (**Shift+Z**) Moves the objects in random directions by random amounts.

- **Scale.** ▢ (**Shift**+**<** or **Shift**+**>**) Shrinks the objects near the cursor. With the **Shift** held down, enlarges the objects near the cursor.

- **Rotate.** ▦ (**Shift**+**[** or **Shift**+**]**) Rotates clockwise the objects near the cursor. With the **Shift** held down, rotates counterclockwise the objects near the cursor.

- **Duplicate (Delete).** ▦ (**Shift**+**D**), Randomly duplicates the objects near the cursor. Duplicates are placed directly over the original so you may not see immediately the effect. Switching temporarily to the *Select Tool* via the **Space** will update the *Status Bar* with the new number of selected objects (newly created objects are automatically added to the selection or *Group*). With the **Shift** held down, randomly deletes objects.

- **Blur.** ▦ (**Shift**+**B**), Blurs objects near cursor. With the **Shift** held down, reduces blurring.

# Tweaking Paths

A variety of *Tweak Tool* modes modify paths. If an object is not a path (i.e., *Rectangles*, *Ellipses*, text) it is first converted to a path. Unlike the *Node Tool*, nodes do not need to be selected.

All path modes share the *Fidelity* parameter. The range for the parameter is from 1 to 100. A low value gives a rough distortion using few nodes, a high value gives a smoother distortion but at the cost of creating large numbers of nodes. Note that any path distortion will affect the entire path, even the parts that are far away from the cursor.

The tool has several known problems. If used on an open path, the path will become closed. It doesn't work well on straight lines or lines with just two nodes.

The following path modes are available:

- **Push.** ⌃ (**Shift**+**P**) Default. Displaces path in direction of drag.

- **Shrink (Grow).** ⋈ (**Shift**+**S**) Insets path near cursor while dragging. With the **Shift** held down, outsets the path near the cursor while dragging. In v0.46 these are separate modes.

- **Attract (Repel).** ✕ (**Shift**+**A**) Displaces path inward toward cursor while dragging. With the **Shift** held down, displaces path outward from cursor while dragging. In v0.46 these are separate modes.

- **Roughen.** ✎ (**Shift**+**R**) Roughens path near dragged cursor.

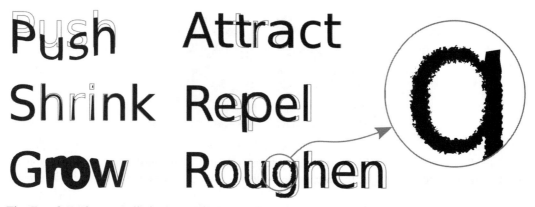

The *Tweak Tool* was applied with a different mode to each of the text objects. In each case the cursor was moved from top to bottom. The mode is indicated by the text. The original text is outlined in red.

A few short cuts exist: **Ctrl** switches temporarily to *Shrink* mode. **Ctrl**+**Shift** switches temporarily to *Grow* mode.

The *Tweak Tool* is very useful for manipulating hatchings.

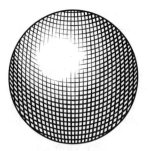

The hatching was created by using the *Interpolate* extension twice to create two quasi-orthogonal sets of lines that were then clipped by a circle. When created, each set of lines belonged to one compound path. The compound paths were broken apart (Path → 🔵 Break Apart (**Shift+Ctrl+K**)) and then the strokes converted to paths (Path → 🖋 Stroke to Path (**Ctrl+Alt+C**)). Finally, the *Tweak Tool* was used in *Shrink* mode to narrow the width of the lines to create a 3D-shading effect.

# Tweaking Colors

The *Tweak Tool* can be used to make small color changes to objects. In doing so, it changes the *Fill* and/or *Stroke* color of an entire object. While it can be used to change the color of *Gradient* stop, it cannot create *Gradients* nor can it modify part of an object leaving the rest alone. This is due to the fundamental nature of vector objects. It can, however, be used to adjust the color of a group of objects, with the objects closer to the cursor changing the most.

Two modes with several options exist for tweaking colors.

- **Paint.** ▣ (**Shift+C**) Paint with current *Fill* and *Stroke* style. When the tool is selected, changing the *Fill* or *Stroke* by using the *Fill and Stroke* dialog or the *Palette* will change only the *Current style* and not any objects. If either *Fill* or *Stroke* are not set, the *Fill* or *Stroke* of tweaked objects will remain unchanged. *New in v0.47*: Holding the **Shift** will invert the color applied.

- **Jitter.** ⬙ (**Shift+J**) Randomize colors. The *Current style* is not used.

The *Tweak Tool* was used to modify a grid of gray squares. Left: In *Paint* mode the tool was used to paint diagonal red and blue lines. Right: In *Jitter* mode the tool was used to add a random color to the squares.

The *Tweak Tool* in a color mode has four options. It can act independently on a color's hue, saturation, lightness (*HSL*) and *opacity*. The options can be toggled on independently by the H, S, L, and O icons next to the *Channel* label in the *Tool Controls*.

# Chapter 12. Spray Tool

*New in v0.48.*

The *Spray Tool* is used to distribute copies of an object (or objects) much like an airbrush would paint drops. Three modes are available in the *Spray Tool-Tool Controls*:

- **Copy mode ( ▣ ):** The distributed copies are separate objects that are independent of each other. Attributes of one object can be changed independent of other objects. This mode is especially useful for creating objects to manipulate with the the *Tweak Tool*.

- **Clone mode ( ▣ ):** The distributed copies are clones of the original object. Changing the attributes of the original object changes the attributes of all copies. The *Fill* color of the original object was changed from yellow to blue after spraying the stars. This mode is moderately less demanding on renderers than the *Copy* mode.

- **Single Path mode ( ▣ ):** The distributed copies are part of the same *Path*. Overlaps of objects are removed. This mode is more CPU intensive during spraying. The source object may need to be converted to a path first.

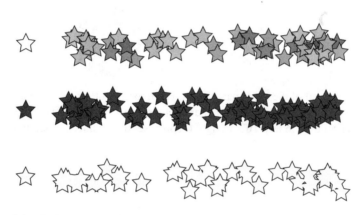

Examples of the three spray modes. From top to bottom: *Copy* mode: The style of each copy can be changed individually as was done here using the *Color Jitter* mode of the *Tweak Tool*. *Clone* mode: All clones must have the same style. If the original object is changed, all the clones are changed in the same way. *Path* mode: The copies are merged into one path with overlaps removed.

To use the *Spray Tool* first select one or more objects you which to spray with the *Select Tool* or any other selection method. Then select the *Spray Tool* from the *Tool Box* ( ↘ ) or use either of the shortcuts: **A** or **Shift**+**F3**. Hold the **Left Mouse Button** down while moving the mouse or the mouse scroll wheel. Once the *Spray Tool* has been selected, you can toggle between the *Spray Tool* and the *Select Tool* using the **Space Bar**.

A number of parameters are available in the *Tool Controls* to modify the behavior of the *Spray Tool*:

- **Width:** Determines the area of the spray (indicated by the orange circle when the *Spray Tool* is selected). The range is from 1 to 100, where 20 corresponds to a radius of 100 screen pixels. As the spray width is defined in screen pixels, zoom can be used to quickly change the size of the spray relative to the size of the drawing. The **Left Arrow** and **Right Arrow** keys can be used to decrease and increase the width at anytime. **Home** sets the *Width* to 1, while **End** sets it to 100.

- **Amount:** Determines how the relative number objects sprayed. The range is from 1 to 100. If the "Use Pressure" button ( ⤓ ) is toggled on, a pressure-sensitive tablet can be used to control the rate objects are sprayed; maximum pressure corresponds to the *Amount* parameter setting. See the *Calligraphy Tool* section for use of a tablet. The **Up Arrow** and **Down Arrow** keys can be used to decrease and increase the (maximum) *Amount*.

- **Rotation**: Adds a random rotation to each copy if non-zero. The setting determines the maximum rotation amount. The range is from 1 to 100 where 100 corresponds to plus or minus 180°.

- **Scale**: Adds a random scale to each copy if non-zero. The setting determines the maximum scaling amount. The range is from 0 to 100 where 100 corresponds to twice the original size.

- **Scatter**: Determines how the items are scattered. The range is from 1 to 100 where 1 corresponds to all the objects being sprayed under the cursor and 100 corresponds an even distribution over the spray region.

- **Focus**: Determines the spread of the scattered items. The range is 0 to 100 where 0 corresponds to all the items being sprayed under the cursor while 100 corresponds to items being sprayed at the edge of the spray area.

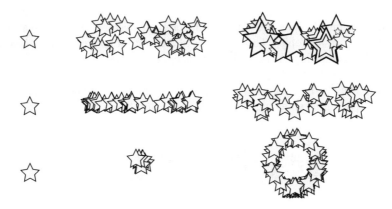

Examples of several of the spray parameters. From top to bottom: *Scale*: Parameter set to 0 on left, 100 on right. *Scatter*: Parameter set to 1 on left, 100 on right. *Focus*: Parameter set to 0 on left, 100 on right (*Scatter* set to 5, cursor jiggled in place).

# Chapter 13. Eraser Tool

The *Eraser Tool* is used to erase parts of a drawing. It has two modes. The *Touch* mode removes objects from a drawing, while the *Cut Out* mode removes parts of objects. To use the tool, either click on the ⬧ icon in the *Tool Box* or use the shortcut **Shift**+**E**.

## Eraser Touch Mode

In *Touch* mode, one uses the *Eraser Tool* to draw a red "touch" line. Any object that the line touches will be deleted when the stroke is finished. To enable *Touch* mode, click on the 🔳 icon in the *Eraser Tool-Tool Controls*.

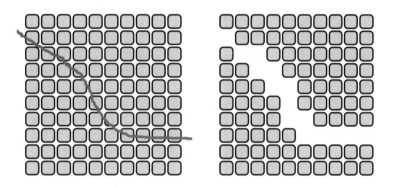

Left: The *Eraser Tool* has been used to draw a red "touch" line over an array of *Rectangles*. Right: Objects the "touch" line crosses are deleted.

## Eraser Cut-Out Mode

In the *Cut-Out* mode, the eraser is used to draw a red path, similar to a path created by the *Calligraphy Tool*. This path is then subtracted from any other paths it crosses. Regular *Shapes* crossed are first converted to paths. This mode does not work on *bitmap* images or directly on *Groups* (enter *Groups* first to use). If many objects are crossed, it may take awhile for the subtraction to be processed.

To enable *Cut-Out* mode, click on the 🔳 icon in the *Eraser Tool-Tool Controls*.

### Use with Tablets

If you are using a tablet with input devices enabled (set to *Screen* mode), the input devices will be pressure sensitive. There is no option to turn off this sensitivity as with the *Calligraphy Tool*. You may find it is better to use the *Calligraphy Tool* in *subtract* mode (hold down the **Alt** key) as there is better control over the pen's parameters. If your mouse only erases a narrow line, check to make sure it is not in *Screen* mode.

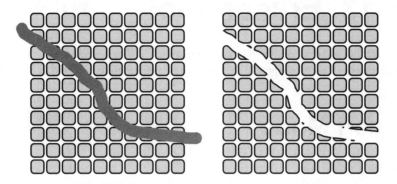

Left: The *Eraser Tool* has been used to draw a red path over an array of *Rectangles*. Right: The area inside the path is subtracted from any objects the path crosses.

# Chapter 14. Paint Bucket Tool

Inspired by the need for cartoonists to color their drawings, the *Paint Bucket Tool* flood fills a region with a color. True to an *SVG* drawing program, the new object is defined by vectors and thus is fully scalable. The region to be filled, however, is defined by the pixels on the screen at the time of the fill. This is best explained by the examples in the sections that follow.

## Simple Use

The simplest use is to fill an area defined by two different objects. Select the *Paint Bucket Tool* ( ✍ , **Shift+F7**) from the *Tool Box* and then click in the overlapping region. A new object is created with the current *Fill* color.

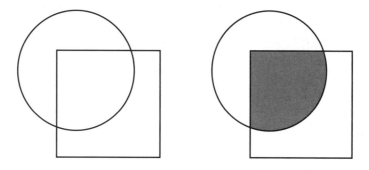

Left: Before *Paint Bucket* fill. Right: After clicking on the overlapping region with the *Paint Bucket Tool* (with the *Fill* color set to red).

The cursor position when clicking determines the starting point of the fill region. The filling algorithm recursively adds neighboring areas to the region until pixels are found that don't meet the criteria determined by the parameters in the *Tool Controls*.

The *Threshold* parameter controls how close a color must match the color (or *Alpha*) under the cursor. Lower thresholds will match a smaller range.

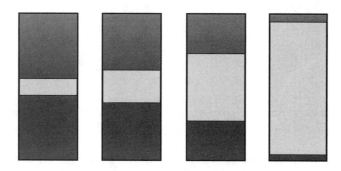

The gray areas have been filled by clicking on the centers of the rectangles with the *Paint Bucket Tool*. From left to right, the *Threshold* parameter was set to 5, 10, 20, and 40. ✪

The *Fill by* parameter controls what color value is used to determine the the color matching. Choices are: *Visible Colors* (default), *Red, Blue, Green, Hue, Saturation, Lightness*, and *Alpha*.

The circles were first filled with a blue to green gradient. The gray areas were created with the *Paint Bucket Tool* by clicking on the centers of the circles. In both cases, the *Threshold* parameter was set to 10. The *Fill by* parameter was set to *Visible Colors* on the left and *Red* on the right. With a value of *Red* the blue and green of the circle are ignored in the color matching, thus the bucket fill area reaches the circle's edge where there is a large change in the red level.✪

Holding the **Ctrl** down while clicking on an object with the *Paint Bucket Tool* will set the *Fill* and *Stroke* to the current style without preforming any filling.

# Filling Fidelity

The filling process works first by determining which pixels should be filled and then tracing those pixels to produce a vectorized path. The tracing process has limited precision which can result in inaccuracies in the filled region. You can improve the filling accuracy several ways. The first way is to zoom in on the region you are filling. Zooming in increases the number of screen pixels in the filled region which results in a more accurate tracing.

The moon man was given a gray fill using the *Paint Bucket Tool*, while the zoom level was 25% on the left and 200% on the right.

The second way to improve the filling accuracy is to expand the fill region slightly in a process akin to "trapping" that printers use to account for small misalignments in their printing plates. This works especially well for cartoons where the fills can be put on a separate *Layer* beneath a *Layer* containing the black lines. The amount of expansion is controlled by the *Grow/shrink by* parameter. As the name suggests, one can both expand and reduce the fill area.

The moon man was given a gray fill using the *Paint Bucket Tool*, while the zoom level was 200%. On the left, no "trapping" was used. On the right the *Grow/shrink by* parameter was set to 1 pixel. The fill was then moved behind the line drawing. On both sides, the region around the eye has been expanded by a factor of four.

# Filling Multiple Regions

Click-dragging the *Paint Bucket Tool* while holding the **Alt** key down across several noncontiguous regions will cause all the regions to be filled. (Not holding the **Alt** down will cause the borders to also be filled.)

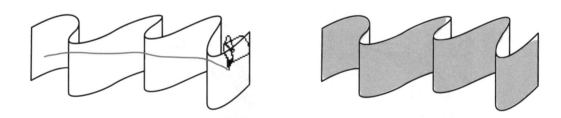

The *Paint Bucket Tool* was click-dragged with the **Alt** key down across the object on the left as shown by the red line. This resulted in the figure on the right.

# Closing Gaps

Small gaps in borders can be "filled" by setting the *Close gaps* to a value other than *None*. This prevents fills from leaking into undesired areas just because there is a small break in a line (as might happen in tracing a cartoon). Note that the gaps are defined in terms of screen pixels so different zoom levels will give different results. Also note, calculating the fill when there are gaps can take some time.

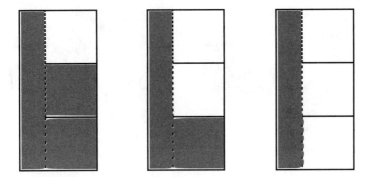

The *Paint Bucket Tool* was applied to the leftmost region in the three figures. The square areas are separated from this region by dashed lines with gaps of 1, 2, and 4 pixels from top to bottom. The *Close gaps* parameter was set, from left to right, to *Small*, *Medium*, *Large*. The filling was done at a zoom of 100%.

# Adding to a Fill

Since the *Paint Bucket Tool* uses pixels to calculate the area to be enclosed, Inkscape will clip the region off-screen to prevent the number of pixels that go into the filling algorithm from becoming too large. If this happens you can either zoom out to do the fill or you can do the fill in pieces. By holding the **Shift** down while clicking you can add to an existing fill. Unfortunately, this can lead to rendering artifacts between adjacent pieces even though they are part of the same path. Two solutions: (1) Set the *Grow/shrink by* parameter to 0.10. This will ensure a slight overlap during the filling process. The overlap is removed in the unioning step. (2) Use the *Node Tool* to adjust the nodes to overlap areas and then use the Path → 🖉 Union (**Ctrl++**) command to remove the overlap.

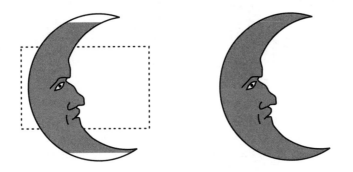

The *Paint Bucket Tool* was applied to the left moon under high zoom. The part visible onscreen is shown by the dotted rectangle. Note the missing fill at the top and bottom. On the right, the missing sections have been added by scrolling in turn so that each missing section was visible onscreen and then with the first filled section selected, **Shift**-clicking on the missing area.

# Chapter 15. Clipping and Masking

Clipping and masking are methods for restricting what part of an object (or *Group* of objects) is visible. For clipping, a *clipping path* defines the visible part of the object, while for masking, the *transparency* or *lightness* of one object determines the opacity of a second object. In both cases, the target object is not changed and can be unclipped or unmasked if needed.

Simple examples of clipping (top) and masking (bottom). The left column shows the text that serves as the clipping path and the text for masking, both overlaying blue rectangles that are the targets of the clipping and masking. In the right column are the results of the clipping and masking.

**Tip**

A clipped or masked object can be edited (transformed, style changed, nodes edited, etc.) while clipped or masked. Objects within a clipped or masked *Group* can also be moved relative to the clipping path or masking object if the *Group* is entered.

**Tip**

The clipping or masking path can be edited without unclipping or unmasking. With the clipped or masked object selected and the *Node Tool* active, click on either the ✂ (clipping) or ⟋ (masking) icons in the *Tool Controls*. *New in v0.48:* The clip or mask path and the object can be edited at the same time. (This only works if the mask path is an actual path and not a shape.)

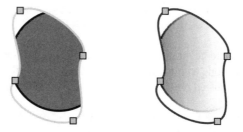

Demonstrating the editing of a clip path (left) and a mask path (right).

*New in v0.48:* By default, Inkscape will clip or mask each object separately if several objects are selected. In the *Clippaths and masks* section of the *Inkscape Preferences* dialog you can change this to have Inkscape first group the objects before applying a single clip or mask.

# Clipping

Any path, regular shape, or regular text object can be used as a clipping path.

To clip an object (or *Group*), select both the object and the clipping path. The clipping path must be above the object to be clipped in *z-order*. Then use the Object → Clip → Set command. To unclip a clipped object, select the object and use the Object → Clip → Release command. The clipping path is then restored as a regular object, placed just above the formerly clipped object in *z-order*.

More than one object (or *Group*) can be clipped at the same time. Just follow the above instructions but include all the objects to be clipped in the selection (with the clipping path on top). Inkscape will store one copy of the clipping path in the *<defs>* section of the *SVG* file for each clipped object; thus, the clipped objects can be edited separately.

When a clipped object is selected, the *Status Bar* will display the type of object clipped along with the word "clipped." The *bounding box* of the clipped object is defined by the intersection of the *bounding box* of the unclipped object with the *bounding box* of the clipping path. (However, if an object inside a clipped *Group* is selected, the unclipped *bounding box* of that object will be displayed.)

# Masking

Any object can be used to mask another object. The opacity and lightness of the mask determines the opacity of the masked objects. A masked object will be fully opaque only at places that are: inside the mask path, where the mask has maximum lightness (i.e., white), and the mask has maximum *Alpha*. So to summarize:

- Regions with minimum lightness (i.e., black) will be fully transparent.

- Regions with minimum *Alpha* (zero alpha) will be fully transparent.

- Regions outside the mask will be fully transparent.

 **Warning**

Masking has a few problems in v0.47 and v0.48. First, masks should use *luminosity* values; instead they use a linear combination of red, green, and blue values. Second, the mask value should be calculated in linear RGB color space; instead it is calculated in sRGB color space. Third, export via Cairo to PDF and PostScript is broken for regions outside the nominal mask area. The first and third problems are fixed in v0.48.1.

To mask an object (or *Group*), select both the object to be masked and the object to be used as a mask. The mask must be above the object to be masked in *z-order*. Then use the Object → Mask → Set command. To unmask a masked object, select the object and use the Object → Mask → Release command. The mask is then restored as a regular object and is placed just above the formerly masked object in *z-order*.

More than one object (or *Group*) can be masked at the same time. Just follow the above instructions but include all the objects to be masked in the selection (with the mask on top). Inkscape will store one copy of the mask in the *<defs>* section of the *SVG* file for each masked object; thus, the masked objects can be edited separately.

When a masked object is selected, the *Status Bar* will display the type of object clipped along with the word "masked." The *bounding box* of the masked object is the same as that of the unmasked object.

# Chapter 16. Filter Effects—Preset

*Filter Effects* [http://www.w3.org/TR/SVG11/filters.html] (*Filters*) are a feature of *SVG* that allow an *SVG* viewer to change the presentation of an object in a well-defined manner such as adding texture to a *Fill*, giving an object a blurred shadow, or modifying the object's color. Inkscape supports almost all *SVG Filter* primitives (see next chapter) and includes many *Preset* (predefined) filters.

## Browser Filter Support

Support of *Filters* is rather new in many web browsers. Don't be surprised to find bugs. Internet Explorer 9 will still not support filters. For work-arounds, see the section called *Supporting Older Browsers*.

This chapter covers *Preset* filters, that is those *Filters* that are preconstructed for your use. The following chapter covers *Custom* filters where you build the filters yourself.

# Use of Preset Filters

Inkscape includes a couple of hundred *Preset* filters. These filters are accessed from the *Filters* menu. To use a built-in filter, just select the object(s) you wish to apply it to then select the *Filter* from one of the sub-menus. A few of the built-in *Filters* have dialogs where you can adjust basic parameters.

With so many *Preset Filters*, finding the correct one isn't easy. It is best just to look through the following examples. Note that most filters fall into one of two categories: those that work with normal objects and those that work with bitmaps. Pay attention to the *Notification Region* for hints on what the filter is suppose to do.

If you have developed your own *Filters*, you can add them as *Presets* by *SVG* files with the *Filters* defined to the `filters` directory (Linux `~/.config/inkscape/filters`). By default, the filters will be added to a *Personal* submenu. You can have more control over where the filters are placed if you define the following attributes:

- `inkscape:label`: Command label.

- `inkscape:menu`: Submenu name

- `inkscape:label`: Tool tip (for *Notification Region*).

Inkscape includes an *SVG* file with samples of all the *Preset Filters*. The file, `filters.svg`, is located in the `examples` directory that can be found in the *File Open* dialog. Be prepared to wait as the file requires processing hundreds of *Filters*.

## Note

All the samples are rendered here using Batik. Missing or incorrectly rendered figures indicate problems either with the *Filter* definition or with Batik.

# ABCs

Best for normal objects.

| Black outline | Clean edges | Diffuse light | Feather | Matte jelly |

| Noise fill | Noise transparency | Roughen | Simple blur | Specular light |

ABCs.✪

# Bevels

Best for normal objects.

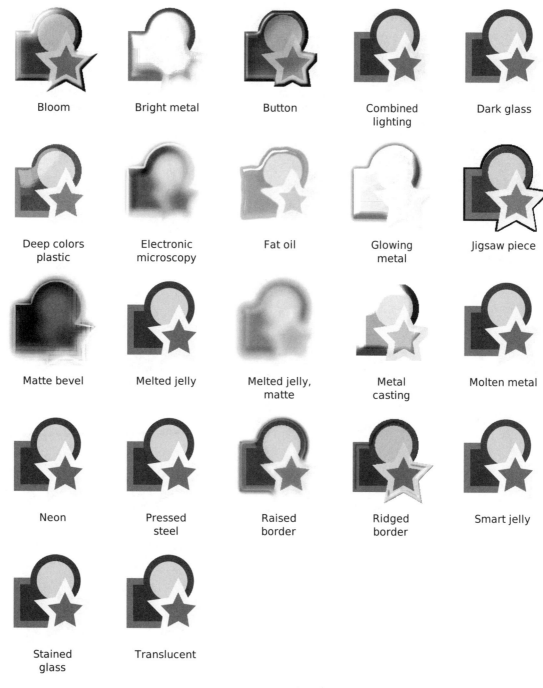

| | | | | |
|---|---|---|---|---|
| Bloom | Bright metal | Button | Combined lighting | Dark glass |
| Deep colors plastic | Electronic microscopy | Fat oil | Glowing metal | Jigsaw piece |
| Matte bevel | Melted jelly | Melted jelly, matte | Metal casting | Molten metal |
| Neon | Pressed steel | Raised border | Ridged border | Smart jelly |
| Stained glass | Translucent | | | |

Bevels.✪

# Blurs

Best for normal objects.

Apparition

Blur content

Cross-smooth

Evanescent

Fancy blur

Motion blur,
horizontal

Motion blur,
vertical

Noisy blur

Blurs.✪

# Bumps

Best for bitmaps, but also useful for normal objects.

| | | | | |
|---|---|---|---|---|
| Bubbly Bumps | Bubbly Bumps, matte | Canvas Bumps | Canvas Bumps, matte | Color emboss |
| Copper and chocolate | Dark Emboss | Emboss | Embossed leather | HSL Bumps |
| HSL Bumps, matte | HSL Bumps, transparent | Plaster | Plastify | Relief print |
| Thick acrylic | Thick paint | Tinfoil | Velvet Bumps | Wrinkled varnish |

Bumps.✪

Bubbly Bumps  Bubbly Bumps, matte  Canvas Bumps  Canvas Bumps, matte  Color emboss

Copper and chocolate  Dark Emboss  Emboss  Embossed leather  HSL Bumps

HSL Bumps, matte  HSL Bumps, transparent  Plaster  Plastify  Relief print

Thick acrylic  Thick paint  Tinfoil  Velvet Bumps  Wrinkled varnish

Bumps.✪

# Color

Best for bitmaps.

Black Light  Colorize  Desaturate  Duotone  Fluorescence

Invert  Invert hue  Lightness Contrast  Moonarize  Quadritone fantasy

Sepia  Soft colors  Solarize  Tritone

Color.✪

# Distort

Best for bitmaps.

Chalk and sponge · Lapping · Pixel smear · Ripple · Rough and dilate

Roughen inside · Torn edges

Distort.✪

# Image Effects

Best for bitmaps.

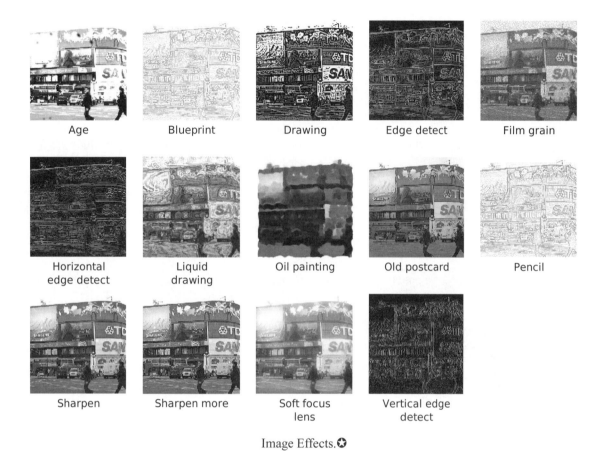

Image Effects.✪

# Image Effects, Transparent

Best for bitmaps.

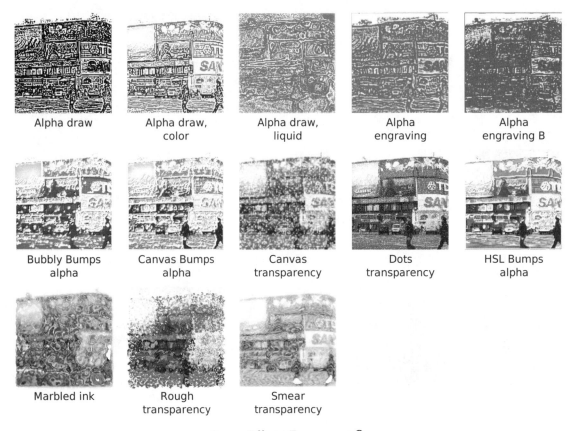

| Alpha draw | Alpha draw, color | Alpha draw, liquid | Alpha engraving | Alpha engraving B |
| Bubbly Bumps alpha | Canvas Bumps alpha | Canvas transparency | Dots transparency | HSL Bumps alpha |
| Marbled ink | Rough transparency | Smear transparency | | |

Image Effects, Transparent.✪

# Materials

Best for normal objects.

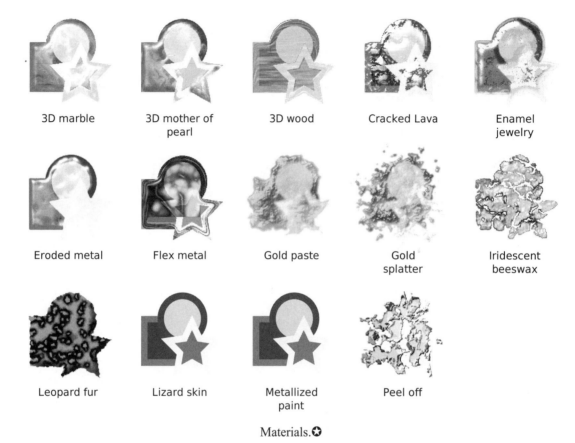

| | | | | |
|---|---|---|---|---|
| 3D marble | 3D mother of pearl | 3D wood | Cracked Lava | Enamel jewelry |
| Eroded metal | Flex metal | Gold paste | Gold splatter | Iridescent beeswax |
| Leopard fur | Lizard skin | Metallized paint | Peel off | |

Materials.✪

# Morphology

Best for normal objects.

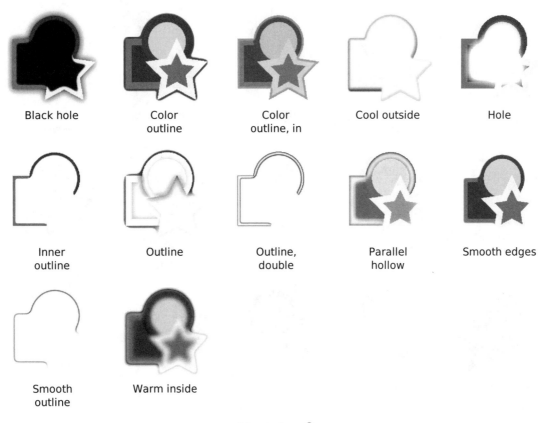

| | | | | |
|---|---|---|---|---|
| Black hole | Color outline | Color outline, in | Cool outside | Hole |
| Inner outline | Outline | Outline, double | Parallel hollow | Smooth edges |
| Smooth outline | Warm inside | | | |

Morphology.✪

# Non Realistic 3D Shaders

Best for normal objects.

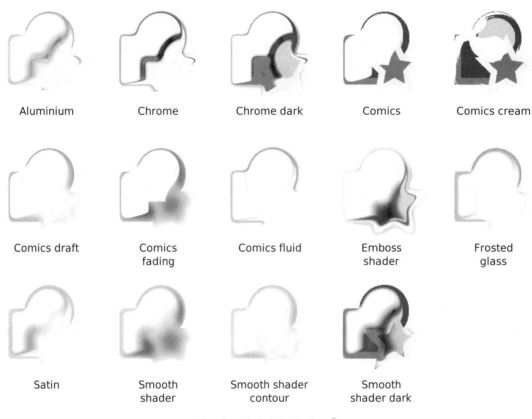

| | | | | |
|---|---|---|---|---|
| Aluminium | Chrome | Chrome dark | Comics | Comics cream |
| Comics draft | Comics fading | Comics fluid | Emboss shader | Frosted glass |
| Satin | Smooth shader | Smooth shader contour | Smooth shader dark | |

Non Realistic 3D Shaders✪.

# Overlays

Best for normal objects.

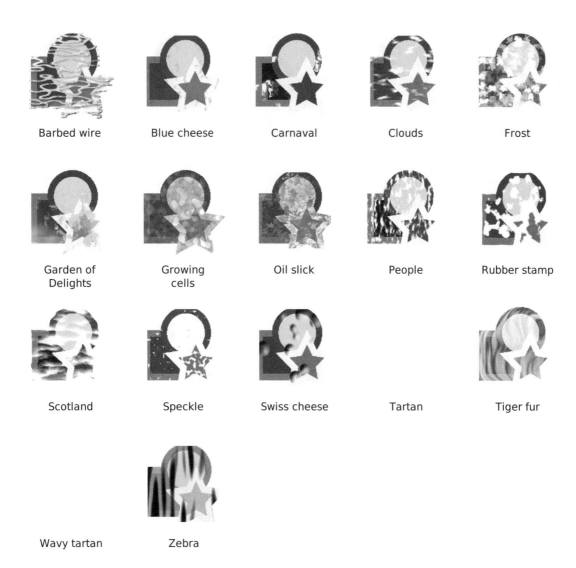

Overlays. Note, a missing figure indicates that Batik could not render the filter.✪

# Protrusions

Best for normal objects.

| Chewing gum | Dripping | Fire | Ink bleed | Snow crest |

Protrusions.✪

# Ridges

Best for normal objects.

| Dragee | Glowing bubble | Matte ridge | Metallized ridge | Refractive gel A |

| Refractive gel B | Thin Membrane |

Ridges.✪

# Scatter

Best for normal objects.

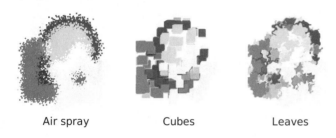

Air spray       Cubes       Leaves

Scatter.✪

# Shadows and Glows

Best for normal objects.

Cutout    Cutout Glow    Dark and Glow    Darken edges    Drop Glow

Drop Shadow    Fuzzy Glow    Glow    In and Out    Inner Glow

Inner Shadow    Inset

Shadows and Glows.✪

# Textures

Best for normal objects.

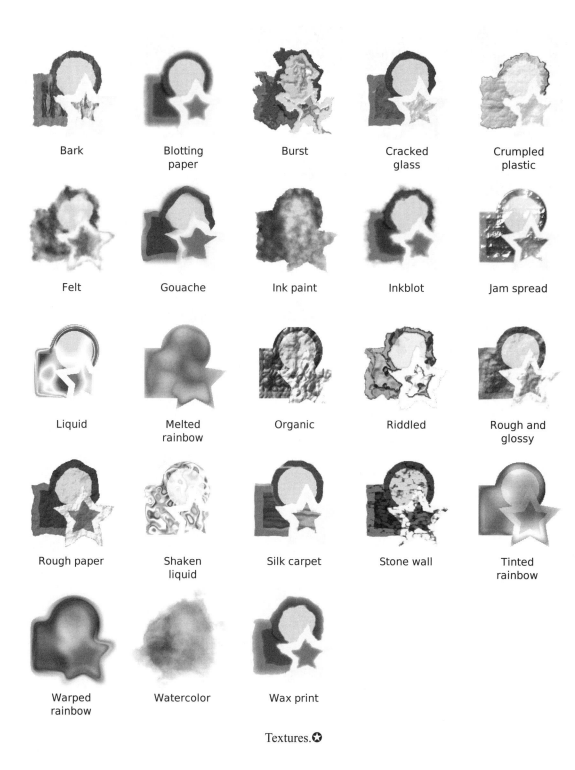

| | | | | |
|---|---|---|---|---|
| Bark | Blotting paper | Burst | Cracked glass | Crumpled plastic |
| Felt | Gouache | Ink paint | Inkblot | Jam spread |
| Liquid | Melted rainbow | Organic | Riddled | Rough and glossy |
| Rough paper | Shaken liquid | Silk carpet | Stone wall | Tinted rainbow |
| Warped rainbow | Watercolor | Wax print | | |

Textures.✪

# Transparency Utilities

Best for bitmaps. Designed for use over another object.

Alpha
repaint

Light eraser

Light eraser,
negative

Monochrome
transparency

Saturation
map

Transparency Utilities.✪

# Chapter 17. Filter Effects—Custom

This chapter covers basic use of *Filters* and how to build up complex *Filters* from the *Filter* primitives.

## Basic Use

*Filters* can be defined and applied through the *Filter Effects* dialog. The *Gaussian Blur* filter can also be used directly through the *Fill and Stroke* dialog. The *Blend* filter can also be applied to an entire *Layer* through the *Layers* dialog.

The *Fill and Stroke* dialog has a *Blur* slider that when moved from zero, creates and attaches a *Gaussian Blur* filter to selected objects. If the slider is reset to zero, the filter is automatically removed and deleted. The same principle works on the *Layers* dialog where a choosing anything but *Normal* creates a *Blend* filter and attaches it to the *Layer*. Setting the drop-down menu back to *Normal* deletes the filter. Filters can also be removed from an object by using the menu entry Filters → Remove Filters.

The *Filter Effects* dialog (Filters → Filter Editor...) is used to build complex *Filters* out of *Filter* primitives. An example of a complex *Filter* is the "Drop-Shadow" filter. The dialog is also used to apply *Filters* to objects.

The source of the graphic used as an input for a *Filter* primitive is either the output of another *Filter* primitive or one of the following sources:

- Source Graphic. Use the object as the source for the *Filter* primitive.

- Source Alpha. Use the *Alpha* of the object as the source for the *Filter* primitive.

- Background Image. Use the region under the *Filter* at the time the *Filter* is invoked.

- Background Alpha. Use the *Alpha* of the region under the *Filter* at the time the *Filter* is invoked.

- Fill Paint: *Not implemented*. Use the *Fill* of the target object as the input to a *Filter* primitive as if the object had an infinite extent. Useful if the *Fill* is a *Gradient* or *Pattern* with transparent or semitransparent regions.

- Stroke Paint: *Not implemented*. Use the *Stroke* of the target object as the input to a *Filter* primitive (see Fill Paint above).

### Need to add "enable-background" tag!

Whenever an input to a *Filter* is specified to be *Background Image* or *Background Alpha*, the *SVG* file must include the "enableBackground" tag to tell the *SVG* renderer it must keep a copy of the background around. Inkscape does not add this tag for you except in the case of using the *Layer* dialog to add a blend. A work-around is to use the *Layer* dialog to temporarily add and then remove a *Blend* filter; this will leave the necessary tag in place.

A filter effect is applied to a region defined relative to the object to which it is attached. By default, the *Filter Effects Region* ranges from −0.1 to 1.1 in units of the object's *bounding box* width and height. This area may not always be sufficient. For example, if a large shift is prescribed in the *Offset* filter, the area must be increased. The area can be adjusted under the *Filter General Settings* tab of the *Filter Effects* dialog. (It can also be set through the *XML Editor* dialog, attributes *x*, *y*, *width*, and *height*.)

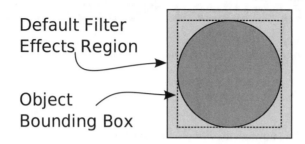

The default *Filter Effects Region* is shown for the red circle.

The *Filter Effects Region* can be defined in terms of the object's *bounding box* or by units in the current user coordinate system by setting the "filterUnits" parameter to "objectBoundingBox" or "userSpaceOnUse". Inkscape currently supports only the use of the first in the *GUI*.

### Color Space For Filters

Inkscape uses the *sRGB* color space with filters. The *SVG* standard specifies that by default, the *linearRGB* color space should be used. This is a known problem with Inkscape. If you wish your drawings to look the same in other *SVG* renderers, you need to manually add the attribute `color-interpolation-filters="sRGB"` to the <filter> tag. (This is already done for the *prebuilt* filters.)

# Filter Effects Dialog

## Adding a Filter

Click on the *New* button on the left to add a new filter. Alternatively, right-click on an existing filter in the *Filter* list to duplicate it. The name of the filter can also be changed by clicking on the name.

## Defining a Filter

A filter is defined by selecting filter primitives from the drop-down list next to the *Add Effect* button. A short description of the filter is displayed when a filter is selected. The description can be toggled on or off under the *Filters* tab of the *Inkscape Preferences* dialog.

Once a primitive is selected, click on the *Add Effect* button to add it to the filter. The input(s) of the filters are automatically attached to the *Source Graphic* or the output of a previously added filter primitive. The default connections are shown as gray lines originating from a triangle right of the filter primitive name. Explicitly defined connections are shown in black.

The inputs of a filter can be reassigned by click-dragging from the triangle at the right of the filter name to one of the columns on the right (e.g., *Source Graphic*), or by click-dragging to another of the filter primitives.

The filter primitives can be reordered by click-dragging a filter primitive in the list to another place in the list.

### Note

Inkscape may fail to update the display when tweaking *Filter Effects* parameters. Nudging the object up and down is sufficient to force an update.

## Applying a Filter

To apply a filter to an object(s), select the object(s) and check the box next to the filter name. Uncheck the box to remove a filter. If multiple objects are selected with different filters, all the boxes corresponding to those filters will be checked.

## Mini Tutorial—A Drop Shadow

Drop shadows are a perfect use for filters. The shadow automatically updates when the source object changes. Here is a step-by-step tutorial on creating a drop shadow:

A drop shadow created using only filters.✪

### Procedure 17.1. Drop Shadow

We will construct a compound filter that creates a drop shadow when applied to a text object.

1. **Add Text**

   Create a text object. In the example, I've used the text "Drop Shadow". Give the text a color. I've used dark red.

2. **Add Gaussian Blur**

   Select the text. Use the *Fill and Stroke* dialog to add a *Gaussian Blur* by dragging the *Blur* slider to a non-zero value. Doing so automatically creates a *Gaussian Blur* filter and attaches it to the text.

   The blurred text has the attributes of the original text, in this case, the dark red color. As the blurred text will become the shadow, we'll change the color to black in a moment.

   We used the *Fill and Stroke* dialog to rapidly create a filter object for the text. Further work will need to be done with the *Filter Effects* dialog. Open the dialog. Select the new filter (with a name like "filter3362") by clicking on it. You should see something like:

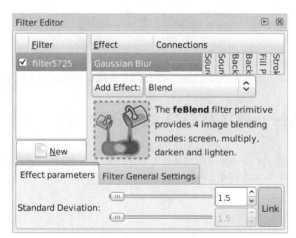

*Filter Effects* dialog after adding *Gaussian Blur* filter.

Let's first give our filter a new name: "MyDropShadow". Clicking on the filter name when selected allows editing the name.

Our filter consists at the moment of a single *Gaussian Blur*, as shown under the *Effect* column. The line connecting a triangle to the right of "Gaussian Blur" label to a square dot in the *Source Graphics* column shows that the input for the *Gaussian Blur* filter is the original source object (in this case the text). The default height of the dialog is too short to show the complete column labels. The dialog can be stretched so that the labels are completely visible.

To get a black shadow, we'll use *Source Alpha* for the input to the *Gaussian Blur* primitive. To make the link, left-drag the mouse from the triangle next to the *Gaussian Blur* label to the *Source Alpha* column. The *Filter Effects* dialog should look like:

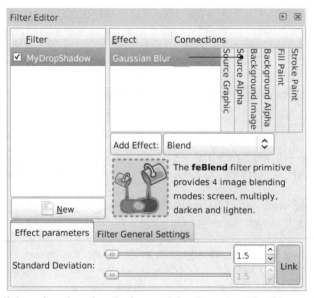

*Filter Effects* dialog after changing the input of the *Gaussian Blur* filter to *Source Alpha*.

The amount of blurring can be changed by using the *Standard Deviation* sliders at the bottom of *Filter Effects* dialog (when the *Gaussian Blur* primitive is selected). There are two sliders: the top for *x* and the bottom for *y*. By default, the sliders are linked together so the blur is the same in both directions. Note that the blur amount (*Standard Deviations*) is defined in terms of pixels in this dialog, while it is defined in terms of a percentage of 1/8 of the perimeter of the *bounding box* in the *Fill and Stroke* dialog.

3. **Add Offset**

The shadow should be shifted relative to the text. This can be achieved through the use of the *Offset* primitive. To add the primitive, select it from the drop-down menu next to the *Add Effect:* button and then click on the button to make the addition. Note the bent line connecting the triangle to the right of the "Offset" entry under the *Effect* column to the "Gaussian Blur" entry above. This (the default) indicates that the *Offset* primitive is using the output of the *Gaussian Blur* primitive as its input. The amount of the offset can be changed by the *Delta X* and *Delta Y* sliders at the bottom of the *Filter Effects* dialog when the *Offset* label is highlighted. Set the offsets both to 3 (pixels). You should see the shadow text shift as the sliders are dragged.

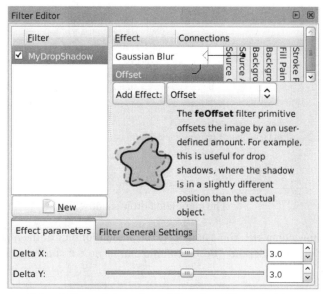

*Filter Effects* dialog after adding the *Offset* primitive.

4. **Add Merge**

Now that we have the shadow, we need to add back in the original text. This can be done with the *Merge* primitive that merges graphics from multiple inputs. Select the *Merge* primitive in the drop-down menu list of *Filter* primitives. Click on the *Add Effect:* button to add the primitive.

When first created, there are no inputs defined. Left-drag the mouse from the triangle at the right of the "Merge" label to the "Offset" label above, to create a link from the output of the *Offset* primitive to the input of the *Merge* primitive.

When an input link to a *Merge* primitive is made, a new, empty input node (triangle) is created. To add back in the original text, unmodified, left-drag the mouse from the empty triangle to the "Source Graphic" column.

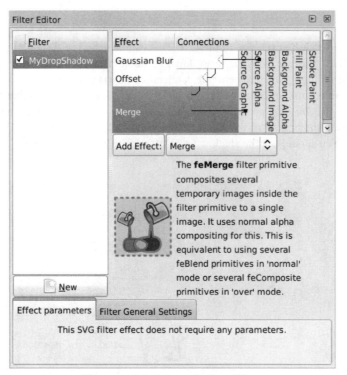

The completed drop-shadow filter.

The drop shadow is now complete. You can modify the amount of blur or the amount of offset by selecting the appropriate *Filter* primitive under the *Effects:* column and using the sliders at the bottom of the *Filter Effects* dialog.

# Color Filter Primitives

Two *Filter* primitives allow the manipulation of colors.

## Color Matrix

The *Color Matrix* primitive maps each *RGB* and *Alpha* value to a new value. The transformation is described by a 5 × 5 matrix with the bottom row fixed, thus a general transformation is described by a 5 × 4 matrix. The fifth column adds a value that is independent of *RGB* or *Alpha*, allowing for nonlinear color correction.

$$\begin{pmatrix} R' \\ G' \\ B' \\ A' \\ 1 \end{pmatrix} = \begin{pmatrix} a_{00} & a_{01} & a_{02} & a_{03} & a_{04} \\ a_{10} & a_{11} & a_{12} & a_{13} & a_{14} \\ a_{20} & a_{21} & a_{22} & a_{23} & a_{24} \\ a_{30} & a_{31} & a_{32} & a_{33} & a_{34} \\ 0 & 0 & 0 & 0 & 1 \end{pmatrix} \begin{pmatrix} R \\ G \\ B \\ A \\ 1 \end{pmatrix}$$

Four types of transformations are defined, of which three are special classes of the first.

- Matrix: The full 5 × 4 matrix is defined. This is the most general case.

- Saturate: The saturation is reduced by specifying one number, $s$. The range of $s$ is 0.0 (completely desaturated) to 1.0 (unchanged). Only the *RGB* values are changed. The exact formula is:

  - $R' = (0.213 + 0.787s)R + 0.715 \times (1 - s)G + 0.072 \times (1 - s)B$;

  - $G' = 0.213 \times (1 - s)R + (0.715 + 0.285s)G + 0.072 \times (1 - s)B$;

  - $B' = 0.213 \times (1 - s)R + 0.715 \times (1 - s)G + (0.072 + 0.928s)B$.

- Hue Rotate: The hue is shifted by specifying one number. Like the *Saturate* case, only *RGB* values are changed. The exact formula is quite complicated. It is not just a red to yellow to green and so on rotation.

- Luminance to Alpha: The luminance is converted to *Alpha* via a fixed formula: $Alpha = 0.2125 \times R + 0.7154 \times G + 0.0721 \times B$ (from ITU-R Recommendation BT709, the HDTV color standard).

Examples of using the *Color Matrix* primitive. From top to bottom: Source object. *Matrix* mode set to swap red and blue. *Saturate* mode with input of 0.5. *Hue Rotate* mode with input of 90°. *Luminance to Alpha* mode.✪

A "negative" can be made by setting the *RGB* diagonal matrix elements ($a_{00}$, $a_{11}$, $a_{22}$) to −1.00 and the top three elements of the fifth column ($a_{04}$, $a_{14}$, $a_{24}$) to 1.00.

Creation of a "negative" using the *Matrix* mode.✪

# Component Transfer

*Partially implemented, No user interface.*

The *Component Transfer* primitive changes the *RGB* and *Alpha* of an object by applying independent functions to each of the *RGB* and *Alpha* input values. The following modes for defining the functions are available: Identity, Table, Discrete, Linear, and Gamma.

# Compositing Filter Primitives

These primitives composite two or more graphics. The graphics may be from an object, a background, or the output of another primitive.

## Need to add "enable-background" tag!

Inkscape has a problem in using one of these filters. When using either *Background Image* or *Background Alpha* as an input to the filter, the "enabled-background" tag must be added to the *SVG* file (this tells *SVG* renderers to keep a copy of the background in memory). This is not done. A work-around is to use the *Layers* dialog to add a *Blend* filter to a *Layer*. The *Layer* blend can then be removed, leaving the necessary tag in place.

## Double counting background

The *SVG* 1.1 specification has a problem when an object is composited with a background that is not fully opaque. The background is included twice (once with the composited image and once as a background). There are three ways to deal with this problem. The first is to avoid using a *Background Image* or *Background Alpha* as a filter input. The second is to replace a transparent background with a solid background (you can use the *Dropper Tool* to replace a transparent *Fill* with an equivalent solid *Fill* [turn off "Pick alpha" in the *Tool Controls*]). The third is to use the *Flood* filter to create a solid white background and include this as the first input to a *Merge* filter (if using a *Merge* filter, include the flood first; if using a *Blend* or *Composite* filter, add a *Merge* filter with the first input being the output from the *Flood* filter and the second input being the output from the *Blend* or *Composite* filter). This solution runs into trouble when it is desired that the overall image have transparency. The *SVG* 1.2 standard corrects this deficiency.

The circle (red) is combined with the background using the *Merge* filter. The background color is black with a transparency of 50%. On the left, the area within the filter region is too dark, a result of the background being added in twice. On the right, the filter region was first filled with white using the *Flood* filter. For this to work with Batik and many other *SVG* renderers, the attribute *color-interpolation-filters="sRGB"* must be added to the <filter> tag.✪

# Blend

The *Blend* primitive blends two overlapping objects or an object with its background by doing a pixel-by-pixel combination using one of five defined blend modes. The five modes are listed below. Except for the *Normal* mode, the result is independent of which object is on top.

For each mode, the mathematical definition is given. In the definitions, *a* corresponds to an object on top of *b*; *c* is the *RGB* color of the object (premultiplied by the *opacity*); while *q* is the *opacity*. Both *c* and *q* range from 0 to 1. Each of the *RGB* colors is combined independently.

- Normal: Top object in front of bottom object as if filter not present. (In fact Inkscape removes the *Blend* filter primitive when "Normal" is selected for a blend added to a *Layer* with the *Layers* dialog.) $cr = (1 - qa) \times cb + ca$.

- Multiply: Top object filters light from bottom object or background. (Like looking through a transparency with color of top object at bottom object.) Examples: Blue object over red object yields black since the blue object filters out all the red light. Cyan object over purple object yields blue since the cyan filters out the red but allows the blue to pass. $cr = (1 - qa) \times cb + (1 - qb) \times ca + ca \times cb$.

- Screen: Top object adds light to bottom object. (As if both top and bottom objects are projected independently onto a screen.) Examples: Blue object over red object yields purple. Cyan object over purple object yields white since cyan contains green and blue and purple contains red and blue. Thus red, green, and blue are present in equal amounts. (Why doesn't the result contain more blue? Because both cyan and purple already contain the maximum amount of blue.) $cr = cb + ca - ca \times cb$.

- Darken: Top object darkens bottom object. $cr = Minimum ( (1 - qa) \times cb + ca, (1 - qb) \times ca + cb )$.

- Lighten: Top object lightens bottom object. $cr = Maximum ( (1 - qa) \times cb + ca, (1 - qb) \times ca + cb )$.

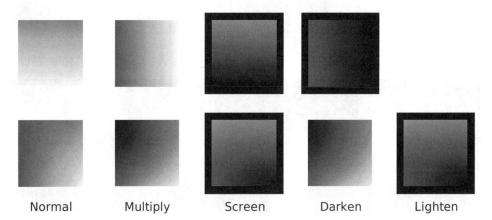

Normal     Multiply     Screen     Darken     Lighten

Top: The blue and red squares contain linear *Gradients* that range from full *opacity* to full *transparency* over a white or black background. Bottom: Blue squares overlaying red squares with different *Blend modes*.✪

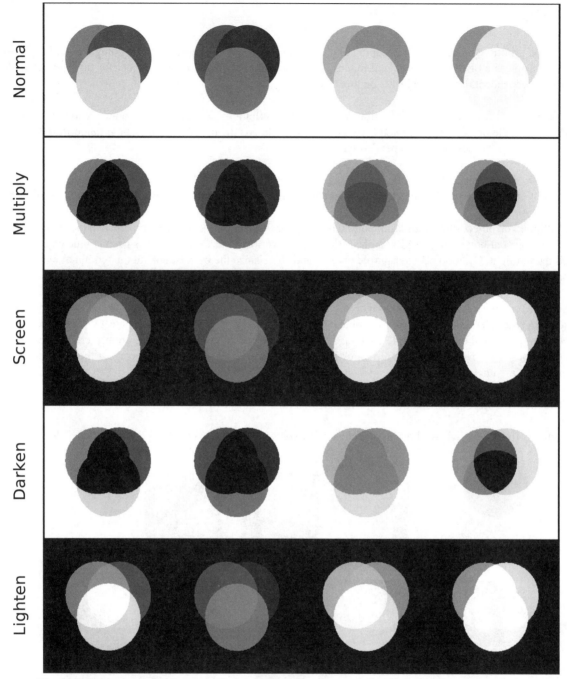

Three circles on top of each other. The same *Blend* has been applied individually to each circle in a set. Note that the circles are on either a white or black background with maximum *opacity*.✪

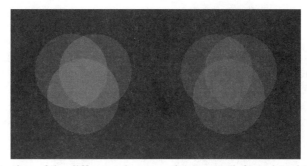

An illustration of the difference between the *Screen* (left) and *Lighten* (right)
*Blend modes*. Each circle has a red value of 128 (50%) and an *opacity* of 128
(50%). If the *opacity* was set to 255 (100%), the two figures would be identical.✪

The *Blend* filter primitive can also be applied to a *Layer* through the *Layers* dialog. In this case, input one is the selected object while input two is set to the *Background Image*.

# Composite

The *Composite* filter primitive allows two overlapping objects or an object and background to be merged pixel-by-pixel according to a mode-dependent rule. See the introduction to this section for problems when using a background as one of the inputs.

The possible modes are:

- Over: The upper object is placed over the lower object. This is equivalent to the normal way overlapping objects are drawn.

- In: The bottom object determines which part of the top object is visible.

- Out: The bottom object determines which part of the top object is hidden.

- Atop: The bottom object determines what part of the top object is visible. The bottom object is also visible.

- XOR: The non-overlapping regions of the top and bottom objects are visible.

- Arithmetic: The inputs *K1*, *K2*, *K3*, and *K4* are used in the equation: result = $K1 \times i_1 \times i_2 + K2 \times i_1 + K3 \times i_2 + K4$ to determine the output; $i_1$ and $i_2$ are the input values of the two source objects.

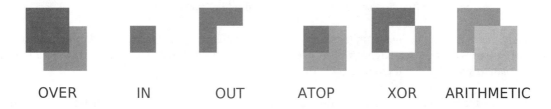

OVER    IN    OUT    ATOP    XOR    ARITHMETIC

Examples of the different modes available in the *Composite* filter primitive. The first input is
the blue square. The second input is a red square derived from the blue square using the *Color Matrix* and *Offset* filter primitives. The parameters for the *Arithmetic* mode are all set to 0.5.✪

# Merge

The *Merge* filter allows the combining of two or more objects or outputs of filter primitives. It works by layering one image on top of another, much as regular objects are layered on top of each other in *z-order*, or, for the case of two inputs, as the *Composite* filter primitive using the "Over" mode.

When the *Merge* filter is added to a complex filter an unassigned input node is created. As each input is assigned, another empty input node is created. This empty node is not included in the *SVG* tree structure.

# Fill Filter Primitives

These primitives provide some type of *Fill* for the filter region.

# Flood

The *Flood* primitive fills the *Filter Effects Region* with a specified color and *opacity*. This filter primitive is most useful when combined with other filters primitives.

An example of using the *Flood* filter. From left to right: 1. A simple circle. 2. After adding the *Flood* filter with a light blue color. Note that the default *Filter Effects Region* is larger than the *bounding box* of the circle. 3. After the addition of a *Composite* filter primitive using the *In* operator. The first input is the output of the *Flood* filter and the second is the *Source Graphic*. 4. The *Fill* of the circle has been changed to the *Cloth* pattern (with the *Fill and Stroke* dialog) and the *Composite* type has been changed to *Arithmetic* with K1 = 0.5, K2 = 0.0, K3 = 0.5, and K4 = 0.0.

# Image

*Partially Implemented.*

The *Image* primitive renders an external graphics file or an internal *SVG* object. It allows more than one object to be referenced in a complex filter (the first being the object attached to the filter).

Unfortunately, this very useful filter primitive is not yet fully implemented in Inkscape with only external images supported. The *GUI* will create a reference with an absolute path to the external image. Use the *XML Editor* to change an absolute path to a relative one if required.

By default, the image is shrunk or stretched to fit inside the *bounding box* of the object to which the filter is attached.

An image applied to two objects with the *Image* filter primitive. The rectangles show the *bounding box* of the objects.

The placement of the image within the *bounding box* can be controlled using the parameters *x*, *y*, *width*, and *height*. The coordinate system is the same as used for the object. The *XML Editor* must be used to modify these parameters. An additional parameter, *preserveAspectRatio*, is not supported by Inkscape.

### Inkscape Implementation Wrong

The *Image* implementation in Inkscape does not correctly position images. Other *SVG* renderers will display the image differently from Inkscape as a result.

An image applied to two objects with the *Image* filter primitive specifying different image regions. On the left, *x* is 60 px and *width* 60 px. On the right, *x* is −60 px and *width* 180 px.

# Tile

*Not implemented.*

The *Tile* primitive fills a rectangular region with a repeated input image.

No options.

# Turbulence

The *Turbulence* primitive allows the creation of artificial textures such as marble surfaces or clouds. It is based on the work of Ken Perlin [http://www.mrl.nyu.edu/~perlin/doc/oscar.html] who won an Academy Award for creating realistic textures with computers. Perlin solved the problem of using random numbers to produce *smooth* random fluctuations in color. A simplified version of his method is to generate random intensities at given intervals and then connect these points smoothly together.

Note that Firefox, Opera, and Batik will render this filter differently than Inkscape if the attribute `color-interpolation-filters="sRGB"` is not added to the filter definition.

The following figure gives an idea of how the filter would be implemented in one dimension:

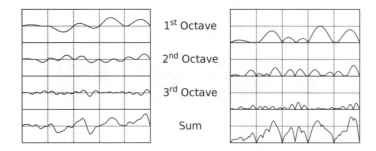

A one-dimensional illustration of the Perlin method of generating noise. *Fractal Noise* is shown on the left and *Turbulence* on the right. The *Base Frequency* is set to 0.05 giving a "wave length" of 20 pixels (indicated by the vertical dotted lines). The contributions from three *Octaves* are shown individually and then summed.

The *RGB* and *Alpha* components are each derived separately.

The components of a *Fractal NoiseTurbulence* filter. From left to right: Red, Green, Blue, Alpha, Combined. There is a black rectangle behind the right half of the latter. The *Color Matrix* primitive was used to extract the individual components.✪

The *Type* menu can be set to either *Fractal Noise* or *Turbulence*. *Turbulence* tends to have more dramatic dark regions as the absolute values of the noise terms are used, creating "visual cusps".[1]

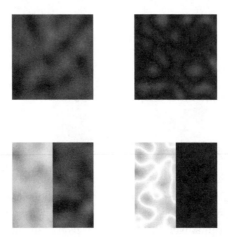

The two types of noise available: Left: *Fractal Noise*. Right: *Turbulence*. Top: Only red channel. Bottom: All channels. There are black rectangles behind the right halves.✪

---

[1]See http://www.noisemachine.com/talk1/22.html.

The *Base Frequency* is defined by default in terms of inverse *Screen pixels*. For example, a frequency of 0.1 would have a "wave length" of 10 pixels. Inkscape cannot yet create resolution independent noise. Reasonable values for this attribute range from 0.01 (a slowly varying texture) to 0.2 (a rapidly varying texture).

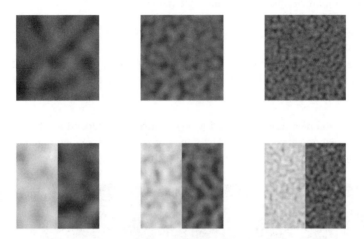

*Fractal Noise* as a function of *Base Frequency*. From left to right: 0.05, 0.10, 0.20, Top: Only red channel. Bottom: All channels, a black rectangle has been placed behind the right halves.✪

The number of *Octaves* determines the complexity of the noise, the more *Octaves*, the more complex. Each *Octave* adds a term with twice the *Frequency* but half the amplitude. Using more than four or five *Octaves* isn't so useful as the spatial and color variations become too small to be seen (and increases the CPU load).

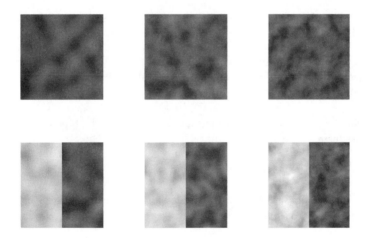

*Fractal Noise* as a function of *Octaves*. All with *Base Frequency* of 0.05. From left to right: 1 octave, 2 octaves, 3 octaves. Top: Only red channel. Bottom: All channels, a black rectangle has been placed behind the right halves.✪

The *Turbulence* primitive uses a pseudo-random number generator. In principle, renderings with different *SVG* viewers should use the same generator and produce the same textures (at the same scale). If you use the filter twice on two identical objects, the textures should be the same. Changing the seed will force the random-number sequence to be different and thus the textures will be different too.

# Lighting Filters Primitives

Two primitives, *Diffuse Lighting* and *Specular Lighting*, are included to simulate light shining on objects. They represent two of the three parts of the Phong reflection model [http://en.wikipedia.org/wiki/Phong_reflection_model] for modeling light in computer graphics. The three parts of the model are:

• Ambient light: The light present everywhere in a scene. In *SVG* this would be represented by a solid *Fill*.

• Diffuse light: The reflection of a light source off a surface that does not depend on the location of the observer. The intensity is a function of the angle between a line connecting the surface to a light source and a line normal to the surface.

• Specular light: The reflection of a light source off a surface that does depend on the location of the observer. For example, the highlights seen on shiny surfaces. The intensity is maximum when the angle between the normal to a surface and the light source is equal to the angle between the normal and the viewer.

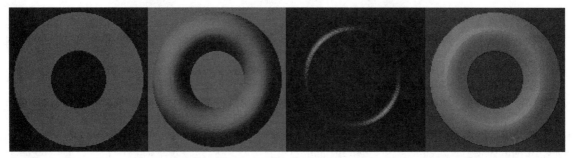

An illustration of the components of the Phong model. From left to right: ambient light, diffuse light, specular light. All light sources combined. The diffuse and specular light source is the same, a red distant light coming from the upper left. The specular image has had a black background added to set off the specular light.✪

The Phong model does not take into account shadows that would be caused by one area of an object on another, that is it does not do ray tracing.

The contour of an object in the *z* (out of the drawing) direction is described by a *bump map* that is defined by the *Alpha* channel of an object. The values of the pixel and the neighboring pixels in the *bump map* define the normal to the surface for the pixel.

The two lighting filters share in common most of their attributes such as the type of light source, its color, and its position; thus we'll discuss them together.

• *Diffuse Color*, *Specular Color*: The color of the light source.

• *Surface Scale*: Sets the scale of the surface in order to calculate normals to the surface. The number represents the maximum height (corresponding to *Alpha* = 1.0) of the surface in the same units as *x* and *y*.

• *Constant*: Diffuse or Specular Reflection Constant: How much of the light that hits the surface is reflected diffusely or specularly. A value greater than 1.0 oversaturates the object.

• *Exponent* (*Specular Lighting* only): Determines how sharp or narrow the specular reflections are. A value of 1.0 (the minimum) suggests a dull surface with wide reflections; as the value increases, the surface appears more polished with narrower reflections.

• *Kernel Unit Length* (Unused): Sets the pixel size used to calculate the reflections (screen pixels are used by default).

• *Light Source*: One of three types of light: *Distant Light*, *Point Light*, or *Spot Light* (see below).

When applying a lighting filter with a large *Surface Scale*, the limited resolution of the *bump map* may create artifacts. These can be removed by applying a small amount of Gaussian blur to the image.

The limited resolution of the *bump map* has resulted in artifacts on the sphere on the left. A small amount of blurring has removed the artifacts on the sphere on the right (the sphere has also been clipped).✪

# Distant Light Source

This light source simulates a light at a large (infinite) distance from the illuminated object. The required attributes are:

- *Azimuth*: The direction (angle) of the light source in the drawing plane. The angle is defined in degrees from the horizontal (*x*) axis in the clockwise direction. Note that this does not match either angle definition used by Inkscape (see the section called *Transformations*). Recall that *SVG* uses a left-handed coordinate system where the positive *y* direction is down.

- *Elevation*: The direction (angle) of the light source above the drawing plane (in degrees).

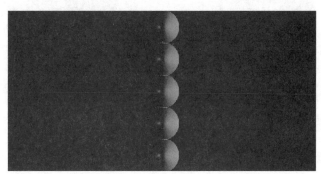

Five spheres illuminated by *Distant Light* sources. The light from the left is a *Specular* reflection, while that on the right is a *Diffuse* reflection.

# Point Light Source

This light source simulates a point light source near an illuminated object. One triple set of numbers (*x*, *y*, *z*) is required to set the *Location* of the light. The units are in the coordinate system of the lit object. Note: *z* represents the distance out of the plane (toward the viewer of the *SVG* drawing) if *x* or *y* are not inverted.

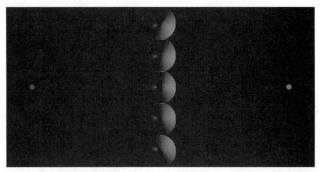

Five spheres illuminated by *Point Light* sources. The light from the left is a *Specular* reflection while that on the right is a *Diffuse* reflection. The small red and blue circles indicate the positions of the light sources.

# Spot Light Source

This light source simulates a point light source near an illuminated object but with a limited cone of light. One triple set of numbers $(x, y, z)$ is required to set the *Location* of the light and another to set the direction the center of the cone points (*Points At*). See previous section for the definition of the coordinate system. The *Specular Exponent* sets how well-focused is the light; the higher the value, the more sharply focused the light. The *Cone Angle* (degrees) defines the maximum angle for the light.

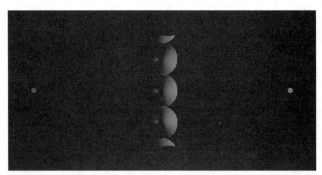

Five spheres illuminated by *Spot Light* sources. The light from the left is a *Specular* reflection, while that on the right is a *Diffuse* reflection. The small red and blue circles indicate the positions of the light sources. The lights are directed at each other. The cone angle is 25°.

# Pixel Manipulation Filter Primitives

These primitives move pixels or blend adjacent pixels.

## Convolve Matrix

The *Convolve Matrix* primitive uses neighboring pixels to modify the color of a pixel. How the pixel is changed is determined by an $N \times M$ matrix with one entry for each neighboring pixel.

$$result = \left( \sum_{i=0}^{i<N} \sum_{j=0}^{j<M} source_{i,j} \times k_{i,j} \right) / divisor + bias$$

The following is an example of a "Gaussian Blur" that uses a 5 × 5 matrix around the center pixel. The *Kernel* is an integer representation of a 2-dimensional Gaussian with a standard deviation of 1.4 pixels. It is normalized by the *Divisor*.[2]

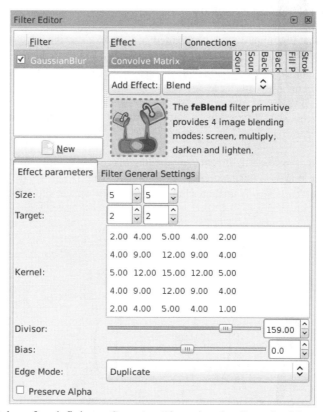

*Filter Effects* dialog after defining a *Gaussian Blur* using the *Convolve Matrix* filter primitive.

The above *Gaussian Blur*, *Convolve Matrix* filter is applied to a photograph.

The parameters for the effect are:

- *Size*: Size of matrix ($x \times y$).

- *Target*: Which matrix element corresponds to the target pixel, default is to center *Kernel* on target pixel.

---

[2]Why define a "Gaussian Blur" using the *Convolve Matrix* filter when a *Gaussian Blur* filter exists? The *Gaussian Blur* filter is designed to blur on a large scale. The *Convolve Matrix* filter works on a short scale, reducing noise from neighboring pixels.

- *Kernel*: The matrix.

- *Divisor*: Scale factor after *Kernel* applied.

- *Bias*: Value added after *Kernel* applied, default 0.

- *Edge Mode*: The method that the input image is extended so that pixels at the edge can be evaluated. The options are: *Duplicate* (the edge pixels are duplicated), *Wrap* (the pixels are taken from the opposite side of the input image), *none* (the extended pixels are given *RGB* and *Alpha* values of zero). At the moment Inkscape does not use this parameter despite it being in the user interface.

- *Preserve Alpha*: If box is checked, *Alpha* will be copied directly from the input graphics. Otherwise, it will be calculated just like *RGB*.

The *Convolve Matrix* primitive is necessarily linked to evaluating pixels. By default, the pixel size is that of the display. This means that the resulting image is not resolution independent. The *SVG* standard provides ways to avoid this through the *filterRes* and *kernelUnitLength* attributes but Inkscape does not yet support them.

# Examples

## Edge Detection

Kernel:

$$\begin{pmatrix} -1 & -1 & -1 \\ -1 & 8 & -1 \\ -1 & -1 & -1 \end{pmatrix}$$

*Divisor* = 1.0, *Bias* = 0.0, *Preserve Alpha* selected.

Edge detection.

## Sharpen

Kernel:

$$\begin{pmatrix} -1 & -1 & -1 \\ -1 & 9 & -1 \\ -1 & -1 & -1 \end{pmatrix}$$

*Divisor* = 1.0, *Bias* = 0.0.

Sharpen.

## Unsharpen

The above "Sharpen" filter is a bit extreme. This "Unsharp" filter is a bit more subtle.

Kernel:

$$\begin{pmatrix} -1 & -1 & -1 \\ -1 & 17 & -1 \\ -1 & -1 & -1 \end{pmatrix}$$

*Divisor* = 9.0, *Bias* = 0.0.

Unsharp.

## Emboss

Kernel:

$$\begin{pmatrix} -2 & 0 & 0 \\ 0 & 1 & 0 \\ 0 & 0 & 2 \end{pmatrix}$$

*Divisor* = 1.0, *Bias* = 0.0.

Emboss.

# Displacement Map

The *Displacement Map* primitive distorts one *bitmap* using another as input. A pixel in the source *bitmap* is translated to a new coordinate via the equations $x' = scale \times (CX(x,y) - 0.5)$ and $y' = scale \times (CY(x,y) - 0.5)$ where *CX* and *CY* are the any of the *RGB* components or *Alpha*, selectable by the *X Channel* and *Y Channel* attributes. The *X Channel* and *Y Channel* can be mapped with different colors.

The *Displacement Map* filter can be used to produce some interesting effects, but figuring out a correct map can be difficult. Many of the *Preset* filters use the output of a *Turbulence* filter to generate random distortions.

In the following examples, the *x* displacement is set to red and the *y* displacement is set to green. The olive green background corresponds to red and green values of 127, which corresponds (almost) to no displacement.

Magnify map (uniform gradients inside of circle).

Magnify.

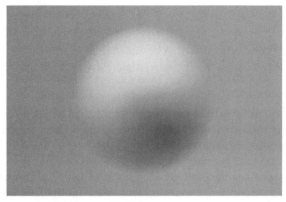

Bubble map.

Bubble.

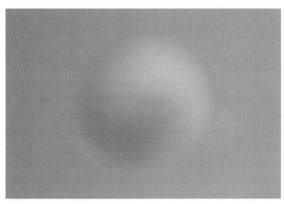

Twirl map.

Twirl.

Ripple map.

Ripple.

See the Stereoscopic Picture example in the next section for another example of using this filter.

## Note

Zero displacement? Not possible in the *SVG* standard. Color and *Alpha* are described by a byte (8 bits). This corresponds to a range of 0 to 255. A zero displacement would be a value halfway between 0 and 255, or 127.5. But these are integer numbers and you can't have a value of 127.5. Take your pick, 127 or 128. In most practical cases, the shift won't be noticeable.

# Gaussian Blur

The *Gaussian Blur* primitive blurs objects. Realistic highlights and reflections can be added to drawings as well as making objects out-of-focus. The primitive creates an output image by using a Gaussian weighted average of the input pixels around the location of each corresponding output pixel.

Internally, the amount of blur is defined in terms of the *blur radius*, which for the mathematically inclined is just the standard deviation of the Gaussian. Technically, a Gaussian function extends to infinity. For practical reasons, the limit of an object's blur is two times the *blur radius* outside the *bounding box* at maximum blur.

The *Gaussian Blur* primitive is highly CPU intensive. The output is a trade-off between speed and quality. One can set the *Blur quality* for the screen display in the *Inkscape Preferences* dialog (File → ⬛ Inkscape Preferences... (**Shift+Ctrl+P**)) under the *Filter* entry. Choosing a low-quality option will affect blurring of thin objects the most. Bitmap export is always done at the highest quality (and thus may be slow). In v0.48, one can set the number of threads used to render the filter in the dialog.

A *Gaussian Blur* filter can be created through both the *Filter Effects* and the *Fill and Stroke* dialogs.

## Blurring with the Fill and Stroke Dialog

Using the *Fill and Stroke* dialog to create a blur is fast and easy. The dialog automatically creates the filter for you (and removes it if the blur is removed). In this dialog, the amount of blurring is defined in terms of a percentage. A blurring of 100% (the maximum blurring allowed) is equivalent to a *blur radius* of 1/8 of the *bounding box* perimeter. For a square *bounding box*, this would be half of a side.

To apply a *Gaussian Blur* to an object, select the object and then adjust the blur with the *Blur* slider near the bottom of the dialog. Only a symmetric blur can be applied with this dialog.

**Tip**

Blurs created through the *Fill and Stroke* dialog depend on the size of the blurred object. To get the exact same amount of blur on different size objects, you can either use the Edit → 📋 Paste Style (**Shift+Ctrl+V**) command (if all the attributes are to be the same) or use the *Filter Effects* dialog to set the *blur radius* (*standard deviation*) to the same values.

Example of using the *Gaussian Blur* filter. The star on the left
has been blurred respectively by 5%, 10%, and 20% to the right.

## Blurring with the Filter Effects dialog

For more sophisticated use of the *Gaussian Blur* filter it is necessary to use the *Filter Effects* dialog. Through this dialog you can create asymmetric blurs as well as have precise control over the *blur radius*. You can also build more complicated filters as demonstrated in the *Drop Shadow* example earlier in this chapter.

# Blurring Examples

## Gradient Blurring

Blurring an object with a *Gradient* softens the color transitions.

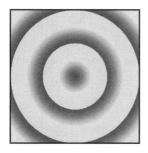 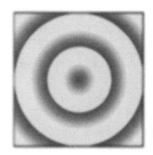 

A *Rectangle* with a radial *Gradient*. Left: no blurring; Middle: 2% blurring; Right: 5% blurring.

## Clipping and Masking

The *Gaussian Blur* primitive is applied to an object before any *Clipping or Masking*. This will give a sharp edge along the clipping path to a blurred object. If you wish the clipped edge to be blurred, put it in a *Group* by itself and then blur the *Group*. If you want a feathered edge to an object like a bitmap, create a white *transparency* mask with the edge blurred.

From left to right: Star with circular *Clip* path not yet applied; *Clip* path
applied to star; star blurred; star put into *Group* with *Group* blurred.

From left to right: White circle mask over bitmap image; blurred circle mask over image; mask applied to image.

## Tile Clones

The *Create Tiled Clones* dialog has an option to vary the *Blur Radius* under the *Blur and opacity* tab.

A sphere cloned with the *Create Tiled Clones* dialog, with *Shift*, *Scale*, and *Blur* changed from their default values.

# Morphology

The *Morphology* primitive "fattens" or "thins" an object. The *Operator* attribute can either be *Dilate* or *Erode*. The amount of change is controlled by the *Radius* attribute. It can have independent $x$ and $y$ values.

Note: Inkscape seems to under do the transform in *PNG* export.

Examples of the *Morphology* primitive. From left to right: Unfiltered object. Dilated object with *Radius* of 4. Eroded object with *Radius* of 4.

# Offset

The *Offset* primitive shifts a graphic by the specified amounts in $x$ and $y$. The classic example is the use of this primitive to create a shadow. See the Drop Shadow example earlier in this section.

This primitive has two parameters: *Delta X*, the offset in the horizontal direction and *Delta Y* the offset in the vertical direction. Note that the positive $y$ direction is in the downward direction (as defined by the *SVG* standard).

If the specified offset is large, the filter region needs to be enlarged. You can increase the filter region under the *Filter General Settings* tab at the bottom of the *Filter Effects* dialog.

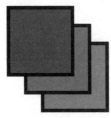

Examples of the *Offset* primitive. The three squares are drawn on top of each other. The green and red squares are then shifted with the *Offset* primitive. The filter region for the green and red squares had to be enlarged.

# Complex Examples

This section features some examples of complex filters built out of primitives.

## Emboss

This example uses the *Color Matrix* to convert a photograph into an *Alpha* layer. The *Alpha* layer is then embossed by the *Diffuse Lighting* filter.

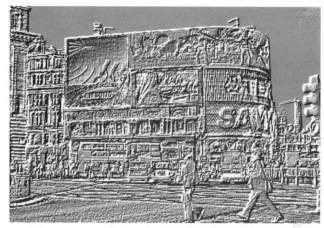

An embossed photograph.

Settings: *Color Matrix*: *In*: Source Graphics, *Mode*: Luminance to Alpha. *Diffuse Lighting*: *In*: Color Matrix output, *Diffuse Color*: White, *Surface Scale*: 10, *Constant*: 2, *Light Source*: Distant Light, *Azimuth*: 45, *Elevation*: 15.

## Neon

This example uses the *Morphology* primitive to create the glow around a neon tube. The glow color is derived from the neon color using the *Color Matrix* primitive. A couple *Gaussian Blur* primitives create the soft feel of the neon and a *Merge* primitive combines the neon and glow together.

A neon sign.✪

Settings: See next figure for overall structure and for *Color Matrix* primitive inputs. *Morphology*: *Operator*: Dilate, *Radius*: 6 (*x* and *y*); *Gaussian Blur*: *Standard Deviation*: first: 6, second: 1.

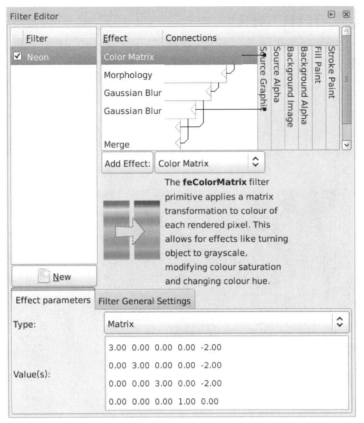

*Filter Effects* dialog for neon effect, showing *Color Matrix* parameters.

# Stereoscopic Pictures

This example uses the *Displacement Map* filter primitive to create a stereoscopic picture. The *Turbulence* primitive is used to generate a picture that is distorted with the *Displacement Map* primitive.

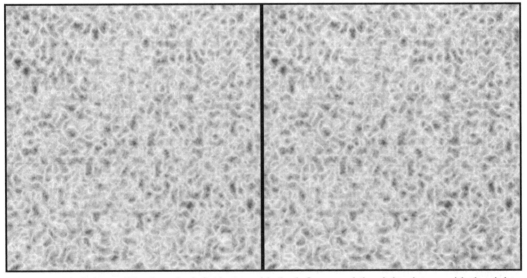

A stereoscopic image. Look at the left picture with the left eye and the right picture with the right eye. It may help to place a sheet of paper vertical and extending from your nose to the line between the two pictures. When your brain combines the two images, a shape should pop out.✪

Settings: Turbulence: *Input*: Source Alpha, *Type*: Turbulence, *Base Frequency*: 0.1, *Octaves* 5, *Seed* 0. Displacement Map: *Input 1*: Turbulence output, *Input 2*: Source Graphic, *Scale:*: 10, *X Channel*: Red, *Y Channel*: Green. Composite: *Input 1*: Displacement Map, *Input 2*: Source Graphic, *Operator*: In.

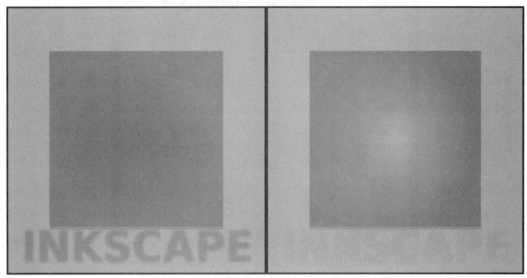

The *Source Graphic*. The red levels control the displacement in the *x* direction.✪

# Solar Flare

*This filter effect displays in Opera 10 but not Firefox 4, Chrome 7 or Batik.*

This example uses the *Turbulence* primitive to modify a radial *Gradient*, thus simulating a solar flare during an eclipse.

A solar flare seen during an eclipse.✪

Settings: Turbulence: *Input*: Source Alpha, *Type*: Turbulence, *Base Frequency*: 0.5, *Octaves* 3, *Seed* 0. Color Matrix: *Input*: Turbulence output, *Matrix*: All 0 except $a_{00}$ and $a_{33}$ are 1. Composite: *Input 1*: Source Graphic, *Input 2*: Color Matrix, *Operator*: Arithmetic, *K*: 0, 1, −0.75, 0.

The *Source Graphic*.

# Chapter 18. XML Editor

The *XML Editor* dialog allows one to directly edit the *XML* description of an *SVG* drawing. (Recall that Inkscape is an *SVG*-based drawing program and that *SVG* is an *XML*-based file format.)

The ability to directly edit an *SVG XML* file is very powerful. It allows the user more control over objects in their drawing such as specifying the exact size or position of an object and by giving access to *SVG* parameters that are not directly or easily available through the Inkscape interface.

## Basic Usage

To edit the *XML* file, open the *XML Editor* dialog (Edit → ⊠ XML Editor... (**Shift+Ctrl+X**)). This will open a window like the following for an empty drawing.

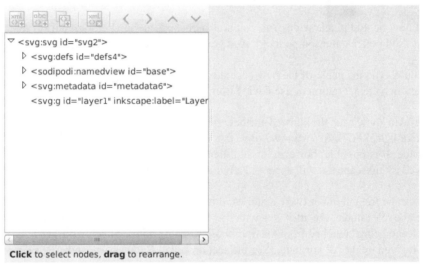

*XML Editor* dialog (with nothing selected).

The "tree" structure of the empty drawing is shown on the left in the dialog. Even an empty Inkscape drawing contains information, including an empty *Layer* ("layer1"). The *Layer*, like all the items listed, is represented by a "node" in the tree. If the layer contained objects, they would be represented by nodes under the layer's node. The objects under a particular node can be hidden in the tree view. To hide and unhide these objects click on the small triangles just in front of a node's name.

Upon adding an ellipse to the drawing, an entry (node) is added for the new ellipse under the formerly empty *Layer* (see next figure). The line is highlighted and the ellipse's parameters are shown on the right. Note that the name of the object is given in the highlighted line (in this case, "path1599").

Now, suppose you would like the ellipse to have a width of 400 pixels (i.e., a radius of 200 pixels in the *x* direction). You can specify this by clicking on the "sodipodi:rx" attribute. The attribute is shown below with the current value in the attribute entry box. Change that value to 200 and then click on the *Set* button (or use **Ctrl+Enter**).

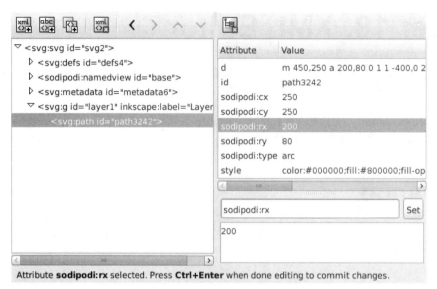

*XML Editor* dialog after changing the width of the ellipse.

The ellipse should now be 400 pixels wide. You could also change the height (sodipodi:ry) and the location of the center of the ellipse (sodipodi:cx and sodipodi:cy). And you can change attributes like the *Fill* color and *Stroke style*.

To add a new attribute, type the name of the new attribute in the upper entry box, enter the value in the lower entry box, and then either click the *Set* button or use **Ctrl+Enter**.

Sometimes it is useful to know what the allowed attributes are for a given type of object. The *SVG* standard is described in detail at the *Official W3C SVG* [http://www.w3.org/TR/SVG/] website. Note that not all the *SVG* standard is currently supported in Inkscape. It is possible, however, to add nonsupported attributes via the *XML Editor*. These attributes may not be displayed by Inkscape but will appear in any program that supports those attributes.

Elements in the Inkscape file fall under two categories: those included in the *SVG* standard and those that are private to Inkscape. In the above example, the attributes with the "sodipodi" tag are internal to Inkscape (the "sodipodi" tag is the result of Inkscape being branched from the Sodipodi program). These attributes are used to calculate the "real" *SVG* path definition given by the 'd' attribute. (See the section called *Paths* in Appendix B, *File Format*.)

The Inkscape internal elements should be ignored by other *SVG* rendering programs. This may not always be true, thus Inkscape includes the possibility to export a drawing without the Inkscape internal elements.

# Editing XML Nodes

The *XML Editor* dialog includes a number of clickable icons to manipulate the "nodes" in the *XML* tree. A description of each icon follows. Some of the things you can do with these commands may not be so sensible.

- ▦ Add XML element node. Add a node. For this to be useful, all the attributes appropriate to the type of node add must also be added.

- ▦ Add XML text node. Can also be used to edit the text in a text object.

- ▦ Duplicate XML node. Make a copy of the currently selected node, including all its daughters. The new node will be placed at the same level and just after the original node. As each node must have a unique *ID*, Inkscape will assign a new *ID*. You can change the *ID* name if you wish.

- ▦ Delete XML element node. Delete a node and all its daughters.

- ‹ Unindent node. Move a node out one level. For a drawable object in a group, this is equivalent to removing that object from that group.

- › Indent node. Move a node in one level. The node will be moved under the closest node above at the same level.

- ⌃ Raise node. Move a node above the previous node with the same parent. Equivalent to changing the *z-order* when the two nodes are drawable objects.

- ⌄ Lower node. Move a node below the next node with the same parent. Equivalent to changing the *z-order* when the two nodes are drawable objects.

- ▣ Delete the selected object attribute.

# Examples

A few examples are given here to show the possibilities of "hand" editing the *XML* file.

## Adding Color to a Marker Arrow

Markers on paths in Inkscape do not inherit the attributes of the path. This is most noticeable for colored paths where the markers are drawn in black. Inkscape now includes the *Color Markers to Match Stroke* extension for changing the color of markers to match the stroke color. This section is kept for pedagogical reasons.

To add color to a marker, open up the *XML Editor*. Select the path with the marker in the canvas window. In the "style" attribute for the line, locate the marker entry (marker-end:url(#Arrow2Lend), for example). Then expand the "<svg:defs>" line by clicking on the triangle at the beginning of the line (if not already expanded). You should see an entry for the marker. Select that entry. The attributes for the marker should be displayed on the right. Select the "style" attribute. Add "fill:#rrggbb" to the attributes in the entry box at the bottom right, where #rrggbb is the *RGB* color in *hexadecimal* form (obtainable from the attributes for the path).

The marker should change color. If it doesn't, then expand the "<svg:marker>" line. Select the path entry and remove any *Fill* and/or *Stroke paint*. For this change to show up, you must save and reopen the *SVG* file.

If you wish to have markers of the same type with different colors, then you must add copies in the <svg:defs> section. You can use the *Duplicate Node* ▣ icon to duplicate a marker entry. Rename the new entry to a suitable name and change the reference to the marker in the path object you want the marker to be associated with. Again the file must be closed and reopened for the changes to be seen.

You are not limited to changing color. You can change other attributes such as the marker size.

A red line with a red marker.

## Underlined Text

Underlined text cannot be added through the normal Inkscape interface, nor will Inkscape display underlines. But you can add underlined text that will be displayed properly by another *SVG* program.

To underline text, open the *XML Editor*. Select the text you wish underlined. Go to the "<svg:tspan>" object found inside an "<svg:text>" tag. If you are selecting part of the text, you may need to add some attribute temporarily (color for example) to create a corresponding "tspan" object; the color can be removed later. Add to the style: "text-decoration: underline".

Here is an example as rendered by the Squiggle program.

## A test of underlined text.

Underlined text example.

# Chapter 19. Tiling

Tiling or tessellation is the covering of a surface with the repeated use of the same shape tile. A typical example is the tiling in a bathroom. In Inkscape, this concept is expanded to include a multitude of options, including progressively changing the tile size, spacing, and orientation.

The tiles are in reality just clones of the source tile or object. Thus the same methods that apply to clones apply to tiles. (See the section called *Clones* in Chapter 4, *Editing Basics*.)

While random use of the *Tile Clones* dialog can produce exquisite patterns, it is useful to understand the fundamentals of tessellation in order to have more control over the final design.

An example of using the *Tile Clones* dialog with a simple calligraphic stroke and the *P6M* symmetry group (see text).

To construct a tiling, open up the *Create Tiled Clones* dialog (Edit → Clone → 🖾 Create Tiled Clones... ).

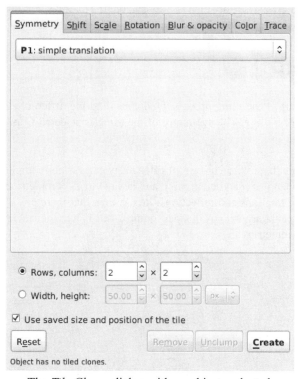

The *Tile Clones* dialog with no objects selected.

At the bottom of the dialog is a fixed section where you can choose the size of the tiling either by the number of rows and columns or by the width and height of the area you wish to cover. The terms *Rows* and *Columns* are only really appropriate for tiling of rectangular tiles (see below). Checking the "Used saved size and position of the tile" forces the tiling to use the size and position of the base tile at the last time the tile was used in a tiling. This preserves the spacing between tiles if the *bounding box* has changed due to editing the base tile. Clicking on the *Reset* button resets most of the entries under the tabs to their default values. The *Remove* button can be used to undo a tiling when the base tile is selected. The *Unclump* button can be used to spread out the clones in a somewhat random fashion (can be repeated). And, finally, the *Create* button creates the tiling.

With a circle and the default values (P1 symmetry, two rows and two columns), you will get the following tiling:

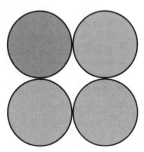

The simple tiling of a circle. The symmetry is "P1" and there are two rows and two columns.

The circle has been replicated four times in two rows and two columns. The original circle is still there, under the top-left cloned circle. The *bounding box* of the circle has been used as the base tile size.

This example is not so interesting, but there are many options under the dialog's tabs that can produce many interesting effects. Each tab will be covered in turn in the following sections.

# Symmetry Tab

The *Symmetry* tab is at the heart of the tiling process. Understanding the different symmetries is necessary to have full control over the outcome of a tiling. The symmetry of the tiling is selected from the pull-down menu under the *Symmetry* tab (see previous figure).

There are three regular geometric shapes that can be replicated to cover a surface completely (without gaps or overlaps). These shapes are: triangles, rectangles (parallelograms), and hexagons. A complete set of tiling symmetries requires taking these shapes and adding rotations and reflections. It is known that there are 17 such tiling symmetries. (See: Wikipedia entry [http://en.wikipedia.org/wiki/Wallpaper_group].) All 17 symmetries are included in the Inkscape *Create Tiled Clones* dialog. The symmetries are shown next.

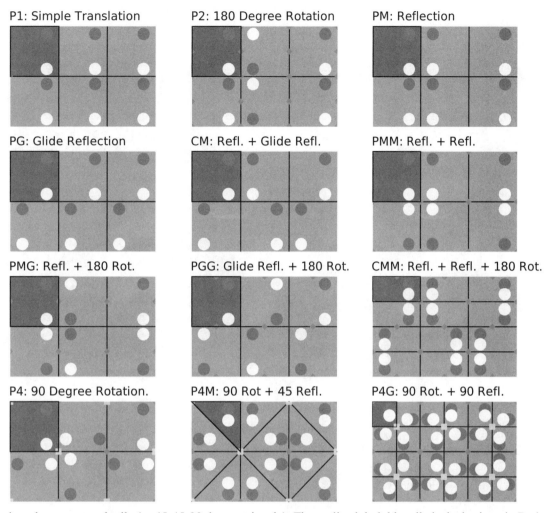

Tilings based on a rectangle tile (or 45-45-90 degree triangle). The outlined dark blue tile is the basic unit. Red and yellow dots show the reflection and rotation symmetries. Points of twofold and fourfold rotational symmetry are shown by pink diamonds and green squares, respectively. The P1 and P2 symmetries also work with parallelograms.

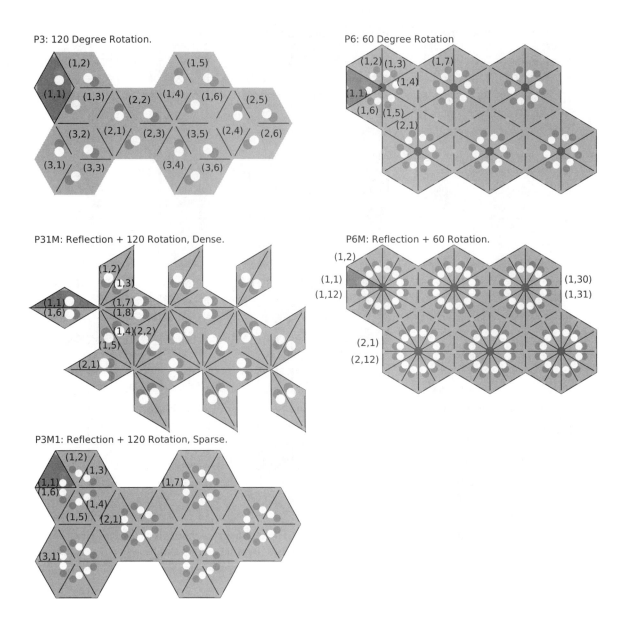

Tiling based on regular subdivisions of a hexagonal. The outlined dark blue tile is the basic unit. All tilings have points of threefold rotational symmetry (orange triangles). Two also have twofold and sixfold rotational symmetries (pink diamonds and purple hexagons). The pairs of numbers indicate the row and column numbers.

The basic tile for each of the 17 symmetries is shown in dark blue in the preceding figures. Inkscape uses the *bounding box* of an object to determine the basic tile size. For rectangular base tiles, the *bounding box* corresponds to the base tile. However, for triangular base tiles, the base tile covers only part of the *bounding box* area. This can result in tiles "overlapping" if an object extends outside the base tile shape (but is still within the *bounding box*) as in the tiling in the introduction to this chapter. Overlapping can also occur if the base tile is altered after the tiles are positioned.

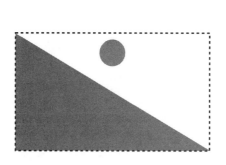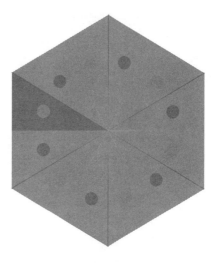

On the left is a triangle and circle that are grouped together. The triangle corresponds to the base tile for a P6M symmetry. Note that the red circle is outside the base triangle but is still within the *bounding box* of the group (and triangle). On the right is a P6M tiling with the triangle and circle. Note how the red circle ends up above some but below other triangles as determined by the order in which the tiling is made.

Inkscape always uses the *Geometric bounding box* to determine the tile size. This avoids problems when creating a triangular tile with a *Stroke* where the *Visual bounding box* doesn't have the same width to height ratio as the *Geometric bounding box*.

If you need to adjust the base tile size after having created a tiling, you can use the *XML Editor* dialog to change the parameters "inkscape:tile-h" and "inkscape:tile-w" (these will appear after you have cloned the object and are used only if the *Use saved size and position of the tile* button is checked).

# Shift Tab

The *Shift* tab allows one to vary the spacing between tiles. With the default parameters, rectangular tiles are arranged so that their *Geometric bounding boxes* are touching. The following options are available to add or subtract space between the tiles:

- *Shift X*, *Shift Y*: Adds (or subtracts) to the tile spacing in units of *bounding box* width and height. A random factor can also be added.

- *Exponent*: Changes the exponent factor $z$ so that position of each tile is $x$ (or $y$) $= (1 + \text{"shift"})^z$.

- *Alternate*: The shift alternates between being added and subtracted.

- *Cumulate*: The previous shift is added to the new shift. For example, if there was a *Shift X* of 10%, normally the space between subsequent tiles would be 10%, 20%, 30%, and so on. With this option, the shifts become 10%, (10+20)% (10+20+30)%, etc. This is useful when one is also scaling the tiles to keep the tile spacing constant. (See the *Scale Tab* section for an example.)

- *Exclude tile*: The tile width or height is excluded in the calculation of tile spacing. This is useful when using the *Rotation* option to put tiles on a circle. In this case, it is a shortcut for specifying a $-100\%$ shift.

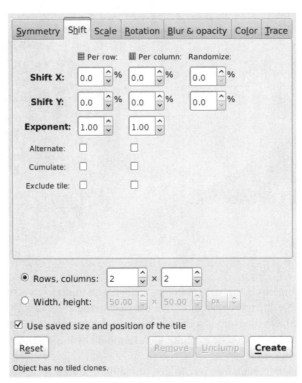

The *Shift* tab of the *Tile Clones* dialog.

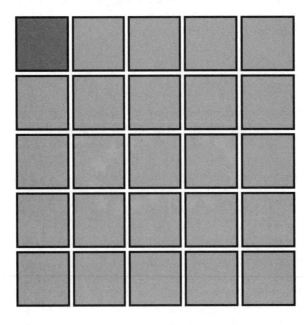

A P1 symmetry tiling with a constant shift of 10% (of the *bounding box*). There is an *x* shift for each column and a *y* shift for each row.

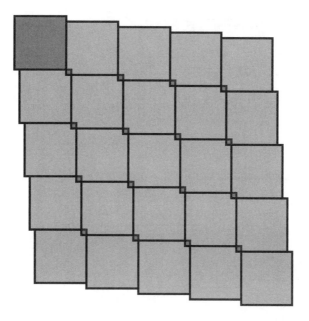

A P1 symmetry tiling with a constant shift of 10% (of the *bounding box*). There is a *y* shift for each column and an *x* shift for each row.

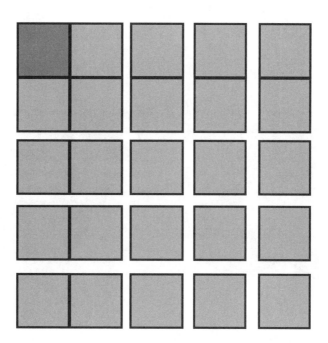

A P1 symmetry tiling with an exponential shift of 1.1 (2% shift in *x* and *y*).

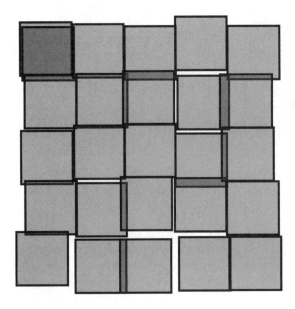

A P1 symmetry tiling with a random shift of 10% (of the *bounding box*) in both *x* and *y*.

Question: What is the symmetry of closely packed hexagons? The answer is P1 as can be seen below. One can use this fact to trivially generate the board for the game Hex [http://en.wikipedia.org/wiki/Hex_%28board_game%29] invented independently by the mathematicians Piet Hein and John Nash.

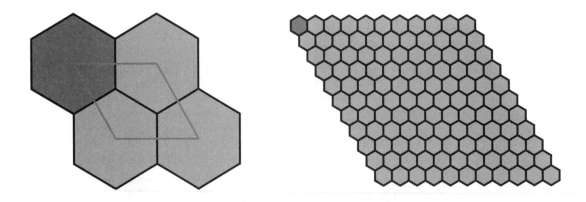

Closely packed hexagons have a P1 symmetry tiling as shown on the left. On the right is the board for the game Hex. To generate both tilings, a hexagon was tiled using a shift in *x* of 50% and a shift in *y* of −25% per row.

# Scale Tab

The *Scale* tab allows one to increase or decrease the size of the tiles depending on the row and column position. The following options are available to scale tiles:

- *Scale X*, *Scale Y*: Scales each tile in terms of percentage. A random factor can be added.

- *Exponent*: Scale each tile with an exponential factor. The nominal scaling S becomes $S^{exponent}$.

- *Base*: Used to create a logarithmic spiral along with *Rotation*. The nominal scaling S becomes $base^{S-1}$ unless *base* is one in which case scaling remains unchanged. Use a value less than 1 for a converging spiral and a value greater than 1 for a diverging spiral. A true logarithmic spiral would use a base of $e$ = 2.718 (or $1/e$ = 0.368). See the *Tile Tricks* section for examples.

- *Alternate*: Alternate scaling up and scaling down tiles.

- *Cumulate*: Scaling is cumulative.

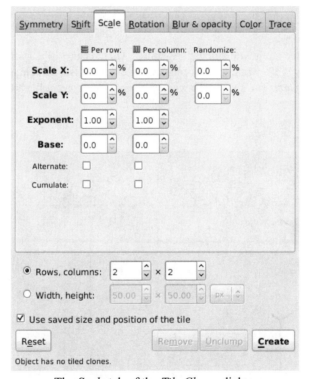

The *Scale* tab of the *Tile Clones* dialog.

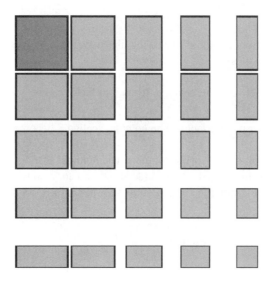

A P1 symmetry tiling with a negative scaling. There is an −15% *x* scaling for each column and a −15% *y* scaling for each row. The scaling is a percentage of the base tile *bounding box*. The spacing between the center of adjacent tiles remains fixed.

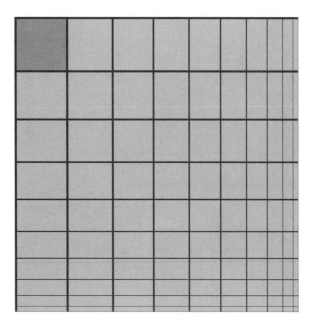

A P1 symmetry tiling with a cumulative negative scaling. There is a −10% *x* scaling for each column and a −10% *y* scaling for each row. There is also a −5% *x* shift for each column and a −5% *y* shift for each row. The *Cumulate* box is checked for both *x* and *y*. A general rule is that to keep scaled tiles just touching, specify a cumulative shift that is half of the scaling (in percent).

# Rotation Tab

The *Rotation* tab allows one to rotate the tiles depending on the row and column position. *Rotation center* is used as the center of rotation. See the *Tile Tricks* section for examples of using a shifted *Rotation center*. The rotation is specified in degrees. The following options are available:

- *Angle*: Rotate by this amount around the *Rotation center*. A random factor can also be added.

- *Alternate*: The rotation alternates between being added and subtracted.

- *Cumulate*: Rotation is cumulative.

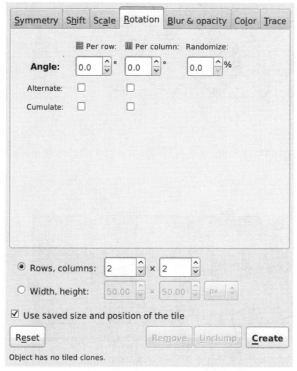

The *Rotation* tab of the *Tile Clones* dialog.

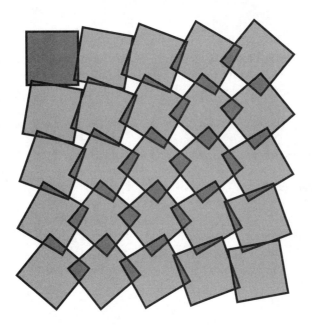

A P1 symmetry tiling with a 10° rotation for each row and column.

A P1 symmetry tiling with a 15° alternating rotation for each row and column.

# Blur and Opacity Tab

The *Blur and opacity* tab allows one to change the *blur* and/or *transparency* of each tile depending on the row and column position.

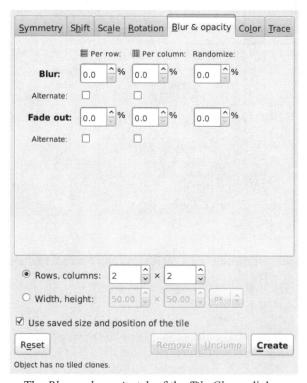

The *Blur and opacity* tab of the *Tile Clones* dialog.

# Blur

A *Gaussian Blur* filter can be applied to each clone with different blurring values.

The blur change is specified in percent. The change in blur can be specified to *Alternate* between a positive and negative value; however, a negative blur value can be entered in the *Per row* and *Per column* boxes. A *Randomizer* factor can also be specified.

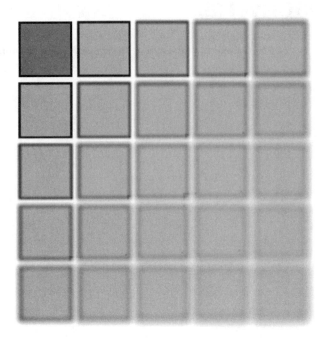

A P1 symmetry tiling with a 2% increase in blur for each row and column.

# Opacity

The opacity change is specified in percent. The change in opacity can be specified to *Alternate* between a positive and negative value. A *Randomizer* factor can also be specified.

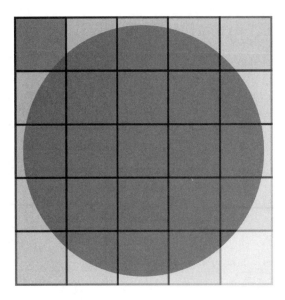

A P1 symmetry tiling with a 10% decrease in opacity for each row and column.
A red circle has been placed under the tiling to illustrate the changes in opacity.

# Color Tab

The *Color* tab allows one to change the *Color* of each tile depending on the row and column position. The color change is specified in percent for each of the three components of a color specified with the *HSL* standard (see the section called *HSL*). The *Hue* repeats itself after a change of 100%. The full scale for *Saturation* and *Lightness* components are each 100%. The changes in the three parameters can be specified to *Alternate* between a positive and negative change. A *Randomizer* factor can also be specified.

Two key points: First, the *Fill* and/or *Stroke paint* must be specified as *Unset* ( **?** ) (see the section called *Fill and Stroke Paint*). Second, an *Initial color* must be specified by using the *Initial color of tiled clones* dialog accessible by clicking on the color button next to the *Initial Color* label.

Note that it is meaningless to have only a shift in *Hue* with a starting color of black or white. This is like trying to walk east from the North Pole.

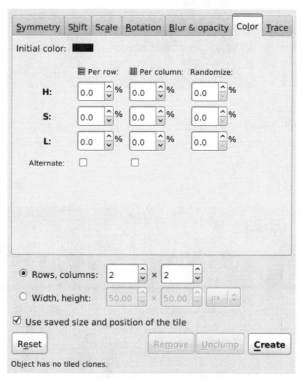

The *Color* tab of the *Tile Clones* dialog.

A P1 symmetry tiling with a 16.7% change in *Hue* per row and a −16.7% change in *Saturation* per column. The starting color is a red with 100% *Saturation* and 50% *Lightness*.✪

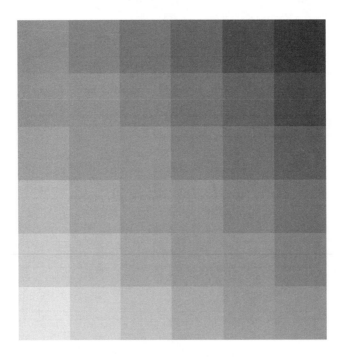

A P1 symmetry tiling with an 8.3% change in *Lightness* per row and a −8.3% change in *Lightness* per column. The starting color is a red with 100% *Saturation* and 50% *Lightness*.

# Trace

The *Trace* tab allows one to set the color, size, and transparency of the tiles by the color or transparency of the objects (including bitmaps) that are placed under the location of the tiling. To enable this feature, the *Trace the drawing under the tiles* box must be checked.

The *Trace* tab has three sections. At the top is a section for specifying what property of the underlying drawing should be used for input. Options include the color, one of the *RGB* components, or one of the *HSL* components. There is also the option to use the *Opacity*, which is the sum of the opacities (*Alpha*) of all objects under the tile.

In the middle of the tab is a section to modify the input value. One can specify a *Gamma*[1] correction or add a randomization factor to the input. One can also invert the input.

The bottom section is for specifying what should be affected by the input. Options include *Presence* (the probability that a given tile will be drawn), color, size, and opacity. The color will only be changed for regions of the base tile that have *Unset* fill.

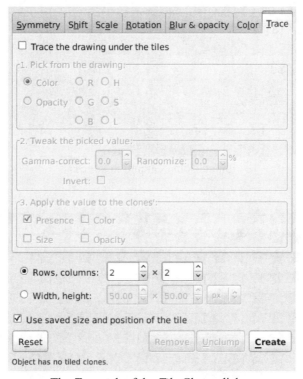

The *Trace* tab of the *Tile Clones* dialog.

The following figures show the effect of some of the possible combinations of input and output options. All the figures use the first rainbow figure as the input drawing. The rainbow is a *radial gradient* with multiple stops. The inside of the rainbow is defined as a white gradient stop with zero *Alpha*. The last outside stop is defined with a red color and with zero *Alpha*. For most figures, a star inside an unfilled rectangle is used as the base tile. The star has been given an *Unset* fill when color is selected in the output.

---

[1] See appendix for definition of *Gamma*.

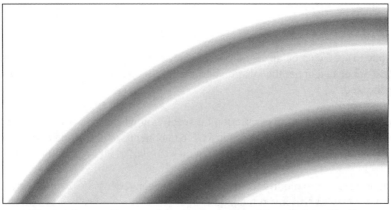

The rainbow pattern used for the background (a radial gradient).

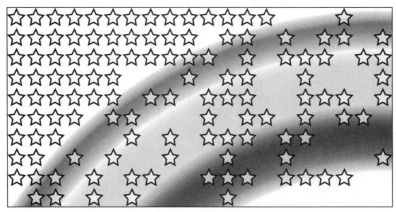

Input: Color. Output: Presence.

Input: Color. Output: Color. Background rainbow has been removed.

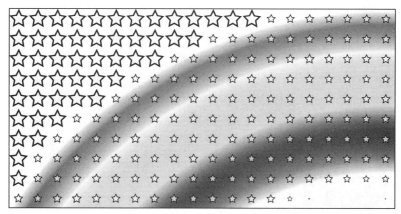

Input: Color. Output: Size.

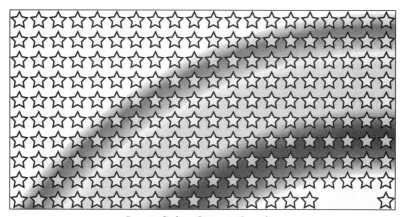

Input: Color. Output: Opacity.

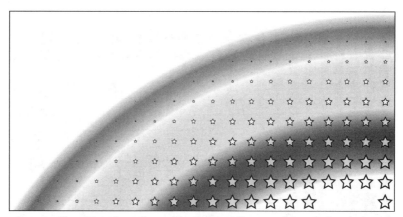

Input: Hue. Output: Size. Note how the red has a hue of zero and purple has the maximum value.

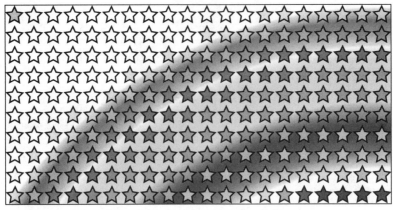

Input: Hue, inverted. Output: Color.

Input: Color, 10% random gamma. Output Color. Changes made to other tabs: Shift: random 10%, Rotation: random 20%. A square base tile with *Unset* fill has been used. The background rainbow has been deleted.

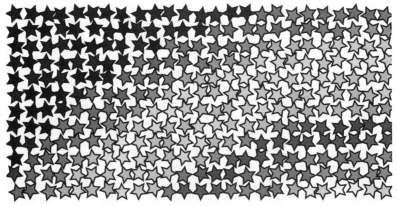

Input: Color, 10% random gamma. Output Color. Changes made to other tabs: Shift: −20%, random 10%, Rotation: random 20%. The number of rows and columns has been increased to compensate for the shift. The background rainbow has been deleted.✪

# Tricks

It is possible to exploit the *Tiling* dialog to produce a number of useful effects. The most interesting is placing tiles along an arc or spiral.

To put a tile along an arc use the P1 symmetry with one row of tiles. Check the *Exclude tile* box. The *Rotation center* is used as the center of rotation.

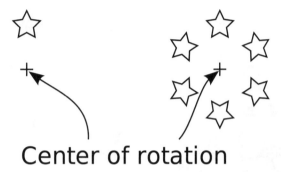

The base tile is drawn on the left, showing the *Rotation center* of the tile. On the right is after a P1 tiling with a per column shift removed by checking the *Exclude tile* box and with a rotation of 60%.

The next figure shows how 12 stars can be put in a circle. This would have been an alternative way of placing the stars in the European Union flag if the stars did not need to be placed with one of their points straight up.

Twelve stars in a circle.

This trick can also place objects along a spiral by specifying that the tile should get larger with each column. One can put the stars on a logarithmic spiral so that the stars don't run into each after several loops.

Stars on a logarithmic spiral. The tile size is increased by 2.5% with *Base* set to 2.7. Each tile is rotated 20°.

Stars on a logarithmic spiral. The tile size is increased by 2.5% with *Base* set to 2.7. Each tile is rotated 20°. The per column shift has been set to 60% (with the *Exclude tile* box checked).

A "P1 symmetry" tiling. 8 rows, 21 columns. Rotation of −11.5° per row and 20.6° per column, *Scale* of 39.3% per row and 24.2% per column with a *Base* of 2.7 for both *x* and *y*. The pattern matches that for a pine cone with 8 rows in one direction and 13 in the other. For the mathematicians: note that 13 times the per column scaling is equal to 8 times the per row scaling and that 13 times the per column rotation minus 8 times the per row rotation is equal to 360°. This is due to the constraint that the 14th star in the first row is the same as the 9th star in the first column.

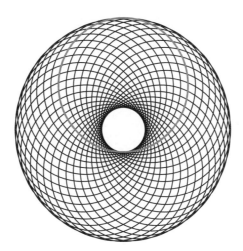

A circle tiled on an arc. The red circle with the *Rotation center* moved off center was the source tile.

# Chapter 20. Tracing Bitmaps

Inkscape has the ability to convert bitmap images into paths via *tracing*. Inkscape uses routines from Potrace [http://potrace.sourceforge.net], with the generous permission of the author, Peter Selinger. Optionally, SIOX can be used as a preprocessor to help separate a foreground from a background.

Tracing an image is not an easy thing to do. Potrace works well for some types of artwork (black-and-white line drawing) and not so well for others (scans from screened color prints). The paths that are created can have thousands of nodes depending on the complexity of the image and may tax the power of your CPU. Using the *Suppress speckles* option can reduce the number of nodes generated by the scan. After the scan, you can use the Path → ≈ Simplify (**Ctrl+L**) command to reduce the number of nodes (but at a cost in resolution). In the latter case, careful tuning of the *Simplification threshold* under the *Misc* section of the *Inkscape Preferences* dialog may be necessary to obtain optimal results.

The result of tracing depends heavily on the quality of the input images. Filtering input scans using Gimp [http://www.gimp.org/] (e.g., Gaussian blur) or mkbitmap [http://potrace.sourceforge.net/] may improve your results.

To trace a bitmap, call up the *Trace Bitmap* dialog (Path → ℗ Trace Bitmap... (**Shift+Alt+B**)). The dialog has three tabs. The first is to select the tracing mode and the second has a list of options.

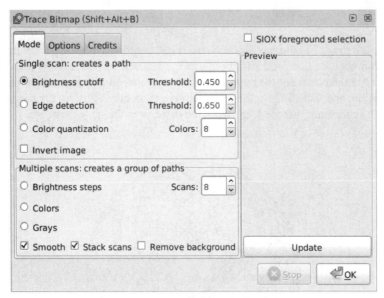

*Trace Bitmap* dialog, *Mode* tab.

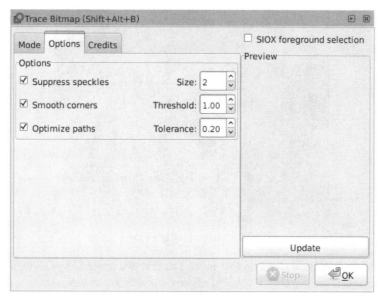

*Trace Bitmap* dialog, *Options* tab.

The *Mode* tab is divided into a number of parts. On the left are two sections: one for *Single* scans, where one *Path* is created, and one for *Multiple* scans, where several *Paths* are created. On the right is a *Preview* window, which can give you a quick idea of what the final scans will look like. A check box at the top right toggles on and off *SIOX foreground selection* (see below).

A number of scanning strategies are available. Each is discussed in a following section. The sections show the results of tracing a black-and-white figure and a color figure. The input figures (from the August 1919 edition of *Vanity Fair*) are shown below. The scans have been passed through the Gimp Gaussian Blur filter to remove the effects of the printing screens.

The source black-and-white drawing.

The source color drawing.

The following part of the chapter is divided into four parts. The first two cover *Single Scans* and *Multiple Scans*. The last two cover options that can be used both with *Single Scans* and with *Multiple Scans*.

# Single Scans

This section covers creating single *Paths* from bitmap images. One option common to all scanning strategies is available: Checking the *Invert image box* will invert the area the created *Path* encloses.

## Brightness Cutoff

Output depends on the *brightness* of the pixels in the bitmap. Brightness is defined as the sum of the red, green, and blue values for a pixel (or the grayscale value for black-and-white drawings). One path is created containing all regions that are darker than the *Threshold* setting. This works well for black-and-white line art.

Brightness. From left to right, the *Threshold* is 0.4, 0.5, and 0.6.

Brightness for a color drawing. From left to right, the *Threshold* is 0.4, 0.5, and 0.6.

# Edge Detection

Output depends on differences in *brightness* between adjacent pixels. A path is created between areas with changes that exceed the *Threshold* setting.

Edge detection. From left to right, the *Threshold* is 0.1, 0.5, and 0.9.

Edge detection for a color drawing. From left to right, the *Threshold* is 0.1, 0.5, and 0.9.

# Color Quantization

Output depends on changes in *color* between adjacent pixels. The *Number of Colors* gives the number of different colors that were used in looking for edges. Only one path is created; what is inside and outside of the path is based on whether the index of the color is even or odd.

Color Quantization for 4, 6, and 8 colors (from right to left).

Color Quantization for 4, 6, and 8 colors (from right to left).

# Multiple Scans

The bitmap is scanned multiple times, each time with a different setting. One path is created for each scan. The paths are stored in a group. The scanning criteria can be *Brightness steps*, *Colors*, or *Grays*. *Grays* uses the *Color* scanning criteria but assigns the resulting paths a grayscale rather than a color. The *Scans* entry box applies to all three scanning criteria. Three options, described in the Options section below, apply to all *Multiple Scans*.

# Brightness Steps

The bitmap is scanned one more time than the specified number (Bug?). The values at which the scans are performed is nontrivial. The lowest (darkest) scan is always done at a brightness threshold of 0.2, the next scan is at a threshold of $(0.2 + (0.9 - 0.2)/n)$. The output level of the darkest region is 0.2 and the lightest is 0.9. Other regions fall at evenly spaced positions in between. If the *Remove background* box is checked, the 90% region is removed.

Multiple scans using the *Brightness* option. From left to right, there are 2, 4, and 8 scans.

Multiple scans using the *Brightness* option. From left to right, there are 5, 10, and 15 scans.

# Colors

The image is traced into the specified number of paths via the following procedure: The number of colors in the bitmap is reduced to the value in the *Scans* entry box using an optimal set of colors chosen via the *Octree Quantization* [http://en.wikipedia.org/wiki/Octree] method. A black-and-white bitmap is created for each color, which is then sent to Potrace for tracing.

Multiple scans using the *Colors* option. From left to right, there are 2, 4, and 8 scans.

Multiple scans using the *Colors* option. From left to right, there are 5, 10, and 15 scans.

# Grays

The tracing principle is the same as for *Colors* but the result is turned into a grayscale image.

Multiple scans using the *Grays* option. From left to right, there are 2, 4, and 8 scans.

Multiple scans using the *Grays* option. From left to right, there are 5, 10, and 15 scans.

# Options

Three extra options are available with *Multiple scans*.

**Smooth.** Selecting the *Smooth* option causes a *Gaussian Blur* to be applied to the **input** bitmap before tracing. This has the effect of smoothing out the difference between adjacent pixels and can be very useful, for example, with scans of screened prints. Too much filtering can lead to loss of detail. The preceding tracings were made without smoothing as the input scan had already been filtered with a *Gaussian* blur in Gimp.

**Stack scans.** The *Stack scans* option determines how the paths are defined. With the *Stack scans* box unchecked, the paths produced do not overlap; with the box checked, each path includes the area of the paths above it in *z-order*. The advantage of unstacked paths is that they are easier to divide into sub-paths, while the advantage of stacked paths is that there are no "holes" between the coverage of the paths. The differences between the two situations is depicted below.

The four paths from a multiple scan with the *Stacked* box checked.

The four paths from a multiple scan with the *Stacked* box unchecked.

**Remove background.** The lowest path in *z-order* is defined as the *background*. Normally, this path has the lightest color. When the *Stack scans* option is chosen, the background path corresponds to a rectangle the size of the scanned image. Checking the *Remove background* box prior to scanning suppresses this path.

# Common Options

This section covers options common to all scanning criteria that are found on the *Options* tab. Two of the options reduce file size while the third produces smoother paths. These are all options that are part of Potrace. Their usefulness will vary depending on the source bitmap.

**Suppress speckles.** Turning on this option removes all paths with a size less than the specified amount. See the *NP Logo* tutorial for an example of its use.

**Smooth corners.** This option produces rounded corners at nodes. The smaller the value, the sharper the corner. A value of 0 is equivalent to no smoothing (i.e., corner nodes connected by straight lines). As the value approaches 1, the number of nodes decreases with the percentage of smooth nodes increasing. The exact behavior is hard to predict.

**Optimize paths.** This option controls merging *Bezier* curves in a scan together, thereby reducing the number of nodes. The *Tolerance* value controls the allowed error in the resulting curve from the merging. The higher the tolerance, the more likely two *Bezier* curves can be merged into one. As *Bezier* curves are required for the merging, the *Smooth corners* option must be used (with a non-zero value).

The red circles are bitmap images and are traced using the *Brightness cutoff* method. From left to right: *Smooth corners* and *Optimize paths* not used: 42 corner nodes; *Smooth corners* used with a *Threshold* of 1.00: 24 smooth nodes and one corner node; *Smooth corners* used with a *Threshold* of 1.00, *Optimize paths* used with a *Tolerance* of 0.20: 4 smooth nodes with 1 corner node.

# SIOX

Simple Interactive Object Extraction or SIOX [http://www.siox.org/] allows one to separate an object from the background in a bitmap image. It acts as a preselection routine for normal tracing. At the moment, only a background region can be specified. In the future, a foreground region will also be definable.

The performance of SIOX depends greatly on the characteristics of the bitmap image. Colored bitmaps where the object is clearly distinguished in color from the background work best.

To use SIOX, check the *SIOX foreground selection* box in the *Trace Bitmap* dialog. The label is a bit misleading as the next step is to select a region that includes the entire object of interest and excludes most of the background. The SIOX algorithm uses the excluded region to characterize the background.

Create a closed path around the object you wish to extract. Give the path a fill if it doesn't already have one. Select both the bitmap image and the path and then trace as usual.

An example of using SIOX. Left, original bitmap image. Middle, image with background exclusion region added. Right, result of tracing. One can see that the background rejection is not perfect as there are similar colors in the background and foreground (e.g., reddish hair on chest).✪

# Chapter 21. Connectors

*Updated for v0.48.*

*Connectors* are lines that "connect" objects, useful for drawing organization charts or flow diagrams. Connectors remain connected even if the objects they connect are moved. Individual objects can be given an *avoid* property that causes connectors to be routed dynamically around them.

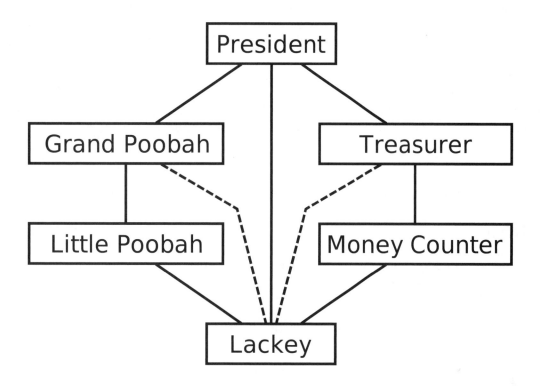

An organizational chart drawn using connectors. The dashed
lines have been automatically routed around other objects.

 **Warning**

There is a bug in v0.48 that causes the connectors to be drawn wrong. Nudging a connected object up and down may cause the connectors to be rerouted correctly.

# Creating Connectors

Connectors are created by the *Connector Tool*. To create a connector, select the tool by clicking on the 🔧 icon (**Ctrl+F2** or **o**) in the *Tool Box*. Then click-drag the mouse from one point on the canvas to another. When the pointer is over an object, a *Connection* handle is shown in the center of the object. Beginning or ending the click-drag on one of these handles will attach the connector to the corresponding object. Alternatively, one can begin a connector by clicking on an empty point on the canvas or on a *Connection* handle and end the connector by a second click. Connectors are drawn so they begin on the edge of the attached object.

By default, connectors will not attach to text objects. This facilitates connections between boxes that frame text. You can change this option under the *Connector* entry of the *Inkscape Preferences* dialog.

# Modifying Connectors

Connectors can be modified several ways. The connectors can be connected or disconnected from objects, the connector line style can be changed, and the routing of the connectors can be changed.

## Connecting and Disconnecting

A connector can be disconnected from an object by dragging an end point away from the object. To do so, first select the connector by clicking on it. Two handles should appear at each end. Drag one of the handles away. The handle will then be fixed to the background. To reconnect a handle (or to move a handle from one object to another), drag the handle to the connection handle that will appear at the center of the object when the cursor is above the object.

## Line Style

All the normal line (path) styles can be applied to a connector, including adding arrows or using a dashed line. To change the line style, use the *Fill and Stroke* dialog (Object → 🖋 Fill and Stroke... (**Shift+Ctrl+F**)).

### Cap Style

Changing the *Cap style* to *Square Cap* may improve the look of a connection to a stroked object.

## Routing

Connectors are automatically rerouted when objects are changed or connectors are added or modified. There are a number of parameters that can be set to control the automatic routing of connectors. These are all accessible from the *Connector Tool-Tool Controls*:

- ⤵ : Clicking on this icon while an object is selected marks the object to permit connectors to cross the object when routed.

- ⤴ : Clicking on this icon while an object is selected marks the object to prohibit connectors to cross the object when routed.

- ⌐ : *New in v0.48:* This icon toggles on/off routing connectors with only horizontal and vertical lines. Clicking it when a connector is selected will toggle the connector to the other mode.

- **Curvature:** This parameter controls the amount of curvature between two straight sections of a connector.

- **Spacing:** This parameter controls the amount of spacing around an object that a connector will not pass through.

- ⋈ : Clicking on this icon will automatically rearrange connectors and connected objects in a "nice" arrangement. The placement is based on the Kamada-Kawai [http://www.boost.org/libs/graph/doc/kamada_kawai_spring_layout.html] algorithm that treats the connectors as springs so that the distance between the *connector* handles are evenly spaced. Only selected objects and connectors will be changed (use **Ctrl+A** to select all objects and connectors). The following parameters/options control this layout. Your mileage may vary.

- **Length:** This parameter controls the "ideal" length of the connectors when automatically rearranging objects and connectors.

- Y : This icon toggles on and off the option that connectors with end *Markers* (e.g. arrows) should point downwards.

- ▥ : This icon toggles on and off the requirement that objects cannot overlap when moved.

# Chapter 22. Extensions

Inkscape can be enhanced by *Extensions*. These are scripts or programs that can be run from inside Inkscape. Most *Extensions* require external programs, usually written in Perl or Python.

Some of the included *Extensions* might be of marginal use to the average user. However, much can be learned by examining the code in order to write your own scripts. Look in the `share/inkscape/extensions` directory for the code.

A few *Extensions* are built into Inkscape; they are located in the source directory `src/extension/internal`. Often, an *Extension* can be used to quickly prototype a feature that may be included natively in a future version of Inkscape. *Extensions* are also a good way to add a feature that may have limited use by the general Inkscape community and thus not warrant the long-term commitment of adding the feature to the main code base.

If an extension doesn't work, it may be that you are missing some external dependency. You can check if this is the case by looking at the log file `extensions-errors.log` in your Inkscape preferences directory (Linux: `.config/-inkscape`, Windows: `Documents and Settings\USER\Application Data\Inkscape`).

*Extensions* can be run live, that is, the script code can be run automatically in the background, responding immediately to changes in parameters. This can both be good (see results of parameter changes immediately) or bad (updating before a parameter is fully modified). Each *Extension* dialog has a button to toggle on and off this *Live Preview*.

It is possible to assign keyboard shortcuts to extensions. See the section called *Custom Keyboard Shortcuts* in Chapter 24, *Customization*.

Extensions are grouped under several broad categories:

- Arrange: Reorder objects.

- Color: Modify the colors of an object or a *Group* of objects.

- Generate from Path: Utilize a path object to create a new object.

- Images: Extract or embed images in an Inkscape file.

- JessyInk: Prepare a presentation viewable in web browsers.

- Modify Path: Modify an existing path.

- Raster: Manipulate the colors in a *bitmap*.

- Render: Create a new object.

- Text: Manipulate text.

- Visualize Path: Extract information about a path.

- *Updated in v0.48*. Web: Add JavaScript parameters or slice a drawing into bitmaps.

Two entries under the *Extensions* menu allow you quick access to the previously used extension. The first, Extensions → Previous Extension, will run the extension with the same parameters. The second, Extensions → Previous Extension Settings... , will pop up the parameters dialog.

# Arrange

This category rearranges objects in a drawing. At the moment there is just one extension in this category.

## Restack

This extension changes the *z-order* of objects based on their position on the canvas. A variety of parameters control how the restacking is done. The *Restack Direction* is set by a drop-down menu in the *Restack* dialog. Options include: *Left to Right*, *Bottom to Top*, *Right to Left*, *Top to Bottom*, *Radial Outward*, *Radial Inward*, and *Arbitrary Angle:*. In the last case the angle is given in the *Angle* entry box where the angle is defined counterclockwise with zero corresponding to left to right. The last two parameters control which point of an object's *bounding box* is used in the restacking process.

The dialog for the *Restack* extension.

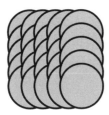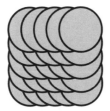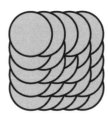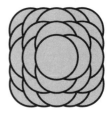

An example of using the *Restack* effect. From left to right: An array of overlapping circles created with the *Create Tiled Clones* dialog. Restacked with direction *Bottom to Top (90)*. Restacked with an *Arbitrary Angle* of 135° Restacked with direction *Radial Inward*.

# Color

This set of extensions manipulates the colors of an object or *Group* of objects. The extensions are implemented through a set of Python scripts (located in the directory `share/inkscape/extensions`). The use of Python scripts is a temporary measure until the capability is incorporated natively into Inkscape. The color mapping is calculated in the *RGB* color space except for the extensions that modify *HSL* values, which are calculated in *HSL* color space.

If no objects are selected, the color change will be applied to the entire drawing. An object's *Stroke* and any *Gradient* are also changed.

## Black and White

*New in v0.48.*

Converts an image to black and white. The extension first calculates brightness (luma) using the YUV [http://en.wikipedia.org/wiki/YUV] color space (for NTSC and PAL standard definition television) and then applies a threshold of 50%.

Left: Original colors. Right: Colors after applying the Black and White extension.✪

## Brighter

Brighten the color of an object or *Group* of objects. This extension has the property of making dark colors more intense but washing out light colors. The effect is subtle so multiple applications may be required.

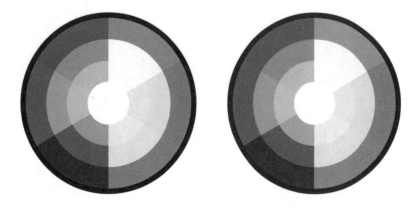

Left: Original colors. Right: Colors after applying the Color Brighter extension.✪

# Custom

This extension allows color custom transformation functions to be defined. Standard math operations are allowed such as +, −, ×, and /. If a resulting value is outside the allowed limits, it is set at the minimum or maximum allowed value.

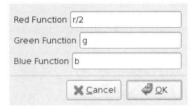

Custom Color Extension dialog set to reduce R (red) to one half.

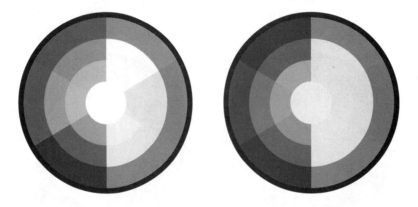

Left: Original colors. Right: Colors after applying the Color Custom extension with the specification that R should be divided by 2.✪

# Darker

Darken the color of an object or *Group* of objects. Each R, G, and B component of a color is set to 90% of its previous value. The effect is subtle so multiple applications may be required.

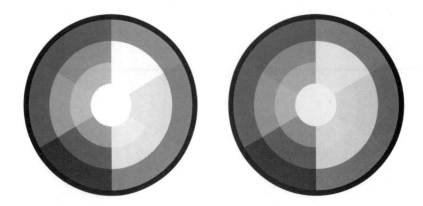

Left: Original colors. Right: Colors after applying the Color Darker extension.✪

# Desaturate

Desaturate the color of an object or *Group* of objects. This sets the values of R, G, and B to the average of the maximum of R, G, and B; and the minimum of R, G, and B. For example, R would be set to (max( R, G, B ) + min( R, G, B ))/2.

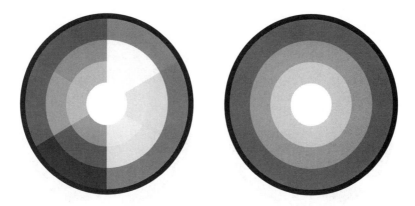

Left: Original colors. Right: Colors after applying the Color Desaturate extension.

# Grayscale

Change the color to a gray using the formula for Luminance used by the NTSC and PAL television standards. This sets the color to a *lightness* (Y) defined by: Y = 0.229 × R + 0.587; × G + 0.114 × B. See the Wikipedia entry for YUV [http://en.wikipedia.org/wiki/YUV] for further information.

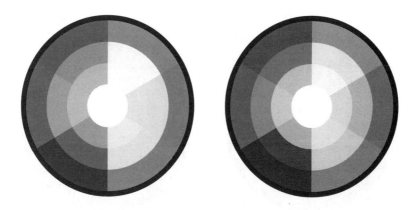

Left: Original colors. Right: Colors after applying the Color Grayscale extension.

# Less Hue

Decrease the hue (see the section called *HSL*) of a color. The hue is decreased by 5% (of the full hue range) or equivalently, a rotation of 18° around the color circle. This, for example, means that a pure red picks up a touch of blue in the *RGB* color space.

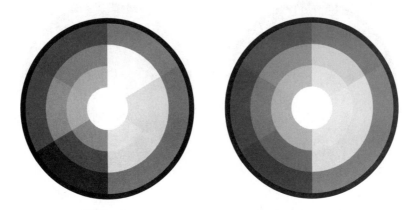

Left: Original colors. Right: Colors after applying the Color Less Hue extension.✪

# Less Light

Decrease the lightness (see the section called *HSL*) of a color. The lightness is decreased by 5% (of the full lightness range). If the lightness is already less than 5%, it is set to 0%. The effect is subtle so multiple applications may be required.

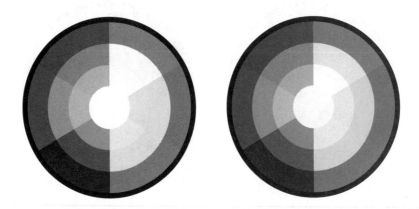

Left: Original colors. Right: Colors after applying the Color Less Light extension.✪

# Less Saturation

Decrease the saturation (see the section called *HSL*) of a color. The saturation is decreased by 5% (of the full saturation range). If the saturation is already less than 5%, it is set to 0%. The effect is subtle so multiple applications may be required.

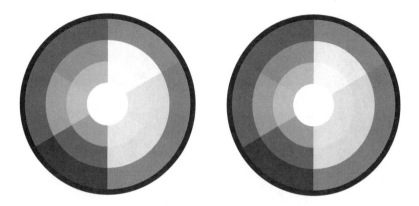

Left: Original colors. Right: Colors after applying the Color Less Saturation extension.✪

# More Hue

Increase the hue (see the section called *HSL*) of a color. The hue is increased by 5% (of the full hue range) or equivalently, a rotation of 18° around the color circle. This, for example, means that a pure red picks up a touch of green in the *RGB* color space.

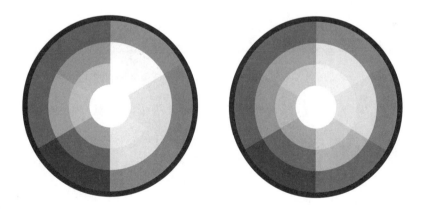

Left: Original colors. Right: Colors after applying the Color More Hue extension.✪

# More Light

Increase the lightness (see the section called *HSL*) of a color. The lightness is increased by 5% (of the full lightness range). If the lightness is already more than 95%, it is set to 100%. The effect is subtle so multiple applications may be required.

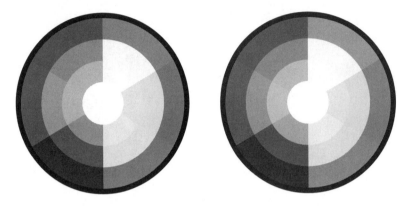

Left: Original colors. Right: Colors after applying the Color More Light extension.✪

# More Saturation

Increase the saturation (see the section called *HSL*) of a color. The saturation is increased by 5% (of the full saturation range). If the saturation is already more than 95%, it is set to 100%. The effect is subtle so multiple applications may be required.

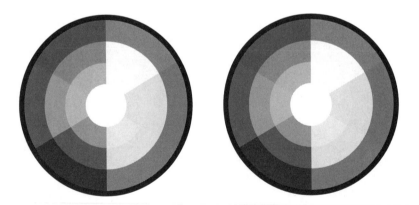

Left: Original colors. Right: Colors after applying the Color More Saturation extension.✪

# Negative

Invert the color. For example, an R value of 64 (25%) becomes an R value of 191 (255−64, or 75%).

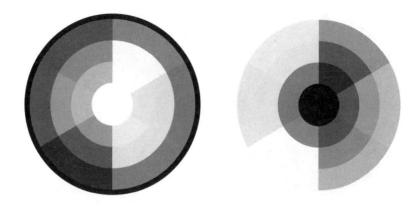

Left: Original colors. Right: Colors after applying the Color Negative extension.✪

# Randomize

Randomize the color of selected objects or all objects if no object is selected. You can choose which of the *HSL* color parameters to randomize (hue, saturation, and/or lightness).

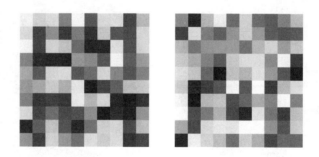

A grid of gray squares after randomizing their colors. Left: Randomizing hue, saturation, and lightness. Right: Randomizing only lightness.✪

# Remove Blue

Set the B value in *RGB* to 0.

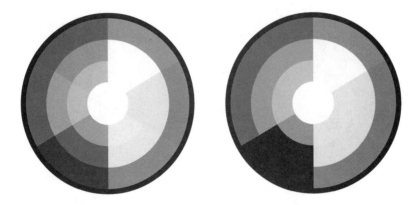

Left: Original colors. Right: Colors after applying the Color Remove Blue extension.

# Remove Green

Set the G value in *RGB* to 0.

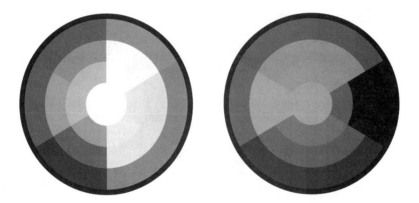

Left: Original colors. Right: Colors after applying the Color Remove Green extension.

# Remove Red

Set the R value in *RGB* to 0.

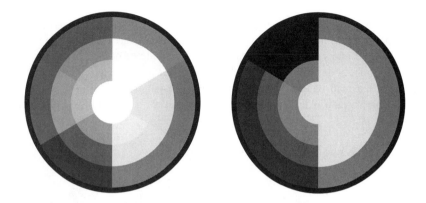

Left: Original colors. Right: Colors after applying the Color Remove Red extension.

# Replace color

Replace a color among selected objects or all objects if no object is selected. Colors are specified in RRGGBB *hexadecimal* form. Color to be replaced must match exactly.

# RGB Barrel

Rotates color (hue) by 120° around the color circle.

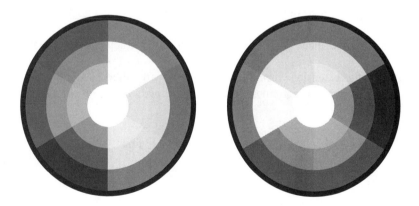

Left: Original colors. Right: Colors after applying the Color RGB Barrel extension.✪

# Generate from Path

This group of extensions creates new objects from one or more existing paths.

## Extrude

Connects nodes in two paths with lines or with polygons. In the case of lines, it simply draws a line between each corresponding node in the two paths (i.e., a line between the first node of one path and the first node of the other path, etc.). If one path has more nodes than the other, the extra nodes are not used. All the lines are sub-paths of one path. In the case of polygons, a quadrilateral is drawn between corresponding adjacent pairs of points on the two lines. Each quadrilateral is a separate path. All the created paths are placed in a *Group*. In both cases, the original paths are not changed.

See the *Motion* for a similar effect utilizing only a single path.

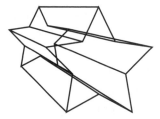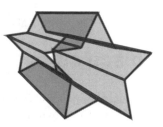

From left to right: Two star paths. After selecting both stars and using the *Line* option. After selecting both stars and using the *Polygon* option.

## Inset/Outset Halo

This extension produces a blurred image of the selected object(s). It works by making multiple copies of the object(s) and insetting or offsetting the path of each copy by a different small amount. The opacity of each copy is set to a small value based on the number of copies made. The copies are embedded in a group that is left above the original object(s).

Why would you want to use this extension when Inkscape now supports filters? Well, filter support in web browsers is still in its infancy. Your *SVG* drawings are more likely to be properly rendered using this extension. The look of the blur is also a bit different.

This extension only works on paths! Convert regular shapes and text to paths before using (Path → ⬚ Object to Path (**Shift+Ctrl+C**)).

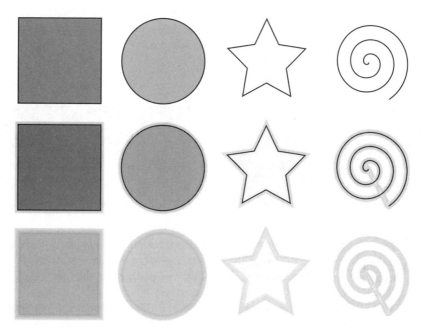

Top: Regular shapes. Middle: Regular shapes after using Inset/Outset Halo extension (*Width*: 5, *Number of steps*: 11). Bottom: After deleting the original objects.

## Text with a blurred shadow.

Text after using the Inset/Outset Halo extension to produce a shadow. The shadow has been
shifted down and to the right. The color of the text was changed after creating the shadow.
The original text was moved above the shadow in *z-order* (*Width*: 5, *Number of steps*: 11).

# Interpolate

Draws a series of lines that interpolate the space between two paths. The options include setting the number of *Interpolation Steps* (in-between lines), an *Exponent* factor that controls the spacing between interpolated paths (zero for
even spacing), specifying if the original paths should be duplicated (*Duplicate Endpaths*), and specifying that the path
style should also be interpolated. Objects need to be converted to paths prior to invoking the extension.

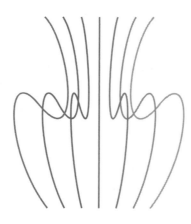

An interpolation between the red and blue lines, with the *Interpolate Style* box checked.

The beginning of the path of one object is matched to the beginning of the other path. This can lead to unexpected effects. The starting point of a path can be found by selecting the path with the *Node Tool* and then using the **Tab** key. If no node is already selected, the first node in the path will be selected.

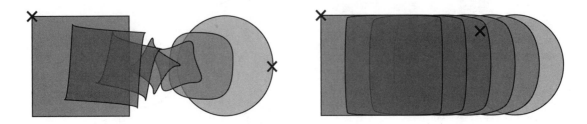

An interpolation between the blue square and a red circle, with the *Interpolate Style* box checked. Left: the start of the two paths (indicated by the crosses) are not in the same relative positions. Right: the circle has been rotated 135 degrees so the start of the two paths are in the same relative positions.

The interpolation extension can also be used to simulate gradients of different symmetries. When calling the extension, the smaller path should be selected first.

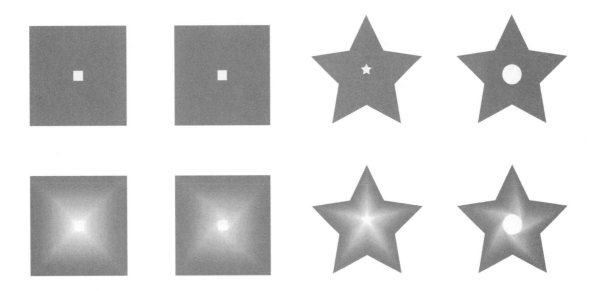

From left to right: Interpolation between two squares in the same orientation; two squares, one rotated 90 degrees; two stars in the same orientation; a star and a circle. The starting paths are shown on top. In all cases, the number of Interpolation steps was set to 25. Note that the smaller path must be selected first.

# Motion

Simulates motion. Draws a copy of the selected object behind the original and then connects corresponding nodes with lines to form a group of closed paths. The direction and offset of the copied object can be specified. The new objects inherit the attributes of the original but can be edited as a group.

 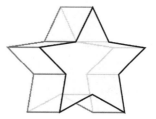

Left: Original object. Right: Object with extrusion. (*Magnitude* of 25, *Direction* of 180.) The *Master opacity* has been set to 0.5 for the new objects.

One can also use this extension to simulate perspective by reducing the size of the copy along with the associated nodes. The steps are:

- Ungroup objects (Object → ▨ Ungroup (**Shift+Ctrl+G**)).

- Combine into one path (Path → ▱ Combine (**Ctrl+K**)).

- Use *Node Tool* to select all nodes associated with copy in back.

- Move nodes toward each other (<, etc.).

- Break apart path (Path → ▱ Break Apart (**Shift+Ctrl+K**)).

- Group objects (Object → ▨ Group (**Ctrl+G**)).

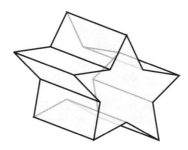 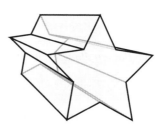

Left: Without perspective. Right: With perspective.

# Pattern Along Path (Extension)

This extension places a pattern along one or more target paths. The pattern can be a single object or a *Group* of objects. See also Chapter 8, *Live Path Effects (LPEs)* for an alternative way of putting patterns along paths.

Copies of the single yellow star are placed along a path. The star is deformed to follow the path.

To put a pattern on a path:

1. **Select the pattern:** The pattern can be a single object or a *Group*. In some cases, you may have better results if you explicitly convert all objects (e.g., *Shapes*) in the pattern to paths.

2. **Select the target path or paths:** Called the *Skeleton* path by the extension author.

3. **Call the extension:** A dialog will open up where various parameters can be selected. After the extension is applied there will be a new path for each object in the pattern. For example, the stars on the line in the above figure are formed by one path.

The *bounding box* of the pattern is used for placing the pattern along the path, with the *bounding box* of one pattern copy touching the *bounding box* of the next copy (if no additional spacing is specified).

When the extension is called up, the following dialog is shown:

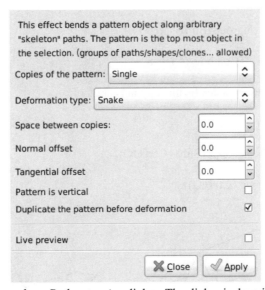

The *Pattern along Path extension* dialog. The dialog is described below.

This dialog has many options that can be set (see figures that follow for examples of use):

- **Copies of the pattern:** You can choose to have a *Single* copy of the pattern placed on the path or multiple copies *Repeated* along the path. The pattern can be *stretched* so that the left edge of the first pattern copy lines up with the start of the *Skeleton* path and the right edge of the last pattern copy lines up with the end of the *Skeleton* path.

- **Deformation type:** Two options are available:

  - **Snake:** The pattern is rotated and deformed to follow the path such that all points with the same horizontal (*x*) position in the pattern will be on the same normal (perpendicular line) to the path, and all points with the same vertical (*y*) position in the pattern will be placed the same distance from the path. If the *Pattern is vertical* box is checked, then the pattern is rotated 90 degrees first.

  - **Ribbon:** The pattern is deformed only in either the vertical or horizontal direction to conform to the path. The direction of the deformation is controlled by the *Pattern is vertical* check box described below.

- **Space between copies:** You can add (or subtract) space between copies of the pattern. The unit is pixel.

- **Normal offset:** The *normal offset* moves the pattern perpendicular relative to the path. Positive values move the pattern to the left relative to the direction of the path.

- **Tangential offset:** The *tangential offset* moves the pattern in the direction of the tangent line to the path.

- **Pattern is vertical:** Checking this box rotates the orientation of the pattern by 90 degrees.

- **Duplicate the pattern before deformation:** With this box checked, the original pattern is left in place. Otherwise, it disappears.

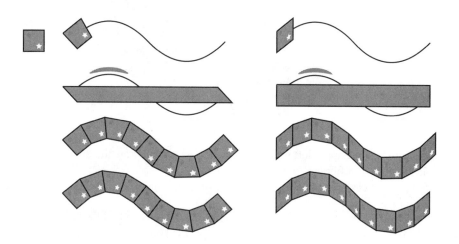

Left: Snake deformation, right: Ribbon deformation. From top to bottom:
Copies of the pattern: Single; Single, stretched; Repeated; Repeated, stretched.

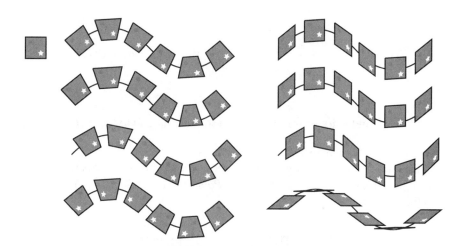

Left: Snake deformation, right: Ribbon deformation. All with spacing of 10 px. From top to
bottom: Spacing only, Normal offset of 5 px, Tangential offset of 10 px, Pattern is vertical.

The *Pattern along Path* is a very useful extension but it does have a few quirks. One is that if the pattern is moved before use, the results may be less than ideal. Another is that different parts of the pattern can be distorted in different ways as seen in figures that follow.

The pattern at the upper left was put on the red path. Note how the distortion of the black outline is different from the blue squares. A solution in this case is to use the *Add nodes* extension to increase the number of nodes in the path of the black square.

The following example shows a pattern placed on both straight and curved paths. If the radius of curvature is too small, the pattern may be grossly distorted.

The pattern at the top of the figure was applied to a straight line and to a curved line (shown in red).

A pattern can be used to create a fancy border as shown below. Care must be taken that the pattern lines up at the corners. This can be done by making the distance between the corner nodes multiples of the pattern width or by breaking the path into disconnected pieces at the corners (use the *Break Path at Selected Nodes* ( ⁂ ) option in the *Node Tool Tool Controls*) and using the *Repeated, stretched* option.

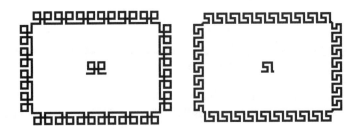

Borders produced with the *Pattern along Path* extension. In both cases, the pattern in the center was put on a rectangle that was converted to a path. On the left, the rectangle side lengths were chosen to be multiples of the pattern width. On the right, the sides were disconnected by using the *Break Path at Selected Nodes* ( ⁂ ) option in the *Node Tool-Tool Controls* on each corner node and the *Repeated, stretched* option was chosen. This ensured that the pattern would line up at the corners properly.

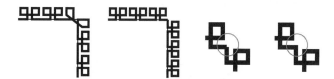

From left to right: A single path with a *corner point*. The lengths of the sides are not multiples of the pattern width; thus, the pattern does not line up at the corner. The path converted to a compound path with two sections by using the *Break Path at Selected Nodes* ( ) option in the *Node Tool-Tool Controls* on the *corner point* node. Using the *Repeated, stretched* option, the pattern width is adjusted so that it lines up at the corner. A close up of corner showing a discontinuity due to the pattern pieces not being connected. A close up of the corner after the two nodes at the corner are connected using the *Join Selected End Nodes* ( ) option in the *Node Tool-Tool Controls*.

Going one step further, a pattern can be applied to a circle. In the following figure, the pattern on the right was applied to a circle (of larger diameter than the solid yellow circle). The resulting path was filled with a radial gradient.

A sun produced by putting a pattern on a circle. The flame path shown on the right was used as the pattern. A small space was added between pattern copies by setting *Space between copies* to 10. (The yellow circle is an independent object.)

One use of the *Single, stretched* option is to put text on a path. The text must be converted to a path first (Path → Object to Path (**Shift+Ctrl+C**)).

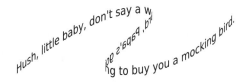

The text was placed along the path using the *Single, stretched* and the *Ribbon* options. The text was converted to a path first.

Another use of the *Single, stretched* option is to create flourishes. (As of v0.47, this is better done by applying the "teardrop" as a custom shape with the *Bezier Tool*. One would not need to add the extra nodes.) The steps are:

• Draw a small circle, convert to a path (Path → Object to Path (**Shift+Ctrl+C**)).

• Create a "teardrop": Convert one node to a corner node and move to right. Adjust node handles to flatten lines.

• Add nodes with *Add Nodes* extension.

• Draw curves with *Bezier Tool* or *Spiral Tool*. Use *Pattern along Path* to put a teardrop along curves.

- Create multiple curved teardrop paths and combine (Path → 🅿 Union (**Ctrl++**)) to form the flourish.

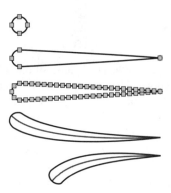

From top to bottom: Circle converted to path. Path with one node moved and handles adjusted. Path with extra nodes added. Teardrop path put on blue curve path. Ditto.

Top: Four "teardrop" paths are in position to be combined. Bottom: The final flourish after combining the paths.

# Scatter

This extension places a pattern along one or more target paths. It is almost identical to the *Pattern along Path* extension except that the pattern is not deformed.

Copies of the single yellow star are placed along a path. The star is not deformed as it is stamped along the path.

Most of the options are the same as for the *Pattern along Path* extension. Those that are different are:

- **Follow path orientation:** The pattern is rotated and to follow the path such that all points with the same horizontal ($x$) position in the pattern will be on the same normal to the path, and all points with the same vertical ($y$) position in the pattern will be placed the same distance from the path. If the *Pattern is vertical* box is checked, then the pattern is rotated 90 degrees first.

- **Stretch spaces to fit skeleton length:** Space is added between pattern copies so they fill evenly the skeleton path.

- **Original pattern will be:** *Moved*: Original pattern is copied, then deleted. *Copied*: Original pattern is copied and remains in place. *Cloned*: Original pattern is cloned, If the original pattern is modified, all patterns along the path will also be modified.

# Voronoi

*New in v0.48.*

Draws Voronoi [http://en.wikipedia.org/wiki/Voronoi_diagram] diagrams. The line segments are derived by distributing sites (points) semi-randomly in an area and then constructing line segments where each point on the segment is equal distance to the two closest sites forming cells around each site.

To use this extension, select a path or object and then call up the extension. There are two settings:

- **Average size of cell (px):** The average cell size (height and width).

- **Size of Border (px):** A positive number greater than the *Average size of cell* results in a pattern that can be tiled smoothly. A negative number removes sites near the edge resulting in larger cells near the border.

After applying this extension, you will have a *Pattern* that is applied to the *Fill* of the object that was selected. The *Pattern* can be shifted, scaled, and rotated like any other *Pattern*. It can also be applied to other objects through the *Fill* tab of the *Fill and Stroke* dialog.

 **Warning**

This extension creates a large object that may overtax your computer.

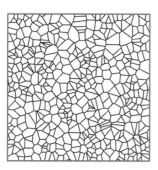 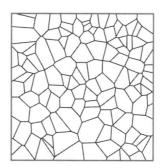 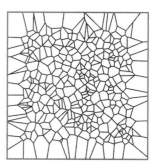

From left to right: Patterns with the default settings (size: 10 px, border: 0 px), with an average cell size of 20 px, with an average cell size of 20 px and a border of -20 px.

 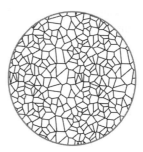

Left: A Voronoi pattern created with an average cell size of 10 px and a border size of 20 px. Right: The pattern applied to a circle. Note the smooth tiling.

# Images

These extensions extract or embed *bitmap* images from or into an Inkscape file.

## Extract One Image

*Updated in v0.48.*

This extension will extract the selected *bitmap* image from the drawing. The destination filename must be given (and not just the path [Bug]). The filename extension (e.g., ".png") is automatically added. As of v0.48, relative paths are relative to the user's home directory.

## Embed All Images

Normally Inkscape keeps references to external graphics files for included *bitmap* images. It is possible to embed the images inside an Inkscape *SVG* file with this extension. Simply call this extension to embed all bitmap images in the file. This may make your *SVG* file quite large. Only *PNG* and *JPEG* files may be embedded.

# JessyInk (Presentations)

*New in v0.48.*

The *JessyInk* package of extensions allows one to use Inkscape to produce a sophisticated web-based presentation, complete with master slides, automatic page numbering, transitions between slides and within slides, and page zooming. *JessyInk* works by embedding JavaScript into your *SVG* file. The JavaScript then manipulates Inkscape *Layers* to run the presentation. Perhaps the best way to see what *JessyInk* can do is to run the demonstration that can be found in the *Featured downloads* section on the JessyInk Home Page.

To use *JessyInk* you first need to add the *JessyInk* JavaScript code to your *SVG* file. This is done by calling up the *Install/Update...* dialog and clicking on the *Apply* button. The code can be removed by using the *Uninstall/remove* dialog.

Once the code is installed, each *Layer* becomes a slide in the presentation. The order of the *Layers* in the drawing corresponds to the order of the slides in the presentation. One slide can be designated as the *Master slide* which will be displayed as background to all the other slides.

### Tip

Keep the *Layer* dialog open while working. Slides can be easily added or moved around in order with the dialog. It helps to give the slides meaningful names.

Keep a web browser open while working. Not only can you easily check your work but you can get an overview of your presentation by using the *Index* mode (toggled on/off by **Ctrl+i**).

## Master Slide

To create a master slide, first create a layer with all the objects you wish to appear on all slides. Give the slide a name using the *Layer* dialog ("Master Slide" is a good choice). Then call up the *Master Slide* dialog via the *Master Slide...* menu entry. Enter the slide name and click the *Apply* button. It is a good idea to lock the slide by clicking on the 🔒 icon in the *Layers* dialog next to the slide name.

You can add a few special *Auto-texts* to the *Master Slide*. The most useful is the *Slide number* which will automatically display the correct slide number on each slide. You can also display the total number of slides (excluding the *Master Slide* and the title (*Layer*) name of each slide.

To add *Auto-text*, put dummy text on the *Master Slide* where you want the *Auto-text* to be located. The *Auto-text* will be displayed with the style of the dummy text. Select the dummy text and then on the *Auto-texts* dialog select the desired type and hit the *Apply* button. You will not see any change to the text in Inkscape but when viewing the presentation in a Web browser, the correct *Auto-text* will be displayed.

## My Inkscape Talk

### Slide Title

#/#

An example of a JessyInk master slide showing a title that will be displayed on all pages as well as examples of *Auto text*. "Slide Title" will be replaced by the *Layer* name of each slide. It is center justified. "#/#" is composed of three separate texts. The first '#' will be replaced by the page number. It is right justified so that page numbers 10 or greater will not overlap with the slash. The second '#' will be replaced by the total number of pages. It is left justified.

# Transitions

Transitions between slides can be added with the *Transitions* dialog. Each slide can have a transition before (*in*) and after (*out*) its display. A default transition type can be assigned to the *Master Slide* which will then be used by all slides that don't have an explicit transition assigned to them.

There are three types of transitions: *appear*, where the slide appears instantly; *fade*, where the slide fades in or out; and *pop* where the slide fades in or out and grows or shrinks. The transition time for *fade* and *pop* can be set in the dialog.

To set a transition effect, call up the *Transition* dialog and the enter the *Layer* name that you which the transition to apply to. Select the transition type and click the *Apply* button. No visible change will be seen in Inkscape.

## Warning

Check whether the computer you plan on using for a presentation is powerful enough to handle the fancier transitions. They can eat up a lot of CPU, especially if using large *bitmap* images or *Gradients* and *Filters*.

# Effects

Effects are similar to transitions, except they apply to things on the same slide. For example, you can have a series of bullet points that appear one at a time. The same types of effects as for transitions are available: *appear*, *fade*, and *pop*. The order in which different effects are applied during a presentation is determined by the *Order* parameter. Effects with the same order number will appear at the same time.

To add an effect, select an object or a *Group* and then call up the *Effects* dialog. Select the type of effect and specify an *order*. Finally, click on the *Apply* button. Again, no visible change will be seen in Inkscape.

## Tip

Think carefully about using effects. Overuse may prove distracting and annoying to your audience. Just because you can do it doesn't mean you should.

# Views

Views are away to zoom in and out to part of a slide. Rotation is also possible. Views can be mixed with effects. The order is determined by the *Order* parameter.

To set a view, add a *Rectangle* to a slide. Removing the *Fill* and adding a light color *Stroke* allows viewing the rest of the slide easily. With the *Rectangle* selected, call up the *View* dialog, set the *Order* parameter and click *Apply*.

# Miscellaneous

There are a few other dialogs available:

- **Keys bindings:** Allows changing the key bindings used during a presentation.

- **Mouse handler:** Allows changing the way the mouse interacts during a presentation.

- **Summary:** Creates a summary of the *JessyInk* script embedded in the *SVG* file.

- **Video:** Allows the embedding of video into a presentation by adding an *HTML5* video tag. Check whether your browser supports the *HTML5* video tag (Firefox 3.6 and later should work).

# Presenting

Once the presentation is finished, it can be opened in any browser that supports *SVG*. The first slide will automatically be displayed. By default use the **Right Arrow** or **Page Down** keys to advance through the presentation. The **Left Arrow** and **Page Up** keys can be used to go in reverse. The **Down** and **Up** keys can be used to navigate without running effects.

There are a few special features available during presentations:

- **Index Sheet:** An *Index Sheet* that shows miniatures of nine slides, with the active slide highlighted, can be called up with the **i** key. Use the arrow keys to navigate through the slides. Pressing the **i** again will return to the presentation at the entrance of the highlighted slide. This allows quick navigation through a presentation.

An example of a JessyInk index view during a presentation. The first slide is the current slide.

- **Drawing Mode:** A *Drawing Mode* can be toggled on/off with the **d** key. In this mode, the cursor becomes a pen. The width and color of the stroke can be controlled with number and alpha keys respectively. (See the *Key binding* dialog for a complete list of keys.) The **z** key can be used to undo a segment.

- **White Board Slides:** Pressing the **n** key while in presentation mode will insert a blank slide. This slide can be used as a whiteboard with the drawing mode.

# Modify Path

The extensions in this section all modify an existing path.

## Add Nodes

Adds nodes to a path, leaving the shape of the path unchanged. The nodes are added evenly spaced. The number of nodes is either specified or by setting a minimum specified spacing. Good for creating scissor lines.

Convert regular shapes to paths before applying.

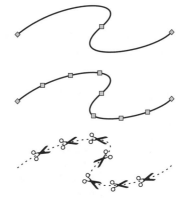

Example of using Add Node. Top: A Bezier curve defined by three nodes. Middle: Same curve after using *Add Node*. Bottom: Curve converted to cut line.

## Color Markers to Match Stroke

Automates changing the *Markers* to match the color of the *Stroke*. The extension makes copies of a *Markers* in the *<defs>* section of the *SVG* file with the appropriate color. This extension is a temporary work-around until the *SVG* 1.2 standard is finalized. The new standard is expected to simplify matching *Marker* color with *Stroke* color.

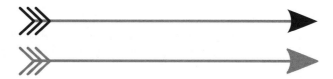

Example of using the Color Marker to Match Stroke extension. The top arrow shows the markers just after changing the stroke color. The bottom arrow shows the results of applying this extension.

# Convert to Dashes

The extension takes a *Path* with *Dashes* and converts each *Dash* into a separate sub-path. This is to allow desktop cutting plotters to cut dashed lines.

# Edge 3D

Adds highlights and shadows to simulate 3D objects like buttons. The extension works by adding paths that are blurred via the *Gaussian Blur* filter and then clipped. The paths have partial transparency, with white for highlights and black for shadows. The extension only works on paths so regular shapes need to be converted first. You may also need to add additional nodes.

Parameters:

- *Illumination Angle*: Sets the angle from which light arrives.

- *Shades*: Sets the number of different gray levels. The path is broken up into sections according to the relative angles of the nodes. A shading path is generated for each level. You must have a least as many nodes in the original path as shades.

- *Only black and white*: If checked, only the lightest (white) and darkest (black) parts are generated.

- *Stroke width*: Not used (fixed internally at 10).

- *Blur stdDeviation*: Sets the blur radius for the *Gaussian Blur* filter in pixel units.

- *Blur width*, *Blur height*: Sets the width and height of the Filter Effects Region [285], the area where the blur is calculated. These parameters are not very useful (you cannot set the *x* and *y* terms). Leave both set at 2.0.

Example of using Edge 3D. Both square and circle were converted to paths. The *Add Node* extension was used to add nodes to the circle. The number of *Shades* is 2 for the square and 4 for the circle.

# Envelope

Distorts a path so that the path's original *bounding box* is mapped to the edges of a quadrilateral. To use the extension, select the path to transform first, then add the quadrilateral path to the selection. Regular shape objects must be converted to a path before transformation.

Left: Original path. Right: Path after mapping *bounding box* to quadrilateral.

The extension works on a single path. The beginning point of the quadrilateral path will determine the orientation of the transformed image. If the image is inverted (like looking through a mirror), reverse the direction of the quadrilateral path with the Path → ⇄ Reverse (**Shift+R**) command.

This extension could be used to produce a pseudo-perspective extension. For real perspective, use the *Perspective* extension.

# Flatten Bezier

This extension converts selected *Bezier* curves to an approximation composed of straight-line paths. The number of line segments used is determined by the *Flatness* parameter. The smaller the *Flatness*, the more line segments are used.

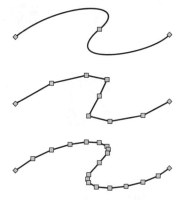

Example of using Flatten Bezier. Top: A Bezier curve defined by three nodes. Middle: After using extension with Flatness of 10. Bottom: After using extension with Flatness of 2.

# Fractalize

This extension turns a straight-line segment into a crooked segment. It works by finding the midpoint of the line segment, adding a node at that point, and then moving the node a random distance perpendicular to the original path direction. This division routine is called recursively depending on the setting of the *Subdivisions* entry in the dialog, doubling the number of resulting segments for each increase by one. The *Smoothness* of the path can also be specified. The magnitude of the perpendicular displacement is a random function with the limits determined by $\pm(Segment\ length)/(1 + Smoothness)$.

The extension will also work on a curved path by turning the path into a series of line segments between the path's nodes.

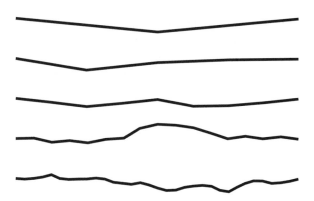

Example of using Fractalize. From top to bottom, the *Subdivision* parameter was increased from 1 to 5. The *Smoothness* parameter was set to 10.

# Interpolate Attribute in a Group

This extension takes the objects in a *Group* or a selection and assigns a value to some attribute of each object, interpolating between two extremes to determine the value. Note that the order of the objects in the *SVG* file determines the order in which the interpolated attributes are assigned. Options include interpolating color, width, height, scale, and position.

Example of using the Interpolate Attribute In A Group extension to interpolate color. There are two groups of five squares. The following parameter values were used: *Attribute to Interpolate*: *Fill*, *Where to apply?*: *Style*, *Start Value*: *#ff0000*, *End Value*: *#000000*, *Unit*: *Color*. The difference between the top row and bottom row is the order in which the squares are included in the *SVG* file.

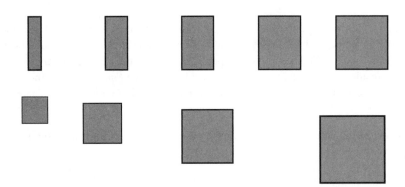

Example of using the Interpolate Attribute In A Group extension to interpolate width and scale. There are two groups of five squares. The following parameter values were used: Top: *Attribute to Interpolate*: *Width*, *Start Value*: *10*, *End Value*: *40*, *Unit*: *No Unit*. Bottom *Attribute to Interpolate*: *Scale*, *Start Value*: *0.5*, *End Value*: *1.5*, *Unit*: *No Unit*. In the last case, the *x* and *y* positions are scaled as a side effect.

# Jitter Nodes

Randomly shift nodes and/or node handles. The *Maximum displacement* parameter controls the magnitude of the randomization. When the *Use normal distribution* box is not checked, the magnitude of displacements will be uniformly distributed between zero and the *Maximum displacement* value (in pixels). When the box is checked, the magnitudes of the displacements will have a *Normal* (a.k.a. Gaussian or Bell curve) distribution with a standard deviation of 0.5 times the *Maximum displacement* value. The Normal distribution option may produce more natural-looking variations in a path. In both cases, the direction of the displacement will be random.

Top: Array of stars created with the *Create Tiled Clones* dialog. Bottom: Same array after applying the *Jitter nodes* extension. Note that the stars must be converted to paths before the extension is applied.

# Perspective

Distorts a path (or a *Group* of paths) so that the path's original *bounding box* is mapped to the edges of a quadrilateral and a perspective extension is applied to the path. To use the extension, select the path to transform first, then select the quadrilateral. Regular shapes and text must be converted to a path before transformation. This extension requires the *Numpy* [http://numpy.scipy.org/] (Numerical Python) package.

The beginning point of the quadrilateral path will determine the orientation of the transformed image; in most cases, the quadrilateral path should be started from the lower-left corner and proceed in a clockwise direction. The **Tab** key will cycle through the nodes in order when the *Node Tool* is in use. If no node is selected, then the starting node will be highlighted on the first use of the **Tab** key. To change the starting node, break the path at the desired start node (v0.47) or one node before (v0.48) ( ⁙ ) and then rejoin ( ⁙ ). To reverse a path, use the Path → ⇄ Reverse (**Shift+R**) command.

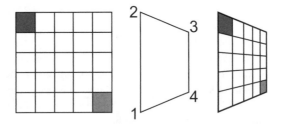

Left: Original path. Middle: Target quadrilateral. The nodes have been numbered to show the normal order in which they should be drawn. Right: Path after mapping *bounding box* to quadrilateral.

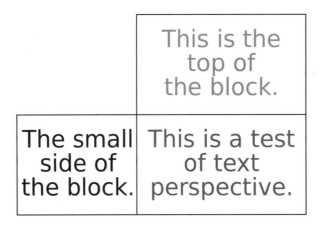

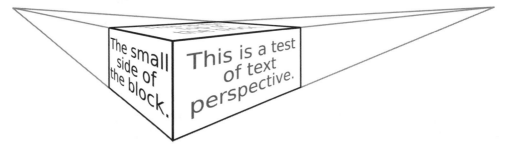

Mapping text to the sides of a block with perspective. The text must be converted to a path. In order to center the text, the text has been grouped with a rectangle (also converted to a path).

# Pixelsnap

*New in v0.48.*

Adjusts paths and rectangles to the pixel grid so that when exported as a bitmap, the lines are sharp. Filled objects are adjusted so that their edges are aligned with pixel boundaries. Paths are first adjusted to have an integer pixel width, and then adjusted so the stroke edges align with the boundaries.

Left: A rectangle and a path, misaligned with the pixel grid. Right: The same rectangle and path after applying the Pixelsnap extension. Both rectangles and paths are 20 pixels wide by 20 pixels high.

# Rubber Stretch

Distorts a path as if the path was stretched vertically or the path was squeezed horizontally. The amount of the distortion is controlled by the *Strength* and *Curve* parameters. Adding extra nodes may produce a better result.

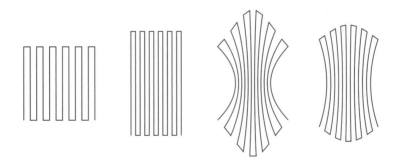

From left to right: Input path (with extra nodes added). After applying the extension with parameters values for *Strength* and *Curve* of 50%, 0%; 0%, 50%; and 25%, 25%, respectively.

# Straighten Segments

Reduces the curvatures of path segments. The amount of straightening can be specified. A *Behavior* value of 1 moves the node handles toward the nodes, a value of 2 moves the node handles to a point one-third of the distance between the node and the neighboring node. There is little visual difference between these two options.

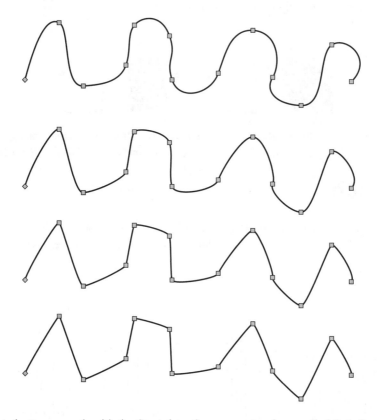

From top to bottom, a path with the *Straighten Segment* extension applied 0, 1, 2, and 3 times.

# Whirl

This extension twists an object around a point, like what might happen if you dropped things in whirling water (except the farther away from the center, the greater the displacement for this extension). The amount of "whirling" is an input parameter. Objects must be converted to paths before applying the extension.

## Tip

The center of view is used for the center of the whirl. To whirl around the center of an object, select the object and then use View → Zoom → ⊕ Selection (**3**) to center the view on the object.

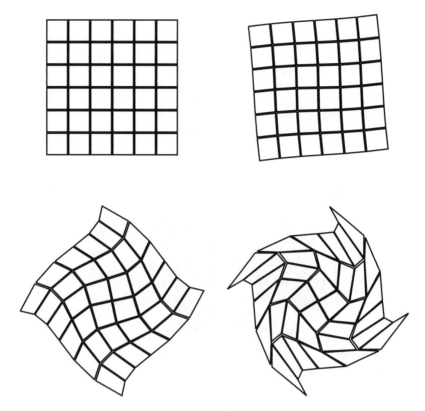

From left to right, top to bottom: Whirl of 0, 1, 10, and 25 units. In each case, the center of the whirl is the center of each array of small squares.

# Raster

This group of extensions manipulates the colors of a *bitmap*. They are handy if you need to make a quick change to a *bitmap* and don't need the power of a full-blown *bitmap* editor like Gimp. The extensions all depend on the ImageMagick [http://www.imagemagick.org] library. After an extension has been applied, the original bitmap, either externally referenced or internal, will be replaced by a modified internal *bitmap*.

Note that these extensions only work on a *bitmap*. Some of the extensions can be duplicated by using *Filters* which also work on all objects and don't permanently change the *bitmap* file.

An example of using the *Implode* extension (with input parameter of 1.0).

List of available extensions:

| | | |
|---|---|---|
| • Adaptive Threshold | • Add Noise | • Blur |
| • Channel | • Charcoal | • Colorize |
| • Contrast | • Cycle Colormap | • Despeckle |
| • Dither | • Edge | • Emboss |
| • Enhance | • Equalize | • Gaussian Blur |
| • HSB Adjust | • Implode | • Level |
| • Level (with Channel) | • Median | • Modulate |
| • Negate | • Normalize | • Oil Paint |
| • Opacity | • Raise | • Reduce Noise |
| • Resample | • Shade | • Sharpen |
| • Solarize | • Spread | • Swirl |
| • Unsharp Mask | • Wave | |

# Render

This set of extensions creates new objects.

## 3D Polyhedrons

This extension generates 3D Polyhedrons. Selecting this extension pops up a dialog with three tabs. The first tab, *Model file*, controls the type of polyhedron that is specified in the *Object* drop-down menu. If *Load From file* is selected, the description in the file specified in the *Filename:* entry box is used. In the *Object Type* tab you can specify if the source file describes the object with edges or faces.

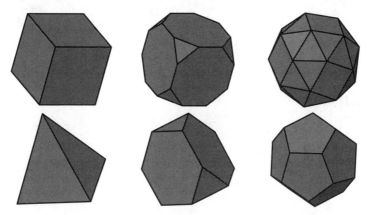

Examples of a few of the available shapes. Top row: Cube, Truncated Cube, Snub Cube. Bottom row: Tetrahedron, Truncated Tetrahedron, Dodecahedron. In all cases, the view was set to a 30° rotation around the *x*-axis followed by a 30° rotation around the *y*-axis. The style was set to show faces.

The second tab, *View*, allows you to rotate the polyhedron. Up to six rotations are allowed (for the mathematicians: why six when any unique rotation can be specified by only three orthogonal rotations?).

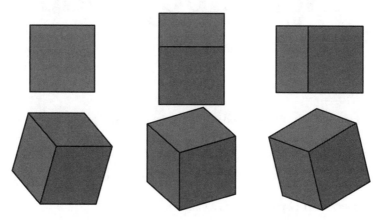

Example of rotating a cube. Top row: No rotations. 30° rotation around *x*-axis, 30° rotation around *y*-axis. Bottom 30° rotation around *x*-axis followed by 30° rotation around *y*-axis, 30° rotation around *y*-axis followed by 30° rotation around *x*-axis, 30° rotation around *x*-axis followed by 30° rotation around *y*-axis followed by 30° rotation around *z*-axis,

The third tab, *Style*, allows you to set all kinds of style parameters, including the *Fill* color and *opacity*. One can also specify if the faces of the polyhedron should be shaded to simulate light striking the object. One can specify the direction from which the light comes. One can specify if the nodes, edges, or faces should be drawn. And one can specify if the "hidden" faces should be drawn (useful if the faces are not fully opaque).

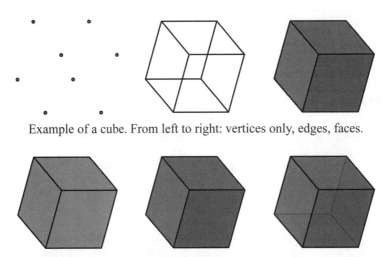

Example of a cube. From left to right: vertices only, edges, faces.

From left to right: No shading, default shading, *Draw back-facing polygons* enabled with *Fill Opacity* set to 75%.

## Alphabet Soup

This extension generates exotic-looking text by recombining parts of characters from mostly the Latin alphabet in a way that the original text is discernible. The dialog has entry boxes for the text, scale, and random number seed. Changing the random number seed will change the parts used to generate the text. This effect is based on code written by Matt Chisholm [http://www.theory.org/artprojects/alphabetsoup/main.html].

Two examples of the Alphabet Soup extension. They differ only in the random number seed used.

## Barcode

This extension generates barcodes. The types of codes that can be generated are:

- EAN8 (European Article Number) 8 digits. A short version of EAN13.

- EAN13 (European Article Number, UPC + 1 digit) 13 digits; one is a checksum. The checksum is calculated.

- UPC-A (Universal Product Code) 12 digits; one is a checksum.

- UPC-E (Universal Product Code) 6 digits; one is a checksum. A compressed representation of UPC-A.

- Code39 (Encodes 26 uppercase letters, 10 digits, and 7 special characters.) Used on packaging.

- Code39Ext (Encodes all 128 ASCII characters.)

- Code93 (Improved version of Code39, used by Canadian Postal Service.)

- Code128 (Encodes all 128 ASCII characters.) Variable length. Includes checksum.

• RM4SCC (Royal Mail 4-state Customer Code, United Kingdom.) Allows letters, numbers, and open/close brackets.

Examples of barcodes.

# Barcode — Datamatrix

*New in v0.48.*

This extension generates a Datamatrix [http://en.wikipedia.org/wiki/Data_matrix_%28computer%29] barcode.

Example of a Datamatrix barcode. The name Inkscape is written with 10 by 10 grids.

# Calendar

This extension generates calendars. There are a variety of options. One can select a whole year or one month. One can choose Sunday or Monday as the starting day of the week, and one can choose which days are considered to be weekend days. One can choose the colors for the different labels and one can change the default names of the months and the days of the week.

## 2011

| January | February | March | April |

Example of a calendar.

# Cartesian Grid

This extension generates Cartesian grids. Options include number of subdivisions, number of sub-subdivisions, linear versus logarithmic divisions, and line widths. For polar coordinates see Polar Grid extension.

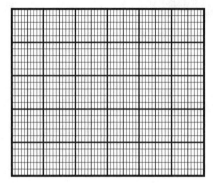

Example of a Cartesian grid.

# Draw From Triangle

This extension is a geometrician's dream. It allows you to create an almost infinite number of constructions based on a triangle. The triangle is defined by the first three nodes in a path (even if the path is not a triangle). The path must be closed and the nodes connected by straight lines.

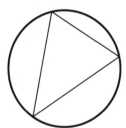 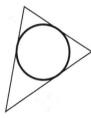 

Examples of using the Draw From Triangle extension. From left to right: Circumcircle, Incircle, Angle Bisectors.

# Foldable Box

This extension draws the pattern for a foldable box as one might use for the input in a desktop cutting plotter (after modifying the paths). The individual sides and tabs are each represented by separate paths which are all in a *Group*.

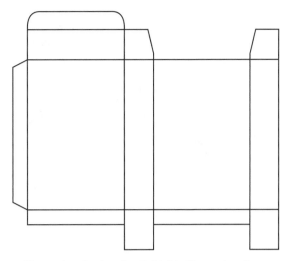

Example of using the Foldable Box extension.

# Function Plotter

Plot a function versus $x$ (horizontal axis). To use, first draw a rectangle to define the width of the $x$-axis and the height of the $\pm 1$ lines of the $y$-axis. Then select the extension. In the pop-up window, enter the $x$ and $y$ ranges. Checking the *Multiply x-range by 2π* box changes the $x$-axis to represent units of $2\pi$, useful for plotting periodic functions. You can either have the routine calculate the first derivative of the function numerically or supply the first derivative yourself.

The function is plotted in the *SVG* coordinate system, which has the $y$-axis upside down. The extension inserts a minus sign automatically to correct for this.

All Python math functions are allowed (as long as they return a single value), including Python random number functions. The *Help Tab* has a list of some of the available functions.

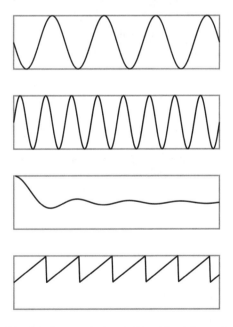

From top to bottom: $-\sin(x)$ with four periods. $\sin(x)$ with eight periods. $\sin(x)/(x + 0.000001)$ with four periods; the first point has been deleted as the first derivative estimate is off. $x -$ floor($x$) with one period. The gray boxes show the location and size of the original rectangles.

When the *Use polar coordinates* option is selected, the *x*-range is set to −1 at the left of the rectangle and +1 at the right side. The *x* values entered in the extension's dialog are used for the angle *domain* (in radians). The *Isotropic scaling* parameter is ignored. *Calculate first derivative numerically* must also be selected.

  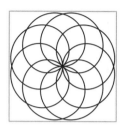 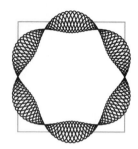

From left to right, all with *Multiply x-range by 2\*pi* selected and *y* range from −1.0 to 1.0:
exp(−0.185\**x*), logarithmic spiral, found often in nature, *x* range from -5 to 0. sin(5\**x*)
with range from 0 to 1. sin(4.0/5.0\**x*), range from 0 to 5. 1+0.2\*sin(3\**x*)\*sin(100.0/7.0\**x*),
*x* range from 0 to 7. The gray boxes show the location and size of the original rectangles.

Note that depending on the version, Python may return an integer if you divide two integers: thus, 4/5 = 0, while 4.0/5.0 = 0.8.

# Gear

Draw a realistic mechanical gear [http://en.wikipedia.org/wiki/Gear]. Three parameters must be given: the *Number of teeth*, the *Circular pitch* (the tangential distance between successive teeth), and the *Pressure angle*. Common values for *Pressure angle* are: 14.5, 20, and 25 degrees. The radius of the "Pitch Circle" is equal to N × P/2π, where "N" is the number of teeth and "P" is the Circular Pitch.

The gear is created around the *SVG* origin and then placed inside a *Group*. The *Group* is then translated so that the center of the gear is at the center of the visible canvas. This makes animating the gear easier as the rotation is then independent of the displacement. An animated clock using these gears can be found on the book's website [http://tavmjong.free.fr/INKSCAPE/].

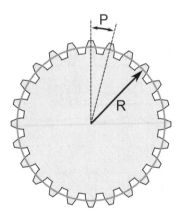

A gear with 24 teeth. The Pitch Circle is shown in blue. The *Circular pitch* is the distance
along the Pitch Circle between the two dotted lines. "R" is the radius of the Pitch Circle.

# Grid

This extension fills the *bounding box* of an object with a grid. The grid spacing and offset can be independently set in the horizontal and vertical directions. The grid line width can also be set.

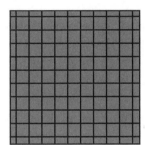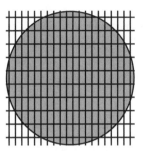

Left: Grid with default settings. Right: Grid with different horizontal and vertical spacings. Note that it is the *bounding box* that is filled by the grid, not the object's area. To fill an area, use a *pattern* or use a *clip path*.

# Guides Creator

This extension creates *Guide Lines* based on the *Page* size. One can choose between three *Preset* options. The first option, *Custom...*, allows one to create evenly spaced *Guide Lines* with the spacing defined by the *Vertical guide each* and *Horizontal guide each* menus. The next *Preset* option, *Golden Ratio*, places *Guide Lines* so that the ratios horizontally or vertically from the *Guide Lines* to the edges of the page are in proportion to the *Golden Ratio* [http://en.wikipedia.org/wiki/Golden_ratio] (approximately 1 to 1.62). The last *Preset* option, *Rule-of-third*, divides the *Page* horizontally and vertically into three equal parts. This is equivalent to using the *Custom...* option with a value of *1/3*.

Enabling the *Start from edges* option will result in *Guide Lines* also being created along the *Page* edges.

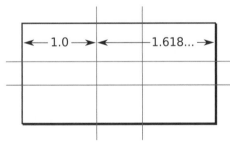

Example of using the Guides Creator extension. The *Page* is shown with the *Guide Lines* created when selecting the *Golden Ratio* preset.

# LaTeX Formula

This extension turns a *LaTeX* string into a path. The string is typed into a dialog box. The extension requires that Ghostscript, *LaTeX*, and Pstoedit to be installed and in the execution path. Pstoedit must include the GNU libplot *SVG* driver or the shareware *SVG* plug-in, available for Windows at the Pstoedit [http://www.pstoedit.com/] website. The resulting formula is rendered as a path.

$$\lim_{n \to \infty} \sum_{k=1}^{n} \frac{1}{k^2} = \frac{\pi^2}{6}$$

An example of a formula generated by the LaTeX Formula extension.

An alternative script for Linux using Skencil for the conversion to *SVG* (avoiding the need for Pstoedit with *SVG* support) is available at the book's website: http://tavmjong.free.fr/INKSCAPE/.

# L-System (Fractal-Lindenmayer)

Draws *Lindenmayer System* [http://en.wikipedia.org/wiki/Lindenmayer_system] structures, developed by Aristid Lindenmayer while studying yeast and fungi growth patterns. It is beyond the scope of this manual to discuss these structures. Just one comment: The *Step* parameter controls the scale of the generated path.

Lindenmayer Systems: From left to right:

Default inputs.

Variant of the Koch curve. Inputs: *Order* 3, *Angles* 90, *Axiom* F, *Rules* F=F+F-F-F+F.

Koch's Snowflake: Inputs: *Order* 3, *Angles* 60, *Axiom* F++F++F, *Rules* F=F-F++F-F.

Sierpinski triangles. Inputs: *Order* 5, *Angles* 60, *Axiom* A, *Rules* A=B-A-B;B=A+B+A.

The rules can be very complex. See the Lindenmayer screenshot [http://www.inkscape.org/screenshots/gallery/inkscape-0.44-lindenmayer.png] for more information.

# Parametric Curves

This extension generates parametric curves. It was derived from the Function Plotter extension and shares many of its parameters.

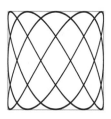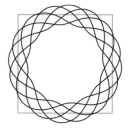

Left: *x-function*: sin(3\*t), *y-function*: cos(5\*t). Right: *x-function*:
sin(t)\*(1.0 + 0.2\*sin(3.2\*t)), *y-function*: cos(t)\*(1.0 + 0.2\*sin(3.2\*t)).

The "Butterfly Curve": *x-function*: sin(t)\*(exp(cos(t)) − 2.0\*cos(4.0\*t) −
pow(sin(t/12.0),5.0)); *y-function*: cos(t)\*(exp(cos(t)) − 2.0\*cos(4.0\*t) − pow(sin(t/12.0),5.0)).

# Perfect-Bound Cover Template

This extension produces a template for a *Perfect-Bound Cover* as found in *Print On Demand* services. The template sets the document to the correct size and creates guides for the front cover, back cover, and spine of the book, including the specified bleed. The dialog allows for specifying a variety of parameters including the number of pages in the book and the thickness of each page. The extension is biased toward English measurements.

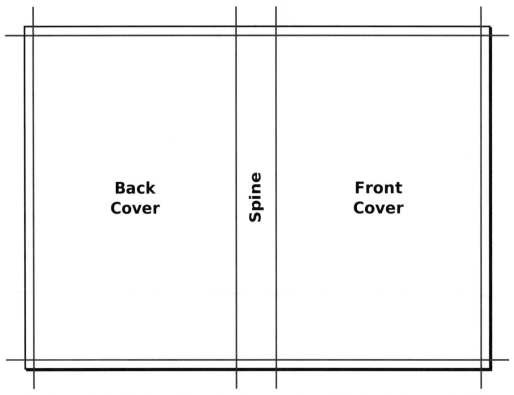

The dialog for the *Perfect-Bound Cover Template* extension.

An example of using the *Perfect-Bound Cover Template* extension with the inputs shown in the dialog screenshot above. The front cover, back cover, and spine regions are labeled. The outer blue lines also show the bleed.

# Polar Grid

This extension generates polar grids. Options include number of subdivisions, linear versus logarithmic divisions, line widths, and angle labels. For Cartesian coordinates see Cartesian Grid extension.

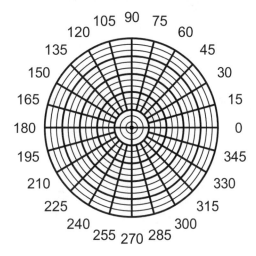

Example of a polar grid.

# Printing Marks

This extension generates printing marks. Options include generating *crop marks*, *bleed marks*, *registration marks*, *star target*, *color bars*, and *page information*. At the moment, the marks are generated "off" the page. The *Selection* option in the *Set crop marks to* drop-down menu in the *Positioning* tab does not work. You will have to enlarge the *Page* and translate the drawing with marks after applying this extension. Note that the printing marks are created on a locked *Layer* named *Printing Marks*.

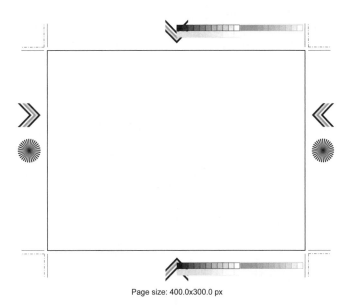

Example of printing marks in use. The rectangle is the *Page* boundary.

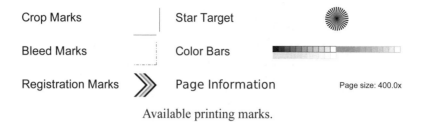

| Crop Marks | | Star Target | |
| --- | --- | --- | --- |
| Bleed Marks | | Color Bars | |
| Registration Marks | | Page Information | Page size: 400.0x |

Available printing marks.

# Random Tree

Draw a random tree made of straight-line segments. This is a classic from *Turtle Geometry* [http://en.wikipedia.org/wiki/Logo_programming_language]. This implementation is rather limited.

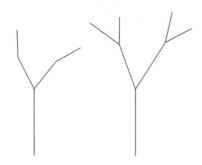

Trees drawn with the *Random Tree* extension.

# Spirograph

Draw a Spirograph [http://en.wikipedia.org/wiki/Spirograph]; that is, an epitrochoid or hypotrochoid curve. Several parameters need to be given: "R", the *Ring Radius*; "r", the *Gear Radius*; and "d", the *Pen Radius*. In addition, one must choose if the *Gear* travels *Inside* or *Outside* the *Ring*. One can also set the *Rotation* angle (the angle of the starting point relative to the center) and the *Quality* (roughly, the number of nodes per loop).

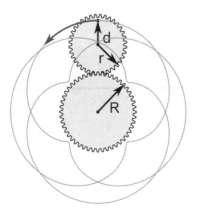

A Spirograph drawing (Epitrochoid). R = 48, r = 36, d = 30.

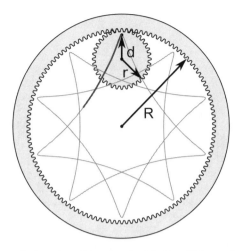

A Spirograph drawing (Hypotrochoid). R = 120, r = 36, d = 30.

The ratio of "r" to "R" determines the structure of the curve. Take, for example, an "r" of 36 and an "R" of 48. The ratio reduced to its simplest form is 3/4. This indicates that the *Gear* will make a total of four "loops" as it circles the *Ring* three times. Simple ratios make simple curves. If you use an *Even-odd fill rule*, the center of the figure will be unfilled if the denominator is even.

Unlike the case with a real *Spirograph* that utilizes plastic gears, it is possible to specify values of "r" and "R" that don't form a *rational number* [http://en.wikipedia.org/wiki/Rational_numbers] ratio. In this case, the curve never closes on itself and is of infinite length. To avoid such infinities, the extension limits the number of nodes to 1000. If the numerator or denominator of the ratio in the simplest form is a large integer, the *Spirograph* may run out of nodes. In this case, decreasing the *Quality* may help.

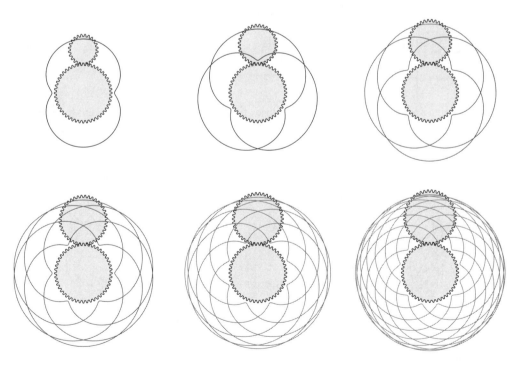

Spirographs (Epitrochoids). R = 48 for all. From left to right, top to bottom: r = 24, 32, 36, 40, 42, and 44; giving ratios of r/R of 1/2, 2/3, 3/4, 5/6, 7/8, and 11/12, respectively. In all cases d = r − 6.

Also, unlike a "real" Spirograph, the Spirograph extension allows "d" to be greater than "r". This results in small loops along the *Ring*.

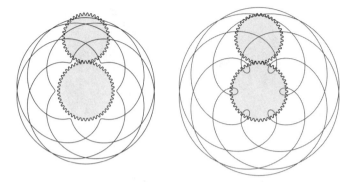

Spirographs with d < r (left) and d > r (right).

# Triangle

This extension generates triangles. Although there are six parameter entry boxes, only three are used at any one time. Which three are used is specified in the *Mode* drop-down menu. Side *c* is always at the bottom.

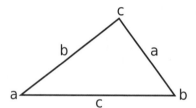

An example of using the *Triangle* extension with the sides and angles labeled.

# Wireframe Sphere

*New in v0.48.*

This extension generates a wire frame sphere using ellipses to represent lines of latitude and longitude. The number of lines can be specified as well as the orientation of the sphere. An option allows the removal of *hidden* lines.

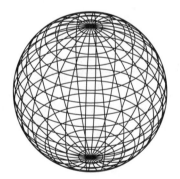 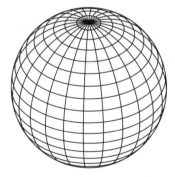

An example of using the *Wireframe Sphere* extension. Left: a sphere using the default parameters (Lines of latitude: 19, Lines of longitude: 24, Tilt: 35°, Rotation: 4.0°, Radius: 100 px). Right: the same sphere but with the hidden lines removed.

# Text

This group of extensions manipulates text. One extension creates a visual representation of Braille text. Another extension, Lorem Ipsum, creates nonsense text. This is useful for mock layouts of text. A third extension does text substitution. Then there is a group of extensions that manipulate case. These are very similar and are treated together.

## Convert to Braille

This extension creates an accurate visual representation of Braille text useful for illustrations. Braille glyphs are substituted for the Latin characters. Note: you must have a font that has *Unicode* Braille glyphs installed on your system (e.g. Deja Vu Sans). Windows users may need to explicitly select that font.

### An example of writing in Braille.

⠁⠝ ⠑⠭⠁⠍⠏⠇⠑ ⠕⠋
⠺⠗⠊⠞⠊⠝⠛ ⠊⠝ ⠃⠗⠁⠊⠇⠇⠑⠲

An example of text generated by the Convert to Braille extension. The top line is the text that was converted.

## Lorem Ipsum

Creates a string of nonsense text that resembles Latin. This is useful in the publishing industry for showing mock layouts of text. The text is generated into a *flowed text* box. If no *flowed text box* has been defined, one is created on a new *Layer* with the size of the page.

Lorem ipsum dolor sit amet, consectetuer adipiscing elit. Suspendisse fermentum. Praesent a eros. Maecenas viverra. Suspendisse viverra placerat tortor. Nam pharetra. Lorem ipsum dolor sit amet, consectetuer adipiscing elit. Integer tempus malesuada pede. Vestibulum ante ipsum primis in faucibus orci luctus et ultrices posuere cubilia Curae; Donec gravida, ante vel ornare lacinia, orci enim porta est, eget sollicitudin lectus lectus eget lacus. Fusce venenatis ligula in

An example of text generated by the Lorem Ipsum extension.

## Replace Text

This extension searches and replaces a string of text by another string in selected text objects. If no text object is selected, it will search and replace text strings in all text objects. Empty text strings can be used in both the text that is searched (to insert text in between all characters) and in the replacement text (to delete a string).

# Split Text

*New in v0.48.*

Normally when text is typed into Inkscape, the text is stored in one *<text>* object with individual lines or parts with different attributes stored in descendant *<tspan>s*. This extension splits a text object into lines, words, or individual letters, putting each line, word, or letter in its own *<text>*. This may make it easier to manipulate the parts.

**Note**

The use of this extension is normally not recommended. By splitting text into separate parts, the semantics of the text is lost. For example, it can no longer be selected as one unit in a web browser or indexed by search engines. *SVG* has been designed to allow text to be manipulated (e.g. individual letters or words having different styles) without losing the semantic value. It is better to rely on these *SVG* features than to break apart text. This is especially true now that the layout of text can be directly adjusted with the *Text Tool-Tool Controls*.

Text as one object.

Split    *into*    *words.*

S p l i t *i n t o* l e t t e r s .

Examples of text split with the Split Text effect and then manipulated.

# Change Case

This group of extensions changes the case of text in selected text objects. If no text object is selected, the extension is applied to all text objects. See the figure below for the available extensions.

| | |
|---|---|
| FlIp CaSe | fLiP cAsE |
| Lower Case | lower case |
| Random Case | ranDOm case |
| Sentence Case | Sentence case |
| title case | Title Case |
| Upper Case | UPPER CASE |

Examples of using the text case extensions. Left is original text; right is text after applying extension.

# Visualize Path

These extensions provide information on a path.

## Dimensions

Adds CAD-style dimension arrows to an object. In v0.47, this extension only works on paths; in v0.48, it also works on *Shapes* and *Groups*. It uses an object's *bounding box* to determine placement of arrows. The arrows and original object are placed inside a *Group*.

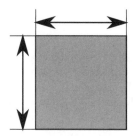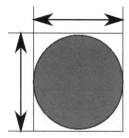

Two examples of using the *Dimensions Extension*. In v0.47, the square must be converted to a path prior to applying the extension.

## Draw Handles

This extension draws the handle lines that one would see if editing the nodes of a path. It would be of more use if it included the drawing of the handle and node symbols.

Top: Bezier curve with three nodes. Bottom: After applying *Draw handles*. (The nodes symbols were NOT added by the extension.)

## Measure Path

*Updated in v0.48.*

This extension measures the length or area (added in v0.48) of a path, printing the length or area alongside the path. A dialog allows many options to be set, including *Measurement Type* (added in v0.48), *Font size*, *Offset* (the distance the text is moved away from the path), *Precision* (number of decimal places shown), *Scale Factor*, and *Length Unit*. In calculating the area, open paths are closed and area is added using an even-odd fill rule. (The area of a donut is the area of the outer circle minus the area of the inner circle if the inner sub-path is in the opposite direction of the outer sub-path; otherwise it is the sum of the two areas.)

A spiral whose path length has been measured using the Measure Path extension. The length of the spiral's path is printed alongside the path. Default options except for *Font size*, which was set to 24 px.

# Number Nodes

This extension numbers the nodes of a path. It is useful for creating an old-fashioned *Connect-the-Dots* puzzle. (It is also an example of how to access the path data in an *SVG* file for writing your own extension.) The original path is turned into a path with no stroke but with dot markers. The dots are then numbered.

The size of the numbers and the size of the dot markers can be specified.

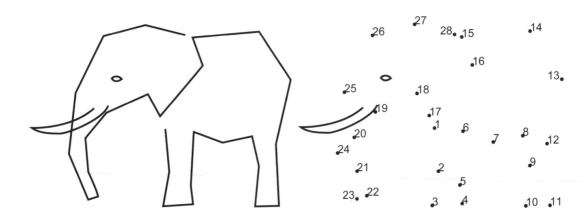

Left: Crude drawing of an elephant.[1] Right: After using *Number Nodes* extension. The positions of some of the numbers have been manually adjusted to remove overlapping.

---

[1] Disclaimer: The use of an elephant should not be construed as an endorsement by the author or publisher of any political organization associated with elephants.

# Web

*Updated in v0.48.*

This category of extensions is useful for preparing *SVG* drawings for use on the Web. There are two submenus. The first is for adding *JavaScript* controls that enable events on one object to change other objects. The second is for cutting an image into multiple parts for use on web pages with the help of *CSS*.

## JavaScript

This submenu has two entries. The first allows events linked to one object (mouse over, clicking on, etc.) to control the attributes of another object. The second allows events linked to one object to transmit that object's attributes to another. These extensions embed JavaScript into the *SVG* file. The JavaScript comes from the *InkWeb* package. To function, the code requires a JavaScript-enabled browser (native support in Firefox, Opera, Safari, Chrome, and Internet Explorer 9, support via plug-in for older versions of Internet Explorer).

## Set Attributes

This extension creates the JavaScript so that an action (clicking on, mouse passing over, etc.) with one object changes the attributes of another object. The list of attributes to change is entered, separated by spaces, in the *Attribute to set* entry box (e.g., fill stroke stroke-width). The action that will cause the change is set in the *When the set must be done?* drop-down menu. The list of new values is entered, separated by spaces, in the *Value to set* entry box. The list of values must match the *Attributes to set* line (e.g., green black 2px). The next option specifies if this action should come before, after, or replace any previously defined actions. The final option determines, in the case where more than two objects are selected, if the first selected object controls all the other selected objects or if the last selected object is controlled by actions on all the other selected objects.

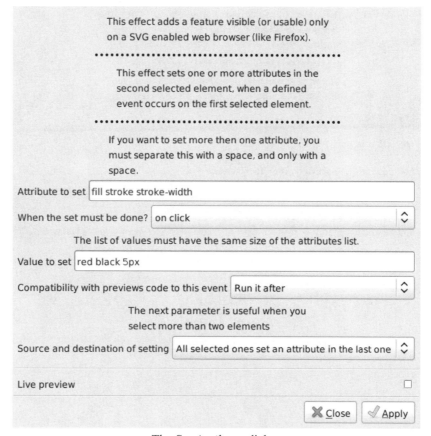

The *Set Attributes* dialog.

An example of using the Set Attributes extension to generate JavaScript code. The two objects on the left, the red square and blue circle, were selected in that order. Then the *Set Attributes* extension was called with the following values: *Attribute to set*: fill stroke stroke-width, *When the set must be done?*: on click, *Value to set*: green black 5px. In a JavaScript enabled browser, clicking on the red square will turn the color of the circle green and set the width of the stroke to 5px as shown on the right.

## Transmit Attributes

This extension creates the JavaScript so that an action (clicking on, mouse passing over, etc.) with one object changes specified attributes of another object to have the same value as the first. The list of attributes to change is entered, separated by spaces, in the *Attribute to transmit* entry box (e.g., fill stroke stroke-width). The action that will cause the change is declared in the *When to transmit* drop-down menu. The next option specifies if this action should come before, after, or replace any previously defined actions. The final option determines, in the case where more than two objects are selected, if the first selected object controls all the other selected objects or if the last selected object is controlled by actions on all the other selected objects.

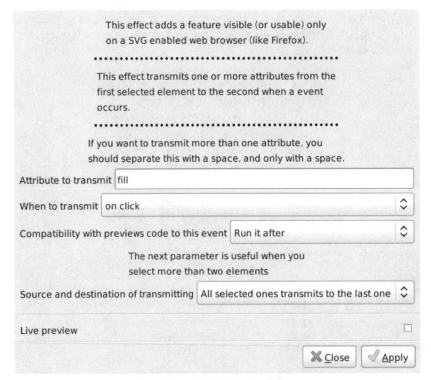

The *Transmit Attributes* dialog.

An example of using the Transmit Attributes extension to generate JavaScript code. The two objects on the left, the red square and blue circle, were selected in that order. Then the *Transmit Attributes* extension was called with the following values: *Attribute to transmit*: fill, *When the transmit must be done?*: on click, In a JavaScript enabled browser, clicking on the red square will turn the color of the circle red as shown on the right.

# Web Slicer

*New in v0.48.*

This extension facilitates slicing a drawing into rectangular bitmaps for use in Web pages. It will optionally export *CSS* and *HTML* code for use with the bitmaps.

There are two steps in using this extension. First, the *Create a slicer rectangle* dialog is used to define a set of named rectangles for the areas that are to be exported. Each rectangle can specify a different target format (*PNG*, *JPEG*, or *GIF*) and optionally, a background color. The rectangles are stored in a separate *Layer* named *Web Slicer*. After defining the rectangles, the rectangle regions are exported using the *Export layout pieces and HTML+CSS code* dialog. A third dialog can be used to add attributes in the *HTML*.

## Create a rectangle dialog

The dialog consists of a number of entry boxes for specifying export rectangles. Note that the placement of the rectangle is not defined in this dialog. After clicking the *Apply* button, a partially opaque rectangle will be created. You move and resize this rectangle to cover the area that should be exported.

- **Name:** Give a name to the export rectangle. The dialog can be used repeatedly with different names to define multiple export regions.

- **Format:** Specify the bitmap format. Different regions can have different formats.

- **DPI:** Resolution of bitmap.

- **Force dimension:** Specify the exact size of the bitmap (in pixels). If specified, the *DPI* setting is overridden.

- **Background color:** Background color for region. This will not be displayed by Inkscape.

Three tabs allow additional parameters to be specified. Note that the *HTML* tab specifies attributes that apply to the export rectangle.

## Export layout pieces and HTML+CSS code dialog

This dialog allows you to specify where the output files should be stored and if *HTML* and *CSS* code should be produced. Note that the *HTML* and *CSS* code is not intended to be the final product but instead allows you to quickly check the output and to generate code that can be pasted into other files. Clicking the *Apply* button does the actual export.

## Set a layout group dialog

This dialog allows you to set attributes that apply to the *HTML* and *CSS* that apply to the group of bitmaps exported. At least one of the *Slicer* rectangles must be selected in order to set these attributes.

## Note

All of the attributes applied to the rectangles and *HTML* export are stored in <svg:desc> tags. These tags are not easy to edit via the *XML Editor* dialog. It may be easier to edit the *SVG* file in a text editor.

# Chapter 23. SVG and the Web

---

**The origins of *HTML5***

The original plan of the W3C was that *HTML* would be phased out for *XHTML*. While similar at first glance, *HTML* and *XHTML* differ in significant ways. *XHTML*, based on *XML* (as is *SVG*), is more strict, every tag must be matched by a closing tag or be self-closing, it is case sensitive, it requires the use of *Name Spaces*. The advantages of this strictness includes: simpler parsers, the ability to "round-trip" *XHTML* to and from different data formats using style sheets, the ability to add items from different specifications (e.g. *SVG*) or custom data structures, and most importantly, the greater likelihood that different browsers would render the content the same since non-compliant *XHTML* files won't render at all. (In contrast, non-compliant *HTML* will usually render, but each browser vendor handles the invalid content in different ways leading to non-consistent results.)

So with all the advantages of *XHTML*, what happened? Well, a certain browser vendor with a large market share did not get onboard. Instead they were content to let their terribly non-compliant browser stagnate, and when they did get the motivation to update it, they again ignored the *XHTML* standard. Today, even with its own browser vendor urging its death, Internet Explorer 6 won't go away as too many intranet applications rely on the non-standard behavior.

With *XHTML*'s adoption blocked, a group of browser vendors got together to extend the *HTML* 4 standard. The result of this work forms the basis of *HTML5*. Seeing the writing on the wall, the W3C joined the effort. While *HTML5* is a great advance forward, much work has had to be done to crowbar in support for *SVG* (and *MathML*). And much work has had to be done (and is still being done) to define how browsers deal with non-compliant *HTML* so that all browsers will render content the same.

---

*Updated for v0.48 and* HTML5.

*SVG* really comes into its own on the Web. The small compact file structure (when compressed and stripped of unneeded items) makes for quick downloads, yet its vector nature results in excellent rendering at any scale. But this is only the beginning. *SVG* plays nicely with other web technologies: *SVG* files can be embedded into web pages, they can contain hypertext links, and they can be can be scripted and animated. And now with *HTML5*, *SVG* will be everywhere.

This chapter introduces *SVG* use for the Web and covers the Inkscape features that help with this use. Inkscape has mostly been developed as a tool for artists and not for web graphics but it is still possible with a little work and knowledge to use Inkscape to create web graphics.

It is not the purpose of this book to cover web design. Only a minimal introduction to animation and scripting is presented. It only touches briefly on some of the tricks that may be needed to get *SVG* files to work on all browsers. It is assumed that the reader has a working knowledge of *HTML*. The following sites are good references (although some of the information is a bit dated) for using *SVG* on the web: SVG Primer [http://www.w3.org/Graphics/SVG/IG/resources/svgprimer.html] and Carto:Net [http://www.carto.net/svg/samples/]. For fun demonstations of the power of *SVG* go to the SVG Wow [http://svg-wow.org/] site.

Support for *SVG* has improved rapidly in Web browsers. Current versions of Firefox, Opera, Safari, and Chrome include almost complete support (Firefox doesn't handle *SVG* fonts and Safari 5 doesn't handle filters). Internet Explorer 9 will offer almost full *SVG* support (missing *SVG* fonts, *SMIL* animation, and filters). Options for users of older Internet Explorer browsers are discussed later.

The upcoming *HTML5* (Hypertext Markup Language, version 5) specification allows "inline *SVG*". *HTML5* defines two different syntaxes: *HTML* and *XML*. All major Web browsers will support *HTML* syntax in the very near future. All major browsers except Internet Explorer (prior to version 9) already support inline *SVG* with *XML* syntax as well as in *XHTML* proper. The major difference between the *HTML* and *XML* syntaxes are that *HTML* does not always require tags to be closed while *XML* does, *HTML* is not case sensitive while *XML* is, and *Name Spaces* are not allowed in *HTML* (except for the *XHTML*, *XLink*, *MathML*, and *SVG Name Spaces* in special cases) while they are required in *XML*. Using closing tags and *Name Spaces* is good practice so it is recommended that you write to the *XHTML* syntax. You also need not strip Inkscape *SVG* of the various items declared in Inkscape and other *Name Spaces*.

### *SVG* Is Case Sensitive

*SVG* being based on *XML* is case sensitive. For example, *viewbox* is not the same as *viewBox* (the latter is the correct attribute name). This may trip up people coming from an *HTML* background. Work is being done to determine how to handle case sensitivity in *CSS* markup.

### Validate Your *SVG* and *HTML*

Validating your *SVG* and *HTML5* ensures that it will be rendered as intended, especially if you create content by hand. The W3C offers an on-line validator service.

For an up-to-date list of which browsers support what, take a look at the When can I use... [http://caniuse.com] website. Chrome is frequently updated (every six weeks!), Firefox, Opera, Safari less so, and, well you probably already know about Internet Explorer.

The sections in this chapter build on each other. The first section covers getting an *SVG* to display on a web page (including options for older browsers). The second section covers how an *SVG* is fitted into a web page. The third covers adding hyperlinks. The fourth section introduces the use of style sheets. The fifth section introduces animation. And a final section covers some features of Inkscape to help produce *SVG*s for the web.

A web page displaying the examples discussed here is available at the book's website [http://tavmjong.free.fr/INKSCAPE/]. Several web pages for testing browser support of *SVG* can also be found there.

# Simple SVG Display

There are many different ways to display *SVG* files in a web page. The simplest way is just to link to an *SVG* file with the <a> tag. Web browsers that support *SVG* will display the drawing by itself. To include *SVG* content as part of a web page one can use one of the following options:

- <object> tag.

- <embed> tag.

- <iframe> tag.

- <img> tag.

- Inline *SVG*.

- *CSS* background.

Each option will be treated in turn. A final section covers a few alternatives for supporting *SVG* on older browsers.

# The <object> Tag

The <object> tag is the primary way to include an external *SVG* file. The main advantage of using this tag is that there is a natural mechanism for displaying a fallback in case the *SVG* is not rendered. The tag requires defining a *data* attribute which is the location of the *SVG* file, normally a relative path. Defining the *type* attribute is highly recommended as it allows browsers to avoid downloading content they do not support. For *SVG* the type is "image/svg+xml". If the *SVG* is not rendered, the browser will try to render the content between the opening &lt;object&gt; and closing &lt;/object&gt; tags. A *PNG* version of the *SVG* would normally be a good choice to put here.

```
<!DOCTYPE html>          ❶
<html xmlns="http://www.w3.org/1999/xhtml">        ❷
  <head>

    <meta charset="UTF-8"/>        ❸
    <title>SVG Included with <object> tag</title>

  </head>
  <body>

    <h1>An SVG rectangle (via <object> tag)</h1>

    <object type="image/svg+xml" data="web_square.svg">        ❹
      <img src="web_square.png" alt="Blue Square"/>        ❺
    </object>

  </body>
</html>
```

❶  *HTML* declaration. With *HTML5* no "dtd" is required.
❷  *HTML Name Space* declaration. Using the *XML* syntax is specified here.
❸  The character encoding of the file, normally `UTF-8` for modern files.
❹  Inclusion of *SVG* file via the object tag. The "image/svg+xml" is the *MIME* type of the included file.
❺  A *PNG* file to be displayed in case the browser fails to render the *SVG*.

There are a couple of known problems with using the &lt;object&gt; tag with Chrome 6 and Safari 5 (which share the same rendering engine). The first is that *SVG*s are displayed with a non-transparent background. The second is that the *SVG*s are often not scaled properly and are displayed with scroll bars. The transparency problem has already been fixed in Chrome 7. The scaling problem will likely also be fixed soon.

# The &lt;embed&gt; Tag

While the &lt;embed&gt; tag was never part of any *HTML* or *XHTML* specification, it is widely supported and used. For this reason it has been included in the *HTML5* specification. It is intended for including content that needs an external plug-in to work. The Adobe plug-in requires the use of the &lt;embed&gt; tag and supporting this tag is the only real reason for its use with *SVG*. There is no fallback mechanism if the *SVG* content is not displayed. Note that Chrome 8 and Safari 5 may require *width* and *height* attributes to avoid scroll bars. Safari 5 also incorrectly displays *SVG*s with non-transparent backgrounds.

Here is an example of using the &lt;embed&gt; tag. Only the *src* attribute is required.

```
<embed src="web_square.svg"/>
```

# The &lt;iframe&gt; Tag

The &lt;iframe&gt; tag, deprecated in *HTML* 4 and *XHTML*, has resurfaced in *HTML5* with the purpose of "sandboxing" content that might pose a security risk. There is no fallback if the *SVG* content cannot be displayed. A *frame* will be drawn around the *SVG*. It can be removed by setting the attribute *frameborder* to 0 (note that this is not valid *HTML5*). The size of the frame can be set using the *width* and *height* attributes. If the size of the frame is too small to contain the *SVG*, scroll bars will be used. Safari 5 incorrectly displays *SVG*s with non-transparent backgrounds.

Here is an example of using the &lt;iframe&gt; tag. Only the *src* attribute is required. Note that a separate closing tag is required and that *XHTML* does not allow anything between the opening and closing tags.

```
<iframe src="web_square.svg"></iframe>
```

# The &lt;img&gt; Tag

The &lt;img&gt; tag is used to embed images. Two attributes are required: the *src* and the *alt* attributes. The latter serves to describe the image in case the image cannot be rendered or viewed (i.e., to someone who is blind).

Here is an example of using the &lt;iframe&gt; tag. Note that the tag is self-closing.

```
<img src="web_square.svg" alt="Blue Square"/>
```

There are two reasons not to use the &lt;img&gt; tag with *SVG*s. The first is that there is no fallback mechanism if the browser cannot render the image. The second is an *SVG* rendered this way is not allowed to run any scripts or have any interaction (e.g. links). One advantage of using this tag is that Safari 5 will handle transparency properly. Another is that it can be used inside an *HTML* &lt;a&gt; object where the other tags will cause the *SVG* to "swallow" mouse clicks.

# Inline SVG

*HTML5* brings with it the possibility to use *SVG* by directly including the *SVG* in the *HTML* file. One could already do this in *XHTML* by using *Name Spaces*. There are a few things to note:

- To include *SVG* using *HTML* syntax you must use a browser with an *HTML5* parser. So far only Firefox 4 and Internet Explorer 9 have *HTML5* parsers. Note that *Name Spaces* are not allowed with *HTML* syntax (except the *XHTML*, *XLink*, *MathML*, and *SVG Name Spaces*). Any Inkscape, Sodipodi, or other *Name Space* declarations need to be removed.

- All the major web browsers except Internet Explorer already support *SVG* with *XML* syntax (as well as in *XHTML*).

- An *HTML5* file normally ends with .html when using *HTML* syntax and .xhtml or .xml; when using *XML* syntax.

Here is an example of inlining *SVG*. The file uses *XHTML* syntax but will also work for *HTML5*. Note that the two *Name Space* declarations are optional with *HTML5* syntax. The *SVG* has been stripped of all unnecessary parts such as items in the Inkscape *Name Space*.

```
<!DOCTYPE html>        ❶
<html xmlns="http://www.w3.org/1999/xhtml">        ❷
  <head>

    <meta charset="UTF-8"/>        ❸
    <title>SVG Inlined</title>

  </head>
  <body>

    <h1>An SVG rectangle inlined</h1>

    <svg        ❹
      xmlns="http://www.w3.org/2000/svg"        ❺
```

```
      version="1.1"
      width="150"
      height="150">
    <rect
width="90"
height="90"
x="30"
y="30"
style="fill:#0000ff;fill-opacity:0.75;stroke:#000000"/>
  </svg>

</body>
</html>
```

❶ *HTML* declaration. (No "dtd" is required.)

❷ *XHTML Name Space* declaration. Required for *XHTML*, optional for *HTML5*. (Note: the name space declaration is identical for both *HTML5* and *XHTML*.)

❸ The character encoding of the file, normally "UFF-8" for modern files. Not absolutely required but highly recommended.

❹ Start of *SVG*.

❺ Required for *XHTML*, optional for *HTML5*.

# CSS Background

It is possible to use an *SVG* as a *CSS* background. One problem is to provide a fallback, necessary for Firefox 3.6 and older as well as Internet Explorer 8 and older. You could display both a *PNG* and an *SVG* on top. If the *SVG* has a transparent background, though, the *PNG* can leak through (a problem at least with Opera when the *HTML* is zoomed). Also, Internet Explorer won't fallback properly. A solution is to use two `background-image` lines; Internet Explorer won't recognize the `none` in the second line, resorting to using the first.

```
body {
  background-image: url('background.png');
  background-image: none, url('background.svg'), url('background.png');
  background-size: 100% 100%;
}
```

# Supporting Older Browsers

The first step in supporting older browsers is to decide which browsers and which versions of those browsers you need to support. We can divide browsers into two classes: Internet Explorer and everybody else. Internet Explorer prior to version 9 does not natively support *SVG* nor does it support *XHTML*. All current or reasonably recent versions of all other major browsers do support *SVG* and *XHTML* although they may not support all of the *SVG* standard (most noticeably is the lack of filter support in Safari 5). So the main question is how to support *SVG* in Internet Explorer? This issue is not unlikely to disappear soon as Internet Explorer users are less likely to upgrade than users of other browsers and in some cases they can't upgrade since they use Windows XP which will not run Internet Explorer 9, or they are using web applications that rely on non-standard features of Internet Explorer 6.

At the moment, the best way to include *SVG* content in a web page is to use the <object> tag with a *PNG* fallback. This is a simple method that will automatically take care of support for older versions of Internet Explorer. If you need to use a pure *SVG* solution, then you need to rely on plug-ins to support Internet Explorer. There are a number of plug-ins that can be used:

• The Adobe plug-in [http://www.adobe.com/svg/main.html]. This plug-in is no longer supported but can still be downloaded. (Adobe lost interest in *SVG* after buying Flash.) It offers fairly complete *SVG* support but it may be difficult to get the plug-in to work. It requires the use of the <embed> tag.

- The Google Chrome Frame [http://www.google.com/chromeframe] plug-in. This plug-in replaces the renderer in Internet Explorer 6, 7, or 8 with the renderer used in Chrome. The plug-in is triggered by including the line: `<meta http-equiv="X-UA-Compatible" content="chrome=1">` in the <head> section of the *HTML* file. If Google Frame is installed, the page will be rendered by the plug-in, otherwise it will be rendered by the normal Internet Explorer renderer. This is a fairly unintrusive way of including the use of a plug-in.

- The svgweb [http://code.google.com/p/svgweb/] JavaScript library uses the Flash plug-in to render *SVG* content. Since most users of Internet Explorer already have Flash installed this is a viable way to support *SVG*. It can also be used to support *SVG SMIL* animation and *SVG* fonts in browsers that don't support those parts of the *SVG* standard. The modifications to the *HTML* file are more invasive than that to use Chrome Frame.

Inlined *SVG* is currently supported by all major browsers except Internet Explorer (before version 9) using *XML* syntax in *HTML5* and in *XHTML* proper. Internet Explorer supports neither so a fallback solution for Internet Explorer must serve *HTML* to Internet Explorer while serving *XHTML* files to everyone else. Inlined *SVG* in *HTML5* using *HTML* syntax requires browsers to have *HTML5* parsers which at the moment only Firefox 4 and Internet Explorer 9 have. The SVG Boilerplate [http://svgboilerplate.com/] project is developing ways to use *SVG* in older browsers, including inlined *SVG* in *HTML*.

And finally, if you are producing vector graphic content programatically, you can look into other means of delivering graphics to older Internet Explorer browsers such as using Raphaël [http://raphaeljs.com/] which uses JavaScript to generate either *SVG* or *VML* depending on the browser.

# Positioning SVG

## Positioning and Sizing Subject to Change

This section is based on current browser behaviour and the *SVG* specification. There is active discussion on changing the specification by the *SVG* standards group.

Now that you know how to get *SVG* to display in an *HTML* file, the next question is how does it get placed? The process is a bit convoluted and the results across browsers are not always the same. There are two steps. The first is to determine the *viewport* or area allocated to the *SVG* by the web page, the second is to determine how the *SVG* fits into the viewport. For this discussion we will assume the *SVG* is being inserted via the <object> tag.

Determining the area of the page that is allocated for the *SVG* is a multistep process:

- If the <object> tag has the *width* or *height* attribute defined in absolute units or in percent, this is the size of the viewport (if only one of *width* or *height* is defined, the other defaults to the same value).

- If the <object> does not have fixed *width* and *height*, then if the *SVG* has fixed *width* and/or *height*, the *SVG* values determine the size of the viewport. The *SVG width* and *height* attributes are set in the Inkscape *Document Properties* dialog.

- If the viewport is still not determined, then if the *SVG width* and *height* are 100%, the viewport fills up the space available to the <object> tag. The meaning of percentage values less than 100% is unclear (browser differ). In Inkscape, you can only set the *SVG width* and *height* to 100% by using the *XML Editor* dialog. The *viewBox* (see below) attribute must be set first.

## *SVG* Width and Height

Think of the *SVG width* and *height* attributes as recommendations to the renderer about the size of the viewport if the *HTML* doesn't define the size. They are *not(!)* always the width and height of the drawing.

Now that the viewport is defined, how the *SVG* is fitted inside that viewport must be determined. Again this is a several step process:

- If the *SVG viewBox* attribute is defined, then the *viewBox* (see below on how to set in Inkscape) is mapped to the viewport according to the value of the *SVG preserveAspectRatio* attribute. The default value of this attribute is *xMidYMid meet* which means that the center of the viewBox is at the center of the viewport and that the SVG is scaled uniformly so that one pair of sides (top/bottom or left/right) of the viewBox coincide with the viewport while the other pair of sides is inside the viewport. See the figure below for the meaning of other possible values.

- If there is no *viewBox* attribute defined, then the *SVG* is mapped so that the upper-left corner of the viewport corresponds to the (0, 0) coordinate of the *SVG* (normally the upper-left corner). The *SVG* is scaled so that one user unit (pixel) corresponds to one screen pixel. Scroll bars may be shown if the *SVG* (as defined by the *width* and *height* attributes) is larger than the viewport.

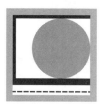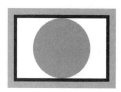

This figure shows how an *SVG* file is placed in an *HTML* page using the <object> tag. The *SVG* is nominally 150 px wide and 100 px tall. It contains a black rectangle with the same dimensions as the nominal size and with a 10 px wide stroke. A circle is placed in the center of the rectangle. A dashed rectangle surrounds the black rectangle. It is outside the nominal *SVG* area. The inside of the gray rectangle marks the viewport (created by setting the *padding* attribute of the <object> to 10 px).

From left to right: <object> *width* and *height* attributes set to 120, *SVG width* set to 150, *height* set to 100, *viewBox* undefined. <object> *width* and *height* attributes set to 120, *SVG width* and *height* undefined (defaults to 100%), *viewBox* set to 0, 0 150, 100. <object> *width* and *height* attributes not set, either *SVG width* set to 150, *height* set to 100, or *viewBox* set to 0, 0 150, 100.

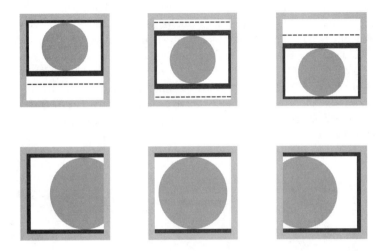

This figure shows how an *SVG* file is placed depending on the *preserveAspectRatio* attribute. One possible value, not shown, is *none* in which case the *SVG* is stretched to fit the viewport. The other possible values take the form: xAYB C, where A and B can have the values *Min*, *Mid*, or *Max*; and C can have the value *meet* or *slice*. The values A and B determine which part of the viewport and *viewBox* are aligned while the value of C determines if the image is scaled so that two edges of the *viewBox* coincide with the viewport while the other two are inside (*meet*) or if two edges of the *viewBox* coincide with the viewport while the other two are outside (*slice*).

The *SVG* shown is the same as in the previous figure. From left to right: Top row: *xMinYMin meet*, *xMidYMin meet*, *xMaxYMin meet*. Bottom row: *xMinYMin slice*, *xMinYMid slice*, *xMinYMax slice*. Note, not all possible combinations are shown.

**To set the *viewBox* attribute in Inkscape:** Open the *XML Editor* dialog and select the *SVG* root element (<svg:svg...>). In an Inkscape created file, the *width* and *height* attributes will have been defined while the *viewBox* will not have been defined. If you open an *SVG* file created by another application the *viewBox* may be defined instead of or in addition to *width* and *height*. If the *viewBox* attribute is already defined, select it from the window on the right. You can then change the values. If it is not defined, click on the text entry box near the bottom of the window, in the same line as the *Set* button. Type in "viewBox". Then in the box below, type in four numbers separated by spaces, the *x* and *y* values of the upper-left corner (normally 0 and 0) and the *width* and *height*. The values are in user units (pixels). Click on the *Set* button or use **Ctrl+Enter** to register your values. Once the *viewBox* is defined, you can modify the *width* and *height* attributes including deleting them or changing them to 100%. Modifying the *Width* and *Height* in the *Document Properties* dialog will now modify the *viewBox* if *width* and *height* attributes are not defined in fixed units, otherwise it will modify the *width* and *height* attributes as well as proportionally modify the *viewBox* attribute.

## Clipping by Viewport

An *SVG* is clipped by the viewport and not by the *viewBox* or the *SVG width* and *height* attributes. This means that objects outside the Inkscape "page" may be displayed in the *HTML* page under some circumstances.

# Adding Links

A link connects *resources*. In the traditional *HTML* framework, these resources would be things like web pages and images that have *URLs*. The *SVG* specification uses *XLinks*, which are more powerful but also more complicated than the original *HTML* links. We'll cover only the most simple use of *XLinks* here and refer you to the *XLink* specification from the *W3C* [http://www.w3.org/TR/xlink/] consortium for more details.

To add a link to an object, **Right-Mouse Click** on the object. Select *Add link* from the pop-up menu. Although nothing will seem to have happened, this will put an <svg:a> wrapper around the object (viewable with the Edit → ▣ XML Editor... (**Shift+Ctrl+X**) dialog).

### Note

The link wrapper <svg:a> acts as a group. To edit a wrapped object, you must double-click on the object to enter the wrapper. It is also possible to create a wrapper within a wrapper by accident. Pay attention to the *Notification Region* or use the Edit → ▣ XML Editor... (**Shift+Ctrl+X**) dialog to keep track of what level you are at.

The attributes of an object's links can be modified through the *Link attributes* dialog that can be opened by selecting the *Link Properties* entry from the menu that pops up from a second **Right-Mouse Click** on the object (this time, you are clicking on the wrapper).

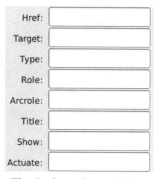

The *Link attributes* dialog.

To link an object to another web page, only the *Href* attribute must be supplied. An example reference is "http://www.w3.org/" (without the quotes) which is a link to the World Wide Web consortium [http://www.w3.org/].

The following listing shows an *SVG* file with a link from the blue square. It can be directly displayed in a web browser or included via the <object> tag in an *HTML* or *XHTML* file.

```
<?xml version="1.0" encoding="UTF-8" standalone="no"?>
<svg
   xmlns="http://www.w3.org/2000/svg"
   xmlns:xlink="http://www.w3.org/1999/xlink"       ❶
   version="1.1"
   width="150"
   height="150">
  <a xlink:href="http://www.w3.org/">       ❷
    <rect       ❸
     width="90"
     height="90"
     x="30"
     y="30"
     style="fill:#0000ff;fill-opacity:0.75;stroke:#000000"/>
  </a>
</svg>
```

❶    The *XLink* name space declaration.
❷    Start of *XLink* object with target of *XLink*.
❸    Source object of *XLink*.

Although the *Link attributes* dialog contains many entries, only a few are of great use. A couple have only one allowed value.

| Href | The location of the referenced object. Clicking on the object will go to the specified link. |
|---|---|
| Target | If there are multiple targets (frames) in the referenced object, this attribute specifies which to use. |
| Type | Specifies the type of link. Only the *simple* link can be used in *SVG*. |
| Role | Specifies the role the resource is intended to have. Must be a valid *URL*. |
| Arcrole | Further specifies the role the resource is intended to have. Must be a valid *URL*. |
| Title | A human-readable description of the resource. Must be a character string. Browsers may show this as a *tool tip* when the mouse is over the object. (It is recommended to use the attribute *title* instead.) |
| Show | Specifies how the resource linked to should be displayed. Valid values are: *new* (open a new browser window), *replace* (replace current browser content), and *embed* (replace the content of the object). It appears that Firefox's behavior for *replace* follows that expected for *embed*. |
| Actuate | Specifies if the resource linked to should be traversed immediately. Valid values are: 'onRequest' (require input, e.g., a mouse click, loading target resource). |

# Using Style Sheets

*SVG* drawings can use *CSS* (Cascading Style Sheets) to control the presentation of the drawing objects. Support for style sheets is in its infancy in Inkscape. One can, however, do a few simple useful things. At the moment, Inkscape can handle only an internal style sheet. External style sheets cannot be used.

In the following example, a *CSS* is used to change the opacity of the blue square whenever the mouse cursor passes over it (when the drawing is displayed in an *SVG*-enabled browser).

```
<?xml version="1.0" encoding="UTF-8" standalone="no"?>
<svg
   xmlns="http://www.w3.org/2000/svg"
   xmlns:xlink="http://www.w3.org/1999/xlink"
   version="1.1"
   width="150"
   height="150">
 <style type="text/css">        ❶
  rect:hover {fill-opacity:1.0}       ❷
 </style>
 <a xlink:href="http://www.w3.org/"
    style="fill-opacity:0.75">      ❸
  <rect
   width="90"
   height="90"
   x="30"
   y="30"
   style="fill:#0000ff;stroke:#000000"/>     ❹
 </a>
</svg>
```

❶   Style sheet start.
❷   Rectangle's hover (i.e., when the mouse cursor is above the rectangle) declaration.
❸   Rectangle's default opacity.
❹   Rectangle's style. Note that "fill-opacity" is not defined here. This allows the attribute to be overridden.

The style attribute can either be added through a text editor or with a bit of difficulty through the Inkscape *XML Editor* (Edit → ▣ XML Editor... (**Shift+Ctrl+X**)) dialog. The *fill-opacity* attribute must be moved from the rectangle and put into a wrapper of the rectangle (in this case the <a> tag).

Steps to add a *style sheet* via the *XML Editor* dialog:

1. Open the *XMLEdit* dialog.

2. Select the top-level entry <svg:svg>.

3. Click on *New element node* ▦ icon.

4. Enter "svg:style" into entry box; click *Create* button.

5. Drag new node above first <svg:g> (layer1).

6. Select <svg:style> node.

7. Enter "type" into *Attribute* entry line (middle of dialog).

8. Enter "text/css" into *Value* entry area (bottom of dialog).

9. Click *Set* button.

10. Click on *New text node* ▦ icon.

11. Enter: "rect:hover {fill-opacity:1.0;}" on right, with a carriage return before and after (which suppresses the quotes).

12. Click on triangle to open <svg:g id="layer1"> node.

13. Click on triangle to open <svg:a> node.

14. Select rectangle, select style attribute, select "fill-opacity:0.75;" and cut (**Ctrl+X**).

15. Select <svg:a> node, add "style" to *Attribute* entry line, paste (**Ctrl+V**) "fill-opacity:0.75" into the *Value* entry area.

16. Save, but do NOT save as a plain *SVG* file as this removes the "hover" attribute from the *CSS* style node. (Bug)

# Adding JavaScript

*SVG* drawings can use JavaScript (ECMAScript) to do complex manipulation of the objects in the drawing. In this example, the style sheet of the last example is replaced by simple JavaScript calls. The *Object Properties* dialog (Object → ▦ Object Properties... (**Shift+Ctrl+O**)) can be used to add the calls.

To modify the previous example to use JavaScript, first remove the *style* section (use the *XML Editor* dialog). Next, open the *Object Properties* dialog. Select the square (make sure the square is selected and not the <a> wrapper, you can do this by first double-clicking the square and then clicking on it again). Then click on the triangle next to *Interactivity* in the *Object Properties* dialog to expose the JavaScript options. Add the following to *onmouseover*: **setAttribute('fill-opacity','1.0')** and the following to *onmouseout*: **setAttribute('fill-opacity','0.75')**. That's it! Do not save as *Plain SVG* as the JavaScript commands will be (erroneously) stripped out. You can save it as *Optimized SVG*.

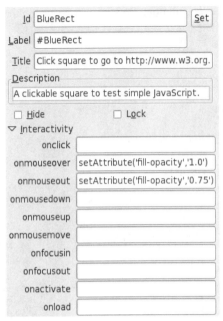

The *Object Properties* dialog showing the JavaScript additions (as well as the *title* and *desc* attribute additions).

While the *Object Properties* dialog is open we can fill the *title* and *desc* attributes. These attributes can be specified for any object in an *SVG* document, including *Groups*. The *title* attribute is intended to be used for a *tool tip*. This is only implemented in some *SVG* browsers like Opera. (Firefox 3.5 will put in the window title area the first *title* found in the document). The *desc* (Description) attribute is used to store a description of the object. It is not normally intended for display. One final touch is to change the *Id* to a more descriptive name. You must click on the *Set* button for changes to these attributes to take effect.

```
<?xml version="1.0" encoding="UTF-8" standalone="no"?>
<svg
   xmlns="http://www.w3.org/2000/svg"
   xmlns:xlink="http://www.w3.org/1999/xlink"
   version="1.1"
   width="150"
   height="150">
 <a xlink:href="http://www.w3.org/"
    style="fill-opacity:0.75">        ❶
  <rect
    id="BlueRect"
    width="90"
    height="90"
    x="30"
    y="30"
    style="fill:#0000ff;stroke:#000000"        ❷
    onmouseover="setAttribute('fill-opacity','1.0')"        ❸
    onmouseout="setAttribute('fill-opacity','0.75')">
     <desc
      id="desc3364">A clickable square to test simple JavaScript.</desc>
     <title
      id="title3362">Click square to go to http://www.w3.org.</title>
   </rect>
  </a>
</svg>
```

❶     Rectangle's default opacity.

❷ Rectangle's style. Note that "fill-opacity" is not defined here. This allows class attributes to be overridden.

❷ JavaScript calls for *onmouseover* and *onmouseout*.

Note that some extensions for adding simple JavaScript are discussed in the section called *JavaScript*.

# Simple Animation

The *SVG* standard provides support for animating drawings both internally through animation elements and externally through scripts. This section will demonstrate a simple animation using *ECMAscript* [http://www.ecma-international.org/] (a standard that JavaScript and JScript are dialects of). Although there are plans for supporting animation in Inkscape, at the moment there is no support. Adding animation requires editing the *SVG* file with a text editor. Note that Inkscape added some limited support for scripts in v0.47 through the *Set Attributes* and *Transmit Attributes* extensions.

In the following *SVG* drawing, the blue square oscillates back and forth (in a supporting *SVG* viewer). The square still changes opacity when the mouse is over it and it still contains a hypertext link.

```
<?xml version="1.0" encoding="UTF-8" standalone="no"?>
<svg
   xmlns="http://www.w3.org/2000/svg"
   xmlns:xlink="http://www.w3.org/1999/xlink"
   version="1.1"
   onload="Start(evt)"           ❶
   width="150"
   height="150">
  <script type="text/ecmascript">        ❷
  <![CDATA[

   var time = 0;
   var delta_time = 25;
   var max_time = 1000;
   var dir = 1;

   var the_rect;

   function Start(evt) {           ❸

     the_rect = evt.target.ownerDocument.getElementById("BlueRect");      ❹
     Oscillate();
   }

   function Oscillate() {

     time = time + dir * delta_time;
     if (time >  max_time)  dir = -1;
     if (time < -max_time)  dir =  1;

     // Calculate x position
     x_pos = (time * 25) / max_time;
     the_rect.setAttribute("transform", "translate(" +x_pos+ ", 0.0 )");      ❺

     // Repeat
     setTimeout("Oscillate()", delta_time)
   }

   window.Oscillate = Oscillate

  ]]>
  </script>        ❻
  <a xlink:href="http://www.w3.org/"
```

```
        style="fill-opacity:0.75">
     <rect
       id="BlueRect"
       width="90"
       height="90"
       x="30"
       y="30"
       style="fill:#0000ff;stroke:#000000"
       onmouseover="setAttribute('fill-opacity','1.0')"
       onmouseout="setAttribute('fill-opacity','0.75')">
        <desc
          id="desc3364">A clickable square to test simple JavaScript.</desc>
        <title
          id="title3362">Click square to go to http://www.w3.org.</title>
     </rect>
   </a>
</svg>
```

❶ Instruction to call script on loading file.
❷ Start of script.
❸ Initialize script.
❹ Get reference to rectangle object (our square).
❺ Set the rectangle's *transform* attribute.
❻ End of script.

# Inkscape for the Web

To be quite honest, making Inkscape convenient for creating *SVG*s for the web has been more of an afterthought. Having said that, many of the great *SVG* examples on the web have started life as Inkscape drawings, as evidenced by tell-tail fingerprints left in the source. This section focuses on ways to prepare Inkscape *SVG*s for the web.

A number of items have already been covered in this chapter. This section covers cleaning up the *SVG* source.

**Vacuuming.** As a drawing is created, items like *Gradients*, *Patterns*, *Markers*, and *Filters* are stored in the <defs> section of the *SVG* file. If you later delete an object with, for example, a *Gradient*, the *Gradient* is not deleted. The File → 🗄 Vacuum Defs command will remove unused items.

**Save as Plain *SVG*.** Inkscape stores a lot of information in the *SVG* file in the Sodipodi and Inkscape *Name Spaces*. The information is useful for editing the file with Inkscape but is not needed for display. It can be removed by choosing the *Plain SVG* option in the drop-down menu in the *Save As* dialog. Note, that this may remove things you want to keep, like scripts.

**Save as Optimized *SVG*.** Choosing *Optimized SVG* in the drop-down menu in the *Save As* dialog will pop-up a dialog that allows you to customize the saved *SVG* file. This works by passing the file through the *Scour* script. Here are the various options:

• **Simplify colors.** Convert all colors to #rrggbb format (or #rgb format if possible). Inkscape already uses this format by default, but if you import a file with say `fill="lightgoldenrodyellow"`, converting the color to `"#fafad2"` could save a few bytes.

• **Style to xml.** Converts *style* attributes to *XML* attributes, e.g. `style="fill:#ff0000"` to `fill="#ff0000"`. Some people argue that using *XML* attributes is better practice. It will probably result in slightly larger files. If you plan on using *CSS* to style objects, don't enable this option. It, may, however be useful if you plan on using your drawing on a mobile phone as the *style* attribute is not supported in the *SVG* Tiny specification. Inkscape always uses *style* attributes.

- **Group collapsing.** Removes *Groups* if they don't have attributes or a <title> or <desc> children. Inkscape created files will not have these unless you have used the *XML Editor* dialog or the *Object Properties* dialog to specifically add them.

- **Enable id stripping.** Removes `id` attributes. Inkscape assigns an id to all objects (e.g. `id="rect3045"`). These attributes are useful when an object is referenced by another (e.g. an object is cloned using the <use> tag) or in referring to an object in JavaScript. Most `ids` are not referenced and can be removed.

- **Embed rasters.** Embeds externally referenced *bitmap* images such as *PNGs*.

- **Keep editor data.** Prevents removal of items in the Inkscape or Sodipodi *Name Spaces* that are useful for editing with Inkscape (e.g., *Grids* and *Guide Lines*).

- **Enable viewboxing.** If a *viewBox* attribute is not present, creates one using the *width* and *height* attributes, and then sets both *width* and *height* attributes to 100%. This is useful if you wish your *SVG* file to automatically scale to use all available space on a web page.

- **Strip xml prolog.** Removes *XML* prolog (i.e., <?xml version="1.0"?>).

- **Set precision.** Sets numerical precision on all coordinates and attributes. Drawings meant for the web rarely need precision greater than three or four decimal places. You can also set the default numerical precision used by Inkscape in the *Inkscape Preferences* dialog in the *SVG output* section (*Numerical precision*).

- **Indent.** Sets the indentation for each *XML* opening (or closing tag). Options are *Space*, *Tab*, and *None*. In all cases, each tag with attributes is placed on one line.

**Use clones.** If you include the same object multiple times in a drawing, you can reduce the file size by using *Clones* (Edit → Clone → ▣ Create Clone (**Alt+D**)), rather than duplicating the object (Edit → ▢ Duplicate (**Ctrl+D**)). The former inserts a reference to the original object while the latter copies the object. References usually take up less file space than copies.

**Simplify the drawing.** Keep in mind how your drawing is going to be viewed. Check that you don't have hidden objects, objects outside the drawing area, or objects that are too small to see. You can use the outline mode (View → DisplayMode → Outline) to help check for such objects. Check that the *Paths* don't have too much detail. (A good example of this is that Wikipedia maps often have orders of magnitude more nodes than necessary at typical viewing scales.) Careful use of Path → ≈ Simplify (**Ctrl+L**) can remove unnecessary nodes.

# Chapter 24. Customization

Inkscape is quite customizable. The easiest way to make customizations is through the *Inkscape Preferences* dialog. More extensive customizations can be made by modifying files in or adding files to the Inkscape preferences directories. The directory for changes shared by all users is `share/inkscape`. The directory for personal changes is `~/.config/inkscape/` on Linux or `%userprofile%\Application Data\Inkscape\` on Windows.

## Inkscape Preferences Dialog

Inkscape is most easily customizable through the *Inkscape Preferences* dialog (File → 🖼 Inkscape Preferences... (**Shift+Ctrl+P**)).

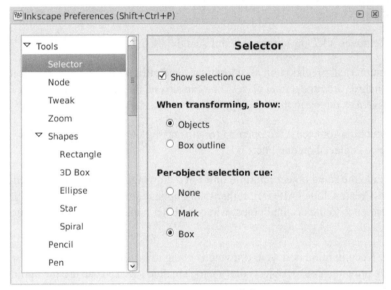

*Inkscape Preferences* dialog.

There are too many options in the dialog to cover here. It is worthwhile to scan through the options under each entry. The most important options have already been mentioned in the text. They include: Setting the *Rotation snap angle* and other scaling parameters under the *Step* entry; determining if transformations should be *Optimized* or *Preserved* under the *Transforms* entry; and setting the *Default export resolution* under the *Misc* entry.

All the preferences are stored in the file `preferences.xml` located on Linux at `~/.config/inkscape/` and on Windows at `%userprofile%\Application Data\Inkscape\`. There are quite a few preferences, some undocumented, that are accessible *only* by hand-editing this file. See the next section for some of these.

## Inkscape Configuration Files

Inkscape can be fully customized through the configuration files, usually located in the `share/inkscape` directory (`/usr/share/inkscape` in Linux).

### Preferences

The user file `preferences.xml` contains all the preferences that are accessible from the *Inkscape Preferences* dialog, as well as quite a few that are not. The file is located on Linux at `~/.config/inkscape/` and on Windows at `%userprofile%\Application Data\Inkscape\`. This section gives information on a few of the latter.

## Alternative Alt Key

Some window managers use **Alt+Left Mouse Drag** and **Alt+Left Mouse Click** for their own purposes, thereby preventing Inkscape from receiving the mouse input. In the group id="mapalt" section you can select an alternative "Alt" key. A numerical value of 1 selects the default "Alt" key. The numbers 2 through 5 select alternative keys. You can see which keys they correspond to by running the `xkeycaps` program available from www.jwz.org [http://www.jwz.org/xkeycaps/].

Alternatively, you can switch the window manager to use another key (such as the "Windows" or "Command" key instead of the **Alt** key. See the FAQ [http://wiki.inkscape.org/wiki/index.php/FAQ].

## Outline Mode Colors

You can specify the colors used in the *Outline Mode* in the group id="wireframecolors" section. Colors are specified in decimal form (converted from a *rgba hexadecimal* value to base ten).

onlight    Default: 255 (#000000ff or black). Color used when stroke crosses a light background.

ondark    Default: 4294967295 (#ffffffff or white). Color used when stroke crosses a dark background.

images    Default: 4278190335 (#ff0000ff or red). Color used to outline images.

clips    Default: 16711935 (#00ff00ff or green). Color used for clip paths.

masks    Default: 65535 (#0000ffff or blue). Color used for masks.

You can force Inkscape to start up in *Outline Mode* by changing the value of *outline* in the group *id="startmode"* to 1.

## SVG Output

A number of preferences control the way content is written to the *SVG* files. They can be found in the group id="svgoutput" section. Most can also be found in the *SVG output* section of the *Inkscape Preferences* dialog.

usenamedcolors    Default: 0. If '0', colors are written as three-digit *hexadecimal* numbers where possible or as six-digit *hexadecimal* numbers if not. If non-zero, colors are written when possible with *SVG color keyword names* [http://www.w3.org/TR/SVG/types.html#ColorKeywords] such as *blue* or *black*. Use of *keyword names* can cause problems with some *Extensions*.

numericalprecision    Default: 8. This is the number of significant digits written out for a number. Lowering the number will save a small amount of space at a cost of precision.

minimumexponent    Default: -8. Any number smaller than 10 raised to this value ($10^{-8}$) is written out as 0.

indent    Default: 2. Number of spaces used for indenting between nested levels of *SVG* tags. A value of '0' disables indentation.

inlineattrs    Default: 0. If '0', attributes are separated by newlines; otherwise, attributes are placed on the same line as their tags.

# Custom Templates

New drawing templates can be added by adding new files to the directory `share/inkscape/templates` (for system-wide use) or to the `templates` subdirectory in your Inkscape preferences directory. The `templates` directory is listed under the *Places* part of the *Save As* dialog. You can directly save any *SVG* file to this directory. Saving the file as `default.svg` will replace your current default template.

### Tip

Objects, gradients, patterns, and so forth, can be added to an empty Inkscape *SVG* file and then saved and placed in the templates directory. When that file is selected in the list of templates, you will have access to all the objects, gradients, and patterns you previously defined.

# Custom Swatches or Palettes

You can add custom *Swatches* (*Palettes*) to Inkscape by adding the appropriate files under the `share/inkscape/palettes` directory. The file format follows the Gimp palettes file format so palettes can be shared between the two programs.

The file format is very simple, as the following example five-color palette file shows.

```
GIMP Palette          ❶
Name: MyPalette       ❷
#                     ❸
  0   0   0 Black     ❹
255   0   0 Red
  0 255   0 Green
  0   0 255 Blue
255 255 255 White
```

❶  Declaration of the type of file.
❷  Name of palette. Shown in list of palettes.
❸  Comment.
❹  List of colors. There is one color per line. Each color is defined as three numbers representing the values of red, green, and blue followed by a name (shown when the cursor hovers over the swatch). The range of values is 0–255, where 255 means that the corresponding color is fully turned on. The above palette consists of the colors black, red, green, blue, and white.

# Custom Markers

It is possible to add custom markers to Inkscape by editing the file containing the marker definitions `share/inkscape/markers/markers.svg`. Here is the definition needed to add a "diamond node" marker. It differs from the diamond markers included with Inkscape in that the center of the diamond is gray and the orientation doesn't depend on the slope of the lines.

```
<marker style="overflow:visible;"                              ❶
   id="DiamondNode"                                            ❷
   refX="0.0"                                                  ❸
   refY="0.0"
   orient="0.0"                                                ❹
   inkscape:stockid="DiamondNode">                             ❺
 <path                                                         ❻
    transform="scale(0.8) rotate(180)"
    style="fill-rule:evenodd;stroke:#000000;fill:#BFBFBF;
        stroke-width:0.5pt;marker-start:none;"
    d="M 0.0,2.5 L 2.5,0.0 L 0.0,-2.5 L -2.5,0.0 L 0.0,2.5 z "
    id="path1234"
    sodipodi:nodetypes="ccccc" />
 <marker>                                                      ❼
```

❶ Start of marker definition. (The "overflow:visible" declaration indicates that the marker should not be clipped if it extends outside a clipping box.)

❷ Name of marker.

❸ Offset of marker origin from node position.

❹ Orientation of marker. If a numerical value, the orientation of the marker with respect to the screen coordinates. If "auto", then it is aligned with the direction of the path at the node (or the average of the directions of the path in and path out if a corner node).

❺ Inkscape id of marker.

❻ The definition of the path of the marker. See the file format for *Paths* in the appendix for more details.

❼ End of marker definition.

For more details, see the Markers section [http://www.w3.org/TR/SVG/painting.html#Markers] of the *SVG* specification.

# Custom Keyboard Shortcuts

You can change the keyboard shortcuts used by Inkscape by editing or replacing the file `share/keys/defaults.xml`.

There are a number of alternative shortcuts available. To use them, simply rename the file to `defaults.xml`.

- ACD Systems Canvas: `acd-canvas.xml`.

- CorelDRAW: `corel-draw-x4.xml`.

- Freehand: `macromedia-freehand-mx.xml`.

- Illustrator: `adobe-illustrator-cs2.xml`.

- Xara: `xara.xml`.

- Zoner Draw: `zoner-draw.xml`.

- Right-handed illustration (for use in drawing on a tablet with a stylus held by the right hand; most commonly keyboard shortcuts are accessible with the left hand): `right-handed-illustration.xml`.

You can also add shortcuts to a `keys/defaults.xml` in your Inkscape preferences directory. These will override any shortcuts defined in the system-wide `defaults.xml` file. See the comments in the default file for more details.

One particularly handy shortcut customization is to bind often-used *Extensions* to keys. Here is an example of binding the / key to the Add Nodes extension:

```
<?xml version="1.0"?>
<keys name="My Customization">
 <bind key="slash" action="org.ekips.filter.addnodes" display="true"/>
</keys>
```

# Chapter 25. Using the Command Line

Inkscape has the ability to batch process *SVG* files without opening up the Graphics User Interface (*GUI*). The available options can be divided into a few categories: general commands, exporting commands (including printing), and query commands. Inkscape will also open PDF files from the command line. The first page in the PDF is imported.

Most Inkscape commands are attached to verbs. Any verb can be called from the command line with the `--verb` argument, allowing complex processing to take place. However, it is not possible to set parameters. A list of all verbs can be obtained using `--verb-list`. It does not appear possible to suppress the *GUI* when using the `--verb` argument.

Here is a simple example of opening a file, selecting an object, flipping it, and then saving the file. The *Star* has an *id* of "MyStar".

```
inkscape --select=MyStar --verb ObjectFlipVertically --verb FileSave --verb
FileClose MyStar.svg
```

The file before running the above command.              The file after running the above command.

Most options have two forms: a short form preceded by one dash and a long form proceeded by two dashes. Some options take parameters that can (usually) be attached to the option with an = sign (e.g., `--export-png=my.png`) or separated by a space (e.g., `--export-png my.png`).

Inkscape has a *shell* mode, entered by calling Inkscape from the command line with the `--shell` option. There are no new capabilities using this command; it is simply to allow one to execute multiple independent commands without restarting Inkscape each time. Here is an example of exporting the `MyStar.svg` to a *PNG*:

```
$ inkscape --shell
Inkscape 0.48 interactive shell mode. Type 'quit' to quit.
>MyStar.svg --export-png=MyStar.png
Background RRGGBBAA: ffffff00
Area 0:0:150:150 exported to 150 x 150 pixels (90 dpi)
Bitmap saved as: MyStar.png
>quit
```

# General Command Line Options

General options:

| | |
|---|---|
| `-?, --help` | Print the help message which lists all command-line options with a short description of each one. |
| `--usage` | Print a list of command-line options showing correct syntax for use. |
| `-V, --version` | Print the Inkscape version number and exit. The version number is also available internally from Help → ♠ About Inkscape. |
| `-z, --without-gui` | Do not use X server. Doesn't seem to play well with `--verb`. |
| `-f, --file` | Usage: **inkscape -f FILENAME**. |
| | Give filename(s) to open upon start-up or for use with other options. The option string (`-f` or `--file`) need not be used. |
| `-x, --extensions-directory` | Print the Inkscape extension directory and exit. Useful for knowing where to install new extensions and checking which ones are included. |
| `--verb` | Call verb when Inkscape opened. If more than one `--verb` given, they will be called in order. |
| `--verb-list` | Print a list of all verb *id*s. |
| `--select` | Select object with given *id*. |
| `--vacuum-defs` | Remove the unused definitions from the <defs> section(s) of an *SVG* file. Also available internally with the File → 🝑 Vacuum Defs command. See the section called *Vacuuming Files*. This option does not create a new file but makes the changes in place. |

# Export Command Line Options

Inkscape can be used to convert *SVG* files to another form. Right now, the command line can be used to generate Portable Network Graphic (*PNG*), PostScript (*PS*), Encapsulated PostScript (*EPS*), Portable Document Files (*PDF*), Enhanced Metafile Files (*EMF*-Windows only), and plain *SVG* files. More options are available from within Inkscape using the *Save As* or *Export Bitmap* dialogs.

The export options can be divided into three classes: those that specify the output format, those that specify the region to export, and those that specify properties such as background color in the exported image.

## Format Options

The output filename must be given (except for the `--print` option).

 **Warning**

Transparency is not supported in exports to *PS* and *EPS* files.

| | |
|---|---|
| `-e, --export-png` | Export a *PNG* file. |
| `-P, --export-ps` | Export a *PS* file. |

| | |
|---|---|
| `-E, --export-eps` | Export an *EPS* file. |
| `-A, --export-pdf` | Export a *PDF* file. |
| `-l, --export-plain-svg` | Export a plain *SVG* file. A plain *SVG* has all the Inkscape-specific information and the *RFD* metadata removed. A program that displays *SVG* files should ignore all such information according to the *SVG* specification, so this option should not in principle be necessary. |
| `-p, --print` | Outputs *PS* data that can be used as input to another program via a pipe (\|) or dumped into a file via >. The parameters to this option must be quoted properly. |

For example, on Linux to send the output to a file, use:

```
inkscape --print '> test.ps' test.svg
```

| | |
|---|---|
| `-M, --export-emf` | Outputs an *EMF* (Enhanced Metafile) file. Only available on Windows. |

# Export Region Options

At the moment, these options only affect bitmap export except the `--export-bbox-page`, which applies to *EPS* exports.

 **Note**

Most PostScript display programs will only display what is inside the rectangle defined by the PostScript *BoundingBox* parameter (if it is set). *EPS* files must contain a *BoundingBox*. It is optional for *PS* files. By default, Inkscape sets the *BoundingBox* to the page area for *PS* files and to the drawing *bounding box* for *EPS* files (both at 72 dpi).

| | |
|---|---|
| `-a, --export-area` | Specifies the rectangular region that should be exported. Requires the co-ordinates of the lower-left corner and the upper-right corner in the format: x0:y0:x1:y1. (The lower-left corner of the drawing has coordinates of 0,0.) The units are in *SVG* user units. |

Example: to export the left half of a 200 by 100 pixel drawing to a *PNG*:

```
inkscape --export-area=0:0:100:100
  --export-png=test.png test.svg
```

| | |
|---|---|
| `-C, --export-area-page` | The area exported will correspond to the area defined by the page. |
| `-D, --export-area-drawing` | The area exported will correspond to the *bounding box* of all objects in a drawing, including any that are not on the page. This is the default for EPS export. Note that `--export-area-page` overides `--export-area-drawing`. |
| `--export-area-snap` | The area exported will be increased outward to the nearest integer value. This option has two effects: (1) If you have aligned all your objects to a pixel grid (to reduce anti-aliasing effects) but the export area *bounding box* is not aligned to the grid, it will ensure that the exported pixmap will be aligned to the same grid. (2) It will ensure that the edges of the drawing will not be clipped. |
| `-i, --export-id` | The area exported will be defined by the *bounding box* of the named object. The exported drawing will include the parts of any other objects that fall within this bounding box. The name of a given object can be found by selecting the |

object from within Inkscape and looking at the *XML Editor*. (Of course, if you do this, you may as well export using the *Export Bitmap* dialog.)

`-j, --export-id-only`  Only the specified object is exported. Must be used with the `--export-id` option. See above. Can be used with `--export-area-canvas` and `--export-area-page`.

# Export Property Options

The first few options are for bitmap exports, while the last few are for *PS* and *EPS* export.

`-d, --export-dpi`  **Bitmap Export.** An exported bitmap will be scaled by the ratio of the given number to the SVG user unit. The default value is 90, which matches the internal scale used by Inkscape; that is, a value of 90 means that one Inkscape pixel corresponds to one exported pixel. A value of 72 means that one Inkscape *point* corresponds to one exported pixel. (See the section called *Inkscape Coordinates*.) This option overrides the `--export-use-hints` option.

**Vector Export.** This option sets the resolution for rasterizing filters. The default values is 90 *dpi*.

`-w, --export-width`  An exported bitmap will be scaled so that the width is equal to the specified number of pixels. Overrides `--export-dpi`.

`-h, --export-height`  An exported bitmap will be scaled so that the height is equal to the specified number of pixels. Overrides `--export-dpi`.

`-b, --export-background`  Use the specified color for the background of bitmap export. Any *SVG*-supported color string may be used (e.g., #ffc0cb, rgb(255, 192, 203), or "pink"). See SVG color keywords [http://www.w3.org/TR/SVG/types.html] for a list of defined colors. If this option is not used, the color specified by the "page-color" attribute in the section "sodipodi:namedview" of the *SVG* file will be used (if it is defined).

`-y, --export-back-ground-opacity`  Use the specified value for the background transparency or opacity. Either a number between 0.0 and 1.0 or an integer from 0 to 255 can be used, where the smaller number in both cases corresponds to full transparency and the larger number corresponds to full opacity. Note: 1 is interpreted as full transparency.

`-t, --export-use-hints`  If you have previously saved an object to a bitmap image from within Inkscape (and saved the file afterward), you can use this option to export the object to a bitmap file with the same name and resolution. Must be used with the `--export-id` option.

`-T, --export-text-to-path`  The text objects should be converted to paths prior to export to a *PS* or *EPS* export. Then ensures that the text will be rendered properly regardless of which fonts are installed on a computer that displays or a printer that prints the resulting file.

# Query Command Line Options

The *query* options allow you to determine position and size information for any object in an *SVG* file. The key here is knowing the *ID* (name) of the object for which you desire the information. The *ID* name must be given. The exported numbers use the *SVG* coordinate system.

Here is an example of finding the *x* position of the *zoom-in* icon in the default icon file on a Linux system:

**inkscape --query-id=zoom_in -X /usr/share/inkscape/icons/icons.svg**

| | |
|---|---|
| -I, --query-id | Specify the *ID* of the object for a query. |
| -S, --query-all | Return a comma separated list of *id*, *x*, *y*, *w*, and *h* for all objects (including *SVG* file, *Layers*, and *Groups*) in file. Each object is on its own line. |

Here is an example from querying MyStar.svg (used in the example at the start of this chapter).

```
svg2293,26.447175,24,97.105652,92.450851
layer1,26.447175,24,97.105652,92.450851
MyStar,26.447175,24,97.105652,92.450851
```

| | |
|---|---|
| -X, --query-x | Ask for the *x* position of an object. |
| -Y, --query-y | Ask for the *y* position of an object. |
| -W, --query-width | Ask for the width of an object. |
| -H, --query-height | Ask for the height of an object. |

# Chapter 26. Challenges

Try your skill at drawing these! Some may not be possible with the current version of Inkscape!

Solutions are given in Appendix D, *Solutions for Challenges*.

## Red Spiral

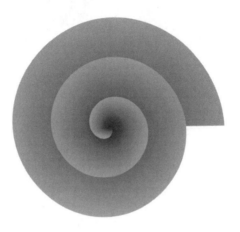

Red spiral with continuous gradient.

## Knot

An exercise in path manipulation.

A knot.

# Squares

Made via simple PostScript program and imported into Inkscape.

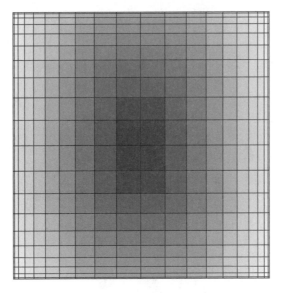

Various size rectangles (size decreases as $1 - x^2$).

# Pine Cone

Made via PostScript program and imported into Inkscape. As of v0.46 it can be done inside Inkscape!

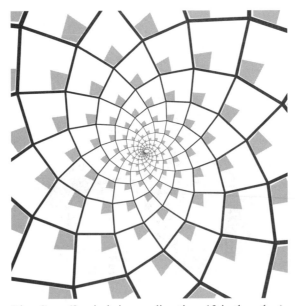

Pine Cone (8 spirals in one direction, 13 in the other).

# Spiral Gyral

Simpler than you think!

Spiral Gyral.

# Appendix A. Inkview

Inkview is a standalone display program for displaying *SVG* files. It can be used to run a slide-show. It is normally shipped with Inkscape.

Inkview can most easily be used from the command line.

Usage: **inkview** `FILE`

where FILE is one or more filenames of *SVG* files (.svg), compressed (gzipped) *SVG* files (.svgz), or *SVG* archive (.sxw, .jar). The archive option has not been tested by the author.

- **Right-arrow**: Show next slide.

- **Left-arrow**: Show previous slide.

- **Up-arrow**: Go to first slide.

- **Down-arrow**: Go to last slide.

- **Esc** or **q**: Quit.

- **F11**: Toggle between full screen and window modes.

- **Enter**: Pop-up window with control buttons (First, Previous, Next, Last).

# Appendix B. File Format

It is not the purpose of this section to describe the Inkscape and *SVG* file formats in detail (for that, look at the *W3C SVG* [http://www.w3.org/TR/SVG/] website). Instead, the purpose is to give an overview that could help the user, for example, edit the *SVG* files with the *XML Editor*.

## Default Template File

Here is a listing of the default template (default.svg):

```
<?xml version="1.0" encoding="UTF-8" standalone="no"?>          ❶
<!-- Created with Inkscape (http://www.inkscape.org/) -->        ❷
 <svg                                                            ❸
   xmlns="http://www.w3.org/2000/svg"                            ❹
   xmlns:sodipodi="http://sodipodi.sourceforge.net/DTD/sodipodi-0.dtd"
   xmlns:inkscape="http://www.inkscape.org/namespaces/inkscape"
   xmlns:xlink="http://www.w3.org/1999/xlink"
   xmlns:rdf="http://www.w3.org/1999/02/22-rdf-syntax-ns#"
   xmlns:cc="http://web.resource.org/cc/"
   xmlns:dc="http://purl.org/dc/elements/1.1/"
   width="744.09448819"                                          ❺
   height="1052.3622047">                                        ❻
  <defs />
  <sodipodi:namedview                                            ❼
     id="base"
     pagecolor="#ffffff"
     bordercolor="#666666"
     borderopacity="1.0"
     gridtolerance="10000"
     guidetolerance="10"
     objecttolerance="10"
     inkscape:pageopacity="0.0"
     inkscape:pageshadow="2"
     inkscape:zoom="0.35"
     inkscape:cx="375"
     inkscape:cy="520"
     inkscape:document-units="px"
     inkscape:current-layer="layer1" />
  <metadata>                                                     ❽
    <rdf:RDF>
      <cc:Work
         rdf:about="">
        <dc:format>image/svg+xml</dc:format>
        <dc:type
           rdf:resource="http://purl.org/dc/dcmitype/StillImage" />
      </cc:Work>
    </rdf:RDF>
  </metadata>
  <g inkscape:label="Layer 1" inkscape:groupmode="layer" id="layer1" /> ❾
</svg>                                                           ❿
```

❶    Declaration of the *XML* version and the character encoding.
❷    A comment. Comments begin with "<!--" and end with "-->".
❸    Start of *SVG* content.
❹    Declaration of *SVG* version and the standards the file adheres to.
❺❻   The width and height of the document page.
❼    Internal Inkscape data, including the color of the page, the zoom factor, and the document units.

❽     Data about the drawing in a format that can be recognized by other programs.

❾     An *SVG* group. This is where the data for objects is put. In this case, the group is empty (other than declaring a label, the type of group, and an id name).

❿     End of *SVG* content.

# SVG Groups with Objects

Here is a listing for an *SVG* group with a rectangle object.

```
<g                                                          ❶
   inkscape:label="Layer 1"                                 ❷
   inkscape:groupmode="layer"                               ❸
   id="layer1">                                             ❹
  <rect                                                     ❺
     style="fill:#0000ff;fill-opacity:0.75000000;fill-r...  ❻
     id="rect1351"                                          ❼
     width="100.00000"                                      ❽
     height="100.00000"
     x="25.000000"                                          ❾
     y="25.000000" />
</g>                                                        ❿
```

❶     Start of *SVG* group.

❷     *SVG* group label. (Displayed in *Layer* pull-down menu if mode type is *layer*.)

❸     *SVG* group id.

❹     Type of *SVG* group (an Inkscape layer).

❺     *SVG* rectangle object.

❻     Rectangle style. (The line has been truncated.)

❼     Rectangle id.

❽     Rectangle width and height.

❾     Rectangle *x* and *y* positions followed by close mark (/>).

❿     Close of *SVG* group.

# Groups of Objects

Here is a listing for three rectangles in a *Group* (the rectangle attributes have been removed for clarity). It can be seen that an Inkscape *Group* is just an *SVG* group, while an Inkscape *Layer* is an *SVG* group with some extra Inkscape parameters.

```
<g                                          ❶
   inkscape:label="Layer 1"
   inkscape:groupmode="layer"
   id="layer1
  <g                                        ❷
     id="g1359">                            ❸
    <rect ... />                            ❹
    <rect ... />
    <rect ... />
  </g>                                      ❺
```

```
</g>                                                        ❻
```

❶ Start of first *SVG* group corresponding to an Inkscape *Layer*.
❷ Start of second *SVG* group corresponding to an Inkscape *Group*.
❹ Three rectangle objects.
❺ End of Inkscape *Group*.
❻ End of Inkscape *Layer*.

# Paths

Here is a listing for a path.

```
<path                                                       ❶
   style="fill:none;fill-opacity:0.7500000;fill-rule:evenodd;stro...  ❷
   d="M 174.0000,113.0000 L 221.0000,113.0000 L 221.0000,91.50000"   ❸
   id="path1370" />                                         ❹
```

❶ Start of *Path* object.
❷ Path style. (The line has been truncated.)
❸ Path commands. The possible path commands are given in the following list. An uppercase letter indicates that the coordinate(s) given are to be interpreted as absolute coordinates; a lowercase letter indicates they are to be interpreted relative to the last point. Parameters are given inside parentheses. Commands may be omitted in some circumstances. For example, "M 20 20 40 40" is to be interpreted as "M 20 20 L 40 40".

For more details, see the *SVG specification* [http://www.w3.org/TR/SVG/paths.html].

M, m         *Move to (x, y)*. Move to a given point.

Z, z         *Close path*. Draw a straight line between last point and first point in path. The lines at the first point will be joined using the current *Join* style.

L, l         *Line to (x, y)*. Draws a line from last point to new point.

H, h         *Horizontal line to (x)*. Draws a line from last point to the point given by the new $x$ coordinate ($y$ coordinate is unchanged).

V, v         *Vertical line to (y)*. Draws a line from last point to the point given by the new $y$ coordinate ($x$ coordinate is unchanged).

C, c         *Curve to (x1, y1, x2, y2, x, y)*. Draws a *Bezier* curve from last point to the point given by the new $x$ and $y$ coordinates. $x1$ and $y1$ are coordinates of handle for old node; $x2$ and $y2$ are coordinates of handle for new node.

S, s         *Smooth curve to (x2, y2, x, y)*. Draws a *Bezier* curve from last point to the point given by the new $x$ and $y$ coordinates. The coordinates of the handle for the old node, $x1$ and $y1$, are calculated assuming the old node is symmetric. $x2$ and $y2$ are coordinates of handle for new node.

Q, q         *Quadratic curve to (x1, y1, x, y)*. Draws a *Quadratic Bezier* curve from last point to the point given by the new $x$ and $y$ coordinates. $x1$ and $y1$ are the coordinates of both the old and new node handles.

| T, t | *Symmetric Quadratic curve to (x, y)*. Draws a *Quadratic Bezier* curve from last point to the point given by the new *x* and *y* coordinates. The coordinates of the old and new handles are the same and are calculated assuming the old node is symmetric. |
|---|---|
| A, a | *Elliptical Arc (rx, ry, x-axis-rotation, large-arc-flag sweep-flag, x, y)*. Draws an *elliptical arc* from the last point to the point given by *x* and *y*. See the *SVG specification* [http://www.w3.org/ TR/SVG/paths.html] for more details. |

❹    Path id and end of path definition.

# Defs

Here is a listing for the <defs> section of an *SVG* file. This is where the definitions for gradients, patterns, markers, etc. are stored. Parts of the definitions have been omitted.

```
<defs                                                    ❶
   id="defs4">
  <marker                                                ❷
     inkscape:stockid="Arrow2Lend"
     orient="auto"
     refY="0.0"
     refX="0.0"
     id="Arrow2Lend"
     style="overflow:visible;">
     ...
  </marker>
  <linearGradient                                        ❸
     inkscape:collect="always"
     id="linearGradient2311">
   <stop ...
  </linearGradient>
  <pattern                                               ❹
     patternUnits="userSpaceOnUse"
     width="320.99999"
     height="289.72575"
     patternTransform="translate(88.07143,25.99358)"
     id="pattern2319">
   <rect ....
  </pattern>
</defs>                                                  ❺
```

❶    Start of *Defs* section.
❷    A marker definition (body deleted).
❸    A gradient definition (body deleted).
❹    A pattern definition (body deleted).
❺    End of *Defs* section.

# Appendix C. Spheres

This section gives diagrammatic views of how the spheres on the book's original front cover were created.

## Sphere with Gradient Shading and Shadow

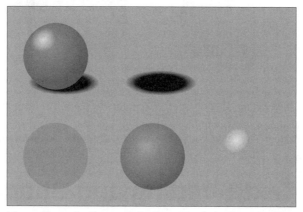

Sphere with gradient shading and shadow. Top left: Completed sphere. Top middle: Shadow. Bottom: The sphere with shadow and highlight layers.

## Sphere with Hatched Shading and Shadow

Sphere with hatched shading and shadow. Top left: Completed sphere. Top middle: Unshaded sphere. Middles: Path used for clipping, raw hatch (single line duplicated via tile-cloning), creation of clipping path from two circles. Bottom: Shadow created from hatches clipped by circle and then squeezed in vertical direction.

# Sphere with Dot Shading and Shadow

Sphere with dot shading and shadow. Left: Completed sphere. Right: Sphere with gradient shading and shadow used as input for tile cloning a dot via the *Trace* tab of the *Create Tiled Clones* dialog. The *Luminosity* (L) was picked from the drawing and used to control the *Presence* and *Size* of the dots. A random value was included on the *Shift* tab.

# Sphere with Text Shading and Shadow

Sphere with text shading and shadow. Text on a path is used for the sphere; flowed text is used for the shadow.

# Appendix D. Solutions for Challenges

Solutions for the challenges are given here.

## Red Spiral

### Procedure D.1. Drawing the Spiral

1. Create a *Grid* and enable snapping to it.

2. Create a three-turn spiral with the *Spiral Tool*, placing the *Outer* handle directly right of the *Inner* handle.

3. Draw a rectangle that passes through the *Inner* handle and encloses the right half of the spiral.

4. Use rectangle to divide spiral (Path → ▣ Division (**Ctrl+/**)).

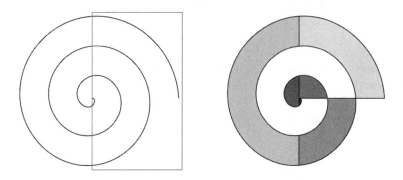

Left: Rectangle encloses right half of spiral. Right: After using rectangle to divide spiral (gray fills added for clarity).

5. Draw rectangle that has upper-right corner at center of spiral and encloses lower-left quarter of spiral.

6. Use rectangle to divide spiral (Path → ▣ Division (**Ctrl+/**)).

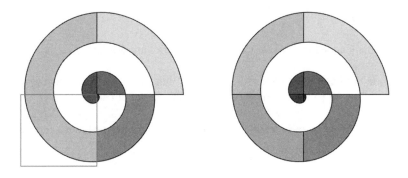

Left: Rectangle (red) encloses lower-left quarter of spiral. Right: After using rectangle to divide spiral (gray fills added for clarity).

7.  Draw duplicate spiral to first spiral. Change number of *Turns* to two in the *Tool Controls*.

8.  Divide new spiral following same procedure as used for first spiral.

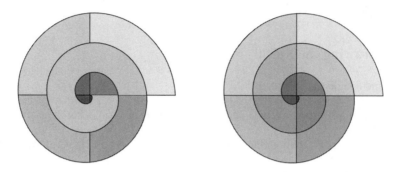

Left: New spiral (red fill added for clarity). Right: After dividing new spiral into pieces (red fills added for clarity).

9.  Add a radial *Gradient* to one section. Set the center *Stop* to black and the outer *Stop* to red. Make sure center handle is at the center of the spiral and each of the outer handles are at the corners of the section as shown below (use node snapping).

10. Copy style of section with *Gradient* and paste to all the sectors (Edit → 📋 Paste Style (**Shift+Ctrl+V**)).

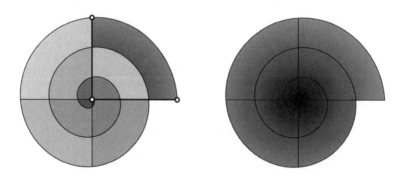

Left: Radial gradient added to one section; gradient handles are displayed. Right: Style copied to all sections.

11. Select section to left of outer-most section (see below). With *Gradient Tool*, adjust gradient by rotating in 90° (be careful not to move center handle). Move outer handles to corners of section.

12. Repeat adjusting gradients in each section. The gradient should be rotated an additional 90° for each adjacent section.

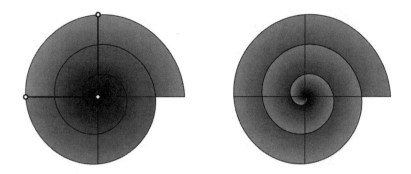

Left: Radial gradient adjusted in one section. Right: All radial gradients adjusted.

13. Remove *Stroke* for all sectors.

14. In theory, you are done, but there is one small problem: At certain zoom levels, you can see white cracks between the sections. These cracks are the result of two problems: The first is that the Inkscape renderer is flawed when two objects abut each other (Batik, Firefox, and Opera don't have this problem). The second is that the spirals are not perfectly drawn.

   The easiest way to reduce the visual effect of this problem is to duplicate the spiral, create a union of all the duplicate sectors, change the color to dark red, and move the new object behind the spiral.

   Perhaps a better, but more complicated, solution is to duplicate the spiral, group the sections, rotate the duplicate a couple of degrees clockwise, put the duplicate behind the original, and adjust a couple of nodes in the duplicate at the outer end of the spiral so the duplicate does not stick out.

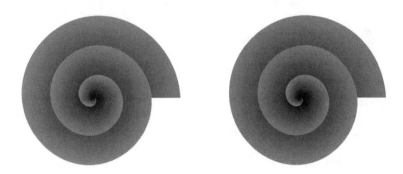

Left: The finished spiral. Right: The finished spiral with a second spiral, rotated and adjusted, behind it.

# Knot

### Procedure D.2. Drawing the Knot

1. Create equilateral triangle with *Star Tool* with 60 px radius.

2. Convert to path (Path → 🖿 Object to Path (**Shift+Ctrl+C**)).

3.  Remove nodes in middle of sides using *Node Tool*.

4.  Drag handle out from top node (**Shift+Left Mouse Drag**).

5.  Convert node to symmetric node (click on ⌐ in *Tool Controls*).

6.  Drag handle while holding down **Control** key to ensure handle is horizontal until handle is 60 px from node (monitor *Notification Region*).

7.  Repeat dragging out handles for other two nodes.

Left: Equilateral triangle. Middle: One handle extended. Right: Completed curve.

8.  Add *Stroke* with width of 12.5 px.

9.  Duplicate, remove one node with *Node Tool*, open *Path* by selecting segment and deleting ( ⋮⋮ ). Change *Stroke* color.

10. Repeat for two other sections.

Left: Stroke widened. Middle: One section created. Right: All three sections created..

11. Duplicate red section; use to divide green section (Path → 🖼 Division (**Ctrl+/**)).

12. Duplicate larger green section; use to divide blue section.

13. Duplicate larger blue section; use to divide red section.

14. Delete small overlapping regions.

15. Recombine sections as shown below (Path → 🖼 Combine (**Ctrl+K**)).

Left: Broken into pieces. Middle: Small intersecting sections removed. Right: Pieces combined into three sections.

16. Add gradients using *Gradient Tool*.

Final knot after gradients added.

# Squares

The obvious way to do this in Inkscape, using the *Create Tiled Clones* dialog, won't work as one cannot control the sizes and spacing properly. Instead, import into Inkscape the following simple *PostScript* program:

```
%!PS-Adobe-2.0
%% BoundingBox: 0 0 500 500
%% Copyright 2007 Tavmjong Bah
%% Squares...

/cell {

    /cell_y2 exch def
    /cell_x2 exch def
    /cell_y1 exch def
    /cell_x1 exch def

    newpath
    cell_x1 cell_y1 moveto
    cell_x1 cell_y2 lineto
    cell_x2 cell_y2 lineto
    cell_x2 cell_y1 lineto
    closepath
    gsave
    fill
    grestore
    0 setgray
    stroke

} def

% Move to center
250 250 translate

% Global constants
/divs    11 def
/boxsize 200 def

% x stuff
/xmul    0 def
/xdiv    divs def
/delxmul 1 xdiv 1 sub div def

xdiv 1 sub {

    /x1      1 xmul 2 exp sub boxsize mul def
    /xmul       xmul delxmul add def
    /x2      1 xmul 2 exp sub boxsize mul def
    /myblue 1 xmul 2 exp sub def

    % y stuff
    /ymul       0 def
```

```
   /ydiv    divs def
   /delymul 1 ydiv 1 sub div def
   ydiv 1 sub {

/y1    1 ymul 2 exp sub boxsize mul def
/ymul    ymul delymul add def
/y2    1 ymul 2 exp sub boxsize mul def
       /myred 1 ymul 2 exp sub def

       myred myblue 0.5 setrgbcolor
x1     y1     x2     y2     cell

myred myblue 0.5 setrgbcolor
x1 neg y1     x2 neg y2     cell

myred myblue 0.5 setrgbcolor
x1     y1 neg x2     y2 neg cell

myred myblue 0.5 setrgbcolor
x1 neg y1 neg x2 neg y2 neg cell

   } repeat
} repeat
showpage
```

## PostScript Programming

Programming in PostScript is easy and fun! Check out the "Blue Book" (*The PostScript® Language Tutorial and Cookbook*) and the "Green Book" (*PostScript Language Program Design*), both available at the Adobe [http://partners.adobe.com/public/developer/ps/sdk/sample/index_psbooks.html] website.

# Pine Cone

As of v0.46, one can do this with a bit of effort with the logarithmic spiral option of the *Create Tiled Clones* dialog. This drawing, however, was done by importing the following *PostScript* program.

```
%!PS-Adobe-2.0
%% BoundingBox: 0 0 600 600
%% Copyright 2007 Tavmjong Bah
%% Spirals...

/cell {

  gsave
    /y exch def
    /x exch def

    x y translate
    x y atan neg rotate
    /mag x x mul y y mul add sqrt 40 div def
    mag mag scale
    newpath
     8.5 0    moveto %
    27    3   lineto
    24.5 27.5 lineto
     0   18   lineto %
    closepath
    stroke

    0.5 setgray
    newpath
      9    1 moveto %
```

```
   15    2 lineto
   14    9 lineto
    6.5  6 lineto %
  closepath
  fill

 grestore
} def

% Move to center
300 300 translate

/mmax   13 def % x repeat
/nmax   30 def % y repeat

/theta   8 13 atan def
/sintheta theta sin def
/costheta theta cos def
/2pi 3.141592654 2 mul def
/e 2.718281828 def
/radtodeg 360 2pi div def

/delx 2pi  8 div sintheta mul def
/dely 2pi 13 div costheta mul def

/myscale 10 def

/n 0 def
nmax {

    /n n 1 add def

    /m 0 def
    mmax {

 /m m 1 add def

 /x n delx mul def
 /y m dely mul def

 /xp x costheta mul y sintheta mul sub def
 /yp x sintheta mul y costheta mul add def

 /radical  e xp exp def
 /ydeg yp radtodeg mul def

 /xpp radical ydeg cos mul def
 /ypp radical ydeg sin mul def

 /xscale xpp myscale mul def
 /yscale ypp myscale mul def

 xscale yscale cell

    } repeat

} repeat

showpage
```

# Spiral Gyral

An interesting use of the *Star Tool*. The "star" has the following parameters: *Corners*: 36, *Spoke ratio*: 0.20, *Rounded*: −0.540. Set the *Fill Rule* to *Even-Odd* ( ). Place concentric circles of various sizes and colors behind the star.

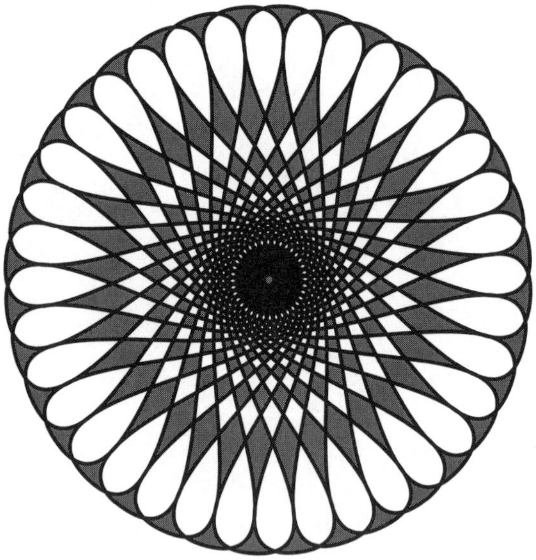

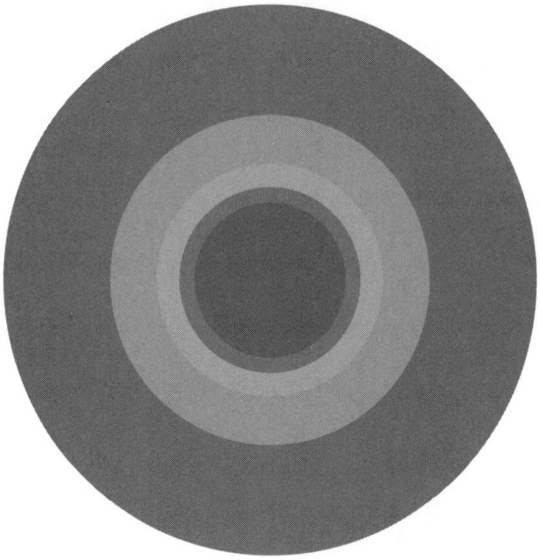

Left: Star, right: background concentric circles.

# Appendix E. List of Dialogs

- File

    - File → ▭ Open... (**Ctrl+O**).

    - File → ▭ Save As... (**Shift+Ctrl+S**).

    - File → Save a Copy... (**Shift+Ctrl+Alt+S**).

    - File → ▭ Import... (**Ctrl+I**).

    - File → ▭ Export Bitmap... (**Shift+Ctrl+E**).

    - File → ▭ Import From Open Clip Art Library.

    - File → ▭ Print... (**Ctrl+P**).

    - File → ▭ Document Properties... (**Shift+Ctrl+D**).

    - File → ▭ Document Metadata... .

    - File → ▭ Inkscape Preferences... (**Shift+Ctrl+P**).

    - File → ▭ Input Devices... .

- Edit

    - Edit → ▭ Undo History... (**Shift+Ctrl+H**).

    - Edit → ▭ Find... (**Ctrl+F**).

    - Edit → Clone → ▭ Create Tiled Clones... .

    - Edit → ▭ XML Editor... (**Shift+Ctrl+X**).

- View

    - View → ▭ Swatches... (**Shift+Ctrl+W**).

    - View → ▭ Messages... .

    - View → ▭ Icon Preview.

- Layer

    - Layer → ▭ Add Layer... (**Shift+Ctrl+N**).

    - Layer → ▭ Rename Layer... .

    - Layer → ▭ Layers... (**Shift+Ctrl+L**).

- Object

    - Object → ▭ Fill and Stroke... (**Shift+Ctrl+F**).

    - Object → ▭ Object Properties... (**Shift+Ctrl+O**).

- Object → 🖰 Transform... (**Shift+Ctrl+M**).

- Object → 🖥 Align and Distribute... (**Shift+Ctrl+A**).

- Object → 🖽 Rows and Columns... .

- Path

  - Path → 🔍 Trace Bitmap... (**Shift+Alt+B**).

  - Path → Path Effect Editor... (**Shift+Ctrl+7**).

- Text

  - Text → **T** Text and Font... (**Shift+Ctrl+T**).

  - Text → SVG Font Editor... .

  - Text → 🔣 Glyphs....

  - Text → 📖 Check Spelling... (**Ctrl+Alt+K**).

- Filters

  - Filters → Filter Editor....

- Extensions

  - Extensions → Previous Extension Settings... .

  - Most extensions have their own dialog.

- Help

  - (None)

- Other

  - Guideline (double-click on a *Guide Line*).

  - Gradient Editor (access from *Fill and Stroke* dialog when a gradient is selected or the *Gradient Tool-Tool Controls*).

  - Link attributes (right-click on object and select from pop-up menu after creating a *link*; see the section called *Adding Links*).

  - Image Properties (right-click on bitmap image and select from pop-up menu).

# Appendix F. Tips for Illustrator Converts

This section is to help those with experience using Illustrator to adapt to Inkscape.

## Key Mappings

Inkscape has its own key mappings optimized for use with the Inkscape *GUI*. However, if you already know the Illustrator key mappings, you might find it easier to use those. To change key mappings, rename the file `adobe-illustrator-cs2.xml` to `default.xml` in the directory `share/keys`.

## Terminology

Inkscape has its own terminology and way of doing many of the things found in Illustrator. Here is a dictionary between the two.

### Illustrator to Inkscape

Anchor Points
: Nodes. Use *Node Tool* to manipulate.

Arc Tool
: *Ellipse Tool*.

Autotrace Tool
: Use *Trace Bitmap* dialog.

Blend Tool
: Use *Interpolate* extension.

Brushes
: Use *Pattern Along Path LPE* or *Pattern Along Path* extension.

Eye Dropper Tool
: *Dropper Tool*.

Hand Tool
: Use **Middle Mouse Drag** with any tool.

Knife Tool
: Draw a "Cutting" path, then use Path → 🖾 Cut Path (**Ctrl+Alt+/**) or Path → 🖾 Division (**Ctrl+/**). See the section called *Path Operations* in Chapter 7, *Paths*.

Marquee Selection
: Use *rubber-band* selection.

Measure Tool
: Use *Measure Path* extension.

Paint Brush Tool
: *Calligraphy Tool*.

Paint Bucket Tool
    *Paint Bucket Tool*.

Palettes
    Dialogs.

Polygon Tool
    *Star Tool*.

Rectangle Grid Tool
    Draw a *Rectangle*, then use the *Construct Grid LPE* or *Grid* extension.

Reflect Tool
    Use *Select Tool* (see the section called *Transformations* in Chapter 5, *Positioning and Transforming*), or from the keyboard, use **h** and **v**.

Reshape Tool
    Use *Node Tool*; see the section called *Sculpting Nodes* in Chapter 7, *Paths*.

Rotate Tool
    Use *Select Tool* (double-click on object to get rotation handles: see the section called *Transformations* in Chapter 5, *Positioning and Transforming*), or from the keyboard, use **[** and **]**.

Scale Tool
    Use *Select Tool* (see the section called *Transformations* in Chapter 5, *Positioning and Transforming*), or from the keyboard, use **>** and **<**.

Scissors Tool
    Draw a "Cutting" path, then use Path → ⬭ Cut Path (**Ctrl+Alt+/**) See the section called *Path Operations* in Chapter 7, *Paths*. If you just want to open a path in one place, create a new node (double-click on path with *Node Tool*) and then click on the ⸬ icon.

Shear Tool
    Use *Select Tool* (double-click on object to get skew handles: see the section called *Transformations* in Chapter 5, *Positioning and Transforming*).

Smooth Tool
    Use Path → ≈ Simplify (**Ctrl+L**) command.

Type Tool
    *Text Tool*.

Zoom Tool
    *Zoom Tool*. You don't need to hold **Ctrl** down when using + and − keys.

# Glossary

alpha

> The transparency of an object (or pixel). If an object with a non-maximal value of *Alpha* is placed over another object, the second object will be visible under the first. In Inkscape, a value of *Alpha* of 255 means the object is completely opaque, while a value of 0 means it is fully transparent (not visible).

Animated Portable Network Graphic (APNG)

> An open standard for animated bitmap graphics, the animated parallel of the *PNG* standard and an alternative to *MNG*. There is support for this format in Firefox 3 and Opera 9.5 but the *PNG* group has rejected this extension to the standard.

Accessible Rich Internet Applications (ARIA)

> An open standard for adding semantic content to web content. This is important for accessibility to those with disabilities. See: the WAI-ARIA [http://www.w3.org/TR/wai-aria/] specification.

baseline

> For text, the line on which most characters (i.e., "x") rest. Some characters such as "p" extend significantly below the baseline. Other characters such as "O" usually extend a small amount below the baseline so that they optically appear to rest on the baseline. Inkscape can align text to a common baseline. Inkscape also uses the word to describe the point at which vertical text is aligned horizontally. The baseline is indicated by a small square when text is selected.

bitmap graphics

> The description of a drawing using pixels (in contrast to vectors). Also refered to as "raster" graphics.
> *See also*: vector graphics.

bounding box

> The smallest rectangular box with sides parallel to the *x* and *y* axis that completely encloses an object. Note: In Inkscape, the *bounding box* is calculated assuming a round stroke *Join* and *Cap* style if the stroke is visible and the *Visual bounding box* option is selected in the *Tools* section of the *Inkscape Preferences* dialog. If the *Geometric bounding box* option is selected, only the nodes are considered in the calculation.

bump map

> A bitmap graphics used to define the contour of a surface so that a lighting effect can be applied. The *SVG* specification uses the *Alpha* channel for this purpose in several of the *Filter* primitives. See: Wikipedia entry [http://en.wikipedia.org/wiki/Bump_mapping].

Cascading Style Sheets (CSS)

> A way of controlling the layout and style of graphics objects (including text) through the use of external files. This allows the separation of content from presentation. It allows documents to be easily adapted for a variety of rendering methods such as printing and web display.

Computer-Aided Design (CAD)

> Use of a computer for techinical design of objects. See: Wikipedia entry [http://en.wikipedia.org/wiki/Computer-aided_design].

Cyan Magenta Yellow Key (Black) (CMYK)

> A method for describing a color by the amount of cyan, magenta, and yellow needed to generate the color. This subtractive color model (where light is absorbed) is most often used in printing. As a good black is difficult to obtain using a mixture of these colors, a fourth ink, the *Key* or black, is also used. See: Wikipedia entry [http://en.wikipedia.org/wiki/CMYK].

dots per inch (dpi)

> The number of pixels per inch when printing or displaying a digitized image. Inkscape has a default resolution for exporting bitmaps of 90 dpi.

ECMAScript

    A standardized language typically used to manipulate elements in an *HTML* page. See Wikipedia entry [http:// http://en.wikipedia.org/wiki/ECMAScript]. JavaScript is an implemenation of the ECMAScript standard as is JScript used in Internet Explorer.

    *See also*: JavaScript.

gamma

    A correction factor to account for nonlinearity in a display device. More technically, the numerical value of the exponent of the power-law correction.

Gaussian distribution

    Also called *Normal distribution* [http://en.wikipedia.org/wiki/Normal_distribution], a mathematical function that describes a distribution found often in statistics (e.g., the distribution of scores on a test). The relevance for Inkscape comes from the use of the distribution in the *Gaussian Blur* filter. The key point is that the color of a pixel is determined by the colors of nearby pixels in the source, weighting the nearest pixels more.

ghostscript

    An open-source PostScript interpreter. See: Ghostscript Home Page [http://www.ghostscript.com].

Graphics Interchange Format (GIF)

    A patented standard for compressing bitmap graphics supported by most web browsers. The open *PNG* standard is technically superior and should be the format of choice for lossless compressed bitmaps.

Graphics User Interface (GUI)

    The interface a computer program presents to the user.

hexadecimal number

    A way of representing a number using base 16 rather than the normal base 10. Very commonly used with computers. The base 10 numbers 0–9 are augmented by the letters a through f (which may or may not be capitalized) representing the numbers 10–15. For example, 31 in base 10 is written as 1F in hexadecimal (1 times 16 plus 15 is 31).

hue, saturation, lightness (HSL)

    A method for describing a color using hue, saturation, and lightness. See: Wikipedia entry [http://en.wikipedia.org/wiki/HSL_color_space].

HyperText Markup Language (HTML)

    The original markup language for web pages. The current version is HTML 4.01. *HTML5* will include inlined *SVG* as part of the standard. See: Wikipedia entry [http://en.wikipedia.org/wiki/Html].

HyperText Markup Language, Version 5 (HTML5)

    The upcoming HTML standard. See: Wikipedia entry [http://en.wikipedia.org/wiki/HTML5].

Joint Photographic Experts Group (JPEG)

    A standard for lossy compression of bitmap graphics supported by most web browsers. More suitable for photographs than line art.

JavaScript

    A language typically used to manipulate elements in an *HTML* page. See Wikipedia entry [http://http:// en.wikipedia.org/wiki/JavaScript]. JavaScript is an implemenation of the ECMAScript standard.

    *See also*: ECMAScript.

kerning

    The process of adjusting the space between letters in text to improve the appearance of the text. A classic example is that the "A" and "v" in "Aviary" should slightly overlap.

LaTeX

    A system for producing high-quality documents commonly used in mathematics and physics documents. LaTeX is built on top of TeX. See: LaTeX home page [http://www.latex-project.org/].

Linear Red Green Blue Color Space (linearRGB)
> A color space where the output intensity of a color is linearly proportional to the input value.
> *See also*: Standard Red Green Blue Color Space.

MathML
> Mathematical Markup Language. An *XML* based language for marking up mathematical notation. Permitted, along with *SVG*, in *HTML5* documents.

Multipurpose Internet Mail Extensions (MIME)
> An Internet standard originally developed for electronic mail that assigns to each type of document content a unique name so that clients (programs) can interpret the data correctly.

Multiple-Image Network Graphic (MNG)
> An open standard for animated bitmap graphics, the animated parallel of the *PNG* standard. Unfortunately, there is little support for this format in web browsers.

name spaces
> The use of tags to define a region in a file where certain definitions are applicable. For example, an *XML* file can contain both *SVG* and *XHTML*. Name spaces keep the two from conflicting with each other.

opacity
> The property of an object that determines the visibility of an underlying object. Opposite of *transparency*.
> *See also*: alpha, transparency.

PDF
> Portable Document Format. A "printing" language created by Adobe that supersedes PostScript. See: Adobe PDF site [http://partners.adobe.com/public/developer/pdf/index_reference.html].

pixel
> Short for picture element. The smallest part of a digitized image that includes all the color information for a region. Computer screen resolutions are typically described as having some number of pixels per inch. The pixel (px) is the default user unit for *SVG*. Inkscape has a default resolution for exporting bitmaps of 90 pixels/inch (ppi). *SVG* viewers typically have a default resolution of either 72 or 90 ppi.

point
> A unit derived from the days when printers used letters carved in metal blocks for printing. Various points have been defined. Inkscape uses the computer point, which is 1/72 of an inch or 0.35277 mm.

Portable Network Graphic (PNG)
> An open standard for compressing bitmap graphics supported by most web browsers.

PostScript
> A printing language created by Adobe. The language can be used to describe a document in a device-independent way. See: Adobe PostScript site [http://www.adobe.com/products/postscript/index.html].

px
> See pixel.

red-green-blue (RGB)
> A method for describing a color using the amount of each primary color present. See Wikipedia entry [http://en.wikipedia.org/wiki/RGB_color_space].

red-green-blue-alpha (RGBA)
> The addition of *Alpha* (transparency) as a fourth component to a *RGB* specified color.

rubber band
> The box drawn when click-dragging the mouse with the *Select Tool* or the *Node Tool* active. The objects or nodes within the box will be selected. The drag must begin over an area without an object or with the **Shift** key held down.

Scalable Vector Graphics (SVG)
> An XML standard for describing a drawing using vector graphics. See: W3C SVG page [http://www.w3.org/Graphics/SVG/].

Standard Red Green Blue Color Space (sRGB)
> A very common standard created by HP and Microsoft for defining color use on monitors and printers. See Wikipedia entry [http://en.wikipedia.org/wiki/SRGB]. The basic property of this color space is that the output intensity for a color (e.g., red) is (roughly) exponentially dependent on the specified input value. All *SVG* colors are defined using this standard. In *SVG*, color interpolation is by default done in the sRGB space except for filters, which is by default done in the linearRGB color space.
> *See also*: Linear Red Green Blue Color Space.

Synchronized Multimedia Integration Language (SMIL)
> A language for authoring interactive audiovisual presentations. See Wikipedia entry [http://en.wikipedia.org/wiki/Synchronized_Multimedia_Integration_Language]. *SVG* can uses SMIL for animation (in addition to JavaScript).

Tag Image File Format (TIFF)
> A file format for storing high-quality images such as photographs or line drawings.

tool tip
> A short dialog shown while the mouse cursor is above some part of window. A typical use is to describe the function of an icon.

transformation matrix
> A $3 \times 3$ matrix that describes how an object is to be transformed. The upper-left $2 \times 2$ sub-matrix controls scaling, rotating, and skewing. While the upper-right $1 \times 2$ sub-matrix controls translations, the bottom row is not modifiable.
>
> An advantage of using transformation matrices is that cumulative transformations can be described by simply multiplying the matrices that describe each individual transformation. Inkscape stores an object's transformation internally as a transformation matrix (which can be seen and modified with the *XML Editor*).
>
> In non-matrix form, we have the transformation: $x' = Ax + Cy + E$ and $y' = Bx + Dy + F$ where $(x', y')$ is the new coordinate of a point at $(x, y)$.
>
> With the above set of equations, it is easy to see that E is magnitude of a translation in the $x$ direction and F is magnitude of a translation in the $y$ direction. For scaling, A and D are the scale factors for the $x$ and $y$ directions, respectively. For a pure rotation, $A = D = \sin(\text{theta})$ and $B = -C = \cos(\text{theta})$ where theta is the angle of the desired rotation. For skewing, C and B control skewing parallel to the $x$ and $y$ axes, respectively.
>
> A *transformation matrix* is always defined with respect to some point. The internal representation is with respect to the internal coordinate system origin (upper-left corner of "page").

transparency
> The property of an object that determines the visibility of an underlying object.
> *See also*: alpha, opacity.

Vector Markup Language (VML)
> An *XML* based language for describing vector graphics. See Wikipedia entry [http://en.wikipedia.org/wiki/Vector_Markup_Language]. VML is supported by Internet Explorer but is deprecated.

Unicode
> A standard for encoding characters for all the world's living languages as well as many historic ones. The character mapping for Unicode can be found at the Unicode [http://www.unicode.org/charts] organization's web pages.

Universal Resource Locator (URL)
> The address of a web page, graphic, etc., on the WWW.

vector graphics
> The description of a drawing using vectors (in contrast to bitmaps).
> *See also*: bitmap graphics.

eXperimental Computing Facility (XCF)
> The native format for Gimp. The acronym comes from the name of the student group at the University of California, Berkeley, that gave birth to Gimp.

eXtensible HyperText Markup Language (XHTML)
> An *XML* markup language for web pages. See: Wikipedia entry [http://en.wikipedia.org/wiki/Xhtml].

eXtensible Markup Language (XML)
> The underlying format for *SVG* files. See: Wikipedia entry [http://en.wikipedia.org/wiki/Xml].

XLink
> *XML* Linking Language. A language for creating sophisticated links between documents. Similar to the simpler *URL*. The *SVG* specification uses "simple" *Xlinks*.

z-order
> The order in which objects are drawn when they overlap each other. Objects drawn on top are higher up in z-order. Unless explicitly changed, the most recent object created is on top.

# Comprehensive Index

## Symbols

Replace Text Extension, 401
Reverse Gradient, 243
Reverse Path, 194
Revert, 110, 134
RGB Barrel Color Extension, 363
Rotation Center, 146
Rotation 145
Rotation Snap Angle, 161
Rows and Columns, 159
Rubber Stretch Extension, 383
Ruler LPE, 206
Rulers, 3, 143

## S

Scatter, 372
Scripts, 353
Scroll Bars, 3
Security Markings, 89
Selection, 134
  Multiple objects, 135
  Tool, 134
  With Find dialog, 136
  With keyboard, 136
  With mouse, 135
Select Tool, 12, 134
Sentence case text extension, 402
Set Attributes Extension, 405
Shadows, 48, 365
Shapes, 161
SIOX (Simple Interactive Object Extraction), 350
Size (Page/Drawing), 6, 110
SK1, 124
Sketch LPE, 206
Slicer Extension, 407
Slices, 116
SMIL Animation, 70
Snap Angles, 161
Snap Bar, 2
Snapping, 152
  Guides, 154
Soup Can, 43
Spheres, 441
Spiral Gyral, 435
Spirals, 169
  Objects placed on, 339
  Tool Controls, 170
  With gradient, 433
Spiral Tool, 94, 169
Spirograph Extension, 398
Spiro Spline LPE, 208
Split Text Extension, 402
Spray Tool, 257
Squares, 161
Star (Polygon) Tool, 17, 167
Stars, 17, 167
  Tool Controls, 169
Star Tool, 96
Status Bar, 3
Steps, 161
Stitch Sub-Paths, 209
Straighten Segment Extension, 384
Stroke
  Width, 173
Stroke Gestures, 249
Stroke paint, 227
Strokes
  Complex, 253
Stroke style, 249
Stroke to Path, 183
Stroke Width, 233, 249
Style Indicator, 3, 233
Style Sheets, 418
Subscript, 222
Superscript, 222
SVG
  File format, 437
  Output Format, 425
Symmetries, 320

## T

Tablet Input, 180
Templates
  Custom, 425
  Default, 110, 437
Tessellation, 319
TeX, 121, 123, 124
Text, 216
  Baseline, 217
  Change Case, 402
  Create, 20
  Creating, 216
  Editing, 219
  Flowed Text object, 218
  Font Family, 220
  Font Size, 221
  Font Style, 221
  In a shape, 225
  Justification, 221
  Kerning, 222, 223
  Letter Spacing, 222
  Line Spacing, 222
  Linked flowed text, 225
  On path, 224, 371
  Orientation, 223
  Regular Text object, 217
  Rotating
    Individual characters, 223

# Index by Menu

## Symbols

# Index by Tool

## Symbols

THIS PRODUCT

informit.com/register

Register the Addison-Wesley, Exam Cram, Prentice Hall, Que, and Sams products you own to unlock great benefits.

To begin the registration process, simply go to **informit.com/register** to sign in or create an account. You will then be prompted to enter the 10- or 13-digit ISBN that appears on the back cover of your product.

Registering your products can unlock the following benefits:

- Access to supplemental content, including bonus chapters, source code, or project files.
- A coupon to be used on your next purchase.

Registration benefits vary by product. Benefits will be listed on your Account page under Registered Products.

## About InformIT — THE TRUSTED TECHNOLOGY LEARNING SOURCE

INFORMIT IS HOME TO THE LEADING TECHNOLOGY PUBLISHING IMPRINTS Addison-Wesley Professional, Cisco Press, Exam Cram, IBM Press, Prentice Hall Professional, Que, and Sams. Here you will gain access to quality and trusted content and resources from the authors, creators, innovators, and leaders of technology. Whether you're looking for a book on a new technology, a helpful article, timely newsletters, or access to the Safari Books Online digital library, InformIT has a solution for you.

THE TRUSTED TECHNOLOGY LEARNING SOURCE

Addison-Wesley | Cisco Press | Exam Cram
IBM Press | Que | Prentice Hall | Sams

SAFARI BOOKS ONLINE

**Inkscape**
Guide to a Vector
Drawing Program
**Fourth Edition**

Tavmjong Bah

# FREE Online Edition

Your purchase of *Inkscape, Fourth Edition,* includes access to a free online edition for 45 days through the Safari Books Online subscription service. Nearly every Prentice Hall book is available online through Safari Books Online, along with more than 5,000 other technical books and videos from publishers such as Addison-Wesley Professional, Cisco Press, Exam Cram, IBM Press, O'Reilly, Que, and Sams.

**SAFARI BOOKS ONLINE** allows you to search for a specific answer, cut and paste code, download chapters, and stay current with emerging technologies.

## Activate your FREE Online Edition at
## www.informit.com/safarifree

> **STEP 1:**   Enter the coupon code: KIHSSZG.

> **STEP 2:**   New Safari users, complete the brief registration form.
>          Safari subscribers, just log in.

If you have difficulty registering on Safari or accessing the online edition, please e-mail customer-service@safaribooksonline.com